COMMUNITY OF PEACE

PITT LATIN AMERICAN SERIES
CATHERINE M. CONAGHAN, EDITOR

COMMUNITY OF PEACE

PERFORMING GEOGRAPHIES OF ECOLOGICAL DIGNITY IN COLOMBIA

CHRISTOPHER COURTHEYN

UNIVERSITY OF PITTSBURGH PRESS

Published by the University of Pittsburgh Press, Pittsburgh, Pa., 15260
Copyright © 2022, University of Pittsburgh Press
All rights reserved
Manufactured in the United States of America
Printed on acid-free paper
10 9 8 7 6 5 4 3 2 1

Cataloging-in-Publication data is available from the Library of Congress

ISBN 13: 978-0-8229-4714-1
ISBN 10: 0-8229-4714-5

Cover photo: Courtesy of the author
Cover design: Melissa Dias-Mandoly

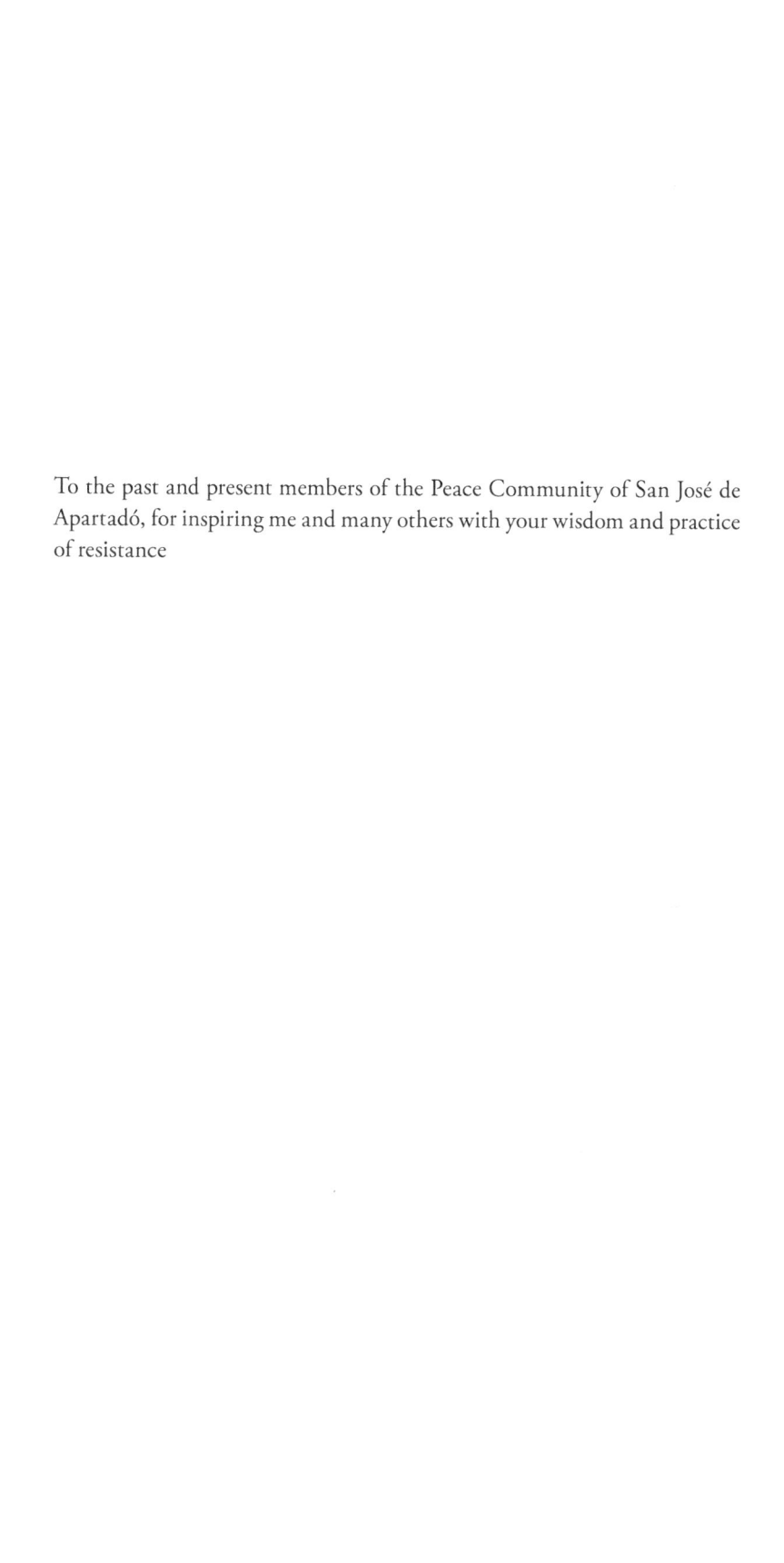

To the past and present members of the Peace Community of San José de Apartadó, for inspiring me and many others with your wisdom and practice of resistance

CONTENTS

Acknowledgements ix

List of Abbreviations xiii

Prologue xv

INTRODUCTION. Peace Communities: Ecological Dignity as Anticolonial Rupture 3

CHAPTER 1. Radical Performance Geography: Embodying Peace Research as Solidarity 25

PART I. WHAT IS THE PEACE COMMUNITY? 39

CHAPTER 2. Returns and Rupture: San José de Apartadó 1997–2016 42

CHAPTER 3. De-indigenized but Not Defeated: Race, Resistance, and Trans-ethnic Solidarity 81

PART II. WHAT IS PEACE? 103

CHAPTER 4. "Peace does not come from them": Antagonisms in Colombia's Peace Conjuncture 108

CHAPTER 5. The Power of Not Participating in War: Radical Trans-relational Peace 131

PART III. WHAT IS POLITICS?   153

CHAPTER 6. "Land is our mother": Alter-territorialities of Ecological Dignity   158

CHAPTER 7. "Memory is the strength of our resistance": An "Other Politics" through Commemoration   193

Epilogue   221

Appendix: Historical Timeline   237

Notes   245

References   251

Index   277

ACKNOWLEDGMENTS

I cannot emphasize enough the extent to which this book is the product of collaborative, collective thinking with members of the Peace Community of San José de Apartadó, other Colombian social movements, fellow protective accompaniers, and academic colleagues. While any error in the text is my own, I would like to acknowledge the many people without whom this work would not have been possible.

I begin by thanking Louis Compoginis from Cabrillo College who was the first to encourage me to study Colombian politics and US policy there, and to eventually travel to the country. I am also deeply grateful to Arnold Bauer and Candace Slater from the University of California who mentored my undergraduate projects and encouraged me to continue doing research in South America. This project would never have been possible without years of support from geographers Claudia Leal and Shawn Van Ausdal, who served as academic mentors of mine since my days as an undergraduate. Along with Andrés Guhl, Claudia and Shawn facilitated an institutional affiliation with the Department of History at Bogotá's University of the Andes during my year of dissertation fieldwork. I am also appreciative of the Inter-American Foundation, Institute for the Study of the Americas, Tinker Foundation, Mellon Foundation, and the University of North Carolina at Chapel Hill's Graduate School for funding my dissertation fieldwork and writing. Funding from the research unit of the Universidad del Rosario contributed toward my revision of the manuscript into a book, while a research grant from the School of Public Service at Boise State University supported its completion. A special thank you to Pitt Latin American Series acquiring editor Joshua Shanholtzer and series editor Catherine Conaghan for supporting its publication by the University of Pittsburgh Press, as well as two incredibly detailed reviewers whose critiques and suggestions helped to greatly enhance my arguments.

As a doctoral student at the University of North Carolina at Chapel Hill, I was honored to have the mentorship of an amazing dissertation committee. During my first semester, Renée Alexander Craft began training me as a critical performance ethnographer, an approach to ethical, creative, and political research without which I cannot imagine my work. Álvaro Reyes guided me in my theorization of race and territory as well as the framework of an "other politics of emancipation" central to my political praxis. Arturo Escobar's scholarship and everyday embodiment of a feminist decolonial politics has contributed to my thinking and acting more than he will ever realize. I am deeply grateful to Altha Cravey and Banu Gökarıksel for their guidance as feminist geographers, who on countless occasions provided critical feedback and encouragement on my written and performance work. Other faculty who supported and shaped my thinking through personal conversations and their courses include Sara Smith, John Pickles, Della Pollock, Gabriela Valdivia, Dottie Holland, Sherryl Kleinman, Scott Kirsch, Larry Grossberg, and Eunice Sahle. I also appreciate Philip McDaniel and Matthew Burns's technical support to assist me in creating the maps included in this manuscript.

I also wish to acknowledge a long list of colleagues and comrades who have accompanied me on this journey. To my fellow participants in the Marxist and Race & Space reading groups—Stevie Larson, Yousuf Al-Bulushi, Adam Bledsoe, Priscilla Ferreira, Willie Wright, Pavithra Vasudevan, Conor Harrison, Laura Gutiérrez, Autumn Thoyre, and Kim Engie—our spaces have truly been an alternative of collaboration and critical thinking counter to the individualism and competitiveness that are all too pervasive in the contemporary university. The same can be said for the care and inspiration I receive from fellow performance ethnographers, with many of whom I cofounded the Hurston Collective for Critical Performance Ethnography: Pavithra Vasudevan, Helen Orr, Seana Monley, Eric Sorenson, Marie Garlock, Kashif Powell, Sonny Kelly, Andreina Malki, Anusha Hariharan, and Elizabeth Melton. I am also especially grateful to Ahsan Kamal for initiating collaborative projects on South-South theory and politics. Further, my understanding of peace was particularly enhanced during my time at the Corporación Universitaria Minuto de Dios, working alongside peace and development scholars Óscar Useche, Ligia Naranjo, Ignacio Holguín, Carlos Eduardo Martínez Hincapié, Amparo Cadavid, Tatiana Gutiérrez, and Angélica Nieto. My work has also benefited greatly from conversations or collaborations with Julieth Albarracín, Diana Gómez Correal, Laura Gutiérrez Escobar, Eloisa Berman Arévalo, Miguel Rojas Sotelo, Marwa Koheji, Anthony Dest, Gustavo Pérez, Jesús Alejandro García, Arlene Tickner, Gwen Burnyeat, Jonathan Aguilar, Bhoj Rai, and members of the collective Estudios de Género en el Sur: Paula Reina, Mariana Silva, Hugo Beltrán, Verónica Castillo, Sofía Guzmán, Karen Yepes, Madelyn Eslava, Laura Calderón, Valentina García, Juanita Roque, and Dania Lombana. Furthermore, Yousuf Al-Bulushi, Stevie Larson, Anthony

Dest, Chelsea Schields, and my mom, Mary Courtheyn, provided critical feedback on draft versions of this manuscript.

A special thank you to all of the members of FOR Peace Presence and RAIS (Red de Acompañantes Internacionales en Solidaridad) whom I worked with in Colombia, and with whom I have shared many beautiful moments and learned so much about political struggle and teamwork: Mayra Sofía Moreno, Amanda Jack, Sarah Weintraub, Camila Nieves, Marcie Ley, Janice Gallagher, Nico Udu-gama, Marion Hiptmair, Jon Patberg, Martín Cranley, Gina Spigarelli, John Lindsay-Poland, Liza Smith, Candice Camargo, Susana Pimiento, Irmgard Ehrenberger, Peter Cousins, Rebecca Gindele, Irene Benítez, Emily Schmitz, Michaela Soellinger, Tom Power, Adilah Nasir, Kevin Coulombe, Danny Malakoff, Julia Drude, Moira Birss, Rita Carvajal, Paul Kozak, Gilberto Villaseñor, Rachel Dickson, Isaac Beachy, David Benítez, Jaime Connatser, Luke Finn, Jake Jenzen, Gale Stafford, Kaya Sugarman, Isabel Moris, Laetitia Sengseis, and Joe DeRaymond. An extra thank-you to Sarah Weintraub, Gale Stafford, Luke Finn, and Mayra Sofía Moreno for granting me permission to use their photos, and to Michaela Soellinger for introducing me to the transrational school of peace research. I am also incredibly grateful to the Operazione Colomba accompaniment team in San José de Apartadó, who gifted me printed copies of two books by Peace Community intellectual Eduar Lanchero.

I am extremely appreciative of the Colombian individuals and organizations who have shared their time and ideas with me over these many years. In addition to the Peace Community, I am grateful to have interviewed or walked with Father Javier Giraldo as well as members of Awasqa, Tierra Digna, ACIN, Hijos e Hijas por la Memoria y Contra la Impunidad, Tierra y Vida, Red Juvenil de Medellín, Acción Colectiva de Objetores y Objetoras de Conciencia, SERPAJ Colombia, Sembrandopaz, COCOMOPOCA, MOVICE, COCOMACIA, San Basilio de Palenque, Marmato, and the Pastoral Social in Quibdó. Also, a very special thank-you to Sebas Patiño, Alejo Vergara, and Julián Londoño for our countless conversations on politics and theory over the years, which so deeply inform my thinking. Finally, my appreciation to Doña Edilma, Don Dorian, and family in Medellín, who so graciously opened their homes to me whenever I needed a place to stay during my years of fieldwork.

As a musician myself, I also wish to recognize Steel Pulse, Bob Marley, Midnite, Hugh Mundell, Public Enemy, and Rush, who through their lyrics exposed me at a young age to critical perspectives on race, colonialism, and capitalism. Thanks to my brother Paul, Justin, Noel, Dustin, Joel, and Dave for introducing me to these artists, who played a key role in opening my mind to the critical theories of violence I now engage in my scholarship.

I cannot end without thanking my mother, father, brother, and godmother Connie Smythe, who have supported my activist and intellectual life throughout all these years. I appreciate your many forms of support and love.

Last, my immense gratitude to the past and present members of the Peace Community of San José de Apartadó, including Doña María Brígida González, Javier Sánchez, Berta Tuberquia Quintero, Jesús Emilio Montoya, Doña Fidelina Sepúlveda Puerta, Jesús Emilio Tuberquia, Eduar Lanchero, and all the others whose names and contributions remain anonymous, with whom I have had the honor of walking and theorizing what dignity and "another world" looks like in practice. I hope this book does justice to the depth and inspiration that your experience of peace truly is.

Due to security concerns, I do not disclose personal interviewees' individual names but refer to them as a "community member," "officer," or "activist," and such. However, I have respected particular individuals' requests to identify them by name, including Jesuit priest Javier Giraldo Moreno, former FOR Peace Presence accompaniers Michaela Soellinger and Luke Finn, as well as Peace Community members María Brígida González and Javier Sánchez, among others. Finally, when voices are transcribed from public events or documentaries, I cite people's names. Commonly cited spokespeople from such sources include Peace Community leaders Jesús Emilio Tuberquia and Eduar Lanchero. I have translated statements made in Spanish into English. The same goes for literature and quotes originally published in Spanish.

Some of the ideas presented here draw from material published previously in distinct forms. Chapter 3 is derived in part from an article published in *Ethnic and Racial Studies* (2019), copyright Taylor & Francis, https://www.tandfonline.com/doi/abs/10.1080/01419870.2018.1554225. Portions of Chapter 6 were published in 2018: "Territories of Peace: Alter-territorialities in Colombia's San José de Apartadó Peace Community," *Journal of Peasant Studies* 45 (7): 1432–59, https://www.tandfonline.com/doi/abs/10.1080/03066150.2017.1312353. A condensed version of Chapter 7 was published in 2016: "'Memory is the strength of our resistance': An 'Other Politics' through Embodied and Material Commemoration in the San José Peace Community," *Social & Cultural Geography* 17 (7): 933–58, copyright Taylor & Francis, https://www.tandfonline.com/doi/full/10.1080/14649365.2016.1139172. This book also draws from ideas that appeared in 2018: "Peace Geographies: Expanding from Modern-Liberal Peace to Radical Trans-relational Peace," *Progress in Human Geography* 42 (5): 741–58, copyright SAGE Publications, https://journals.sagepub.com/doi/abs/10.1177/0309132517727605.

LIST OF ABBREVIATIONS

ACIN	Asociación de Cabildos Indígenas del Norte del Cauca (Association of Indigenous Councils in Northern Cauca)
AGC	Autodefensas Gaitanistas de Colombia (Gaitanista Self-Defense Forces of Colombia)
AUC	Autodefensas Unidas de Colombia (United Self-Defense Forces of Colombia)
ELN	Ejército de Liberación Nacional (National Liberation Army)
EPL	Ejército Popular de Liberación (Popular Liberation Army)
FARC-EP	Fuerzas Armadas Revolucionarias de Colombia—Ejército del Pueblo (Revolutionary Armed Forces of Colombia—People's Army, or FARC, for short)
FOR	Fellowship of Reconciliation
FORPP	FOR Peace Presence
JAC	Junta de Acción Comunal (Communal Action Board)
MOVICE	Movimiento de Víctimas de Crímenes de Estado (Movement of Victims of State Crimes)
PCN	Proceso de Comunidades Negras (Black Communities Process)
RECORRE	Red de Comunidades en Ruptura y Resistencia (Network of Communities in Rupture and Resistance)
SERPAJ	Servicio Paz y Justicia (Service of Peace and Justice)
UP	Unión Patriótica (Patriotic Union)

PROLOGUE

In February 2015 my local community in Chapel Hill, North Carolina, where I was a graduate student at the time, was shaken by a massacre. Three Muslim university students were assassinated by their next-door neighbor, an Islamophobic white man. We held a vigil to denounce the killing and commemorate the victims. Months later, on the day that I began to write this manuscript, another massacre in the United States occurred. It compounded the multitude of cases of police and para-police killing black people that were being publicly denounced in Ferguson, Missouri, and beyond. On June 17 Dylann Roof, a twenty-one-year-old white male, killed nine African Americans of the Emanuel African Methodist Episcopal (AME) Church in Charleston, South Carolina. An important site in the long black liberation movement, Charleston's AME Church had been burned to the ground during a slave rebellion in the 1820s, with subsequent pastors referencing this history of resistance in their sermons. In 2015 they would suffer another attack. Sitting in on a bible study group, Roof shot Pastor Reverend Clementa Pinckney, Sharonda Coleman-Singleton, Cynthia Hurd, Daniel Simmons, Myra Thompson, Reverend Depayne Middleton Doctor, Ethel Lance, Susie Jackson, and Tywanza Sanders.

Presente.

As news emanated from Charleston, I could not help but remember the stories and presence of those killed in two massacres in the Peace Community of San José de Apartadó, Colombia. This is a group of approximately one thousand campesinos (rural, small-scale farmers), who are primarily the descendants of indigenous peoples. Since 1997 in the war-torn region of Urabá, they have committed to communal work and participated in human rights networks to resist forced displacement and co-optation by paramilitary, army, and guerrilla forces. On July 8, 2000, in the village of La Unión, six Peace Community work coordinators were lined up and shot by paramilitaries as a Colombian army helicopter hovered overhead. One of the six, Rigoberto Guzmán, a member of the Community's leadership council, refused the paramilitaries' order to kneel, and they shot him standing up.

P.1. The 2000 massacre in La Unión: Painting by María Brígida González, titled, "We will never forget the memory of our martyrs. As women we have the right to demand justice for our victims and for the people who think about constructing a country where the civilian population's rights are not violated." Author photo, with artist's permission.

The others who were killed were Jaime Guzmán, Humberto Sepúlveda, Elodino Rivera, Diafanor Díaz, and Pedro Zapata.

Presente.

On February 21, 2005, in the settlements of Mulatos and La Resbalosa, a joint military and paramilitary operation killed eight more campesinos. The attackers cut up their victims' bodies with machetes, including three children and Peace Community leader Luis Eduardo Guerra. In 2009 demobilized paramilitaries testified about the massacre. They said that after killing the adults, they were ordered by National Army commanders of the 17th Brigade to kill one-year-old Santiago and five-year-old Natalia because it was best to eliminate these witnesses to the massacre before they grew up to become guerrilla rebels (*Semana* 2009; Giraldo Moreno 2010): Natalia Tuberquia, Santiago Tuberquia, Sandra Muñoz, Alfonso Bolívar Tuberquia, Bellanira Areiza, Deiner Guerra, Luis Eduardo Guerra.

Presente.

This word *presente* is commonly voiced when commemorating the dead in Latin America. It is also used in the United States and elsewhere during gatherings in solidarity with migrants and those killed by political violence, especially those assassinated by Latin American armed forces trained by the

PROLOGUE

P.2. Resistance remembered: Community painting of the 2000 La Unión massacre victims. Author photo.

US military. Among the largest such encounters is the annual School of the Americas Watch protest and vigil, held each November in Columbus, Georgia.

When I hear, say, or write "presente," I feel something. Yet it is not something that I can rationally explain. I feel it. None of the individuals named above from the Peace Community or Charleston's Emanuel AME Church are people whom I knew personally. But I can feel that they are there, that they are here. Consistent with Diana Gómez Correal's (forthcoming) findings about the connections that relatives maintain with loved ones who were killed by political violence, the dead continue to exist, and not only as a belief in the minds of those who remember them (de la Cadena 2015). Having participated in commemorations of the 2000 and 2005 massacres in San José de Apartadó, I feel a special connection to these victims who defied militarism. By evoking people, spirits, and histories of violence and resistance, the enunciation of *presente* can nurture communion with the dead as well as togetherness and solidarity among those who struggle for a world of justice and dignity (Taylor 2020). This interconnectedness is not inevitable but is produced through the solidarity-creating power of commemoration.

Memory is among the Peace Community's core principles, which they enact by commemorating their communal history. In particular, they memorialize those campesinos who have been killed in the course of Colombia's war. Enunciating the names of the victims, and the values they died for, is a performative act through which actors joined by witnesses create meaning and political power. As Peace Community member Doña Brígida González said in my first fieldwork interview, "Memory is the strength of our resistance" (personal interview 2011).

I am not part of the Peace Community or Charleston's Episcopal community. I do not belong to their organizations or racial class. My connection is different. I have worked with the members of the Peace Community since 2008, when I first lived there as an "international protective accompanier" with the Fellowship of Reconciliation Peace Presence (FORPP, or FOR for short). Facing intense levels of violence, the Peace Community invited FOR to place a team of permanent observers in the village of La Unión. In 2002 the first accompaniers arrived to serve as witnesses to the community's process in the hopes that their presence would deter attacks by armed groups. We would accompany groups harvesting crops or resettling abandoned villages, community pilgrimages to commemorate massacres, and leaders traveling to other villages or cities to meet with fellow farmers or their diplomatic networks. Our work also included writing reports about the human rights situation in San José and meeting with members of the Colombian government, international embassies, and human rights institutions. After working in FOR, I enrolled in graduate school to analyze the significance of the Peace Community's resistance as part of my broader intellectual project to theorize how social change occurs and to create alternatives to militarism and injustice. Given the many years I have worked in solidarity with the Peace Community, I feel a particular responsibility to critically reflect on my role there and on what I do beyond San José, in terms of the consequences of my accompaniment and research.

In other words, I am living and implicated in the same world. As a white middle-class male from the United States, I am not the target of such violence. And I use the word *target* intentionally. In Spanish the word *blanco* has two seemingly unrelated meanings: white and target. Upon further reflection, however, those two meanings *are* related, albeit in opposition to each other. To be "white" in the modern-colonial world means precisely to *not* be the target of systematic or gratuitous violence (Fanon 2008; Wilderson 2010). This is exactly why peace communities and other human rights defenders in the Global South invite people like me to serve as "unarmed bodyguards" (Mahony and Eguren 1997). Protective accompaniment by white people and citizens of the Global North seeks to prevent human rights violations by offering a physical presence alongside threatened communities and conducting political advocacy with state authorities to encourage respect for human rights (Koopman 2011, 2014; Pratt 2008). In so doing, accompaniers spread the experiences and ideas of those social movements to a broader audience. This is a task that I have continued as an academic, including with this book.

Accompaniment is a strategy used by threatened human rights defenders in countries of the Global South. But it is also a strategy by activists in the Global North to intervene against their governments' policies abroad, especially US military aid in Latin America. Due to the Plan Colombia package signed in 2000, Colombia became the largest recipient of US military assistance in the Western Hemisphere. While the deal also supported development initiatives through USAID and reforms of Colombia's judicial system, approximately 68 percent of the more than $11 billion package has been military assistance: helicopters, aerial fumigations of coca crops, intelligence collaboration, and training soldiers (Lindsay Poland 2018; Tate 2015; Londoño 2015). Plan Colombia built from long-standing ties between the two countries, including but not limited to the Drug War (Hylton 2006; Gill 2004). Such assistance has been linked to discursive depictions in the United States of Colombia as both an "exemplary democracy" as well as "another Vietnam" in need of help (Murillo 2004). Despite human rights stipulations in the agreement and supposed vetting systems against training soldiers implicated in violations, research has shown a positive correlation between US training and Colombian soldiers' killings of civilians, which number over five thousand since Plan Colombia went into effect (Fellowship of Reconciliation and Colombia-Europe-U.S. Human Rights Observatory 2014). Protective international accompaniment is therefore a method for activists—from the United States in this case—to witness the impacts of military aid in order to document and resist its effects.

Are the experiences of the Emanuel AME Church and Peace Community related? How are Charleston, San José de Apartadó, and countless other cases of violence connected? Some might argue that each case is the product of its unique and complex context. Surely each will have its own particularities, but both groups are nonetheless comprised of racialized subjects targeted for their histories of resistance. Meanwhile, government officials commonly deny any systematic nature to such violence by deeming such massacres as "senseless," the result of "a few bad apples" or "mentally ill individuals" (A. Butler 2015; Tate 2007; Sullivan, Berman, and Kaplan 2015; *Washington Post* 2015). But is there no sense to these killings?

A global analytical lens reveals common threads: racialization and colonialism, as well as states' refusal to directly acknowledge or face these connections. One of my goals in this book is to explore the role of racism in violence against the Peace Community in order to participate in the global movement to theorize race and end white supremacy. Another goal is to detail San José de Apartadó's affirmative project of peace. Its resistance to war for over two decades is an example of the plethora of social movements, especially in Latin America, which continue to challenge systematic killing within the modern world. San José's intense commitment to continually memorialize its organizational history and those who have been killed in the process also highlights the role of memory performance in political struggle. In a time when racist violence seems only to escalate, from the killings of Marielle Franco and Berta Cáceres to George Floyd and Breonna Taylor, memorializing the histories and strategies of resistance is as imperative as ever. In an attempt to analyze the significance of the Peace Community after having been honored to witness their construction of peace for over a decade, I offer this book as an addition to this memory project.

COMMUNITY OF PEACE

INTRODUCTION

PEACE COMMUNITIES

Ecological Dignity as Anticolonial Rupture

In October 2013 a group of rural communities from across Colombia gathered together in a small village within the hills of San José de Apartadó to participate in workshops about resisting the country's ongoing war. San José is located within Colombia's Urabá region, which is adjacent to the border with Panamá. A site of intense armed conflict between National Army soldiers, paramilitary death squads, and guerrilla insurgencies for decades, Urabá has been among Colombia's most war-torn areas. It is also where one of the country's most emblematic oppositions to war emerged: the Peace Community of San José de Apartadó. Facing threats, assassinations, and forced displacement, campesinos (small-scale rural farmers)[1] in San José declared themselves a "peace community" in 1997. They vowed to refuse supporting armed groups with information, supplies, or food. They committed themselves to making decisions autonomously from the armed groups and to participating in work groups that would harvest crops and resettle abandoned villages. San José is one of a number of communities in Colombia that have resisted armed conflict by creating autonomous peace zones, while also participating in a solidarity network that brings such groups together. This network meets periodically in what they call the Campesino University of Resistance, in which campesino, indigenous, and black communities share knowledge about agroecology and human rights to inform their strategies of resistance to forced displacement.

The 2013 Campesino University gathering was preceded by days of hiking through San José's hills to confront paramilitaries in adjacent villages who had induced another round of forced displacements with threats and the kidnapping of a youth. Various indigenous and campesino communities from around the country, as well as journalists and international allies, including me, joined the march. We hiked through thick mud and across rivers to reach villages up to five hours apart. The paramilitaries fled into the hills and refused to face our caravan, but we nonetheless heard them trigger gunshots into the air in the distance. We encountered a few remaining families living in what were otherwise abandoned villages. They thanked the Peace Community for its solidarity and requested more such visits in the future.

Back on Peace Community land, Campesino University workshops ensued. One topic of discussion was the "peace process" currently under way between the Colombian government and Latin America's longest-standing guerrilla group, the Fuerzas Armadas Revolucionarias de Colombia—Ejército del Pueblo (FARC-EP, Revolutionary Armed Forces of Colombia—People's Army). Some people in attendance expressed hope that a peace accord would help de-escalate attacks against rural communities and human rights defenders. Others were skeptical, pointing out that the National Army and paramilitary death squads continued to operate throughout the country. A Peace Community leader observed, "The people believe that in Colombia we are moving toward peace. But it is really to a peace of cemeteries," in which killings continue unabated. This sarcastic comment provoked laughter among the group, implicitly mocking the dominant discourse pronouncing that "peace" was on its way.

The conversation shifted to a discussion about communities' respective strategies amid this context. A Peace Community leader stated that they would continue their existing strategy that combines collective farming and solidarity work locally as well as collaborations with other communities. He proceeded to say, "We are an example of peace, demonstrating that peace is possible." An international solidarity activist interjected with a skeptical tone, "But, forgive me. What peace can you really live in with all of these armed groups operating in the surrounding areas?" San José's leader responded, "We are not going to wait for the armed groups to come to an agreement. We are going to be an example of peace whether they continue to attack us or not. To show that, yes, peace is possible. You have a problem if you wait for it from them. Day-to-day, we don't need the armed actors to come to an agreement" (field notes 2013). This perspective mirrored what I heard repeatedly in interviews with Peace Community members: peace is not when the war ends, but when people withdraw their participation in war and instead work collectively to build community and solidarity.

This book is an attempt to theorize peace alongside the Peace Community. The debate between the community leader and international observer exemplifies the question at the core of this manuscript: What does it mean to seek peace outside of the dominant channels of state politics? Is grassroots peace possible when people continue to be surrounded and attacked by armed groups? Doesn't peace require treaties between armed actors to end war? Indeed, we usually think of peace as a utopian "tranquility," "no war," or "harmony" without conflict. And an "eternal" or "perpetual" peace is supposedly tied to harmony within and between states established through peace accords (Kant 2012). Why, therefore, is the Peace Community dismissive of the prospects of the peace process between the FARC and the Colombian government, two actors who have attacked them? How do racialized groups like campesinos of indigenous descent understand and attempt to create peace amid violence and exclusion? San José's analysis seems to parallel critiques that argue that anything called "peace"—in the highly unequal and exploitative societies we live in—seems more reflective of what we deem to be violence: the victory of one armed group over another (Foucault 2003; Dalby 2014); the repression of dissent against injustice (Ross 2011); or entrenched hierarchies of patriarchy, racism, and capitalism (Daley 2014; Darling 2014; Gelderloos 2007). Nevertheless, San José continues to articulate its resistance politics through the language of peace. What does peace mean to them? How do they create that peace in practice? And is peace really possible in today's global conjuncture permeated by military conflicts, genocide, sexual assault, and poverty?

PEACE IN AND AGAINST THE MODERN WORLD

Answering these questions about the possibility of peace requires a global perspective that accounts for the ways that the pursuit of peace is enmeshed in the dynamics of the modern world. Drawing from the theoretical framework of decoloniality, when I speak of the *modern world*, I refer to the sociopolitical "civilization" that emerged out of the European colonization of the Americas. It is best termed *modernity-coloniality* to emphasize the constitutive nature of colonialism in modernity (Quijano 2010; Mignolo 2010). This world-system celebrates equality, individualism, nation-state sovereignty, democracy, universality, and progress. But it has always been structured by unequal and exploitative core–periphery relationships inherent to capitalism, which I understand as a political economy in which the means of production are monopolized and harnessed for endless accumulation (Marx 1976; Wallerstein 2004; Rosenthal 2019). Capitalism and modernity at large are also structured by hierarchical dualisms of men over women, reason versus emotion, humans exploiting nature, white over black/indigenous, and civilization versus barbarism (Escobar 2018; Martínez Hincapié 2015). Modernity is thus both an era (Dussel 2000) and an "attitude" (Foucault 1984; Dietrich 2012) constituted by divisions rooted in exploitation and domination.

While formal colonialism by empires over other peoples is now the exception rather than the norm, the logic of colonial power endures, which Aníbal Quijano (2000) calls the "coloniality of power." It persists in the form of ongoing racial and gendered dehumanization and discrimination; exploitative labor relations tied to concentrations of control over land, natural resources, and political power by a relatively small number of state and transnational corporate actors; controls over knowledge that delegitimize existing or imagined alternatives to capitalist markets or patriarchal gender norms; and militarized policing of societies to maintain these hierarchies (Quijano 2010; Mignolo 2010; Lugones 2010). Achieving anything worthy of being called peace often seems impossible, given how systematic racial and patriarchal violence has become in the modern-colonial world.

Nevertheless, this system of domination is not absolute. Racialized women and men have resisted coloniality throughout its more than five-hundred-year history. To be clear, this is not to brand subjugated peoples as "unmodern," because it is precisely the knowledge, skills, migrations, and labor of colonized black slaves and indigenous peoples in the Americas—who mined silver and processed sugarcane—that was the basis for the original accumulation of wealth appropriated by European colonial powers to consolidate a modern-capitalist world-system (Rivera Cusicanqui 2012). The modern "civilized subject" was constituted in relation to its racialized "other" (Fanon 2008; Quijano 2000; Silva 2007; Maldonado-Torres 2010). Beyond simply experiencing subjugation, to be "anticolonial" or "decolonial" entails resistance to oppression. The concept of "anticolonial rupture" names ideas and practices that break free from individualism, patriarchy, racism, capitalist exploitation, and/or state domination. In other words, decolonial rupture is a question of political movements that liberate themselves from dehumanization and subjugation in the modern world.

In the context of the current alter-globalization movement, which insists that "another world is possible" (Santos 2006), scholars and social movements have increasingly affirmed that "other worlds" are indeed being created or already exist (Walsh 2010; Escobar 2018; Ceceña 2012; Blaney and Tickner 2017). Examples in Latin America include movements by precarious workers as well as indigenous and black communities who preserve or forge autonomous anti-statist forms of political organization, in addition to noncapitalist and reciprocal human–nature or labor relations (de la Cadena 2015; Escobar 2008; Mora 2017; Oslender 2016; Gonçalves 2006; Zibechi 2010, 2012). Indicative of what might constitute true peace, I conceptualize these practices and knowledges as *ecological dignity*: nonexploitative and dignified relations among all beings to ensure the sustainability of life (Courtheyn 2018a). My use of the term *dignity* is inspired by many Latin American communities—including San José de Apartadó—who use this concept in their struggles against dispossession and oppression (Santos 2014). This concept parallels what Mariana Mora (2017) identifies as the Zapatistas' "*kuxlejal* (life-existence) politics" or what other scholars call "relational ontologies" (Blaser 2010; de la Cadena 2015; Escobar 2018), in which political and cultural ways of living in the world reflect interdependent relations between humans, nature, and the cosmos. I prefer the term *ecological dignity* because it specifically names the types of relations that constitute these political ways of being as *dignified* interrelationality among all of an ecosystem's beings. As the world today faces socioecological crisis due to climate change and unabated violence against people of color and women, illuminating and advancing such alternatives are critical. Most decolonial scholarship highlights ethnic black or indigenous peoples, but nonethnic communities can also break with coloniality. My contention in this book is that campesinos in San José de Apartadó are yet another example of ecological dignity. Understanding the Peace Community's approach to peace offers a window into the practice of anticolonial rupture.

MODERNITY-COLONIALITY IN RURAL COLOMBIA

Analyzing the dynamics of a decolonial politics in a rural Colombian community requires a contextualization of the period of intensified political violence in which the Peace Community emerged. Colombia is an acute case of social antagonism in the periphery of the modern world-system. Particular actors advance the coloniality of power through violent appropriations and maintenance of control over land, labor, and the state. Meanwhile, other groups mobilize resistance to defend life and land. Colombian history is marred with cycles of violent repression of subaltern movements which resist capitalist exploitation by asserting political and economic self-determination (Fals Borda 2009; Hylton 2006; Murillo 2004; Ospina 1997; Roldán 2002). As a simultaneous effect and cause of this standoff, government army forces, right-wing paramilitary death squads, and left-wing guerrilla insurgencies[2] have engaged in armed conflict for much of the past half-century, resulting in at least 220,000 assassinations and an array of human rights violations (Grupo de Memoria Histórica 2013). As of December 2019 Colombia had the world's second-largest internally displaced population at almost 6 million people (International Displacement Monitoring Centre 2020).

Of particular concern for my story here is the period of intensified social conflict and political violence in the 1990s. This era saw the consolidation of a hegemonic economic and sociopolitical class in Colombia, which Nizih Richani (2002) calls the "narco-bourgeoisie." Emerging from economic and political actors tied to illicit narcotics, the narcobourgeoisie's origin does not perfectly coincide with Colombia's traditionally powerful families or the country's industrial bourgeoisie. Comprised of a variety of actors such as drug traffickers, large landowners and cattle ranchers, paramilitary groups, the military, and conservative political factions (Richani 2002), this socioeconomic class exhibits a capitalist logic of "accumulation by dispossession" (Harvey 2005). Consistent with extractivist accumulation strategies seen in many parts of the world during the neoliberal era, Colombia's narcobourgeoisie seeks ongoing wealth generation beyond nar-

I.1. San José de Apartadó within the Urabá region: San José is in the department of Antioquia on the border with Córdoba department. Map by author.

cotics production alone by appropriating more and more land suitable for agribusiness (especially oil palm and cattle ranching) or land that is coveted for its mineral reserves (such as gold and coal) (Richani 2007, 2012; Escobar 2008; Dest 2021). In particular they target lands in the so-called "frontier" (Ballvé 2020), which are frequently racialized as "no man's land" (García 1996) and barbaric "savage territories" (Serje 2005). In reality, these are places already settled by indigenous- or African-descendant campesinos. Such areas are thus connected to markets and unwittingly prepared for extractivist production by entrepreneurs if campesinos can be dispossessed of their land. This repeats a pattern in rural Colombia going back to the post-1850s boom of Colombia's agricultural export economy, when business entrepreneurs began appropriating campesinos' land and labor in frontier zones to produce coffee, sugarcane, bananas, and beef for the world market (LeGrand 1986). Since the 1930s Colombian state policy has consistently sided with large landowners over small-scale farmers, thus contributing to unequal distributions of land as well as patterns of campesino migrations into new frontier areas (LeGrand 1986; Fajardo Montaña 2002; Hylton 2006; Reyes Posada 2009). Amid the escalating armed conflict of the 1990s, the military and paramilitary wings of the narcobourgeoisie targeted areas with guerrilla presence, thus combining economic and political motives (Romero 2006; Richani 2012). The Colombian narcobourgeoisie epitomizes the coloniality of power because it is an imposition of patriarchal and capitalist logics of exploitation and domination. But this process does not occur without resistance. One of the places where the struggle between the narcobourgeoisie and campesinos has played out since the late 1990s is San José de Apartadó.

PEACE COMMUNITIES

San José is a *corregimiento* (rural district) with thirty-two *veredas*, roughly translated as villages or dispersed settlements and the smallest administrative unit in Colombia. This corregimiento is located in the municipality of Apartadó, which falls within the Colombian department of Antioquia. Apartadó is within the Urabá region, which comprises parts of the departments of Córdoba, Antioquia, and Chocó that are in close proximity to the Gulf of Urabá and adjacent to the border with Panamá. The region's strategic value increased with the advance of illicit and extractivist commodity chains tied to neoliberal globalization. Urabá serves as a drug and arms trafficking corridor to and from North America, while its plentiful rivers and fertile farmlands are harnessed to cultivate banana and oil palm as well as hydroelectric power (Aparicio 2012; Ballvé 2020; García de la Torre et al. 2011). San José de Apartadó is located within the hills of the Serranía de Abibe (Abibe Range) between the city of Montería to the east in Córdoba and the lowland banana-producing zone that includes the city of Apartadó to the west.

Small-scale farmers seeking land began migrating to the Abibe Range in the 1960s from the Upper Sinú River area in Córdoba and towns in Antioquia south of Urabá. These farmers identify as campesinos and are primarily the descendants of indigenous peoples. Some of them had survived the civil war between the Conservative and Liberal Parties known as *La Violencia* (The Violence, 1946–1957),[3] which was particularly acute in zones, such as Dabeiba, of conflict between land entrepreneurs and cam-

I.2. Gulf of Urabá viewed from the Abibe Range, where San José is located. Photo by author, Julia Drude, and Moira Birss.

pesinos. La Violencia contributed to another wave of campesino dispossession through the transition to capitalist agriculture (Fajardo Montaña 2002; Roldán 2002). By the mid-1990s migrants to San José de Apartadó had made it a productive and thriving area in which campesinos harvested a multitude of crops, including cacao, avocado, and maize. They had also organized an economic cooperative called Balsamar. State military forces under the command of the National Army's 17th Brigade were present in San José, but the district had also become a stronghold of the left-wing Unión Patriótica (Patriotic Union) party and the FARC guerrilla group.

In 1996 the National Army, in conjunction with paramilitaries from the Autodefensas Unidas de Colombia (AUC, United Self-Defense Forces of Colombia), launched an offensive to take control of San José de Apartadó. This was part of military operations across the Urabá region led by 17th Brigade commander Rito Alejo del Río and the governor of Antioquia, Álvaro Uribe Vélez, who in 2002 would be elected president of Colombia in a triumph of national hegemony for the narcobourgeoisie (Romero 2006; Richani 2007). In military operations throughout San José's villages in 1996 and 1997, army soldiers "warned" the campesinos that *mochecabezas* (those who cut people's heads off, referring to paramilitary death squads) were in pursuit, recommending that campesinos leave. In waves of evictions caused by army and paramilitary operations over the course of those two

I.3. Peace Community billboard: "The Community freely: Participates in community work. Says no to injustice and impunity. Neither participates in the war directly or indirectly nor bears arms. Does not manipulate or pass information to any of the parties." Photo by author, Julia Drude, and Moira Birss.

years, the area's villages were abandoned. Among other assassinations, army soldiers and paramilitaries killed Bartolomé Cataño, a Patriotic Union member who had founded San José as a corregimiento and coordinated the economic cooperative. The majority of San José's residents fled to cities and many never returned. Elsewhere in Urabá, such as parts of Chocó, agribusiness ventures in oil palm followed in the wake of the campesinos' forced displacement. Indicative of the consolidation of the narcobourgeoisie in this period, such land grabbing projects were carried out by a coalition of drug traffickers, paramilitary death squads, sectors of the Colombian government and military, and national and international corporations pursuing profits in agribusiness and extractivism (Ballvé 2020; Grajales 2011; Richani 2005, 2007, 2012).

In San José de Apartadó five hundred campesinos taking refuge in the district's town vowed to resist further displacement and to return to their villages. Building from existing practices of communal organization as well as strategic thinking with solidarity allies in Colombian human rights organizations and the Catholic Church, San José's campesinos declared themselves a "peace community." They committed to not bearing arms, neither passing information nor collaborating with any armed group in any way,

I.4. Father Javier Giraldo Moreno (center) narrating a massacre commemoration in Mulatos, San José de Apartadó. Author photo.

denouncing injustice and impunity, and working in collective groups. They began raising signs that displayed these commitments in order to mark Peace Community villages and farms as civilian zones. In so doing they rejected the presence of all armed groups in their spaces and affirmed their refusal to collaborate with *any* such group—including guerrillas as well as state and paramilitary forces—since colluding, fraternizing, or living with one would make them a target of the other.

Armed actors, especially those tied to the state, responded with vehement attacks against the Community.[4] As of 2010 the number of assassinations in San José de Apartadó numbered 210. These are documented by Javier Giraldo Moreno (2010) in his book *Fusil o toga, toga y fusil* (Rifle or Robe, Robe and Rifle). Father Javier, as he is affectionately known, is a Jesuit priest and lawyer who has accompanied and advised the Peace Community since its founding.[5] Assassinations in San José are traced all the way back to an army massacre of eight campesinos and the forced disappearance of three others in 1977. Indicative of the paramilitary's project to eradicate any dissent against the state—and in particular against the narcobourgeoisie—the number of killings intensified following the founding of the Peace Community in 1997. Of the documented 210 deaths from 1977 to 2010, the Community attributed 186 killings to the military and paramilitary and 24 to the FARC. By March 2019 the Peace Community affirmed a total of 307 deaths to date (Comunidad de Paz de San José de Apartadó 2019). This is an astounding number for a population which has oscillated around one thousand people since 1997. With massacres and threats, paramilitary, military, and guerrilla groups have thwarted various Peace Community attempts to resettle their villages and induced repeated displacements since 1997 from villages such as La Unión, La Esperanza, and Mulatos. Among the most notorious cases is the 2005 massacre in Mulatos and La Resbalosa, in which a joint army and paramilitary operation beheaded and cut up the bodies of eight people. They included three children and Community leader Luis Eduardo Guerra, who was also its interlocutor with the state at the time. Afterward the Community reaffirmed and broadened its *ruptura* (rupture) with the state. In 2003 the Community was a founding member of the Red de Comunidades en Ruptura y Resistencia (RECORRE, Network of Communities in Rupture and Resistance). Given state impunity with respect to human rights violations and the assassination of many people who had testified in previous investigations, San José de Apartadó was among four communities as part of RECORRE which declared their rupture with the state judicial system (Comunidad de Paz de San José de Apartadó et al. 2003; Lindsay Poland 2018).

In this era of increasing political violence and threats of forced displacement, San José inspired other declarations of civilian neutrality to the war across Urabá in the late 1990s. These included the peace communities of San Francisco de Asís and Nuestra Señora del Carmen, as well as humanitarian zones, spaces where civilians could take refuge during combat, in Cacarica and Curvaradó (García de la Torre et al. 2011; *Vida, dignidad y territorio* 2003). Meanwhile, other initiatives associated with the peace communities movement organized themselves under different titles, such as "association," "laboratory," or "experience of peace." Renowned grassroots peace initiatives across rural Colombia in recent decades include the municipal constituent assemblies of Micoahumado, Mogotes, and Tarso, as well as a plethora of autonomist campesino-indigenous-black communities, as in Santander and northern Cauca, among other places (Hernández Delgado 2004, 2012; Rojas 2007; Mitchell and Ramírez 2009; Lindsay Poland 2018). However, two decades later San José de Apartadó is the only organization to continue resisting under the name of "peace community."

After two decades since its founding, the Peace Community had expanded across eleven villages. To this day they continue to assert their self-determination by putting up signs that mark their spaces. They created an organizational structure to make decisions independently of the armed groups: every Community member is part of a work group, with each having a coordinator; each village has weekly meetings and a coordinator who facilitates decisions about communal projects; an elected Internal Coun-

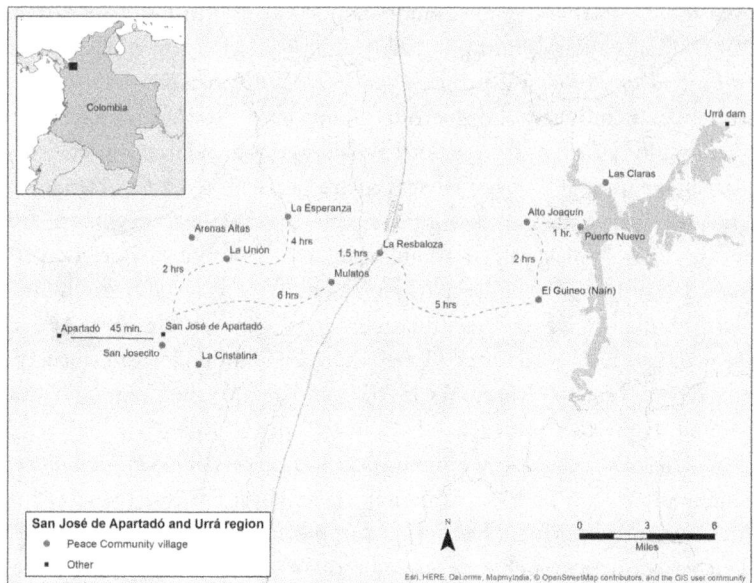

I.5. Walking the Peace Community: This map shows approximate walking times between Peace Community settlements and travel time by jeep between Apartadó and San Josecito during the dry season. Times can increase during or after heavy rains due to the difficulty of crossing rivers or mud patches. Map by author.

cil provides leadership in strategic decision making and its members serve as representatives who communicate with other actors; ultimate decision-making power resides in a community-wide assembly in which all members meet periodically. Furthermore, the Peace Community created an autonomous education system in which local and invited teachers educate children about community history and agroecology. They continue to struggle to maintain and remake their livelihood as campesinos by farming the land in groups. Through a combination of private and communally owned land, they cultivate organic cacao for national and international markets in addition to a variety of food crops such as corn, beans, and plantains. They have also initiated experiments in food sovereignty by creating agricultural centers and self-sufficient family farms. Community members participate in a weekly workday to build homes, repair trails, and harvest communal crops. They continue to denounce injustice, impunity, assassinations, and threats through press releases, commemoration pilgrimages to the sites of massacres, and monuments of stones that are painted with victims' names. They have built a solidarity network with other Colombian campesinos, human rights defenders, and peace activists from other countries. The latter include international observers known as "protective accompaniers" who are invited to live in the community and report to the diplomatic corps and human rights community.[6] Finally, they strategize as well as share seeds and knowledge with other rural racialized communities in a trans-ethnic Campesino University of Resistance. Despite recurrent threats, the Peace Community continues its unarmed resistance to displacement and its struggle for peace.

Together these actions nurture ecological dignity: just and sustainable relationships between humans and the land, the living and the dead, and among communities in resistance. I contend that the Peace Community thereby enacts a politics of decolonial rupture with the coloniality of power. By resisting the narcobourgeoisie land grab, they refuse to concede to the dictates of state domination and capitalist accumulation logics at the heart of modernity-coloniality. Meanwhile, their peace practice fosters communal and ecological sustainability through networks with racialized communities to counter dehumanization and ethnic divisions, thus building an alternative intercommunal structure of autonomy and solidarity.

This endeavor for dignity parallels other Latin American struggles, such as the Zapatistas, Landless Workers Movement (MST), and Piqueteros in Mexico, Brazil, and Argentina, respectively, who have framed themselves as "national liberation," "landless," or "unemployed worker" movements. San José's particular form of resistance, articulated as a "peace community," specifically tenders the question about how to create peace amid the systematic violence against nonwhites, women, the poor, and nature that constitutes today's global socioecological crisis. Colombia is a productive place from which to theorize peace, with intensified debates about its meaning in relation to the country's recent "peace process" between the Colombian government and the FARC-EP. In addition to the narcobourgeoisie land grab, the peace process is another contextual phenomenon central to my analysis of the Peace Community.

THE PEACE PROCESS

In 2012 Colombia inserted itself into the global peacebuilding spotlight when the administration of President Juan Manuel Santos (2010–2018) announced negotiations to end over fifty years of armed conflict with the FARC, Latin America's largest and longest-standing guerrilla insurgency at the time. People met the news with a variety of reactions.

On the one hand, some Colombians viewed the announcement with skepticism, partially due to the failure of previous dialogues between the state and the FARC, the most recent being the 1999–2002 process under the Andrés Pastrana administration (Chernick 2009). Former president Álvaro Uribe (2002–2010) became the most visible critic of the peace process. He insisted on the continuation of his administration's strategy of either

I.6. Peace as political discourse. U Party billboard: "'There is no way to peace, peace is the way'—A.J. Muste." Author photo.

militarily annihilating the "terrorists"—his preferred term for both guerrillas and human rights defenders—or forcing them to surrender.

On the other hand, many Colombians and non-Colombians celebrated the news. This camp included those who had demanded a negotiated solution to the armed conflict since before the Pastrana negotiations (Isacson and Rojas Rodríguez 2009). They argued that a new peace process could finally lead to the end of a war between the FARC and the government spanning more than five decades (Rueda, Alvarado, and Gentili 2016). Although President Santos had been expected to continue the former administration's hardline policy after he had served as Uribe's minister of defense, Santos married his political rhetoric and program to peace (Gómez Correal 2016). His political party, commonly known as The U Party,[7] erected billboards throughout the country with different peace quotes by figures such as Buddha and A. J. Muste alongside the party slogan "¡Unidos, como debe ser!" (United, as it should be!).

As the talks progressed, divisions persisted between a "pro-peace" movement fueled by human rights organizations across the country and what became known as the "No" movement led by Uribe's far-right Democratic Center Party. Then in August 2016 the FARC and government negotiators announced that they had reached a peace accord. It included agreements on integral agrarian development, political participation for opposition parties, illicit drugs, victims, and ending the armed conflict. While a slim majority of voters rejected the accord in a national plebiscite in October, an amended accord that integrated the critiques of the "No" movement was ultimately approved by the Colombian Congress in November. In June 2017, as one of the first tasks of its implementation, the FARC officially laid down its arms.

Many insisted on a subsequent accord with the smaller but still active Ejército de Liberación Nacional (ELN, National Liberation Army) guerrilla group. Additionally, despite the supposed demobilization of the paramilitary AUC in 2006, "new" paramilitary groups who subsequently rearmed (or in fact had never disarmed) continued to operate and target human rights defenders across the country (Human Rights Watch 2010; Programa Somos Defensores 2020). The government's peace process with the AUC was fiercely critiqued for failing to dismantle paramilitarism or assure truth and reparations for victims, thus essentially legalizing the narcobourgeoisie's appropriation of wealth and capital (Hristov 2009; Richani 2007). Many Colombian popular organizations argued that more profound sociopolitical transformations would be needed if there was going to be real and lasting peace.

In this context debates about peace began pulsating throughout Colombia, as different sectors manifested their particular understandings and projects. One vision affirmed the need to finally assure the state's monopoly on the legitimate use of force by demobilizing the guerrillas and ending the "internal armed conflict." Others argued that peace required the fulfillment of state-guaranteed rights to political participation and basic services like education, health care, and housing for excluded populations. Various actors also argued that peace would be created through reconciliation and national unity through a process of transitional justice, which would conduct highly selective trials on "exemplary" cases of human rights abuse. Many victims' movements, however, were critical of the transitional justice model and affirmed the need for victimizers' convictions and community-based memory work. Meanwhile certain government, corporate, and development sectors argued that peace would allow for the intensification of the country's economic development model spearheaded by large-scale mining and agribusiness. Finally, amid their ongoing resistance to forced displacement and active combat, campesinos of indigenous and African descent insisted on their communities' self-determination and dignity. In fact, while the "peace process" captured the national and international headlines, this latter group of communities had been resisting war and forging grassroots forms of peace for decades.

Interestingly, two of these major approaches to peace—formal peace treaties between states and armed groups versus peace as a lived politics of ecological dignity—intersect around one date: March 23. This was the date by which the Colombian government and FARC negotiators were set to reach their final accord after over three years of talks. In September 2015 the state and FARC announced preliminary agreements on four of their major agenda topics. They announced they would have a final agreement six months later on March 23. Coincidentally, March 23 is also a significant date for peace in Colombia for another reason: this was the same day when San José's campesinos had founded the country's first peace community in 1997. March 23 thus represents two approaches to peace: a "peace process" between the state and guerrillas through a negotiated accord and implementation period each with a proposed completion date versus a peace community that has a beginning date and ongoing practice of peace. The former reflects peace as a finalized condition, while the latter insists on peace as a continual process.

While the FARC and government eventually reached an agreement, they failed to meet their March 23, 2016, deadline. This is illustrative of the fact that, as I argue, peace does not work with completion dates by which it will be "achieved." Conversely, in March 2016 the Peace Community celebrated its nineteen-year anniversary with a gathering of its members, an example of lived peace regardless of what state and armed actors do. They wrote in their subsequent press release, "Nineteen years living as a Peace Community has taught us that guns are not necessary to construct internal democracy and solidarity. Our project of life has been rooted in hope and not in tyranny, and therefore walking in dignity every day has permitted us to live these years without turning to subjugation. These 19 years are a light of hope before a world that is further and further from the minimal feeling of humanity that should emanate in society" (Comunidad de Paz de San José de Apartadó 2016a). In other words, the Peace Community affirms that peace should not be relegated to armed actors' treaties but is built through everyday practices of solidarity. Their position is an invitation to theorize peace from multiple perspectives. Considering the ways that violence can persist despite formal peace accords, one of the goals of this book is to analyze the extent to which particular visions and projects of peace advance coloniality or ecological dignity.[8]

RADICAL PERFORMANCE GEOGRAPHIES OF PEACE IN COLOMBIA

People often assume that peace is created through military operations or state diplomacy. Colombia is a particularly interesting country in which to research peace, given its current multitude of competing visions and projects. During the "peace process" conjuncture, many proposals centered on assuring state legitimacy correlate with Johan Galtung's (1996) canonical peace studies concept of "negative peace" as the simple absence of direct violence. This contrasts with his more robust notion of "positive peace," which combines the absence of direct, cultural, and structural violence with the simultaneous realization of social justice. Other praxes of peace, such as those of communities in resistance like San José de Apartadó, exceed that rubric and map onto alternative framings, such as Wolfgang Dietrich's (2012) notions of "energetic peace" as ecological harmony, or an array of normative "moral peaces" that emphasize rules of behavior to ensure hospitality or salvation in the afterlife. Drawing from the emergent geographies of peace literature (McConnell, Megoran, and Williams 2014), I argue that peace should not be reduced to a utopian future or seen as a condition that will be achieved once and for all. Rather, it is a question of ongoing (and potentially already-existing) *processes*, which are inherently spatial because they always take place in geographical spaces. Such socio-spatial processes are entangled in debates over how peace is understood by different actors and how it should be produced across space and time.

In this Introduction, without much initial thought, I instinctively included pictures of billboards as representations of the government's and Peace Community's competing visions of peace. Billboards are a form of territorially marking space, which in this case are used to advance particular political processes of peace through a governmental peace process or community autonomy. Peace imaginaries are therefore fundamentally questions of territory and politics. Within the dominant modern imaginary, demarcating geographical space to determine who has territorial control where—as in nation-state sovereignty—is implicitly seen as a precondition for peaceful relations among peoples. Meanwhile, peace is a discourse of power employed to generate support for one's cause, trumpeting the virtue of one's vision and position (Ross 2011; McConnell 2014), whether that be state sovereignty or a civilian safe zone. In other words, peace is a spatial discourse and practice and a performative act. Peace signs are a territorial performance in which the interaction between their creators and viewers produce signification.

Complementing Judith Butler's (2004a) approach to "performativity" in which people recurrently reenact—and in rarer instances potentially subvert—gender roles and identity positions, I use the term *performance* in the sense of staged and vernacular acts before a witness through which meaning is collectively created (Madison 2010, 2012). Following Kelly Oliver (2001), this "bearing witness" is not to dichotomously divide "performers" and "witnesses" into "subjects" and "objects"; rather, it is to signal their relational role in the coproduction of meaning. This is congruent with Butler's (2004a) recognition that gender (or peace politics) "is real only to the extent that it is performed" (161). Building from Dwight Conquergood's (1985) concept of "dialogical performance" between investigators and interlocutors in ethical collaborative research processes, performance is always a dynamic and relational dialogue across people and beings. Communities of peace are relational and collective. They perform their opposition to war through continual and embodied practices. While both the formal "peace process" and the campesino "peace community" wield the term *peace*, these uses are better understood as "friction" (Tsing 2005), where the same word is interpreted quite differently and utilized toward differing ends.

Is the Peace Community's performance of peace simply a reproduction of the Colombian nation-state's territoriality that advances the coloniality of power, which seeks to dominate the population and the environment by exerting its control over a bounded area? To be sure, the Peace Community resists eviction from its land by attempting to block armed groups from entering its spaces. Nevertheless, I argue that a closer look at San José's campesino peace centered around food sovereignty, commemoration of the dead, and solidarity networks reflects the "relational autonomy" (Ulloa 2012) that scholars have identified in many indigenous and black communities across Latin America, which seeks not to exploit nature or dominate populations but instead to cultivate reciprocal and dignified ecological reproduction among all beings (Zibechi 2012; de la Cadena 2015; Mora 2017; Escobar 2018). Ecological dignity is created through this dialogical performance between humans and the earth, social movements in solidarity with one another, and intellectuals with communities in resistance. San José de Apartadó's set of spatial practices, places, and values creates a particular type of territory through which a political subject is produced. This territorial formation reveals that territory should be conceived of as more than mere sovereign control and domination over a space (Delaney 2005; Foucault 2007; Fernandes 2009; Sánchez Ayala 2015); rather, it entails the production of collective subjects (Gonçalves 2006; Reyes and Kaufman 2011; Colectivo de Sentipensamiento Afrodiaspórico 2015). In this case, instead of the nationalistic and capitalist subjects produced by today's liberal nation-states, the Peace Community's alter-territory nurtures and is nurtured by subjects committed to autonomy, solidarity, and dignity.

If the current modern-colonial world is structured by global crises, inequality, and dispossession, then peace as *living in community with dignity* requires a specific politics of rupture, whose network of alter-territories goes beyond hegemonic forms of politics limited to electoral representation and reforming the state. Challenging the coloniality of power involves radical forms of politics in which people liberate themselves from dehumanization and oppression (Fanon 1965, 2004; Rancière 2010). Scholars have called such processes of subjective transformation and the creation of dignified living conditions an "other politics" of emancipation (Grupo Acontecimiento 2012; Denis 2012; Ceceña 2012; Gutiérrez 2012). In using the term *radical*, I refer to political forms that go to the root of the problem to put the entire (modern-colonial) system in question toward "anti-systemic" ruptures and alternative worlds (Escobar 2018; Madison 2010; Wallerstein 2004). San José is also useful for rethinking race beyond the multicultural perspective limited to ethnic identities and cultures, and instead from a structural perspective about hierarchies of (de)humanization, including the role of antiracist coalitions in emancipatory politics.

Peace Community members frequently say that "memory is the strength of our resistance" when asked about how they have survived against enormous odds or why they continue to commemorate the dead in a variety of forms. Following this line of thinking, memory is central to radical forms of peace, territory, and politics. Rather than a reactive act anchored in the past, I understand memory to be a spatial practice in the present, rooted in place and landscape, which is related to the past and future (Bal 1999; Halbwachs 1992; Mills 2010; Till 2005; Ricoeur 2004). Memory can be both a "strategic practice" where traumatic history is deployed for sociopolitical goals, as well as a "difficult return" of bringing into the present the presence of people and past events through naming and symbols (Simon, Rosenberg, and Eppert 2000). Of course not all memory work is emancipatory. It can be mobilized for xenophobic or other dangerous ends, resulting in reactionary violence and genocide (Bal 1999; Benjamin 2007b). It can also function to silence ongoing structural violence when the past is memorialized in a way to claim that inequalities and exploitation have been overcome (Tyner, Alvarez, and Colucci 2012). In other words, mainstream peace and justice mantras of "never again" are insufficient as long as structural conditions of capitalist-racist-patriarchal violence persist (Depelchin 2011; Acevedo 2009; Mamdani 2004).

Anything worthy of being called peace therefore must be relational and radical. Inspired by the Peace Community's array of practices, I call this *radical trans-relational peace*: ecological dignity nurtured through the dialogical performance of solidarity across communities. A radical trans-relational peace is constituted by a form of politics that is rooted in ecological dignity both *within* and *beyond* the people and beings in question. It is relational in three senses: First, radical peace rejects the modern division between "humanity" and "nature" through an alter-territoriality that seeks mutual life rather than the domination of "land." These commitments are seen in San José's rejection of extractivism and the Community's work for sustainable agriculture. Second, through particular forms of memorialization, such as the Peace Community's pilgrimages and stones to commemorate the dead, relational peace eschews both retaliatory killing that reproduces the cycle of violence and the separation between "the living" and "the dead" by nurturing the "agency of the dead" (Gómez Correal, forthcoming). Third, radical peace speaks to relational space among social movements. This refers to communities who encounter and nurture one another in solidarity networks to resist modern-colonial patriarchy, racism, and capitalism, which is especially impactful when uniting campesino, indigenous, and black communities who suffer racialized violence but who can also be divided by the hegemonic ethnic lexicon. This peace is not produced by groups in isolation from one another, but through solidarity, understood here as political collaborations across difference that challenge oppression (hooks 1984; Scholz 2008). Ecological dignity is produced through the dialogical performance of radical peace, in which solidarity between people and land, the living and the dead, and among communities in resistance rupture with relations of violence toward just and sustainable life worlds.

This book is a radical performance geography of peace. It ethnographically traces the political imaginaries and territorial practices of the Peace Community of San José de Apartadó in order to illuminate anticolonial politics and new ideas of peace. This exercise attempts to make theoretically explicit the arguments that San José's campesinos perform through their words and actions, and to explore the theoretical implications of the concepts they enunciate. While Community members name "the state" and "capitalism" as their antagonists, rather than colonialism directly, my contention is that their discourses and practices nonetheless reflect ruptures with coloniality.[9] This is not to say that they are disconnected from global capitalist markets and the colonial matrix of power altogether. However, in the Community's political vision of peace and territorial practices, I find examples of them refusing to submit to the power relations of capitalism and coloniality rooted in exploitation, dehumanization, and dependency, while also forging alternatives to them through solidarity networks, collective work, and food sovereignty projects.

For me, *rupture* does not mean that "de-linking" from colonial violence comes from isolationist strategies (Mignolo 2010). Outright separation is almost impossible in today's globalized political economy. It is true that the most pressing concern of our times might be whether or not coloniality and capitalism can be eclipsed while people are still enmeshed within them (such as radical movements' engagement in state politics or international markets). But that is a broader theoretical question that cannot be answered by the Peace Community's experience alone and is thus beyond the scope of this project. My purpose here is to illuminate an already existing alternative to coloniality in an array of Peace Community conceptions and practices. In the process, along with other Latin American communities in resistance, they contribute to the articulation of new liberatory concepts while also reworking modern ones with decolonial meanings, such as dignity, autonomy, territory, and peace, with the last being of particular interest in this book. Ultimately my goal is to illuminate the role of political resistance, solidarity, and memory performance in this radical community of peace.

BOOK OUTLINE

The book is organized into three parts, preceded by this Introduction and Chapter 1. The latter, "Radical Performance Geography: Embodying Peace Research as Solidarity," details my methodological framework in and beyond the field. Rooted in my experience as an international accompanier in San José de Apartadó, I call it *radical performance geography*. I also conceptualize the importance of solidarity in my research as a dialogical performance for ecological dignity.

Part I, "What Is the Peace Community?" explores the historical trajectory and political significance of the San José de Apartadó Peace Community. Chapter 2, "Returns and Rupture: San José de Apartadó 1997–2016," tells the story of the Peace Community's emergence and evolution. It situates the armed conflict in San José within broader struggles over land, community autonomy, and political representation in Colombia. I contend that the Peace Community's autonomous peace praxis constituted a political break with the dominant strategies of the Colombian Left rooted in electoral politics or armed struggle. Supplementing this focus on social movement strategy by placing these dynamics within the context of the global modern-colonial structure of race, Chapter 3, "De-indigenized but Not Defeated: Race, Resistance, and Trans-ethnic Solidarity," interrogates the racial dynamics of land struggles and anti-campesino violence in Urabá and Colombia more broadly. Analyzing how San José de Apartadó's campesinos and their indigenous and campesino counterparts in the Campesino University of Resistance understand the war, I explore the extent to which certain campesinos remain racialized despite lacking an explicit ethnic identity. I also illustrate how trans-ethnic solidarities undermine racial hierarchies meant to dominate but also divide the subaltern. To complement this section, I include an appendix at the end of the book which offers a timeline of San José de Apartadó's history.

Part II, "What Is Peace?" offers an intervention in peace theory based on diverse understandings of peace in Colombia. Chapter 4, "'Peace does not come from them': Antagonisms in Colombia's Peace Conjuncture," examines contrasting notions of peace during the peace negotiation period, including voices from the Santos administration, the armed forces, and an array of social justice activists. Among the many divisions surrounding the "peace process," I argue that Colombia's current struggle for peace is undergirded by antagonistic territorialities that pit the modern-colonial political economy of extractivism against ecological dignity. Chapter 5, "The Power of Not Participating in War: Radical Trans-relational Peace," turns to a comprehensive presentation of Peace Community members' definitions of peace. I place their critiques of state-driven peace projects in relation to the logic of modernity-coloniality, while drawing from their conceptions of peace as the active decision to withdraw support for the war's armed groups and the construction of community to articulate my notion of a radical trans-relational peace.

Building from Part II's focus on Colombian social movements' *definitions* of peace, Part III, "What Is Politics?," moves to the Peace Community's *practice* of peace as a case of an "other politics" of emancipation. Chapter 6, "'Land is our mother': Alter-territorialities of Ecological Dignity," explores the Peace Community's production of an alter-territory through solidarity caravans, resistance networks, and food sovereignty initiatives in agricultural centers and self-sufficient family farms. Building from the growing literature that retheorizes territory beyond the nation-state given indigenous and African-descendant groups' demands for "territory" as they confront land grabbing in Latin America, the chapter offers a conceptual framework for analyzing diverse territorial formations. Chapter 7, "'Memory is the strength of our resistance': An 'Other Politics' through Commemoration," traces the relationship between the Peace Community's politics of peace and their forms of embodied and material commemoration through pilgrimages to massacre sites, painting stones with victims' names, and folk paintings of Community history. I illustrate how San José de Apartadó's massacre commemorations and painted stones reject vindictive violence and nurture a liberatory politics through internal and external solidarity.

I conclude the book with an Epilogue that provides an update on events in San José de Apartadó since the completion of the first draft of this manuscript in 2016, the same year the peace agreement was signed by the government and the FARC. It offers a final reflection on the Peace Community's ongoing significance in Colombia's post-accord context and for theorizing anticolonial peace.

CHAPTER 1

RADICAL PERFORMANCE GEOGRAPHY

Embodying Peace Research as Solidarity

An anticolonial geography of peace requires an appropriate methodology that integrates critical analysis and political action. In agreement with Silvia Rivera Cusicanqui (2012), "there can be . . . no theory of decolonization, without a decolonization practice" (100). If I intend to create and live in a just world, then I have to enact critical theory through my research practice. Combining critical spatial theory and performance ethnography, I call my methodology *radical performance geography*.

The first component is structural analysis rooted in critical and radical human geography, feminist geopolitics, critical race theory, and decoloniality, in order to understand the context in which peace movements take place. Informed by a Marxist critique of capitalism (Marx 1976), critical development studies (Escobar 1995), and world-systems analysis (Wallerstein 2004), critical geography adds an explicitly spatial lens to critical theory's analysis of states, capitalist core–periphery relations, neocolonialism, and social movements (Harvey 2001, 2012; Gregory 2004; Routledge 2008). Meanwhile, radical geography considers the spatial dynamics of alternatives outside dominant systems, such as noncapitalist economies (Gibson-Graham 2006) and anarchism's non-statist politics (Springer 2012). Building from critical geography, the subfield of feminist geopolitics attends to the militarization-state-resistance nexus by foregrounding the embodied practices of those experiencing or resisting war, which reveals the interdependence of global, national, local, and personal processes of power (Dowler and Sharp 2001; Fluri 2011; Koopman 2008; Mayer 2004). Moreover, critical scholarship on race attends to how certain populations are marked as "less than human" and struggle for liberation (Fanon 2008; Gilmore 2002; Goldberg 2009), with the subfield of black geographies adding a spatial lens to the places and practices of blackness (McKittrick and Woods 2007). This complements the feminist approach for an intersectional analysis of the multiple violences that structure the modern world-system as well as subversion to violence through spatial and political practice. The framework of decoloniality situates these processes of oppression and liberation within the global history and logics of patriarchal and racist power in the modern-colonial world (Quijano 2010; Mignolo 2010; Lugones 2010; Dussel 1985). Critical theory is thus essential for both deconstructing how phenomenological conditions are structured by sociohistorical power relations and creating emancipatory alternatives to them (Gómez Correal and Pedraza 2012). This book therefore highlights the Peace Community's everyday practices of peace, which are understood in relation to broader processes of global violence and struggle, such as today's resistance by racialized peoples to state-corporate enterprises' land grabbing in new resource frontiers.

My second methodological point of departure is critical performance ethnography, which Soyini Madison (2012) deems "critical theory in action" (16). Understanding the performative aspects of research is particularly crucial for geographers, because we not only write about and analyze space; we also perform and create space. As a performance geographer, I use the written word as well as my body in space as a mode of inseparable investigation, analysis, and presentation. My work is *critical* by rejecting orientalist ethnography's complicity in conquest and the pretension of an outsider observing "over the shoulders" of a research "subject-object" (Conquergood 2002). As a geographer I am inevitably a participant in the construction of particular forms of peace through my presence and publications. I take such political stakes seriously by highlighting community members' voices and merging my analysis with the critical theory necessary to fully grasp their praxis. It is essential to link ethnography with critical theory in order to situate local processes within global relations of power that structure and are structured by them. However, this works both ways, where ethnographic action research is a means to put academic theory into practice. Therefore this is *performance* geography in that I recognize how my body as a researcher marching in a community mobilization or interviewing government officials performs international solidarity with peace communities and is interpreted as such by both social movement organizations and armed actors. As part of the global climate and racial justice movement, my intent is to utilize the fieldwork process of research itself as a *radical* political act against neocolonial militarization by increasing the safety and visibility of racialized communities struggling for alternatives to the social and ecological violences at the root of today's global crisis. Moreover, I understand the interview not as an extraction of data but as a performative space of dialogical knowledge production; the back-and-forth conversation of a semi-structured interview allows for continual reflection and clarification as well as the formation, critique, and crystallization of theory (Madison 2012; Pollock 2005). I present my experiences and Peace

Community voices with poetic transcriptions and staged performance pieces toward more embodied renderings of ethnographic research and political struggle; these put the body and the word in motion for innovative presentations to a broad array of fellow academics, research interlocutors, and government and social movement actors.[1] All of these methods reflect a quest for "dialogical performance" between researchers and interlocutors (Conquergood 1985) toward the coproduction of knowledge against oppression.

Such deeply reflexive, embodied, and collaborative work calls attention to the political implications of our presence and publications as researchers. A dynamic toolkit of performative methods offers creative ways of conducting fieldwork and presenting findings that complement written work for ethical and effective scholarship. Radical performance geography therefore integrates critical geographical theory and performance methods into a comprehensive methodology to not only analyze places but also more consciously *embody* and *produce* spaces of peace through research. In this chapter, I detail my methodological process.

SOLIDARITY

I emphasize *radical* in the naming of my methodology for full disclosure about what drives my theory and politics. Personal experiences and political leanings can limit or enhance our abilities to interpret or comprehend particular phenomena and political projects. For instance, during a speaking tour in the United States, Peace Community leader Jesús Emilio Tuberquia (2011) was asked about the role academics can play in their process. He responded by stating that such outsiders often misunderstand: "They write in their summaries that we are anarchists. *No, we are a project of life*." Reflecting on critiques I have heard over the years of the Peace Community as a courageous but still "parochial" or "unrealistic" alternative, I sense that researchers and accompaniers primarily focused on the modern state system of electoral representation and realpolitik geopolitics have difficulty interpreting the Peace Community's practice as more than a limited retreat within the system. Given San José's autonomous peace praxis, I argue that to fully appreciate the depth, significance, and possibilities of the Peace Community, we have to approach it from the perspective of a radical anti-systemic politics (Wallerstein 2004) that exceeds what seems politically and socially "realistic."[2] Indeed, much of my subjective political formation took place as an accompanier in the Peace Community, exposing me to such a politics of "rupture" and convincing me to take such alternatives to electoral politics and armed struggle seriously.

Research with a community in the middle a war zone such as San José de Apartadó is often conditioned on solidarity with the organization in question, for security or other reasons. In line with what bell hooks (1984) calls "Sisterhood" in the feminist movement and Sally Scholz (2008) calls "political solidarity," I use the term *solidarity* to refer to collaboration across difference that challenges oppression, which is rooted in a political commitment to struggle and transformation. What is commonly referred to as the solidarity movement in the United States is rooted in alliances (often by white people) with those excluded from the national body politic: racialized people, undocumented migrants, resistance movements in the Global South (Russo 2019). Sara Koopman (2011) calls alliances that strategically use geopolitical networks to impede violence against communities in resistance "alter-geopolitics." Depending on the nature of the interaction, such solidarities can reproduce white privilege and saviorism (Boothe and Smithey 2007; Koopman 2008) or foster a dialogical performance among people committed to justice and dignity (Koopman 2011). Anticolonial solidarities must be a transformative process that politicizes, creates new subjectivities, and fosters innovative political strategies and tactics (hooks 1984; García Agustín and Jørgensen 2016; Featherstone 2012).

Attention to the dialogical performance of solidarity also helps elucidate the dynamics of ecological dignity in Peace Community food sovereignty initiatives and Campesino University trans-ethnic networks, but my focus in this chapter is on the dynamics between communities in resistance and allies and researchers. Being *in solidarity* does not mean *in total agreement* with a counterpart's organizational strategy. Notwithstanding, I wish to disclose that my objective here, as an outsider, is not to provide a comprehensive account of all of the internal workings of the Peace Community. Similar to Arturo Escobar's (2008) work with the Colombian Proceso de Comunidades Negras (PCN, Black Communities Process), I am a nonmember and view my role as a scholar to explain San José de Apartadó's significance toward evaluating our current conjuncture and strategies of social transformation, rather than meticulously critiquing the Community's internal dynamics. The appropriate space for such dialogues is directly with Peace Community members and their Internal Council, rather than through this book. Here I agree with Anna Tsing (2005): "My ethnographic involvement with activists taught me the restraint of care: There are lots of things that I will not research or write about. I do not mean that I have whitewashed my account, but rather that I have made choices about the kinds of research topics that seem appropriate, and indeed, useful to building a public culture of international respect and collaboration" (xii). Such ethical protocols are essential to protect against the potential harms of research through dialogue, care, and discretion, without compromising one's commitment to critical analysis.

1.1. Dialogical performance: Interview with Doña Brígida González in San Josecito. Author photo.

EMBODYING PEACE RESEARCH IN AND BEYOND THE FIELD

As a geographer of peace who is a former international accompanier in Colombia, I am situated as an active participant in the Peace Community's process that builds from my historical relationship with them. I first arrived in San José de Apartadó to serve as a protective accompanier, working for seventeen months, from 2008 to 2010, with what was then the Fellowship of Reconciliation's Colombia Peace Program. This program later became the independent organization FOR Peace Presence, where I served on the board of directors from 2013 to 2019. With the exception of 2015, I visited San José de Apartadó every year from 2008 to 2020 and have spent a total of just under two years (twenty-three months) there. This is part of the six years I have studied and worked in Colombia for more than the past decade.

To inquire into people's ideas of peace, memory, and territory, I conducted sixty-eight semi-structured interviews across Colombia between 2011 and 2018. Reflective of local practices of communal debate and decision making, ten of these were group interviews involving two to five people concurrently. In the Peace Community I interviewed a total of twenty-seven members from eight of their eleven settlements, and I had repeated interviews with six of these members. These interviewees included eleven women and sixteen men of various ages. Some were founding members of the Community while others had joined only in recent years. For additional perspectives, I interviewed twenty-one members of other Colombian communities and social movement organizations, four army and police officers, and seven protective accompaniers, for a total of sixty-nine people interviewed altogether.

Adapted as appropriate for the particular interviewee or group, my questionnaire included the following: How do you define peace? How do you understand the roots of the war? What is your perspective on the state–FARC peace talks? Why do you commemorate history or victims in the ways that you do, and how do those memory practices affect your organizational process? What is the relationship between memory and peace? What do land and territory mean to you, and how do they relate to peace? What is your relationship with state agencies as well as other Colombian and international organizations? What is international accompaniment, and how do you evaluate it? How have your organization's strategic practices emerged or changed over time? What have you learned from other organizations, and what lessons can you offer for other peacebuilding initiatives?

Interviews can also be a form of political accompaniment. One visit to an army base was particularly memorable. At the beginning of a trip to Urabá in September 2013, I emailed and faxed a letter to the region's military authorities to announce my arrival to the region, copied to my research sponsors and collaborators. This followed the protocol of international accompaniment organizations, who send such advisory letters to law enforcement agencies and the diplomatic corps to increase visibility of their movements and the safety of those they accompany. When I went to the military base to schedule an interview in April 2014, I was able to arrange a meeting on the spot with one of the commanders. I remember reflecting on how easy it was to get access, given my position as an international researcher and the power that connoted; it felt even easier to get a meeting as an academic than it was while I was an accompanier in frequent contact with these officers. I brought my introduction letter with me and presented it to the people I asked for interviews. After glancing over it, one officer passed the letter off to a lower-ranking official for her to take into another room and review. He asked me about my time as an FOR accompanier, which he had seen indicated on the letter, and proceeded to call the current team's cell phone to ask if they knew me. When the lower-ranking officer returned, he asked her what the letter said, and she responded that it explained what I had verbally told them, that I was there from the University of North Carolina doing research about peace and wanted to speak with them. We continued to talk, until he suggested I interview other officers within the brigade, which I did. I interviewed Colombian army and police officers not only to include their perspectives in this geography of peace, but

RADICAL PERFORMANCE GEOGRAPHY 31

1.2. Fieldwork sites in Colombia. Map by author.

also to disclose my presence in the area and embody my political network as a form of potentially dissuading attacks against the Peace Community.

To complement my interview inquiries about how people defined peace, I investigated the embodiment of peace by witnessing daily practices and events. Recognizing the ways my body projected international solidarity, I understood this as co-performative action research. In addition to San José de Apartadó, I visited artisanal gold miners in Caldas; Afro-Colombian community associations in Chocó and Bolívar; campesino organizations in Sucre, Bolívar, and Caldas; land restitution activists in Antioquia; community organizers and urban Hip Hop youth collectives in Medellín; youth conscientious objectors in Medellín and Bogotá; nonviolent reconciliation trainers in Barranquilla; as well as trade activists, human rights defenders, state crimes victims' organizations, and representatives of the Colombian Congress in Bogotá. In multi-organization gatherings in San José de Apartadó and at university events in Colombia and the United States, I also interacted with representatives of indigenous communities from Cauca, Chocó, Cesar, and La Guajira; Afro-Colombians from Cauca; campesino communities from Quindío and Cauca; and victims and human rights organizations from Bogotá. Such encounters also served up many informal yet insightful conversations about peace, memory, territory, race, and politics.

To complement the Peace Community experience, this book cites personal statements as well as the public or written works of a variety of other organizations. Interactions with organizations such as the Red Juvenil de Medellín (Youth Network of Medellín) and Tejido Awasqa Conciente (the Conscious Cultural Weave collective, sometimes written as Tejido Awasqa Cultural and commonly referred to as simply Awasqa) provided urban youth perspectives on peacebuilding. Presentations and publications by Tierra Digna—Centro de Estudios para la Justicia Social (Land of Dignity Research Center for Social Justice) were particularly useful to understand the context of Colombian economic, environmental, and military policies. I also draw from evaluations of the government–FARC peace process by victims movements such as Hijos e Hijas por la Memoria y Contra la Impunidad (Sons and Daughters of Memory and Against Impunity) and Movimiento de Víctimas de Crímenes de Estado (MOVICE, Movement of Victims of State Crimes); land restitution activists from Tierra y Vida (Land and Life), originally founded as the Asociación de Víctimas para la Restitución de Tierras y Bienes (ASOVIRESTIBI, Association of Victims for Restitution of Land and Assets); the campesino organization in Sucre known as Sembrandopaz (Planting Peace); as well as Afro-Colombian organizations such as Consejo Comunitario Mayor de la Organización Popular Campesina del Alto Atrato (COCOMOPOCA, Community Council of Campesino Popular Organization of the Upper Atrato river region) and Consejo Comunitario Mayor de la Asociación Campesina Integral del Atrato (COCOMACIA, Community Council of the Integral Campesino Association of the Atrato river). Interactions with SERPAJ Colombia (the Colombian branch of Servicio Paz y Justicia, or Service of Peace and Justice, which is a part of the International Fellowship of Reconciliation network) added an analysis of the peace process from the perspective of active nonviolence. Finally, representatives of the Asociación de Cabildos Indígenas del Norte del Cauca-ACIN CXAB WALA KIWE (ACIN, Association of Indigenous Councils in Northern Cauca), among other indigenous com-

1.3. Radical performance geography: Producing space through research on a Holy Week commemoration pilgrimage along the Apartadó–San José road. Photo by Gale Stafford, with permission.

munities, frequently highlighted the racial dynamics of resistance to war in Colombia.

Co-performative action took various forms. For instance, I participated in multiple anniversary gatherings and commemoration pilgrimages where Peace Community members hiked to the sites of massacres and recounted those histories. I also joined a rural caravan that marched across various villages in San José de Apartadó to challenge paramilitary and military harassment and kidnapping. In addition to such large-scale events, there were also times when I accompanied, by semiformal petition, individual Peace Community leaders during trips outside of San José to buy supplies in the city of Apartadó. Indicative of why they seek such presence given the risks they face in (para)military-controlled areas, on one such trip a leader was threatened while buying groceries as I waited outside. The aggressor said, "Those gringo sons of bitches, do you think they will be accompanying you all the time?," before proceeding to kick the leader's shopping basket and mutter "escolta" (bodyguard)—referring to me—as he left the store (Comunidad de Paz de San José de Apartadó 2014a). As he relayed the interaction to me afterward, he noted that such threats made international

1.4. Performing solidarity: Peace Community members watching a greetings video from former FOR accompaniers. Author photo.

presence essential for them to move around, affirming that he could have been assaulted and killed otherwise, since paramilitary groups have lists of identified social justice leaders (field notes 2014). This is radical performance geography at work: mobilizing the protective power of researcher presence alongside threatened activists as a co-performance of resistance. There was also my work in my own organization within the international solidarity movement. As a former FORPP accompanier and member of the organization's board of directors, I provided auxiliary support for the accompaniment team over the years. I was an accompaniment trainer, while also sharing my security analysis and programmatic advice upon consultation. I also served as a coleader of delegations in Colombia and coorganizer of speaking tours in the United States. In other words, co-performative action is radical performance geography both with external allies and within our own movement organizations.

The Peace Community, FOR accompaniers, and I also designed a collaborative memory photo project. This facilitated a reflection on how international accompaniers and my own research influence and contribute to the Community's collective memory. This project arose from accompaniers' and the Community leadership council's recognition that in many cases we had been the only ones with cameras and thus a source of photographs of particular events and people. We were key chroniclers of history, as FOR accompanier Sarah Weintraub put it (personal communication 2013). In 2014 I delivered 2,500 digital photographs collected from accompaniers' archives to the Community to use as they wished, such as the possibility of creating digital archives or memory boards for events, schools, and libraries, as well as their memory museum under construction. I then created slideshows and organized three photo-viewing events in different villages. The slideshows opened with a video in which former FOR accompaniers sent greetings to the Community after having departed. To conclude the event itself and during the following days, these memory slideshow and video events inspired subsequent conversations with community members about past events, particular people (living and deceased), and the role researchers and accompaniers play in documenting San José's history—not only for the outside world but also by returning and re-presenting these materials within the community to induce ongoing remembrance, reflection, and motivation to continue the struggle.

Also drawing from the performance ethnography repertoire, as a cofounder of the Hurston Collective for Critical Performance Ethnography at the University of North Carolina at Chapel Hill during my doctoral coursework, I created a series of staged theater performances about displacement, commemoration, and accompaniment that I use to present San Jose's history and my experiences there with other audiences, such as academics, students, and nongovernmental organizations (NGOs). For instance, "If We Remain on the Land" reenacts the Peace Community's formation, forced displacement, and first village return, in which participants play community members and armed actors. Its script is composed of excerpts of the Peace Community's self-written history (Comunidad de Paz de San José de Apartadó 2005a). In addition to the sensations of being forcibly moved and then actively returning from one side of the stage to another, performers and audience witnesses frequently comment on how intense it is to be taken or see others taken from the group, plus observing the group's numbers drastically decline as more and more folks are pulled away by the military, thereby reflecting the drastically high number of assassinations in San José de Apartadó. I have used such pieces in scholarly conference presentations, classroom lectures, and accompanier trainings. This pedagogy of role-play, poetic transcription, and audience participation serves to nurture collective and engaged learning spaces. In addition, I organized events in two villages of San José de Apartadó during my fieldwork to stage these performances, in which Community members and accompaniers performed roles. I organized these events to seek critique about the appropriateness of my presentations of their stories and of international accompaniment. Community members responded by affirming their value as educational memory events in and for the community itself, in which newer members and children

1.5. "If We Remain on the Land": Co-performing a performance piece of historical memory with Peace Community members and international accompaniers. Author photo.

had an additional medium through which to learn about the organization's principles and history.

My sources also included news articles from local (*El Heraldo de Urabá*) and national (*El Tiempo, Semana, El Espectador, Noticias Uno Colombia*) outlets; Peace Community communiqués available on their website, www.cdpsanjose.org; and documentaries of the Peace Community available on DVD and online, such as *Hasta la última piedra* (Until the last stone) (Lozano 2006) and *Hope for Colombia: The Grace Pilgrimage 2010 Bogotá* (Buenaventura 2011). In July 2014, when a significant portion of my fieldwork had been completed, I reviewed my findings with the Peace Community leadership council, receiving additional feedback and permission to proceed writing about and performing my core observations and arguments. All of these methods together reflect an approach to research as a dialogical performance of solidarity, which takes place between theory and method; across word, text, and body; and between accompaniers or researchers and communities in resistance.

While I do not claim to have fully enacted an anticolonial method in this project, I do hope that these reflections will be helpful for others who are also engaging in the never-ending work to decolonize our methodologies. To that end, I wish to conclude this chapter by clarifying how I understand and frame this research to be participatory, and how it is not. This is relevant given the often uncritical claims regarding the "participatory" nature of certain projects (Pain and Francis 2003). Similar to Sara Koopman (2008), I conceive of this as research not *of* but *with* this community, but in a particular way. It was not participatory action-research (PAR) in the sense of mutually designed questions, methods, and publications (Fals Borda and Rahman 1991).

First, I came to this work with my particular intellectual questions, guided by specific scholarly debates taking place in universities and among social movements today. For example, I joined FOR Peace Presence and later pursued doctoral research driven by my long-held questions about peace and politics, specifically, to evaluate nonviolent and armed strategies of social change for sustainability and peace. Conversely, my conceptual interrogation of territory and land emerged in graduate school through the academic literature on the discourses, production, and significance of territory in contemporary Latin America. My attention to the dynamics of memory arose over time from my experiences accompanying Peace Community commemorations, while academic colleagues encouraged me to more deeply analyze the spatial and political aspects of such practices. My attention to race began in accompanier-training workshops on the complex and contradictory nature of racial and citizenship privilege in international solidarity work. Later, in an academic working group on race and space, I was able to integrate a racial focus into my project to analyze the racial dynamics of not only accompaniment, but Colombia's war and resistance more broadly. That is to say, academic interests informed by political commitments drive this ethnography of peace.

Second, the Peace Community's Internal Council never requested that we co-structure the project's thematic focus, particular questions, and methods in accordance with PAR. When I broached this possibility with them, their response was to reaffirm the importance of an outside researcher's documentation of their process. They then redirected the topic of conversation to how my presence could be best utilized while in San José. As I reflected on this with fellow ex-accompanier Gwen Burnyeat, who was also there conducting an ethnography, we deduced that the Peace Community was not concerned with codirecting our academic projects, maybe due to a level of trust regarding what we would write and perform based on our historical relationships with them (field notes 2014). While they value such written works as contributions to what they frequently call the "justice of history," they prioritized the collaboration of concrete acts on the ground rather than of written works alone. I therefore consider this project to be participatory co-performance through particular contributions that are embedded within the Peace Community process: walking with them in pilgrimages, supporting FOR's accompaniment team, collecting and returning accompaniers' photos, and spreading written work about the significance of their resistance.

As a book, this work is inherently an intervention to enrich academic discourse about geographies of peace, memory, territory, race, and politics. While my methodology of radical performance geography emphasizes the embodied performance of political theory through solidarity and social movement action, it is also driven by the task of intervening in intellectual debates that are central to political transformation. To that end I now turn to the significance of the Peace Community's rupture with electoral representation and armed struggle through the production of an autonomous politics and a trans-ethnic resistance network.

PART I

WHAT IS THE PEACE COMMUNITY?

After an hour and a half walk down through tropical hills, I reach the Peace Community settlement of San Josecito. This is a settlement of about 150 people, with houses of mostly wooden walls and dirt floors. I have made this walk many times before, and like every other, it leaves me tired, and my back and socks sweaty. It will feel good to sit down. . . .

I head to the house of a Community member to have a conversation about memory and dignity in the Peace Community. This will be my first official research interview. Nationally and internationally known, she is María Brígida González, affectionately called Doña Brígida. I arrive at the house, recognizable by the flowers at its entrance—pink and red petals hovering over green stems. I go inside, and she greets me with a hug and smile. She proceeds to show me some of her recent pieces of art: a painting about Community villages threatened by the nearby Urrá dam projects and beaded bracelets that spell Comunidad de Paz.

The village was calm and quiet when we began to talk, with the only noise an intermittent rooster crow or Community member stopping by to say hello. Soon, however, someone started pumping merengue music SO LOUD, to the point that I had to lean closer to hear her words. I was nervous as I continued to listen and ask questions, hoping my voice recorder was still picking up her voice. . . .

When I go *there,* and I say to people: "dignity."
How do you want me to explain it?

Okay.
What is a life of dignity?

For the Peace Community.

For the Peace *Community?*
Well, it is having *shelter, health,* which is part of *life, education,* and land where you can farm. And *to grow stronger,* in yourself. In order to *reject,* everything that is counter to dignity.

(A MERENGUE SONG IS BLASTING,
"¡VAMOS AHORA, VAMOS AHORA!")

Dignity is being in settlements that don't allow the armed public forces *here*.
And *we are here*.
For example, this, Why is it called San Josecito *of Dignity*?
Because when we came from San *José*, we came to *build*. Here.
We are constructing *dignity*. To not live alongside the armed actors.
That is dignity.
           Not giving in to the system, *correct?*
Not *giving in* to the system.
                  Not . . .
Not, *not*,
not *compromise yourself,* not
                 be complicit.
Yes. And not be complicit. In the atrocities, and in all the demagoguery of the government.
That is dignity.
                (personal interview 2011)

Dignity is a central key word in the Peace Community lexicon. This interview excerpt introduces how I began to understand dignity from the Peace Community's perspective. Doña Brígida signaled a number of the components of this complex concept. There is the issue of meeting basic material needs, including shelter, health, life, education, and land. She continued by mentioning "not living alongside the armed actors" or being complicit in the "atrocities" and "demagoguery of the government." Dignity thus also incorporates the idea of truth. This involves being true to one's own convictions as well as a commitment to Truth itself, which in this case is the reality of political violence and discourse. She also mentioned "growing stronger in yourself," which refers to a personal element of growth and transformation as a subject with agency, in what we can imagine to take place in a number of other ways: politically, spiritually, and communally, among others. This understanding of dignity inspired what became central to my conceptualization of peace, which I understand as a radical and relational process of building ecological *dignity* through solidarity practices and networks. Indeed, the different aspects indicated by Doña Brígida encapsulate the core values and practices that make the Peace Community what it is. A core aspect of this conception of dignity is rupture with the practices and discourses of state militarism.

The history of this struggle and how it relates to political resistance and racialization is the focus of Part I. Reflecting on its relationship with broader social movement strategy in Colombia, Chapter 2 traces the Peace Community's formation and evolution through its first twenty years in its struggle against land grabbing by the narcobourgeoisie. Considering the question of state and social movement relationships, I ponder the significance of San José's insistence on autonomy. As a break with the typical forms of politics by the Colombian left to reform or indeed take over the state through elected representation or armed struggle, my contention is that the Peace Community's rupture with the armed groups and the state represents a decolonial form of politics. Chapter 3 offers a racial analysis of anti-campesino violence in Urabá and the Peace Community's national resistance network. I render how Community members and their partners in the Campesino University understand the war against them and consider the relationship between political violence and race as well as the extent to which certain nonethnic communities—in this case, San José's campesinos—might also be racialized and subvert racism through trans-ethnic solidarity.

CHAPTER 2

RETURNS AND RUPTURE

The Peace Community 1997–2016

The tropical jungle path below my feet is a mix of brown, gray, and green. Light brown dirt alongside patches of dark brown mud mix with gray rocks; some are pebbles, others the size of two fists. The path's edges rise up in grasses, ferns, and other leaves that range in color from deep dark green to almost yellow, which are backed by the browns of tree trunks. Bup . . . bup . . . bup . . . bup, the sound of our steps, adds to the constant and faint but high-pitched voicing of the forest: insects, chirping birds, and flowing water. Splash splash splash, the hooves of the horse carrying a Peace Community member ahead of me cross a stream and pierce the water. My rubber boots then make contact, ga-lush, ga-lush. . . . Looking up, a flower jumps out of the foliage, opening up with its pink, white, and red petals. Ooh, the foul smell of the excrement the horse ahead just left behind, and then a return to the refreshing, heavy, and slightly sweet aroma of the humid jungle.

We stop to take a drink from our water bottles or the stream. Ahh, the attempt to drink quickly causes drops to roll down my chin and neck. Campesinos wipe their sweaty brows with the cloth towels they keep over their shoulders. A few hours of hiking remain, so the rest is short. A high-pitched call "Vamos!" to resume our walking is followed by a deep yell "Mula! mula!" to the donkeys. And, with that, the trot of hooves, and rubber boots, resumes.

Our semi-silent saunter is replaced by talk of almost having reached a house along the way. Soon enough, after climbing up from a riverbed to higher ground, we see the thatched roof and light brown walls of wood cut from the surrounding hills. Palm trees surround us, and the host takes his machete from its black case covered with yellow and red designs, hanging from his waist, to chop open the green shell of a coconut, revealing its white flesh interior, and clear, sweet water. Next, we reach a body of deep green water and board a small boat. There is much commotion: everyone in our party of more than ten people is chatting about the hills through which we have walked until now, and the reservoir we are about to cross.

We smell the exhaust from the motor as we rev up to travel. From the canals of this lagoon, we emerge onto the Urrá reservoir, created by the Urrá hydro-

RETURNS AND RUPTURE

2.1. On an accompaniment from La Resbalosa to Naín, Córdoba. Author photo.

electric project in southwest Córdoba. Its wave-less light blue hue spreads wide into the horizon. The black dog of a nearby resident of the reservoir's shores paddles along feverishly with our wooden motorboat. We pull up to a muddy shore. Backpacks are passed from one person to next from the boat to land, and then carried up a slight incline to a family's home. Night is rolling in, as are mosquitos to electric lightbulbs and our sweaty skin. The buzz of insects is drowned out as greetings are exchanged between new acquaintances and old friends.

Over the next few days spanning late February and early March 2010, our delegation of Peace Community leaders and international accompaniers meets campesinos who have just recently joined the Peace Community. We had departed from Peace Community settlements in Mulatos and La Resbalosa to march into the neighboring department of Córdoba. Located on the shores of the Urrá reservoir or in the surrounding countryside, we encounter new Peace Community members in the veredas of Naín, Alto Joaquín, Puerto Nuevo, and Las Claras. A member from Alto Joaquín describes the process of joining the Peace Community, "We knew about the work of the Peace Community of San José de Apartadó. The farmers in this region organized meetings to discuss the possibilities of joining. Then, Community members came to meet with us to fully explain its principals. We feel much stronger and safer now that we are part of the Peace Community."

2.2. On the Urrá reservoir during a FORPP delegation. Author photo.

During its first eleven years of existence, the members of the Peace Community shared a common history: displacement in 1996 and 1997 from their farms and settlements in the district of San José de Apartadó, followed by the subsequent struggle to return to their homes, be it to La Unión, La Esperanza, or Mulatos. However, these new members from Córdoba are neither victims of that particular displacement nor relatives of the families who founded the Peace Community. But that is not to say they do not share a similarly tragic story. To the contrary, they do, albeit under different circumstances.

In the mid-1990s, the Colombian government authorized a massive hydroelectric project known as Urrá (after the name of the company, Urrá S.A.). Construction began in 1998, and this dam of the Sinú River flooded 7,400 hectares and displaced almost six thousand people. According to a Peace Community member from Las Claras, "This lot here where we are standing has been my family's since I was a child. Then came Urrá and massive displacement. People were offered a very small amount of money for their homes. Those who wouldn't sell were threatened by paramilitaries. They killed lots of people. We fled from here in 1995 to a town nearby. It was also dangerous there, and there was no work, so we returned here in 2003." This plot of land is located on ground still above the reservoir. Its incredibly rich soil is planted with various crops, such as rice, sugarcane, cacao, and pineapple.

However, in 2007 Urrá S.A. and the Colombian Ministry of Mines and Energy began to promote the construction of another dam, known as the Sinú River Project, or Urrá II, which would inundate over fifty thousand hectares, seven times as much as the first Urrá dam. A struggle about Urrá II ensued

2.3. Autonomous peace: Community meeting in Córdoba. Author photo.

between different Colombian government agencies. In June 2009 the Ministry of Environment denied the hydroelectric proposal on grounds that the new reservoir would encroach into part of the protected Paramillo Natural Park. Other concerns included the adverse social consequences for the inhabitants of the area, who include not only Peace Community families, but also other campesino and indigenous Emberá-Katío communities. Nevertheless, the project's proponents remain undeterred. Despite the Environmental Ministry's ruling, the president of Urrá S.A. states that in order to begin construction as planned in 2011, he will appeal to the Consejo de Estado (National State Council) for approval. A resident of Puerto Nuevo tells me that the farmers in the region fear being forcibly removed from their homes by 2011, and that "if they go ahead with Urrá II, about one hundred thousand families will be displaced." Given the widespread resistance to Urrá II on ecological and social grounds, it has yet to be constructed.

The Peace Community was founded in San José thirteen years ago to defend itself from displacement and violence. It is now extending its resistance to the encroachment of the armed groups and megaprojects across even more area to include farmers in Córdoba.

Many residents here have already been threatened for deciding to organize themselves with the Peace Community. A youth from Las Claras says, "I recently had to stand up to the army and guerrillas and tell them that I am a Peace Community member. And I therefore do not collaborate with or share information with the armed groups." In fact, just prior to our visit Peace Community communiqués dated January 18 and February 21, 2010, recorded instances of army soldiers in Naín and paramilitaries in Las Claras, respectively, threatening civilians (Comunidad de Paz de San José de Apartadó 2010).

Still, throughout the four settlements common sentiments among the new Community members are excitement and hope. Members in Alto Joaquin say, "We are farmers, and we want to work. This rich land gives life and food. We are happy to be part of this community because the Peace Community defends the rights of the campesino population. Previously when there were threats, we had to leave, and that was that." According to a man from Las Claras, "there is more security now due to international support and accompaniment. When there are threats, internationals will bear witness and respond." A man from Alto Joaquin adds, "We hope that as the other farmers see how we work as a community, they will join as well. There are threats, but we are going to resist being kicked off our lands again." (edited from my field notes 2010)

This ethnographic vignette describes one of the most strenuous and inspiring accompaniments I have ever done in Colombia. It involved hours of trekking through rivers and mountains, while also witnessing an unprecedented expansion of the Peace Community from its heartland in Apartadó, Antioquia, to the Urrá dam region in Córdoba. Such an expedition would have been unimaginable a decade before, considering the violence leveled against San José de Apartadó's campesinos from the late 1990s onward as part of the state and narcobourgeoisie's attempt to take over the Urabá region. This chapter details the evolution of the Peace Community from its initial stance against forced displacement to a consolidated resistance organization spanning multiple villages by the time of the 2016 peace agreement between the Colombian government and FARC.

To narrate this history of the Peace Community, I foreground the voices of two of its most influential leaders, Luis Eduardo Guerra and Eduar Lanchero. Their pronouncements are interspersed with supplementary statements by other Community members, my own commentary, and historical references. As a complement to this historical background, see the Appendix for a timeline of San José de Apartadó history.

Luis Eduardo Guerra was one of the Peace Community's founding members and most respected leaders. He was a fixture on the Community's leadership board, called the Internal Council. He was also among its most well-known leaders internationally, having traveled to Europe and the United States on speaking tours. For example, he spoke at the School of the Americas vigil in November 2002 in Columbus, Georgia. Luis Eduardo was among the victims of the 2005 massacre in Mulatos, after having been the Community's delegated interlocutor with the state. This chapter

2.4. Luis Eduardo Guerra commemorated. Photo by Mayra Sofía Moreno, with permission.

integrates excerpts of his final interview conducted by the Italian Solidarity Network just prior to the massacre, in which he chillingly affirmed, "Today we are speaking, tomorrow we can be dead," right before he would in fact be killed (Red Italiana de Solidaridad 2005). The Community frequently plays the audio in full during the annual 2005 massacre commemoration in Mulatos.

2.5. Organic intellectual: Eduar Lanchero, second from the left, with Community members at the renovated school in La Resbalosa. Author photo.

Eduar Lanchero was a native of Bogotá who, along with Father Javier Giraldo and Sister Clara Lagos, was one of the Colombian advisers of the Peace Community from its early days as members of the Comisión Intercongregacional de Justicia y Paz (Intercongregational Justice and Peace Commission). While officially an *asesor* (consultant), Eduar was beloved by Peace Community members and was considered one of its greatest leaders. This chapter integrates excerpts of statements from a documentary about the Peace Community and Lanchero's two books, in which he offered a political theorization of the Peace Community (Buenaventura 2011; Lanchero 2000, 2002). He epitomized the figure of the "organic intellectual" (Gramsci 1971). His analysis and leadership as an intellectual embedded in a struggle shaped and were fundamentally shaped by the movement. Precisely for this reason Lanchero was among the most threatened people associated with the Peace Community. Indeed, one of the reasons we were asked as international accompaniers to join the 2010 trip to Córdoba detailed above was to provide protection for Eduar, who was one of the delegation's leaders. After suffering repeated bouts of malaria from his time in San José de Apartadó and ultimately cancer, Lanchero passed away in July 2012. He had informed his family that he wanted to be buried in the Peace Community. The day after his death, hundreds of campesinos went to meet his casket as it arrived to San Josecito (Giraldo Moreno 2012), where his tomb remains today.

2.6. Eduar Lanchero's tomb in San Josecito. Author photo.

The use of their statements is a means to embrace Eduar's and Luis Eduardo's "agency of the dead" (Gómez Correal, forthcoming), which is evident in Peace Community commemorations as well as this text: their words continue to create history and truth. Drawing from these narratives and other sources, this chapter traces the history of the Peace Community's first two decades of existence. It situates the formation of the Peace Community within the political crisis in Colombia and Urabá in the late 1990s, in which the traditional radical approaches to social change through armed struggle or electoral party and policy campaigns directed at taking control of the state had proved futile. Consistent with many campesino and ethnic communities' growing rejection of armed groups' and the state's control in this period, San José de Apartadó's praxis of autonomy reflected the forging of a creative and alternative mode of politics. The Peace Community's survival for over two decades since the army-paramilitary onslaught exhibits an anticolonial politics that refuses to be displaced by the needs of capitalism and state hegemony.

CRISIS OF POLITICAL FAILURE

Understanding the emergence of the Peace Community in the late 1990s requires contextualizing this historical moment of political crisis in Colombia. The crisis was rooted in a failure of the dominant forms of counter-hegemonic politics to change Colombia's historically exclusive political and economic structure. Two of the most emblematic attempts at social change in the twentieth century by the Colombian Left were the FARC-EP guerrillas and the Patriotic Union (UP, Unión Patriótica) party. Both were strategies to reform or take control of the state but by different means: insurgent armed struggle and electoral party politics, respectively. The FARC was central to the formation of the UP, as a civilian party that would contribute toward combining "todas las formas de lucha" (all forms of struggle) alongside an armed insurgency. However, the two should not be equated as different wings of the same organization. The UP was comprised of a diverse coalition of actors rather than simply being a wing of the FARC. Understanding each organization's focus separately is crucial to analyzing the Peace Community's rupture with both strategies.

Following the assassination of Liberal guerrillas who demobilized at the end of the civil war between Conservatives and Liberals known as La Violencia, the FARC was founded in 1966 to defend themselves from further attacks by the state military. Indeed, according to Forrest Hylton (2006), during the La Violencia period, "communist enclaves were the only territories where life was *not* regulated by terror," where frameworks for conflict resolution, land use, civil marriage, women's equality, and indigenous rights were established (46). The FARC emerged from such roots of campesino communism during the post–La Violencia period. In the era known as the National Front, the leadership of the Conservative and Liberal parties agreed to rotate the presidency in order to avoid partisan violence and ensure political stability. Yet this bipartisan governance also locked out any alternative political parties, including those to the Left.

This was the Cold War era, when the Colombian government advanced the US-informed Plan Lazo, a counterinsurgency project to kill suspected communists. The most infamous military operation was in 1964 in a communist hamlet in Marquetalia, Tolima. In response, some of the campesinos under siege who escaped organized themselves into a mobile guerrilla army (Hylton 2006). The FARC's political platform had historically been focused on two issues: agrarian reform and increased political participation for campesinos and the poor. In subsequent decades the FARC expanded into a variety of Colombian departments and came to include revolutionary students, unemployed youth, and leftist politicians fleeing persecution (Chernick 2009). Their largest expansion took place in the era of the booming cocaine economy, from which the FARC earned income initially by taxing coca leaf growers at the beginning of the commodity chain before becoming intermediaries between coca farmers and narcotraffickers (Ortíz 2006). While the coca trade potentiated the FARC's growth, the organization's role in the illegal drug trade should not to be confused with that of the Medellín and Cali cartels or subsequent narco-paramilitaries, who vertically integrate and control production and trafficking (Camacho Guizado 2006; Tate 2015). It should also be noted that the FARC never truly represented a threat to take over the Colombian state militarily. Despite its expansion into 13 percent of the country's municipalities covering up to 40 percent of Colombia's area as of 1998, those areas accounted for "less than 10 percent of the population, none of its industry, and remarkably little infrastructure" (Tate 2015: 53). Nevertheless, the FARC—along with the Ejército de Liberación Nacional (ELN, National Liberation Army)—represented the most radical wing of Colombia's political Left demanding social transformation.

In their practices, however, the FARC could hardly be considered a political alternative for addressing Colombia's inequality and exploitation. Marc Chernick (2009) is correct to assert that the FARC was not a purely "communist" movement; it was influenced just as much by Colombian liberalism as Soviet communism. Supporting coca production contradicts the search for an alternative to capitalist socioeconomic relations. Teófilo Vásquez (2011) remarks, "The FARC does not want to realize that social reproduction based in the coca economy creates precarious social identities, more subject to economic interests than to strong political identities and ideas, which are an indispensable condition for a project in which political discourse and rhetoric are in fact central" (416). While coca has afforded many Colombian campesinos a means of survival income amid increasing precarity during the neoliberal era, coca production follows a capitalist logic and pushes farmers into further submission to armed drug trafficking groups, thus undermining collective logics of governance and work. Anthony Dest (2021) argues that the "anti-culture of coca"—a term used by an Afro-Colombian Community Council leader in Cauca critical of coca production—contributes to advance the coloniality of power.

I recall Peace Community farmers in Las Claras, Córdoba, telling an international delegation in 2011 how the FARC insisted that they grow coca, since this was the best available income generator and thus campesino survival strategy. Peace Community campesinos denounced this, arguing that growing the coca leaf, while not ecologically destructive on its own, invites Drug War–driven government fumigations, which cause substantial damage to the soil and water. The radicality of the Peace Community's eschewal of growing coca cannot be underestimated in a country where it has become one of the main campesino crops. Consistent with Dest's (2021) analysis, Peace Community campesinos said that they rejected growing coca because it led farmers to cede authority to the actor to whom they were selling, be it the guerrillas, paramilitaries, or police or army officers, all of whom are active in the coca trade in Urabá's rural areas and small towns (field notes 2008, 2011).

However, that is not to say that guerrilla and paramilitary control are equal. While paramilitaries work against communities' self-organization, the FARC promoted communal living and work. However, their form of community was not voluntary. It was mandatory and forced. Breaking their rules for "living in a dignified and honest community" resulted in fines, while "capital offenses"—including being an informant for another armed group, rape, repeated drug abuse, falling asleep while on duty, or using a weapon against another FARC combatant—were punished by execution (Tate 2015: 117, 249). In its attempt to resist state domination, the FARC reproduced the hierarchical social relations of sovereign power while perpetuating a cycle of indoctrinated and retaliatory violence (Sánchez 2006).

In contrast, the Patriotic Union party emerged as an attempt to shift Colombia's unequal and exclusionary social and political structure through electoral politics and subsequent policy reform. The party was founded in 1985 by an array of guerrilla fighters—including from the FARC—who sought social change through the ballot box. It also included other people from the Colombian Left, such as urban intellectuals. It arose in the historical conjuncture leading up to 1988, when city mayors in the country's municipalities would be elected for the first time by popular vote rather than being appointed by the national president. The UP succeeded in winning multiple municipal elections. However, paramilitary campaigns—coordinated, supported, or tolerated by the Colombian armed forces—subsequently assassinated over three thousand UP party leaders across the country from 1985 to 2000, including two presidential candidates, in what has been called a political genocide (Gomez-Suarez 2017).

In fact, Apartadó was one of the municipalities where the UP party won the city council and then implemented an array of social investment programs, including in the corregimiento of San José de Apartadó, whose UP city council delegate was ultimately a victim of the genocide. Wherever one's sympathies lie regarding the Patriotic Union's project, it ultimately was an ineffective strategy for political change—not due to its own program but rather due to the limits of electoral politics in a context of increasing paramilitarism amid the consolidation of the narcobourgeoisie.

The extermination of the UP was another case of the historical inability of Colombian opposition parties to achieve widespread reforms, due in part to the staunch resistance by the Colombian elite. The Colombian "elite" is not a homogenous group, of course. The emergence of the narcobourgeoisie exemplifies this, because it arose less from traditional ruling families or industrial elites and more from middle- and lower-class sectors who generated wealth through illegal economies like drug trafficking or work as paramilitaries (Richani 2007, 2012). Colombian elites have been divided among themselves in various moments of the country's history, with some advocating for progressive social reforms. Nevertheless, most of these possibilities have been thwarted by either the elites ultimately reuniting with one another to reaffirm a collective resistance to change or regional groups impeding the materialization of national-level reforms through the use of paramilitary repression. Examples include the failure to achieve pro-campesino land rights or agrarian reform (LeGrand 1986; Hylton 2006) as well as violence against indigenous and black communities, despite legal recognition of these groups and their territories (Castillo 2004; Dest 2020; Fals Borda 1975; Lame 2004; Oslender 2016). In fact, renowned scholar Gonzalo Sánchez (2006) has argued that there is nothing positive to commemorate in Colombian history. He notes that the most widely commemorated event is one of tragedy: the Bogotazo uprising following the assassination of popular Liberal presidential candidate Jorge Eliécer Gaitán in 1948. Furthermore, considering the virulent attacks from different sectors of society against the 2016 government–FARC peace accord, it appears unlikely that even such a historical agreement lauded by the international community and many in the national peace movement will fulfill its promise and emerge as a source of national pride.

This is not to say that state-oriented politics of party movements and armed struggle are *inherently* ineffective. "Effectiveness" depends on a particular political movement's objectives and conjunctural possibilities (Churchill 2007). While the guerrillas are the group most often critiqued for their combination of "all forms of struggle," it is actually the paramilitary groups who best combined an armed movement with electoral politics in order to effectively advance their ideological project (Romero 2006). This exemplifies how, in the dominant forms of sovereign power and modern politics, war can be "politics by other means" (Clausewitz 1982), but hegemonic politics is indeed "war by other means" (Foucault 2003).

When the narcobourgeoisie's paramilitary offensive intensified in the 1990s, San José's campesinos could have doubled down with armed resistance alongside the FARC or reaffirmed the quest for state reforms through the UP or another party. But they did neither, seemingly responding to the need for alternative forms of politics amid this antagonism. Following Frantz Fanon (2004), writing about the phase after anticolonial movements earn national independence, in war contexts "everybody therefore has violence on their minds and the question is not so much responding to violence with more violence but rather how to diffuse the crisis" (33). Fanon asserts that the principal confrontation is not the battle against colonizers and oppressors; a true decolonial revolution is constituted by new ways of being, thinking, and acting. This speaks to the need for transitions from merely reactive actions against injustice to affirmative projects of solidarity and dignity. The divergent strategy of San José de Apartadó's farmers to organize themselves as a peace community, rather than arming themselves in self-defense or forming a new political party, suggests the impasse facing those two dominant methods of political change in Colombia in the late 1990s. In response the Peace Community forged another type of emergent politics.

FORMATION OF THE PEACE COMMUNITY IN 1997

In an interview recorded just before his death, Luis Eduardo Guerra was asked to begin by explaining the conditions in which they organized themselves. He noted the waves of evictions in the villages of San José amid a context of increasing paramilitarism and its attack on popular movements in the region:

> This was as a consequence of all the *conflict* that there was in the region. Since '95. *All* of the development of the paramilitary project. The extermination of the Patriotic Union, the Communist Party, and in general, all of the popular organizations that there were in the region. When this extermination took place, through blood and fire from the military and paramilitary forces, the campesino communities in San José de Apartadó—those of us who inhabited the villages—we were left totally *alone*. And suffering all the aggressions of the army. And of the paramilitaries. The large majority of [those living in] the thirty-two veredas that existed had to move away. (Red Italiana de Solidaridad 2005)

In the years preceding the founding of the Peace Community, Urabá had become one of the foci of the state and paramilitary's counterinsurgency project, which included attacking not only guerrillas, but also residents living in guerrilla-controlled places as well as popular or leftist social organizations. Violence began to escalate in Urabá during the 1980s, especially in the lowland banana plantation zone where armed groups disputed control over production and union organizing, including paramilitaries work-

2.7. Legacies of the Patriotic Union: This former health center was built in Mulatos as part of the UP party's social investment in health and education infrastructure in San José de Apartadó during the 1990s. It was renovated to be a mini health center and grain storage building in the Peace Community's Luis Eduardo Guerra Peace Village. Author photo.

ing in conjunction with corporations such as Chiquita to confront banana worker unions tied to guerrilla groups (Aparicio 2012; García 1996). This is consistent with entrepreneurs' speculative accumulation strategy across the country to use military and paramilitary forces to destroy campesino and union organizations; acquire undervalued land in guerrilla regions; and then reap profits from mineral extraction, agribusiness, or land speculation (Richani 2007, 2012; Hristov 2009, 2014; Morris 2019; Ballvé 2020). By the early 1990s national organizations began to attend to the intensification of human rights violations in Urabá (Aparicio 2012).

The Patriotic Union had widespread support in the region, given its pro-campesino development program, and San José was a strong voting bloc for the party. In addition, Bartolomé Cataño, who had founded the corregimiento of San José de Apartadó, was a UP councilor to the Apartadó City Council. San José's villages benefited greatly from the policies of the Patriotic Union governments. The district saw social investments, including the construction of health centers and schools, even in villages far afield. Under the administration of Mayor Gloria Cuartas Montoya beginning in 1995, the municipal government began installing electricity and running water. These projects followed in the wake of decades of rural development programs carried out by regional and international development agencies, including the Urabá Development Corporation and the Netherlands government (Aparicio 2012). However, the UP projects were interrupted by the paramilitaries' killing campaign against Patriotic Union members and displacements of San José's farmers. At the time of the mass displacement in 1996, only San José town and the village of La Unión had running water and electricity. The extermination of the Patriotic Union party meant the end of these social investments, and most of San José's settlements remained without these amenities as of 2016.

As part of their larger campaign across Urabá, the paramilitaries and the army targeted San José de Apartadó because it was a historical stronghold of both the Patriotic Union and the FARC, whose 5th Front was reportedly founded there in 1973 (García de la Torre et al. 2011: 300). This project built from prior campaigns such as the Plan Retorno (1986–1989), in which banana businessmen, cattle ranchers, drug cartels, and the state's armed forces allied with one another against the FARC and any campesinos, community leaders, and organizations deemed subversive (Burnyeat 2018). Congruent with a critique of the enforced death of "necropolitics" (Mbembé 2003), Eduar Lanchero analyzed the logic of such paramilitarism, which rejects plurality and difference: "Paramilitarism is a way of life where power is above life. And therefore it exterminates life in many ways. In the same respect, all forms of resistance have to be extinguished. The resistance of civilian communities is extinguished. Human rights activists are threatened and murdered. There is a total control over society. So there is something which they call a *limpieza* [cleaning or cleansing of undesirable peoples], which means to kill everyone who does not fit within their scheme" (Buenaventura 2011).

Alliances between different actors in Urabá epitomized the consolidation of the narcobourgeoisie across the country in this period, including agribusiness corporations, cattle ranchers, paramilitary forces, the military, and government officials (Richani 2002; Hristov 2009; Ballvé 2020). With respect to armed groups, the military and paramilitary operations of the late 1990s in Urabá occurred amid a confluence of Antioquia's governmental leaders who were united by their counterinsurgency aim: Governor Álvaro Uribe Vélez and 17th Brigade army commander Rito Alejo del Río. Additionally, fierce antiguerrilla leader Carlos Castaño of the paramilitary Autodefensas Unidas de Colombia (AUC, United Self-Defense Forces of Colombia) was based in neighboring Córdoba (Romero 2006). Carlos's brother and fellow AUC leader Vicente Castaño described their state building and accumulation aims in no uncertain terms: "In Urabá we have oil palm crops. I, myself, was able to get businesspeople to invest in those projects that are long-term and productive. The idea is to take the rich to invest in this type of project in different parts of the country. To bring the rich to these zones is for the state institutions to arrive. Unfortunately, state institutions only go along with these things when the rich are there. We have to take the rich to all the regions of the country and that is one of the missions that all the commanders have" (*Semana* 2005). Such military operations and capitalist investment in frontier regions—that entail the eviction of campesinos already living there—advanced what Orlando Fals Borda (1975) had decades earlier called the "decomposition of the campesino."

Apartadó's campesinos reacted to the mass evictions from their lands by marching to the municipal city center and occupying its stadium from June to July 1996. They denounced forced displacement in San José de Apartadó and called for an end to state violence. A governmental verification commission documented ninety-one state crimes between May and August 1996, including joint military and paramilitary action, forced displacement, and the destruction of crops. All of these crimes still remained in impunity as this book went to press. The march had been organized by San José community leader Bartolomé Cataño. He was then assassinated on August 16, 1996 (Giraldo Moreno 2010).

With the extermination of the region's leftist and grassroots social organizations, such as the Patriotic Union, the farmers in San José sought an alternative political strategy. Luis Eduardo Guerra proceeded to describe the reaction of those who remained after the initial displacements and how they responded to their increasing isolation through alliances with the Catholic Church and national human rights organizations:

> And us—those who were there, *still in eleven veredas*—decided to look for support in the Church. To see what we could do. [We had to decide] if we were going to let [the armed actors] kill us *there* [or] if we would have *to leave*. The large majority of us had nowhere to go. And that is where we searched for a *possibility*. . . . With the help of the Church, some other organizations, [and] national NGOs . . . we made the proposal of what initially were humanitarian territories. To concentrate ourselves there and ask for the respect of the armed actors, including the state, the paramilitaries, and the insurgency. (Red Italiana de Solidaridad 2005)

The idea of forming "humanitarian territories" emerged in a series of workshops facilitated by the local Catholic diocese as well as Colombian NGOs, including the Intercongregational Justice and Peace Commission and the Centro de Investigación y Educación Popular (CINEP, Research and Popular Education Center). This proposal was rooted in the United Nation's Universal Declaration of Human Rights and international humanitarian law, which affirm the right of civilians to not participate in wars against their will. This progressive sector of the Catholic Church, including those in the Liberation Theology tradition (Welch 2007), was involved in similar community organizing initiatives across Colombia during this period (Tate 2015). This is one of the three primary "vectors" Juan Ricardo Aparicio (2012, 2015) identifies as fundamental to creating the conditions for the possibility of the Peace Community to emerge in this particular place and time of neoliberal governmentality: a Colombian Left directed by unions as well as the progressive wing of the Catholic Church committed to defend and protect "victims" and "the poor." The Peace Community's inaugural declaration was also accompanied internationally by a Dutch parliamentarian and the Dutch NGO Paz Christi (Burnyeat 2018), which reflected a continuation of the Netherlands' work toward rural development in Urabá and San José as well as the role of global solidarity in the Peace Community process more broadly.

Of course the ability to create an organized resistance to war was also enabled by San José's farmers' decades of community organizing experience. Aparicio (2012) signals this as another vector of the Peace Community assemblage: a tradition of Colombian campesino migrants struggling for autonomy. In this case it can be traced at least as far back as families in San José who had survived La Violencia. Elder Community members, such as Jesús Emilio Montoya, frequently recounted in conversations and interviews with me how they had survived living in the forest for four years after fleeing attacks by the state and Conservative paramilitary forces of that era before migrating to Apartadó in search of land (field notes 2020). Many of San José's elders were quite aware of the dynamics of armed conflict and could draw on lessons about how taking up arms in self-defense often intensifies violence (Roldán 2002). Additionally, in San José itself campesinos were undoubtedly influenced by political education from the FARC as well as in workshops facilitated by the Unión Nacional de Oposición (UNO, National Union of Opposition) and the radical Sincelejo wing of the Asociación Nacional de Usuarios Campesinos (ANUC, National Association of Campesinos) (Aparicio 2012), with the latter being a protagonist in the agrarian reform movement demanding land titles for campesinos (Zamosc 1986).

Locally San José's farmers had organized into village-level *Juntas de Acción Comunal* (JAC, Communal Action Boards), the smallest governmental administrative unit in Colombia. They had also developed a robust and district-wide socioeconomic program in the Balsamar Cooperative, which managed the buying and selling of cacao beans and developed communal projects (Burnyeat 2018). The campesinos drew from decades of self-organization since settling the area in the 1960s. Paralleling settler practices in frontier zones across Colombia's Andean region (LeGrand 1986), large groups of farmers living in or adjacent to a given village would work on one family's farm one day and then move to another family's plot the next. San José's campesinos frequently recall how this form of collaborative work, known as *convite*, would conclude each harvest with village celebrations. The commitments to collective work and solidarity that would come to define the Peace Community were therefore reconfigurations of already existing campesino practices.

Even so, I find Luis Eduardo Guerra's emphasis in the quote above on the word *possibility* quite telling. It appears dialectically opposed to the apparent "impossibility" of an alternative strategy beyond displacement, armed self-defense, or policy reform. This is a sentiment I encounter frequently among the Peace Community. Their survival or construction of an alternative is never taken for granted. It is always an experience of contingent possibility, constructed in daily practice and through strategic decisions, epitomized by their innovative strategy to organize themselves as a peace community in 1997. Another then-member of the Internal Council, Renato Areiza, speaking from the village of La Unión, reiterated the key role of the Catholic Church's regional bishop (who notably brought knowledge and inspiration from his experience with ecclesial base communities in Brazil [Aparicio 2012]):

> This was a village. There were pool halls, stores, bars, all the things you would find in a village. In '97, the paramilitaries had advanced in all of [Urabá] and across the entire *country*, you could say. They had already been displacing people from the other villages, like La Esperanza, Las Nieves, Porvenir, Mulatos. . . . *We were worried*. We saw that the people from veredas further up the mountain were displacing, and so, we wondered, "*What about us?* Are they also going to kick us out too?" So, we asked Bishop Isaías Duarte Cancino for advice, for an *idea*. He told us, well, we need to form *neutral zones*, so that the armed actors don't enter. And so we said, *okay*. (Lozano 2006)

While inspired by indigenous communities in the region declaring themselves neutral in the armed conflict earlier in the decade, San José ultimately decided against naming its organization with the language of "neutrality." While many Community members continue to refer to their neutrality and its importance—Luis Eduardo will do so, below—their official designation was not as a "neutral zone." They intentionally and strategically named themselves a "peace community," for reasons described by Father Giraldo Moreno (2010):

> Throughout the year of 1996, various *neutral communities* were being established, for the most part among indigenous groups of Antioquia. But by the end of the year, there was a strong debate about the word "neutrality," since there were interpretations that only considered this possible in relation to the illegal armed groups and not with regard to the official army. For many, however, the fusion between the National Army and the paramilitaries was so evident, and their methods of barbarism so identical, that there was no way to make

a distinction between the armed groups. For that reason, they opted for the denomination of *Peace Community*, that says NO, equally, to all the armed groups. (35, emphasis original)

This diverted from then-governor of Antioquia Álvaro Uribe's proposal of "active neutrality." In 1996 Governor Uribe attended a meeting of delegates from communities across the Urabá region, including San José. He proposed that they organize themselves as *Convivir* (living together) communities, an organizational model he was implementing across the department. Officially called Servicios Especiales de Vigilancia y Seguridad Privada (Special Services of Surveillance and Private Security), they were designed for civilians to break their links with the guerrillas through an alliance with the National Army (Giraldo Moreno 2007). Residents would arm themselves against guerrilla attack and inform state forces about the guerrillas' movements. In effect, these civilians would become paramilitaries themselves or, at the very least, become governed by paramilitary and army units (Tobón 1997). Indeed, demobilized paramilitary Éver Veloza García, alias "H.H.," famously declared in 2008 during his testimony as part of the Justice and Peace Law linked to the AUC demobilization: "Let's not tell lies, all of the Convivir were ours" (Comisión Colombiana de Juristas 2008).

San José de Apartadó refused to become a Convivir allied with the state and paramilitaries. Influenced by religious values tied to the Catholic Church, this framing as a "peace community" was also significant by creating a different organizational goal, expectation, and praxis than the mere "neutrality" of a "humanitarian space" of refuge. In addition to withdrawing support and legitimacy for external armed actors, a "peace community" also defines what will constitute the group *internally*: communal life and solidarity.

Luis Eduardo proceeded to describe the concrete actions associated with their declaration: "When we finally organized ourselves and made the declaration, it was March 23, 1997. We signed the commitment to not participate in the war, to not collaborate with any armed actor" (Red Italiana de Solidaridad 2005). The rules included not passing information to any of the armed parties as well as denouncing injustice and impunity (Comunidad de Paz de San José de Apartadó 2005b). Later that year, after suffering further attacks by (para)militaries and guerrillas, they added "participate in community work" to their core commitments. These are listed on signs that mark Community villages and farms.

In subsequent years, they have incorporated additional rules. These include not drinking alcohol within San José de Apartadó, due to the fact that intoxicated individuals often induce armed groups' intervention to resolve disputes and are also more likely to commit domestic violence. They also

2.8. Peace Community billboard with additional commitments: "The Community freely . . . does not consume alcohol. Says no to illicit crops [and individual] reparations to victims." Author photo.

prohibit growing illicit crops, such as coca, which have become increasingly common in the Abibe Range and whose production brings the campesino under the authority of the guerrillas and paramilitaries who purchase or traffic them. Additionally, they refuse to receive individual reparations to victims from the state—such as those offered by the 2011 Victims and Land Restitution Law legislated by the Juan Manuel Santos administration—without systematic justice. The Peace Community's refusals reflect a series of ruptures with armed groups and state hegemony, thus confronting economic and political logics in the coloniality of power.

Even today, the original principles roll off the tongues of Community members almost verbatim when they speak: "Not participate directly or indirectly in the war. Not collaborate with any armed actor. Participate in community work." They know them by heart, and visitors hear them repeatedly when talking to Community members. This reflects Community members' intense belief in these principles, which is the product of the communal process of deciding what those regulations would be. Father Giraldo gave an account of this process: "It was a profoundly democratic process. Each norm was written out, discussed in each family, and then discussed house by house, on street corners. Later there were assemblies and then it would return to a second process of discussion by family, neighborhood, and assembly. And for that reason, it is a *reglamento* [set of rules] of much consensus" (Moncada Hurtado, Ossa, and Caro Morales 2011a). Eduar Lanchero (2002) provided his own perspective: "The desolation was brutal but the resistance remained alive, because it was not a process sustained by a certain number of leaders but was a historical movement of an entire community in which everyone believed, from the oldest to the youngest" (49).

Given the support of the Catholic Church as well as different NGOs, the members of the newly formed Peace Community hoped to be respected by the armed groups and be able to remain in their homes and farms. However, Renato Areiza described what immediately followed: "And so, we signed a declaration where it would be registered that we agree to being neutral. And we signed it on March 23 of '97. Which we can say, for us, was *fruitless*, because the following *week* there was an *intense* joint military and paramilitary attack" (Lozano 2006). San José's residents frequently recount how army soldiers responded by bombing the villages with helicopters. Troops patrolling the villages infamously told farmers that they had five days to leave before the *mochecabezas* (those who cut people's heads off) would arrive. In fact, paramilitaries arrived only three days later, killing many of those they encountered (Comunidad de Paz de San José de Apartadó 2005a; Giraldo Moreno 2010; Masullo Jiménez 2015). Frank Safford and Marco Palacios (2002) implicitly infer the coloniality of such operations by describing the "spirit of conquest" that "infuses the military when it imposes public order on regions 'dominated by communism'" (282).

Luis Eduardo Guerra described the armed actors' reaction to San José's declaration and the Community's subsequent response: "As a consequence, what happened was an even *stronger* repression. There was the mass displacement of those eleven veredas, where they faced *massacres*, where [the army/paramilitaries] gave timetables to displace the people, so that people would displace, with threats that they would *kill them*. From then on, we all concentrated ourselves here in the town of San José de Apartadó" (Red Italiana de Solidaridad 2005). The process of forced displacement in San José de Apartadó thus occurred in two rounds, prior to which the district reportedly had over seven thousand inhabitants. The first mass displacement took place during the paramilitary incursions of 1996, when the majority of inhabitants left. The second took place *after* the remaining campesinos declared themselves a peace community. In the wake of the attacks the week after the founding of the Peace Community in March 1997, only ten families remained in the town of San José, with the other ninety having fled (Burnyeat 2018).

Father Giraldo gave his analysis on the attacks following San Jose's farmers' declaration as a peace community, "I interpret it as a response by the state, affirmed through its actions, which said, 'We don't want this type

TABLE 2.1. KILLINGS IN SAN JOSÉ DE APARTADÓ BY YEAR, 1977-2012.

Year	Number of killings pre–Peace Community	Number of killings post–Peace Community	Total number of killings	Percent of all killings 1977–2012
1977	12		12	6%
1992	3		3	1%
1996	12		12	6%
1997	6	44	50	24%
1998		13	13	6%
1999		4	4	2%
2000		26	26	12%
2001		8	8	4%
2002		21	21	10%
2003		1	1	0.5%
2004		7	7	3%
2005		18	18	8.5%
2006		5	5	3%
2007		11	11	5%
2008		1	1	0.5%
2009		5	5	3%
2010		1	1	0.5%
2011		9	9	4%
2012		3	3	1%
Percent of all killings 1977–2012	16%	84%		
Total	33	177	210	100%

Source: Table by author using data from a San José de Apartadó Peace Community postcard listing the names and dates of each killing up to 2012. This list was derived from the Center for Research and Popular Education's (CINEP) database. For details of each killing to 2010, see Giraldo Moreno (2010).

of communities. And so that other communities do not become motivated to do the same, we are going to exterminate this one by drowning it in its own blood'" (Lozano 2006). In other words, as Luke Finn (2013) argues, when the Peace Community rejected all forms of violence and put the state's violence on par with that of non-state armed groups, it provoked violent retaliation by calling the state formation itself into question, because the state is precisely defined by its ability to exert legitimate force over its population (Weber 1946).

Then, on October 6, 1997, the Peace Community began to suffer attacks from FARC guerrillas as well. During a *comunitario* (community workday) in La Linda, three Peace Community members, including Internal Council leader Ramiro Correa, were assassinated by the FARC's 5th Front due to the Peace Community's new refusal to sell any goods to the guerrillas. Lanchero (2002) described the aftermath:

> It is impossible to describe the days that followed, the weeping and desperation. The loneliness was immense, and the energy was at rock bottom. The idea of leaving San José caused terror, and it was visible that the social fabric that was still just returning had been torn. The task of reconstruction looked even more difficult because everyone was moving about on their own: the workshops, work, analysis, and gatherings of joint reflection had been left behind. The search for community had been clouded by the smell of death.
>
> Terror left a clear lesson: communal and organizational work was seen as a danger. To participate was a death threat. During this rough period nobody attended meetings or workshops. In the community workdays, they were only able to bring together three people at a maximum. It was disheartening to see the proposal of a different economy destroyed, of an experience for dignity in the middle of war. (52)

While most attacks against the Community have come from the military and paramilitary—and as a result the Community's denunciations are mostly directed at the state—the Peace Community was not only a rejection of becoming informants for the state in Governor Uribe's Convivirs, but also a rupture with the guerrillas, who had been a traditional authority in the zone for decades.

Peace Community member Jesús Emilio Montoya, affectionately called Montoya, described the arrival of the FARC and the Ejército Popular de Liberación (EPL, Popular Liberation Army) to San José de Apartadó decades earlier:

> The first guerrilla group here was men following Tiro Fijo [Sure Shot or Manuel Marulanda, founder of the FARC]. The first innocent person they killed was a nurse. . . . Then came the EPL. . . . They said they came to defend us because we were defenseless, poor, and they did not want the rich people to abuse us. Instead they said that we had to arrive at equality, where the rich person was less rich, and the poor person was less poor. That was what they told us. But look at them afterwards and now, what they did, when [the EPL demobilized in 1991]. They joined the paramilitaries. . . . Later, the FARC . . . asked [me once when we passed on a trail], "Are you with us?" I responded, "But we don't want any army." . . . They said goodbye and we kept walking. . . . Their forces kept getting bigger, the 5th, 57th, 58th Fronts. . . . They would exploit the campesino and

even kill. They said that the time would come when the state would put us in the middle of war. . . . I would tell them, "I am a working person [not aligned with any armed group]. And that's the truth." (personal interview 2012)

Montoya's narrative exemplifies an insistence on working autonomously without interference from any armed groups, a sentiment that strongly defines not only the Peace Community but also many of Colombia's campesinos, which Aparicio (2012) calls "a liberal tradition of campesino settlers struggling for their autonomy" (281). Moreover, it is reflective of a "principled" rather than merely "strategic" nonviolence, in which nonviolence is not merely a means to an end but in fact a moral lifestyle (Burrowes 1996; Teixeira 1999; Schock 2005). Former Internal Council member Jesús Emilio Tuberquia deconstructed militaristic politics: "There are people who believe that guns protect them, but that is a lie. That is a very big misunderstanding, right? Because guns are not designed to safeguard the life of people, but to destroy it, put it to an end" (Moncada Hurtado, Ossa, and Caro Morales 2011a).

Of course most civilian noncombatants tend to cooperate with an armed actor—whether or not they sympathize with the actor's cause and presence—if there is only one where they live.[1] In such regions there tend to be low levels of direct violence because the armed actor's authority is uncontested and killing its base likely does more to delegitimize the group than maintain support for it. However, when a rival armed group enters to contest the area, high levels of violence tend to ensue. The invading force targets the residents as "followers" of the other group, while the group traditionally controlling the area will react with increasingly harsh treatment against those suspected of collaborating with or shifting their allegiances to the new group (Roldán 2002; Vásquez and Vargas 2011; Tate 2015).

The formation of peace communities was a strategy to break from such hegemonic control and resist attack amid a confrontation between armed actors. In San José de Apartadó, following the killings by army, paramilitary, and guerrilla forces in 1997, only a small group continued to resist through the peace community strategy. To continue with Luis Eduardo Guerra's narration: "*Some* of us continued in the process, about 630 people. *Others* did not, they left. Because they *no longer believed* that they would respect us. And from then until now, this has been a situation of resistance. Because we have had massacres, selective assassinations—we are speaking about how they have assassinated more than 130 people among us. From the civilian population. Various leaders of the Community" (Red Italiana de Solidaridad 2005). I find it revealing that Luis Eduardo emphasized the words "*some* of us" and "*others*." He pointed to divergent reactions to the ongoing violence. Luis Eduardo was not saying that the "others" were misguided in their assessment of the situation; the prediction that the armed groups would continue to attack the unarmed population proved correct. He signaled a different distinction at play here. It is not that people's analysis of the conflict diverged; rather, it was folks' way of reacting to that violence. This speaks to a fundamental distinction between those who chose—and continue to choose—to participate in the resistance as a peace community, and others who chose to flee or have subsequently opted to leave the organizational process. Indeed, this is the contrast between merely seeking to survive amid modern-colonial dehumanization and dispossession versus forging an anticolonial politics against it.

The creation of the Peace Community itself, as the formation of an autonomous space free from armed control, represented a new political path advanced by those committed to it. On the one hand, rather than consolidating the FARC's authority in self-defense against the army-paramilitary onslaught, the Peace Community eschewed armed struggle and broke with the insurgency. On the other, they also distanced themselves from electoral party politics. Gwen Burnyeat's (2018) ethnography of the Community offers two indicative quotes. One member explained, "I voted only once in my life. For Bernardo Jaramillo [of the UP]. Because the people said, we're going to have a president. Then they killed him and we saw that voting was useless. I felt my vote had contributed to him being killed. I will never vote again, in order not to be part of that problem" (165). And then, having witnessed the extermination of the Patriotic Union whose programs had indeed promoted campesino well-being, another member reflected on the remaining options: "Political candidates promise things and then don't fulfill them. We don't vote. We don't believe in politicians" (165). In other words, they came to deem so-called representative democracy amid Urabá's armed conflict futile. Instead they sought survival and dignity through self-governance and solidarity networks. Nonetheless, sustaining this politics of autonomy would require ongoing struggle, the creation of a dignified socioeconomic program, and the consolidation of a "community" itself.

PEACE COMMUNITY EVOLUTIONS 1998-2016

The Peace Community's process illuminates how it is often only a few individuals whose actions can galvanize or benefit a larger group, to paraphrase FOR accompanier Mayra Sofía Moreno (personal communication 2011). Speaking to the importance of leadership during crisis, Eduar Lanchero (2002) described what happened in the wake of people's deep depression following the October 1997 massacre by the FARC: "One Friday afternoon, there was a community meeting in the chapel. Only seven people came. But . . . they formed the first work group, an organizational structure that would be generalized across the community. It was a resurgence of a solidarity economy amid the ashes of war. [And] the group had a concrete goal: to return to La Unión" (52). As mentioned earlier, the commitment to participate in community work was not among the initial Peace Community rules in the March 23 declaration. Rather, it was officially adopted during a community assembly on November 21, 1997. According to Community members' recollections of this meeting shared with me over the years, Eduar himself was the person who called the meeting. Lanchero was a particularly inspiring leader, speaker, and writer, whose role in galvanizing San José's farmers to persist in their resistance cannot be underestimated. As often occurs in meetings between the urban intellectual and rural communities in resistance (Fanon 2004), there was a profound process of mutual inspiration and learning. On the one hand, the Peace Community's struggle deeply inspired Lanchero, who, according to Father Giraldo, "found in the Peace Community what he was searching for" (personal interview 2013). On the other hand, San José's farmers were deeply moved by Eduar's leadership and words on what he deemed to be the significance of their actions. One of his many moving insights states: "Every tree planted was an action against the war because it was saying no to displacement. It was a form of refusing to abandon the land, to reaffirm life and strengthen the dignity of the community that, in spite of death, was taking its first steps to once again sustain itself autonomously and independently" (Lanchero 2002: 51).

The preceding quotes speak to the emergence of work groups and village returns as core elements of the Peace Community process. The work groups have been interpreted as "the fundamental motor of its economic strategy, a practical mechanism to reflect and make decisions in the collective interest" (Proietti 2007: 16). Meanwhile the Community itself has asserted, "To speak about our community's work groups is to speak about its development and essence; they reflect . . . our construction of a new society" (Comunidad de Paz de San José de Apartadó 2005a: 17). "This dynamic has permitted us to put into practice the principle of solidarity and of unity" (Comunidad de Paz de San José de Apartadó 2005b: 15).

The Peace Community further strengthened their work groups in the wake of a series of paramilitary blockades of the Apartadó–San José road in 1997, 2000, 2002, and 2004 (Comunidad de Paz de San José de Apartadó 2005a). Effected through paramilitary *retenes* (check points), these blockades inhibited San José's farmers from bringing in food and supplies. Former Internal Council member Diana Valderrama described the Community's response:

> As a community we had an experience, which was an economic blockade. They assassinated all the drivers of the Apartadó–San José road, and then no drivers would come up, causing panic. We spent three months without food. They

wouldn't let food or anything come up. What enabled people to survive? We sustained ourselves because people had their crops. Nobody went hungry because if I didn't have [food, another] *compañero* did. We shared whatever we had: yucca, plantain, something. We were prepared, even though we didn't know this could happen, because we at least had food. We realized that this sort of thing could happen again. But since we live in the countryside, we have our farms and all we need to buy are basic goods. (Lozano 2006)

The strengthening of their food sovereignty was coupled with an emphasis on building a community rooted in collectivity and solidarity. Valderrama continued, "We saw that there were many women, head of households on their own, because their husbands had been disappeared or killed in front of them. We saw the necessity to no longer work individually, every owner of their farm sustaining themselves without worrying about their neighbor. 'My' problem became 'our' problem. Out of that was born the idea to work in work groups, where you harvest together and then all the profits are shared" (Lozano 2006).

One might interpret the Peace Community as being fundamentally "a group of peasants who, above all, organized themselves to seek protection from armed groups' violence" (Masullo Jiménez 2015: 21). Yet while the goal of survival might have driven the initial formation of the Peace Community in 1997, the organization's emphasis on solidarity, dignity, and self-sufficiency through collective work signals the enhanced complexity of what this political process has become. This is not merely a question of "endurance" or "momentary" ruptures (Povinelli 2011; Aparicio 2015), but what I witness as the production of a coherent politics struggling to break with individualism and dependency at the root of modernity-coloniality. According to former Internal Council member Wilson David, "*no aguantamos, resistimos* [we do not endure, we resist]. Because . . . resistance implies generating the possibility of another world to the logic of death" (Comunidad de Paz de San José de Apartadó 2007: 80). In other words, consistent with the alter-globalization slogan of "Another world is possible," there was a subjective shift in San José de Apartadó from mere survival to the creation of a different world through the community process. Rooted in their analysis of a paramilitarized Colombian state (Burnyeat 2018), this search for another world beyond state politics broke with common campesino strategies to simply become independent producers within a capitalist economy by making demands for land titles or protection from the national government (LeGrand 1986).

Agricultural work groups are not the Peace Community's only form of collective work. Another is the weekly community workday, known as the *comunitario*, which parallels what is known in other communities, such

2.9. Return to the first village: Painting by Doña María Brígida González depicting the return of displaced Peace Community members to La Unión in 1998. Author photo, with artist's permission.

as the Nasa, as a *minga*. During these workdays Community members of all ages come together to complete a particular communal project, such as constructing homes, repairing or forging trails, or harvesting crops. Lanchero (2002) offered his analysis of this collectivity as he recounted the first Peace Community return to an abandoned village:

> Despite all the death, the community continued to maintain its strength because the return to La Unión was now a reality. They reconstructed the houses. Beginning to clear the jungle and plant crops was not easy but the people were strengthened by the knowledge that they were reconstructing the community fabric. This was an important moment in the organizational process. It was learned that suffering was shared and overcome in solidarity. They confronted the conflict economically, but beyond mere money, that meant a relationship with nature, with the conflict, with the community, and beyond. . . . The blood and tears soiled the land, but the taste of life and dignity flourished in the bananas and cacao, and no pest could destroy the fruit of an alternative and solidarity economy in the Peace Community of San José de Apartadó. (53–54, 56)

In the months after returning to La Unión in March 1998, the Peace Community resettled Arenas Altas and La Esperanza. However, additional hardships would lie ahead. Between 2000 and 2002 La Unión alone would suffer three more forced displacements, one induced by the July 8, 2000, massacre of six work group coordinators, including Internal Council member Rigoberto Guzmán. With a military helicopter flying overhead, paramilitaries occupied the village and then separated the women and children from the men. They subsequently picked out the male work group coordinators from their hit list, which paramilitaries notoriously create with the names of those they plan to kill. Peace Community members recall how those Community leaders had met with officials of the 17th Brigade only days earlier. The paramilitaries ordered the men to kneel down. But Rigoberto Guzmán refused. Community members lucidly recall how he said to the paramilitaries, "I do not have anything to be ashamed of. In the Peace Community, we are civilian campesinos. If you are going to kill me, then kill me standing up," which the paramilitaries did (see Giraldo Moreno 2010: 55).

The 2000 La Unión massacre was preceded by another in San José town in February of the same year, in which paramilitaries killed five campesinos. Such massacres coincided with retaliations in the region by the AUC following the FARC's destruction of its central camp in the Upper Sinú region of Córdoba adjacent to Apartadó in December 1998, upon which AUC leaders declared that they would recover state territory lost to guerrillas (Romero 2006). This exemplifies how armed groups do not mostly kill each other's combatants but instead unarmed civilians whom they perceive to sympathize with or support their enemy (Roldán 2002). In response to these attacks and state discourse affirming that the Peace Community was a front for the FARC, the Community stopped meeting with the military. A governmental commission following the 2000 massacre proceeded to investigate human rights violations in San José de Apartadó. However, despite testimony given by many San José residents, the commission did not lead to any judicial sanctions or convictions.

The Peace Community would eventually respond to such impunity by entering into a *ruptura* (rupture) with the Colombian state. This "rupture" was announced in 2003 with the creation of the Red de Comunidades en Ruptura y Resistencia (RECORRE, Network of Communities in Rupture and Resistance). Launched in September of that year during a meeting of indigenous and campesino communities in San José de Apartadó, they declared their refusal to provide any further testimony to the judicial branch of the government until systemic impunity ended (Comunidad de Paz de San José de Apartadó et al. 2003).

In 2005 the Peace Community would sever its communication with the Colombian state even further. On February 21, 2005, a joint military and paramilitary operation killed eight campesinos in two separate massacres in the villages of Mulatos and La Resbalosa. Among the victims was Luis

Eduardo Guerra, who had been the Community's interlocutor with the state regarding the placement of a police post in San José de Apartadó. While the government wanted to locate the police post within the town of San José, the Peace Community insisted that the post be placed somewhere else along the Apartadó–San José road. The Peace Community argued that a police station inside the town would violate their community principles of not living alongside any armed actor and would put the community in the middle of cross fire when guerrillas attacked the police post. Following Luis Eduardo's death, former Antioquia governor and then-president of Colombia Álvaro Uribe announced that the police post would be installed in April 2005. As denounced by then–Internal Council member Renato Areiza during a Community meeting in 2006, "the police did not come to protect the civilian population, but rather that the civilian population protects them" (Lozano 2006).

The entire population of San José's town center abandoned it and began building a new settlement fifteen minutes down the road by foot. Constructed from scratch on private Peace Community land, it was named San Josecito de la Dignidad (Little San José of Dignity). In the wake of the February massacre, President Uribe once again stigmatized the Peace Community as a front for the guerrillas in a public statement on March 20, 2005, during a visit to Urabá:

> Peace communities have the right to exist in Colombia thanks to the rights accorded by our political system. But they cannot, as is practiced in the Peace Community of San José de Apartadó, obstruct justice, reject the armed forces, prohibit the sale of licit items, or restrict the freedom of the citizens who reside there. In this Community of San José de Apartadó there are good people, but some of its leaders, sponsors, and defenders are being gravely accused by residents there of being auxiliaries to the FARC and of utilizing the Community to protect this terrorist organization. (Asociación Campesina de Antioquia 2008; Masullo Jiménez 2015: 57)

President Uribe incorrectly blamed the FARC for the massacre and did not even condemn it or offer condolences to its victims. Instead this public address reiterated his defamation of the Peace Community (Asociación Campesina de Antioquia 2008).

In response to this series of events and persistent impunity, the Peace Community announced four conditions for ending their ruptura and resuming dialogue with the Colombian state. The first was an apology from the Colombian presidency for stigmatizing comments against the Peace Community, including those on May 27, 2004, and March 20, 2005. They demanded the removal of the police post from San José town as the second condition. Third, they called for a truth commission comprised of national and international agencies to investigate the reasons behind impunity for human rights violations in San José de Apartadó, including why a Special Investigation Commission carried out in 2000 had failed to lead to any judicial cases or convictions. Ending military and paramilitary killings and harassment in the district's humanitarian zones and Peace Community settlements was the final condition.

Humanitarian zones had been proposed in February 2005. They were designed as spaces where civilians could take refuge during combat so as not to have to flee all the way to Apartadó, San José, or other population centers. Mostly located in schools, these safe-space zones were located in at least seven veredas within the district, including Mulatos, Alto Bonito, Buenos Aires, Bellavista, La Linda, La Cristalina, Miramar, and Arenas Bajas. The Peace Community demanded that the armed groups respect the humanitarian zones, even though those villages were not active Peace Community settlements. Many of these residents were not members because they did not comply with all of the organization's commitments, such as participating in a weekly community workday or refraining from consuming alcohol. Even so, the Peace Community continued to demand that the armed groups respect these unarmed campesinos' right to safe spaces. However, the humanitarian zones eventually ceased to function after many of their coordinators were assassinated in subsequent years. In addition to the February 2005 massacre in Mulatos that occurred ten days after the zones were announced, between 2005 and 2007 paramilitaries killed humanitarian zone coordinators Arlén Salas, Edilberto Vásquez, Francisco Puertas, and Dairo Torres, among other residents of these veredas (Fellowship of Reconciliation 2007; Giraldo Moreno 2010). In the words of Burnyeat (2018), the Community's "rupture" was rooted in and reflective of its "radical narrative" of a paramilitarized, corrupt, and illegitimate state; this discourse consolidated itself ever more with each attack.

Amid these recurrent violations rulings by the Inter-American Court of Human Rights and the Colombian Constitutional Court (the highest courts in the Western Hemisphere and Colombia, respectively) have backed the Peace Community's position to remain neutral in the conflict. They call on the Colombian state to take the first steps toward reestablishing dialogue. Yet as of 2016 only one gesture toward meeting these conditions had been made, when then-president Juan Manuel Santos offered an apology for Uribe's comments in December 2013 (*El Espectador* 2013). The Community responded that this alone did not meet their conditions, because Santos had failed to invite them to be present for the announcement, as stipulated (Comunidad de Paz de San José de Apartadó 2013b). San José's position is akin to Glen Sean Coulthard's (2014) observation about indigenous peoples' resistance to reconciliation programs amid ongoing dispossession: "I argue that in the context of ongoing settler-colonial injustice, Indigenous peoples' anger and resentment can indicate a sign of moral protest and political outrage that we ought to take seriously, if not embrace as a sign of our critical consciousness" (22). The Peace Community's refusal to compromise their demands or accept an incomplete apology is another manifestation of its implicit anticolonial posture.

Attacks against the Peace Community are not limited to physical aggressions but include an array of diverse tactics, including paramilitary blockades of the Apartadó–San José road as well as defamatory campaigns. Luis Eduardo Guerra described the state's different forms of aggression: "We have looked to all of the institutions of the state at the national level. We have even proposed investigative commissions. And the results have been *none. All* those assassinations are in impunity. The current situation is that, practically, what we see is a new strategy to continue *attacking us*. There is the *economic blockade,* there are *threats* made openly by paramilitaries and army officers" (Red Italiana de Solidaridad 2005). Notice his attention to impunity. As accompaniers frequently hear in diplomatic meetings, international embassies in Colombia continue to place the burden for reestablishing dialogue on the Peace Community rather than on the state, which contradicts the Inter-American Court's and Colombian Constitutional Court's rulings. Luis Eduardo continued:

> And although this is denounced nationally and internationally, nothing happens. We have been very clear about these principles. We have maintained a position of neutrality with respect to the insurgency. But, nonetheless, what they say is that we continue to be organized directly by the insurgency, that we receive direct orders from the insurgency in order to discredit the state and denounce the state. And to say that "it is only the state that violates human rights" . . . is a lie, any way you look at it. Because what we have said publicly and what we continue to say is that *among* those 130 killings, the subversion also has a big participation. In more than twenty cases. We don't have anything to hide from any of the armed actors. The only thing that we ask for is respect for those who are part of the civilian population. . . . Even at the level of the *embassies themselves*, who say, "[The government has] a total *willingness*; it's the communities who oppose the government's presence." When that is a complete lie. And that "[the government forces] are not violators of human rights, that the human rights violators are the insurgency," when we have said, look, there is a very clear example: How many deaths do we have? In how many have the paramilitary forces participated? Why is *all* the paramilitary structure in the Urabá region supported? So, I think it is a *difficult situation* . . . because economically and politically, the government is working *very hard* against the communities. Especially against San José de Apartadó. (Red Italiana de Solidaridad 2005)

The Peace Community is challenging the legitimacy of all violence against the unarmed population, including that of the guerrillas as well as the state's supposed legitimate use of force. In his interview Luis Eduardo signaled that the prime state strategy against the Peace Community became more complex to include defamation campaigns and judicial impunity. In fact, the only convictions for all of the human rights violations in San José de Apartadó were of paramilitaries and army officers who conceded to their participation in the 2005 massacre that killed Luis Eduardo Guerra. The highest-ranking officer convicted was an army captain, rather than the 17th Brigade commanders—trained by the United States, it should be noted—who planned the February 2005 Operación Fénix and ordered the executions, according to demobilized paramilitaries' testimonies (*Semana* 2009; Lindsay Poland 2018).

There has not been another mass killing in the area since the double massacre in Mulatos and La Resbalosa in 2005, but the state and paramilitary forces as well as guerrillas continued to attack. Residents have been forcibly displaced on repeated occasions, as in the village of La Esperanza (Comunidad de Paz de San José de Apartadó 2008; *El Tiempo* 2015; Radio Macondo 2015). Selective assassinations continued, such as the killing of Bernardo Ríos on the eve of the Peace Community's fourteenth anniversary in 2011 (Comunidad de Paz de San José de Apartadó 2011). Meanwhile, paramilitary and army forces, including then-commander of the 17th Brigade Germán Rojas, have continued to threaten to exterminate the Peace Community, including an attempted assassination of the Community's legal representative in 2017 (Comunidad de Paz de San José de Apartadó 2014a, 2017a).

The state apparently reevaluated its strategy after the 2005 massacre. When the police post was installed in the town of San José in April 2005, the police patrolled an empty village because all the town's residents had relocated to San Josecito (Lozano 2006). In the coming years the Álvaro Uribe administration began to promote social investments in San José de Apartadó through his executive branch development agency, Agencia Presidencial para la Acción Social y la Cooperación Internacional (Presidential Agency for Social Action and International Cooperation, popularly known as Acción Social). This agency's objective was to provide displaced populations with humanitarian aid. San José de Apartadó was soon announced as one of the pilot project areas, along with numerous indigenous communities, many of which were precisely those refusing the presence of the state's police and army forces.

Acción Social began to finance housing construction in and near San José town. More and more people began to move to San José, including many from surrounding cities like Apartadó, but also including some who left San Josecito and the Peace Community. Export-oriented teak plantations began to cover the hillsides surrounding San José town. As part of its periodic humanitarian events held in the town, in 2009 Acción Social handed out beans imported from the United States, although this is the easiest crop to grow in the area. Peter Cousins (2009), a FOR accompanier reporting on the event, compared this to "taking coal to Newcastle." Ex-mayor Gloria Cuartas Montoya (2007) interpreted such social investment as a new tactic in the wake of still-occurring assassinations, as part of the strategy to break the Peace Community's neutrality and resistance by enticing campesinos to live in the police-controlled town. A Peace Community leader reflected, "For years after our declaration as a Peace Community, we asked for social investments from the government following the extermination of the Patriotic Union. Yet it is only now, after the Peace Community vacated the town of San José, that the state makes social investments there" (field notes 2014).

Community members note that such social investments come with a price. The town of San José became a site of frequent combat, with subsequent FARC attacks on the police post and adjacent military training site (Lozano 2006). Even the non–Peace Community Communal Action Board formed in the town in 2009 has denounced ongoing police and army harassment (Junta de Acción Comunal—Corregimiento de San José municipio de Apartadó 2009).

Moreover, according to Peace Community Internal Council member, Berta Tuberquia Quintero, "humanitarian aid creates dependency. [Acción Social] gave out seeds, but they were genetically modified seeds" (group interview 2014). Referring to seeds with the terminator gene, member Javier Sánchez added:

> There is a kind of bean seed. Where these beans are cultivated, they put in a lot of chemical fertilizer. They are brought here and planted. They do not produce. If they do produce, it is only a minimal amount, and you cannot plant them again because the seeds do not have that ability. They are adapted to chemical fertilizer. Therefore they are not going to work in this ecosystem, in our soil and climate. Nevertheless, the company wants to make these sales—it is in their interest, you see—where we buy seeds, plant them, and then have to continue buying them over and over. These are seeds that do not work for us. . . . It's profit for them, but destruction for us. (Fellowship of Reconciliation 2011)

Peace Community members and many of their sympathizers (Cuartas Montoya 2007, 2014; Altieri 2007; Pérez 2007) argue that such social investments are in fact tools to undermine the campesinos' subsistence and autonomy. In so doing, such programs buttress capital accumulation by creating dependency on the market and the state.

Internal Council member Jesús Emilio Tuberquia summarized their lack of faith in the state: "When they shoot people, well, we do not believe in that state or in the public forces who act in that way. Leaving behind widows, orphans, so much misery, . . . displacements, . . . burning homes, robbing our livestock, horses, harvests. The public forces with the paramilitaries steal food, rape our women, have carried out massacres, selective killings, and robberies. The constant death threats against us. The trumped-up judicial charges, which they wield against us, being the victims" (Moncada Hurtado, Ossa, and Caro Morales 2011a).

Luis Eduardo reflected on the volatility of the Peace Community's resistance, including his chilling assertion about speaking one day and dying the next, just before his own assassination: "We have always said, and in this we have been clear, as of today we are *resisting*. And [we] still [are] in this project to continue resisting and defending our *rights*. We do not know until when. Because what we have lived during our entire history is that today we can be speaking, tomorrow we can be *dead*. That today San José de Apartadó is there, tomorrow the majority of the people can be *displaced*. Because there could be a massacre there of thirty people. . . . Here in this region *everything* is possible" (Red Italiana de Solidaridad 2005). However, the Peace Community's resistance is not only *against* displacement and assassination, but is also constituted by the production of an alternative, as he explained, "But while we are here, our projects of life continue. . . . We are also looking to partner with other communities nationally, other communities who are resisting, and how among all of us, we can design our own project of *life*. There is the University of Resistance, which we call Communities in Resistance. It doesn't mean that we are in an armed resistance. Our resistance is against the *state*, let's be clear, but an *unarmed* resistance. It is a civilian resistance" (Red Italiana de Solidaridad 2005). By affirming unarmed resistance, Luis Eduardo alluded to a simultaneous break from guerrilla politics. He also referred to RECORRE, which had been launched only two years before this interview in 2005, and mentioned the Campesino University of Resistance, whose first session was a monthlong gathering in Arenas Altas in August 2004. Luis Eduardo explained their significance: "That is why our project continues. . . . Where economically in these communities it is very difficult to resist. But we continue having economic *proposals* to do *projects*, which guarantee that we have food and that we have a minimal *dignity* as people, to continue resisting. Because there is a very clear saying that says, 'As long as the stomach is *full*, we can think, and we can do a lot. But when the stomach is empty, *everything* comes to an end'" (Red Italiana de Solidaridad 2005). Notice the words he emphasized the most with intonation in these final two passages: *resisting, dead, life, state, projects*, and *full* (stomach), counterposing the death system of the state to resistance communities' vision of life through unarmed resistance, solidarity, and projects that meet material needs. RECORRE and the Campesino University have continued to function for more than a decade. The Peace Community has put knowledge learned in these spaces into practice in its agricultural centers and self-sufficient family farms. The "rupture" is thereby not only about refusing collaboration with the armed groups and the state judicial system; it also ruptures with the political logic of modern-colonial domination that drives them.

Asserting independence from the guerrillas involved ongoing trials and tribulations, which I witnessed in my initial year as an accompanier. There were waves when the 5th Front of the FARC re-exerted its presence in and around particular villages before Peace Community leaders responded by reasserting their autonomy. In the preceding years FARC forces, under the command of alias "Samir," assassinated various Peace Community members (Giraldo Moreno 2010). In one notorious incident Samir's band almost killed an Internal Council member and Eduar Lanchero as they accompanied a return to a displaced village. Indeed, Samir continued his aggressions after he turned himself in and began working with the armed forces, becoming a key public spokesperson defaming the Community alongside state officials (field notes 2008; Comunidad de Paz de San José de Apartadó 2009).

Nonetheless, in 2012, as I joined a Community member to overlook a village, she said, "Look around: We've won." I asked her to explain. She responded, "You don't see anyone with arms anywhere. The armed groups don't enter any longer; they respect us. We are stronger than before. More and more people are participating in the comunitario. We've won [control of this village]" (field notes 2012). Having earned their autonomy was a common refrain during that particular visit of mine, a full fifteen years after the founding of the Community, which testifies to the intense commitment and perseverance involved in emancipation.

Community goals and values have evolved over time as well. A leader emphasized their increasing attention to the ecological aspect of peace:

> In the founding of the Community, our priority was to return to and remain on our lands through nonviolent resistance. However, over the past two years, our principles have grown from simply not collaborating with any armed group to a focus on not replicating in any way the logic of the armed groups. In other words, to not simply reject violence in order to survive in the midst of war, but to work together even harder to develop a true social and economic alternative of peace. This has meant more harmony with the environment, such as cultivating our crops organically and building agricultural centers where we harvest medicinal plants available in the region. We are continuing to evolve more and

more into a true "community" with nature and with each other. (Courtheyn 2015)

Another communal project to rupture with the state has been to found Community-run schools. One of their primary educators has been a Catholic nun who has worked in solidarity with the Peace Community for years, although most of the teachers are Community members themselves. Reflecting on the impacts of such Community-based education, a member described changes in students' artwork over time: "The children have lived all of the aftermath of the war. [Initially] they wouldn't draw anything but helicopters and armed groups shooting. Dead people. . . . They are injected with it. . . . [But] now they draw the environment, rivers, nature" (Moncada Hurtado, Ossa, and Caro Morales 2011b). One of the teachers expounded on this by talking about the relationship between nature, the curriculum, and Community and state education:

> We are with the children in the countryside, in the school, teaching them about the rivers, plants, the territory of the Community, the sites of memory. So, the children are always in contact with nature. . . . They have a garden in which they work two days each week. . . . They like this education more. . . . They gravitate more to what they are learning. [Learning] which seed is from which tree. . . . They gain a love for it. . . . The land. The rivers. "Let's go fishing" with the family. And they get their hands dirty because they know how. . . . [But the traditional education of the state] tells the children: "You should be a lawyer, an engineer [rather than a campesino]." And they plant that idea in the children. (personal interview 2014)

The Peace Community hereby works to produce a subject who does not see land as something to be engineered or legislated. And they counter the dominant state discourse that a "better future" is to be found in the city rather than the countryside.

Over the course of its many years of existence, the Peace Community has returned to many abandoned villages and has also expanded beyond its original area within the municipality of Apartadó. When the Peace Community returned to Mulatos and La Resbalosa in 2008, three years after the massacre in which Luis Eduardo Guerra was killed, its members began to increase dialogue with campesinos farther afield in the neighboring department of Córdoba. A campesino in the farm of El Guineo in the vereda of Naín who was resisting pressures to grow coca joined. Word spread to surrounding campesinos in Alto Joaquín, Puerto Nuevo, and Las Claras, some of whom joined as well. Through this process the Community expanded beyond the corregimiento of San José de Apartadó in Antioquia to include campesinos living on the banks of the Urrá dam reservoir, constructed in

1998 in the neighboring municipality of Tierralta in Córdoba department. Out of the ashes of a completely displaced corregimiento in 1997, the Peace Community extended to eleven villages as of 2016: San Josecito, La Cristalina, La Unión, Arenas Altas, La Esperanza, Mulatos, and La Resbalosa (in San José de Apartadó, Antioquia), plus Naín, Puerto Nuevo, Las Claras, and Alto Joaquín (in Tierralta, Córdoba). As of 2011, according to an internal census, the Peace Community had 1,162 members committing to its principles (Moncada Hurtado, Ossa, and Caro Morales 2011a). Despite all of the attacks against it, this life project of peace persists.

Violence in Urabá since the 1990s reflects another wave of conflict between small-scale farmers and land entrepreneurs seeking to appropriate recently settled frontier lands. Such conflicts have occurred throughout the country since the agricultural export boom during the 1850s to the 1920s. However, San José de Apartadó is not simply a repeat of those dynamics. Unlike many entrepreneurs before them, the narcobourgeoisie did not seek to appropriate property titles to settled land in order to exploit campesinos as tenant labor. The economic and political context had shifted to neoliberal logics of outright displacement in order to extract mineral resources or install agribusiness, which do not require an already-present labor force but are carried out by proletarianized workers, oftentimes brought in by paramilitaries and corporations themselves. Diverting from many other Colombian campesino movements, the Peace Community broke with any hope of support from the central government, which they deemed to be a paramilitarized institution. This might be interpreted as an expression of campesino exhaustion with demanding assistance from the state after decades of agrarian policies that sided with land entrepreneurs over small-scale farmers.

In contrast to the majority of Colombia's campesinos who were displaced and took refuge in stadiums, towns, and cities across the country during (but also prior to and since) the late 1990s, the Peace Community's insistence on remaining in and returning to its villages deviated from the norm (Aparicio 2012; Masullo Jiménez 2015). Their refusal to submit to the logics and demands of the state and narcobourgeoisie exemplifies an anticolonial politics that ruptures with the coloniality of power. The Peace Community is reflective of the broader trend of autonomous social movements across Latin America eschewing political change through traditional political parties, in what has been called an "other politics" of emancipation (Grupo Acontecimiento 2012). As such, they represent an alternative to modern politics' limited options of "the ballot or the bullet," to use the words of Malcolm X (2007).

By rejecting both the state-paramilitaries *and* the guerrillas, and then committing to communal solidarity, the Peace Community presents an alternative to authoritarian politics. The cost for doing so has been immense, as shown by the number of assassinations and waves of forced displacement. Yet in contrast to repressive state-paramilitary orders or mandatory and hierarchically organized community work in FARC zones (Tate 2015), participation in the Peace Community is voluntary, which enables a different type of political subject forging both autonomy and solidarity. If the FARC is indicative of a *reactive* action against campesino dispossession, then the Peace Community reflects a "scission" (Fanon 2004; Reyes 2012a) that ruptures with the dominant forms of modern-colonial politics to construct an *affirmative* politics of life and dignity through autonomy from armed groups, political parties, and the state. While the political failure of those dominant methods of social change in Colombia is one key factor shaping the Peace Community's search for an alternative, my next chapter turns to another central component in Colombian social antagonism—race—to offer an analysis of San José's trans-ethnic solidarity network.

CHAPTER 3

DE-INDIGENIZED BUT NOT DEFEATED

Race, Resistance, and Trans-ethnic Solidarity

> I asked a Peace Community member, "Why do you think there is a war? What are the armed groups' interests?"
>
> "Because the Peace Community denounces what they do." (personal interview 2013)

This query became one of my core interview questions, along with how Peace Community members understand peace, territory, and memory. In asking this question I was curious how Community members analyzed the reasons behind the violence against them. I wondered about the extent to which they would explain the reasons for the war in terms of Urabá's geostrategic location and the coveted resources in the lands where they live. Indeed, many members affirmed the economic roots of the war, tied to struggles for land, water, and minerals. The quote above was the first answer that deviated from this explanation, asserting that *the war against us is because we denounce the war.* My initial reaction was: "But what is the root of that war to begin with, which is denounced? Are not the condemnations contingent upon a prior war to begin with?"

Yet as I proceeded to ask this question more and more, I noticed that Community members would generally stress one or both of these two explanations: they are attacked for the richness of their land coveted by outside interests and for their denunciations of the state's violence. I kept thinking that the true "root" of the war would have to be the first: a war over resources, which is denounced, spurring further repression against that movement. Yet Community members' repeated assertions of their being targeted because they stand up to the state began to signal another dynamic at play. I realized that I was limited to thinking in a simplistic chronological fashion, along the lines of "Which is it? Which comes first, the denunciations or the war being denounced?" I began to understand how there is no "one" moment in the recent past to which the war can be traced or a specific date "when the war against us began."

That is not to say that there are no specific dates to point to. There were the mass displacements of 1996, which induced the remaining farmers in San José de Apartadó to search for a political strategy to remain in their villages. From March to October 1997, following their declaration as a Peace Community, military and paramilitary repression as well as a massacre by FARC guerrillas caused the abandonment of the entire district. We could also point to the National Army's killing and forced disappearance of eleven campesinos in La Resbalosa in July 1977, which Community members point to as the first massacre in the area, and a preface for what was to come (Giraldo Moreno 2010: 13–20). Or we could reference how decades prior—as elder members frequently mention—many of the eventual founders of the Peace Community fled assassinations and homes set ablaze in other regions of Antioquia during the La Violencia period. The point is that this war has seemingly always existed for these campesinos. The quote that opened this chapter also signals how their act to organize themselves as a Peace Community, rather than throwing water on the fire of war as intended, fueled further attacks. When Community members signal both resource conflicts *and* their denunciations of the state as the drivers of war, they thus infer that the violence is linked to specific economic and geopolitical interests that are part of a larger system of annihilation that intensified due to their oppositional stance as a community of peace.

Studies of the Peace Community tend to begin their historical context with the military-paramilitary onslaught in 1996 (Masullo Jiménez 2015; Pardo Santamaría 2007; Giraldo Moreno 2007), as I did in this book's Introduction and Chapter 2. Yet this war against campesinos can be traced to the racialized partisan violence of the La Violencia period (Roldán 2002), which was itself part of a longer history of land conflict between entrepreneurs and campesinos in frontier zones that goes back to the agricultural export boom beginning in the 1850s (LeGrand 1986). However, I contend that these violent periods of confrontation in frontier regions are rooted in a coloniality of power whose origins are even older (Quijano 2000). It emerged out of the Spanish Conquest of indigenous peoples in present-day Colombia, from whom most Peace Community members are descended. By imposing a logic of capitalist dispossession justified by racist classifications of the subaltern population and of the regions in which they live, the coloniality of power is at the root of ongoing violence against indigenous descendants today. If we seek to identify "when the war began," we should analyze how the legacies of the racial regime that emerged out of the colonial period shapes violence and resistance today.

Even though San José's campesinos do not identify as indigenous or black, might they nonetheless be racialized within this global modern-colonial system? Does the violence against them follow a racist logic? And what is the significance of the Peace Community's solidarity network with other campesino as well as indigenous and black communities? In this chapter, by situating resistance in San José in relation to the global structure of race and Latin American racial formations, I add a racial lens to analyze how Peace Community members and their allies in the Campesino University understand the violence against them.

CAPITALIST WAR, INTERNAL ENEMIES, AND RACE

The violence in San José de Apartadó is undoubtedly tied to the capitalist political economy of extractivism and land grabbing by the narcobourgeoisie. Many Peace Community members affirmed this connection between the war and economic interests. One leader put it this way: "These lands are very rich. And for that reason, they are fighting over this land and want to kick us out, because of the richness that we have. Especially pure air [and] pure water. And the Abibe Range is very rich . . . in what has to do with coal, many minerals. Gold, et cetera. And they are already handed over to a multinational [corporation]" (Moncada Hurtado, Ossa, and Caro Morales 2011a). In one of my interviews I asked, "Why do they want to displace you?" She responded, "Because they say that the area belongs to them, that they have to control this whole area. I don't know why. The highway that they are building to discover, what is that called?" "A mine," I replied. She continued, "Yes, mines. They evict us from here and they end up positioned. That's why we have to struggle to not leave" (personal interview 2013). Another Peace Community leader, in a presentation to an international delegation, situated this conflict over land in relation to the neoliberal era of free trade agreements:

> This whole war has an objective: free trade. To kill the people in the social organizations, to annihilate the indigenous communities and unions because we demand rights. To kill many in order to subjugate the rest, because they have to exploit the mines, gold, oil, water, and minerals, and as campesinos we do not want to leave the land. For the government, they have to kill us. The story of so many years of war is due to this. To pave the way for enrichment and wealth. As campesinos, Afro-Colombians, and indigenous peoples, we do not need petroleum to live, according to our ancestral practices, but we are now obliged to because the United States and Europe need it. With the free trade agreements there will be many more deaths than until now. The needs of the United States and Europe increase. But the communities are going to resist, although the others are the ones with the guns. (field notes 2012)

Congruent with this narrative about the logic of capitalism driving attacks in San José, Community member Jesús Emilio Montoya bluntly stated that it is a "capitalist war" of rich against poor (personal interview 2018). In accordance with the work of various scholars (Escobar 2008; Gonçalves 2006; Ulloa 2012), Peace Community discourse parallels Pablo Dávalos's (2011) conception of "competing territorialities" between neoliberal extractivism versus indigenous and black communities' resistance.

It is not only a war due to state and corporate interests in capital accumulation and resources; the war is also a business itself in which transnational corporations foment Colombia's profitable "war system" (Richani 2002, 2005; Altieri 2007). The Peace Community is quite aware of this dynamic. According to member Doña Brígida González, "many governments, in Europe and America, are interested in the war! Why? Because there are grand weapons manufacturing powers whose capital is in guns. If wars end, then to whom are they going to sell the guns? Given this, will there ever be peace one day?" (personal interview 2013). Therefore business interests in new resource frontiers and the weapons economy are crucial conditions shaping the war in San José de Apartadó. The Peace Community's resistance to the narcobourgeoisie's accumulation project is indisputably a class antagonism. However, capitalist accumulation has always been tied to racialized dehumanization, divisions, and dispossession (Robinson 2000). Since race and class mutually constitute one another in Latin America (Zapata Olivella 1989; Quijano 2000), it is imperative to consider how race also plays into this case of anti-campesino political violence.

While the profit motive of the capitalist political economy is a definitive factor, the repression of dissent throughout Colombia's colonial and postcolonial history is not solely a question of generating or preserving material wealth (Rojas 2002; Escobar 2008). Scholars have signaled how repression against autonomous communities and the inability to achieve progressive reforms in the country are rooted in the Cold War ideology of the "internal enemy," who was understood as anyone who threatened the existing order, such as guerrilla insurgents, but also including all political dissidents: unionists, radical intellectuals, and campesino movements (Gómez 2007; Giraldo Moreno 1996; Romero 2006). Diana Gómez Correal (forthcoming) speaks of Colombia's "hegemonic emotional habitus of hate" rooted in the modern-colonial project of hatred against all those who are "other" to the nation or who question the status quo. This is indeed a key component of the country's unresolved social contradiction or "agrietamiento structural" (structural crack or break) (Guzmán Campos, Fals Borda, and Umaña Luna 1962). Of course this hegemonic emotional habitus of hate directed against the nation's "internal enemies" is not merely a Cold War phenomenon. It is rooted in the colonial formation of the Colombian nation-state (Gómez Correal, forthcoming) and its original enemy: the racialized subject.

Colombian and Colombianist scholars have begun to pay more attention to the role of race in this structural crack (Wade 1993; Roldán 2002; Applebaum 2003; Serje 2005; Lasso 2007; Mosquera Rosero-Labbé, Laó-Montes, and Rodríguez Garavito 2010). Despite increasing recognition of indigenous and black communities' existence and rights since Colombia's pluri-ethnic Constitution of 1991, racist attacks against these groups persist (Dest 2020; Restrepo 2018; Riaño-Alcalá 2015; Wade 2017). Yet the limited attention to how nonethnic groups might also be racialized seems to presume that lacking an ethnic identity precludes racist discrimination and violence. I challenge this assumption by considering the extent to which racism nonetheless structures the violence against nonethnic mestizo ("mixed-race") campesinos, such as in San José de Apartadó.

Race is not a biological reality but a social construct historically produced through colonialism (Fanon 2008; Quijano 2000; Silva 2007); *racialization* refers to the process whereby cultural differences are then marked as biological inferiority (Mora 2017). Along with gender and class, race is a social hierarchy of modernity, comprised of humanity's poles from "civilized" to "barbaric," with those marked as "less than human" predisposed to premature death, both physically and socially (Gilmore 2006). Race is fundamentally a question of *threat*: who is dehumanized and threatened *by* the system, but also who is a threat *to* the system by constituting a potential alternative to it (Goldberg 2009; Moten and Harney 2011).

Race has always been a political and spatial category. It is a question of territoriality, the political relationship people have with space (Courtheyn 2018b). For the European colonizers of the Americas, you were only "human" if you *dominated* space by *demarcating* it. Thus emerged the distinction between the black and indigenous colonized subjects being "in a state of nature" like animals versus the white colonizer and its country's "citizens" participating in human "civil society" (Reyes and Kaufman 2011; Wilderson 2010). Rather than merely a question of phenotype or ancestry, race emerged as a distinction among humans mediated by the hegemonic notion of territory, as a demarcated space controlled by a particular group. The white European identity was not a preexisting one; it was produced in the Atlantic world through the colonizers' mutual identification as "not indigenous" and "not black" (Quijano 2000; Allen 2012). Additionally, "moral topographies" of environmental determinism emerged (Taussig 1987; Wade 1993), marking "primitives" in relation to the "inhospitable" climates they live in. Such regions are especially pronounced in Colombia, with Urabá being a prominent example (Leal León 2010; Serje 2005).

One means to understand race as a political and territorial question is Frank Wilderson's (2010) racial triad of white, red, and black: Whites occupy the "civilized" position, as those who own property and are members of the civil society. Within the structure of modernity, blacks are ontologically "slaves." They have no spatiality of their own and are thus to be owned and exploited by whites. Blacks can also be owned by the intermediary group, the "red" indigenous "savages," who are recognized as having had land and exerting sovereignty over space in the past (Wilderson 2010). Indigenous people were deemed to live in "a state of nature" rather than in a modern civil state, but they could be potentially saved through conversion to Christianity (Reyes and Kaufman 2011; Watanabe 2016). Wilderson (2010) posits that indigenous peoples were racialized *between* whites and blacks because European colonialism did not fully deny them a claim to humanity; indeed, indigenous peoples were "colonial subjects" in many parts of colonial Spanish America, a condition that was denied to black slaves (O'Toole 2012; Rappaport 2014). Nevertheless, this hierarchy of dehumanization did not exist in the same way everywhere, because there are cases where blacks were considered by certain Latin American elites to be "closer to civilization" than indigenous peoples, as during the Colombian independence era (Lasso 2007). These arguments thus speak to a leeway toward or away from civil society that racialized groups have depending on the practices of assimilation or resistance that they adopt. In other words, my contention is that racialization is not solely tied to ancestry or phenotype, but *politics* as well, in which racial slurs and attacks are especially wielded against racialized peoples who resist oppression and threaten the system's racist status quo (Fanon 2004; Goldberg 2009; Moten and Harney 2011; Harney and Moten 2013).

MESTIZAJE AND MULTICULTURALISM

In the Latin American colonial context, lacking large populations of European-descendant workers and exhibiting greater extents of "racial mixing" than in contexts of explicit segregation like the United States and South Africa, racial divisions manifested through a broad array of categories, including the *casta* paintings of colonial Mexico and postindependence mestizo and ladino classifications (Watanabe 2016). Surely, the meanings associated with categories such as black, indigenous, and mestizo have not remained static since the colonial era. These social classifications have had quite different connotations in distinct places and times: for example, in the colonial era of Spanish South America, *black*, *Indian*, and *mestizo* often referred less to phenotype than to an array of other characteristics, such as noble lineage or religion (Rappaport 2014). Nevertheless, the sometimes ambiguous use of these fluid legal classifications by both colonial authorities and racialized subjects was crucial to "the making of race" and consolidation of colonial rule (O'Toole 2012), which then solidified over time into the modern-colonial structure of race.

As a "coloniality of power" (Quijano 2000), such identifications functioned to divide and disarm the racialized subaltern. Even national developments against racial discrimination failed to overcome racism. Latin American nationalistic projects of *mestizaje* and *mestiçagem* (where the nation became defined by its supposed "racial mixture" and racial democracy) were less about plurality than whitening, in which subjects would become "more civilized" by becoming mestizo—whether through miscegenation or simply acculturation—rather than indigenous or black (Chaves and Zambrano 2006; Goldberg 2009; Wade 1993). In Colombia, where the category of mestizo did not prevail as a common identifier after independence, claims to national citizenship have often been made by asserting racialized regional identities, such as "antioqueño" tied to Antioquia or "caucano" in Cauca, which nonetheless correspond to a national homogenization project privileging whiteness (Applebaum 2003). This is tied to the "myth of racial harmony" that prevailed in postindependence Colombia, in which racial equality was made legal doctrine but also foreclosed affirmations of ethnic difference as well as indigenous and blacks' denunciations of ongoing discrimination (Lasso 2007). While the white-indigenous-black triad is most clearly evident in contexts of explicit racial segregation, Latin America's racial formations—despite varied classifications and identifications—nonetheless correspond to these same poles (Wade 1993; Sheriff 2001). The *structural* base of racism has endured despite Latin America's more fluid *symbolic* boundaries (Sheriff 2001; Wade 2017). Race undoubtedly manifests differently in particular places and times, but the continuities of dehumanization across diverse contexts in the Americas and beyond speak to the global nature of the modern-colonial race structure (Silva 2007; Maldonado-Torres 2010; Bacchetta, Maira, and Winant 2019). In other words, the "red savage" and the "black slave" remain less than human (Wilderson 2010), whereas "mestizos" or "campesinos" include many who attempt to assimilate into the dominant white civil culture by ridding themselves of their indigeneity or blackness.

There are exceptions to this whitening mestizaje, of course. For some mestizaje does not necessarily mean getting rid of all indigenous cultural practices, as "indigenous mestizos" in Peru demonstrate (de la Cadena 2000). Meanwhile Indians, blacks, and mulattoes in Costa Chica, Mexico, have lived together, forged an identity as *morenos*, and shared knowledge of agrarian, spiritual, and healing practices, thus forging an "antiwhite" mestizaje in opposition to regional "white" elites (Lewis 2016). Yet these transgressive mestizajes are exceptions that prove the rule.

While some racialized peoples did move up the "social ladder" through urbanization and modern education (de la Cadena 2000), the shift to mestizaje reconfigured the social hierarchy in a way that simultaneously hardened lines of exclusion against those asserting an indigenous or black identity and "homogenized" the population at large, hiding persistent racial discrimination and violence against "mixed-race" or "de-ethnicized" populations (Alberto and Elena 2016; Goldberg 2009; Lasso 2007; Leal León 2010; Moreno Figueroa 2008; Vargas 2004; Wade 1993). In Colombia campesino has worked in a similar fashion to the category of mestizo by connoting an identity that is supposedly detached from any ethnic connotation and no longer indigenous or black.

The era of multiculturalism beginning in the late twentieth century brought a new dynamic, in which some indigenous and African descendants, who had not previously identified as such, began to "re-ethnicize" by "legalizing" black and indigenous identities (French 2009). In Brazil, Peru, and Colombia, for instance, such groups have struggled for inclusion and recognition of their cultural differences and political rights, earning victories in the multicultural policies of pluri-ethnic governments or subsequently taking advantage of them (Chaves and Zambrano 2006; French 2009; Poole 2016; Warren 2001). Whereas mestizaje demanded de-indigenization and de-Africanization as a means to "civilization" and access to societal privileges, the era of multiculturalism—coinciding with neoliberal governance that cut public welfare programs—actually affords more rights to recognized ethnic minorities than to much of the population at large (Chaves and Zambrano 2006; Moreno Figueroa 2008; Wade 2016). The "re-indigenization" movement has spurred conflicts over the "veracity" of such ethnic claims, both between communities and governments—considering the implications for communities' ability to block extractivist development projects based on territorial rights (Bebbington 2009; Dávalos 2011)—as well as among ethnic and peasant groups themselves (Dest 2019; Poole 2016; Tsing 2003). For instance, while the Colombian state initially granted ethnic rights to the Pastos of Putumayo and the Muiscas of Suba, Bogotá—seemingly not expecting many communities to identify their racialized and discriminated position—as this movement grew, the state began to reverse such legal recognitions (Chaves and Zambrano 2006; Paschel 2016). Therefore racialized exclusions continue to target oppositional political and territorial practices. The slipperiness of anti-indigenous and antiblack mestizaje versus multiculturalism's acceptance of cultural—rather than politically radical and anti-extractivist—affirmations of blackness and indigeneity facilitates ongoing violence against indigenous- and African-descendants (Hale 2006; Rahier 2014; Rivera Cusicanqui 2012; Smith 2016; Dest 2020). This is the case whether it is camouflaged discrimination against de-ethnicized mestizos or the denial of indigenous/black rights to recognized communities.

RACIALIZATION AND CAMPESINOS IN URABÁ

To what extent is the war against San José de Apartadó Peace Community's farmers—whose identity as (nonethnic) campesinos is tied to land rather than an indigenous or African phenotype—nevertheless structured by racism? Congruent with the arguments of twentieth-century indigenous leader Manuel Quintín Lame (2004), Cristina Rojas (2002) demonstrates that postindependence Conservative and Liberal elites—despite different perspectives on land policy and religious versus secular governance—were united by their shared hate of the nonwhite population, given their mutual concern with the "will to civilization" to advance the European project of modernity, a preoccupation which superseded their aspirations for the accumulation of wealth. This is not to deny that indigenous peoples oftentimes allied themselves with the Conservative party in defense of landholdings established during the colonial period or blacks with the Liberal Party against slavery (Fals Borda 1975; Hylton 2006; Lasso 2007). While the postindependence myth of racial equality buttressed elites' rejection of any claims of discrimination by indigenous and African descendants (Lasso 2007), a racist logic persisted in the dominant discourse about differentiated regions.

Urabá, where the Peace Community is located, was indeed one of the regions considered to be among Colombia's uncivilized *territorios salvajes* (savage territories) (Serje 2005). After the 1905 territorial reordering of Colombia's administrative units, Urabá's central corridor became part of Antioquia, giving the department a *salida al mar* (exit to the [Caribbean] sea) at the Gulf of Urabá. Claudia Steiner (2000) describes the central Antioquian government's establishment of control in Urabá as a "colonial encounter," defined by the imposition of antioqueño (Antioquian) and *paisa* (another identifier for people from this region) values and practices to produce a Catholic, conservative, "hard-working," and progressive subject there.

Urabá as the "frontier" marked it as a peripheral space supposedly "unknown" by the core (Sánchez Ayala 2015; Ballvé 2020). Clara Inés García (1996) references the dominant discourse: "'*Urabá era la tierra de nadie*' [Urabá was the land of no one] or, in other words, of anyone who had the capacity to impose themselves over others" (29). Reflective of race as a spatial category, "savage territories" and "the land of no one" signal a colonial understanding of space: if there is not a modern administration of space through private property and state institutions, then there is effectively "no one" there. Reflective of modernity's "coloniality of being" (Maldonado-Torres 2010), the inhabitants of such regions occupy the "zone of nonbeing" (Fanon 2008) outside of the white civil society (Wilderson

2010). Of course there *were* real people there, but these discourses reveal that these zones *were not yet colonized*. They remained peripheries yet to be subjected to primitive accumulation.

Branding peoples and regions "savage" does not tell us anything about those made "other" or what the actual inhabitants think and do; rather, these discourses are a reflection of and window into what the *core* thinks. For Margarita Serje (2005) they are "the mirror of the nation-state." They reflect an understanding of politics and governance as "sovereign power" (Foucault 2003), where those supposedly living "in a state of nature" and amid a Hobbesian war of all against all must be disciplined by sovereignty: set arrangements of who controls what and whom (Reyes and Kaufman 2011). Therefore the core's description of these zones as areas where the predominating logic was "Quítate tú pa' ponerme yo" (Get out so I can insert myself) (Aparicio 2012) is indeed reflective of the dominant modern imaginary, which insists on disciplining these areas into a particular territorial and political formation, where the nation-state achieves exclusive control (Serje 2005; Reyes and Kaufman 2011; Ballvé 2020). Marking certain people and places "other" through spatial terms (even if not explicitly racially signified) is another means to conceal race and perpetuate racism.

Most Colombian authors describe areas like Urabá as zones of "colonización" (Aparicio 2012; García 1996). Yet the sense with which they use this term is not to refer to colonialism but what I would translate into English as *settlement*, which in this case refers to the arrival of small-scale farmers and subsequently capitalist entrepreneurs (LeGrand 1986; Kalmanovitz 1995). Nevertheless, in agreement with Nancy Applebaum (2003), I argue that this use of *colonización* or colonization is especially appropriate, even if certain authors do not intend to argue as such. For decades Urabá has indeed experienced a process of primitive accumulation. Urabá's strategic location for drug and arms trafficking to and from North America, its fertile land, banana plantations, and water and mineral reserves coveted by state, corporate, and rebel interests make it a contested site of violent land grabbing and state making (Ballvé 2020). Unlike places such as Hispaniola or Potosí, Urabá was never fully colonized during the Spanish Conquest (Steiner 2000), yet its current war manifests colonial conquest today.

Such regions are discursively produced as "disease-ridden" and "dangerous" as well as the sites of incredible riches. Steiner (2000) quotes a description of the "riches" in the Pacific department of Chocó, whose northern region is part of Urabá, from the *El Antioqueño* newspaper in 1904: "In Chocó everything is fabulous. Its forests are curdled with the most valued resins, of almost inappreciable woods. . . . Cotton and sugarcane grow there in a truly incredibly way. And at the entrances to its mountain ranges and riverbeds there shines a lustful change to the eternal nightmare of men.

It is an immense camp for all the industries; it is the future of Colombia" (8). This depiction emphasizes natural resources that can be extracted and commodified for capitalist accumulation but does not mention the value of the people who settled Chocó. According to this logic, these regions can be the future of prosperity for the nation, but not if left in the hands of "the natives." As an inference that "indigenous people are incompatible with modern politics and development," take Colombian senator Paloma Valencia's recent proposal that Cauca department be "divided in two. One indigenous department and another for the mestizos" (*El Colombiano* 2015), a statement immediately branded as racist by commentators. What did Valencia mean by "mestizos?" She seemed to infer nonindigenous or white mestizos like herself rather than "indigenous mestizos" who actively practice indigenous rituals (de la Cadena 2000). What about the campesinos in San José de Apartadó? They neither conduct indigenous cultural rituals nor identify as indigenous and could thus be classified as mestizos. Would that make them white mestizos like Senator Valencia?

But they are clearly not white, revealing racial divisions among Colombian mestizos. The history of migration to San José de Apartadó discloses the indigenous roots of its settlers. The campesinos who settled in and founded San José de Apartadó migrated from various places. One group came from the Upper Sinú River region in the southern part of Córdoba department. Others arrived from an array of municipalities in the department of Antioquia between Urabá and the city of Medellín, such as Dabeiba and Cañas Gordas. Elder Peace Community members described communication and commercial networks in the Nudo de Paramillo zone that linked communities in Dabeiba with others in the Sinú. The eventual founder of the corregimiento of San José de Apartadó, Bartolomé Cataño, traversed this region as a youth; to his fellow campesinos in Dabeiba, he transmitted information from communities in the Upper Sinú about productive lands in Apartadó, which then contributed to migrations from Dabeiba and neighboring municipalities (field notes 2020). Located about halfway between Medellín and Apartadó, Dabeiba became a major hub for migrant workers who built the Highway to the Sea, whose construction began in the 1920s to connect Medellín to the Gulf of Urabá. Others found jobs in agriculture to supply the market in Medellín. It then became a site of violent conflict during the La Violencia period (Roldán 2002), with some of the survivors migrating to Apartadó during the following decades.

Similar to Urabá, the Dabeiba region had also been the target of the Antioquian government's campaign to spread the "raza antioqueña" (Antioquian race) and paisas' "superior" Catholic religion and customs of conservatism and "hard work" (Steiner 2000). *Paisa* and *raza antioqueña* are code words for whiteness, given many paisas' insistence that they are the "most European" among Colombians (Steiner 2000; Rojas 2002; Applebaum 2003). Both state education and the Catholic Church played a role. Steiner (2000) documents how the Catholic missions framed their goal as "the reduction, evangelization and civilization of the indigenous tribes" (86) who were living in the areas surrounding Dabeiba and Frontino, whose cooler climate the Spanish priests preferred. Future migrants to Urabá, who would found the Peace Community decades later, are likely descended from those indigenous groups or were migrants to Dabeiba from indigenous and African-descendant communities elsewhere. By the time they migrated to Urabá from Dabeiba in the wake of state and church "civilization" programs, however, they identified as campesinos and antioqueños rather than indigenous, although notably not as paisas aligned with claims to whiteness. A similar process likely occurred with migrants to what became San José de Apartadó from the Sinú region, who now identify as antioqueños but came from an area in the Nudo de Paramillo where indigenous communities remain prominent. One Peace Community leader originally from Dabeiba explained to an international delegation, "By nature, we are of indigenous blood, and we carry that within us" (field notes 2012). Even though San José's campesinos do not *identify* as indigenous, they are nevertheless *indigenous descendants* who were the product of "de-indigenization" by whitening policies and over the course of migratory movements.

In fact, *antioqueño* and *campesino* appear even more effective for projecting racelessness—where racial categories are denied altogether (Goldberg 2009)—than terms such as *mestizo* and *ladino*, which explicitly remain dialectically related to *indigenous* or *indio*. Unlike ladinos, however, the Peace Community's campesinos do not serve conquest (Watanabe 2016) but instead continue to resist it. That is, San José's antioqueños are *not* the same racially as the white antioqueño entrepreneurs Peter Wade (1993) contrasted with blacks and Caribbean mestizos in the Chocó part of Urabá or the antioqueño paisa coffee farmers associated with whiteness (Hylton 2006). San José de Apartadó's campesinos are more akin to a sector of paisas in the Coffee Region who affirm indigenous and mestizo ancestries to contest the myth of paisa settlers' white origins (Applebaum 2003).

It bears repeating that race is not only a question of phenotype but one's position within the hierarchy of modern society. In this process of becoming Antioquian campesinos, did San José's farmers move up the social ladder like some mestizos, such as certain urban women in Cuzco, Peru (de la Cadena 2000)? Do Antioquian elites in Medellín and national leaders now treat them as equals? The virulent physical and discursive attacks against them attest to the contrary.

For an example of how counterinsurgency and race rhetoric blend together—an exemplary case of the "internal enemy" logic rooted in an "emotional habitus of hate" (Gómez Correal, forthcoming)—take the arguments of Fernando Vargas Quemba (2006), founder of the National Committee of Victims of the Guerrilla and adviser to the Colombian armed forces. In his 2006 book, *Comunidades de paz: Estrategia de guerra; Caso San José de Apartadó* (Peace communities: War strategy; Case of San José de Apartadó), he claimed that the Peace Community was ultimately a Soviet-style "gulag" (29) and "not a camp of peace but a concentration camp" (39). He proceeded, "It is correct to say that this community of San José is of negritudes. It must be said that they are also African immigrants as well. Whatever brings fruit to the discrediting campaign against the Army is good for them" (197). "When indigenous communities today reclaim respect for their culture, it is not clear to which culture they refer: to the pre-Columbian savage and enslaving one; or the one defended by the Spanish Crown; or the modern one, a mix of tribal rituals with a communist tendency" (196). Vargas Quemba thus racially marks the Peace Community as a band of black and indigenous communist savages who block the progress of the Colombian armed forces. The then–peace adviser of Antioquia, Jaime Fajardo, vocalized a less direct yet nonetheless racialized insult of the Peace Community in 2005 when he said in the name of the state, "We repudiate that *ghetto*" (*El Colombiano* 2005). While San José's farmers do not profess an ethnic identity, they cannot escape their phenotype or ancestry. Within the global racial structure the Peace Community aligns politically with indigeneity, given its members' indigenous roots and identity tied to a particular relationship with the land. However, indigeneity is just as much about a connection to the power relations of ongoing migrations and networked territorial struggles due to settler colonialism (Bryan 2009; Ng'weno 2013; Radcliffe 2017), which are also indicative of the experience of San José's campesinos. Campesinos can be racialized as white or not white depending on the time and place, but also on their politics. This is a reminder that race is not reducible to those threatened because of their phenotype alone but is also linked to the "threat" that groups like the Peace Community pose to the existing order of capitalist development by forging a political alternative of intercommunal autonomy and solidarity.

Correlating with conceptions of racialization as a double-edged process of suffering dehumanization while also threatening the system with alternatives, Community member Doña Brígida González analyzed the relationship between campesinos, the state, wealth, and wisdom:

> The poor . . . for states and for the [Colombian] state, we are trash. We are trash. We are not part of the society. The state . . . has totally abandoned small-scale subsistence farming. And education. Why? Because it believes and thinks that the campesino does not know how to read or write, is stupid, and is not capable

of demanding anything. And it turns out that they are mistaken. Because maybe someone does not know how to read or write. But he or she sees, listens, and analyzes.... We are poor, but we are not poor; we are rich! Because we have our abilities and wisdom. We know how to teach many things, and these are *riches*! ... How many unhappy rich people are there? They aren't happy even with all the comforts that they have. (personal interview 2013)

Her words implicitly reflect a racialized position by asserting that San José's campesinos are excluded from civil society based on discourses that deem them stupid and disposable.

Peace Community leader Jesús Emilio Tuberquia (2011) similarly analyzed the way that state education contributes to undermining campesino ways of life. He argued, "Official education by the Colombian state has been harmful for campesino communities. Taking our kids to public school does not serve us and leads to our displacement. In state education, human beings and campesinos are devalued, because for you to be valued as a human you have to displace to the city or leave the country in order to be recognized." Jesús Emilio's terminology of devaluation speaks to the dehumanization of Colombian campesinos, in which their only way to be recognized as fully human is to shed their rural way of life. Without using racial terms directly, this nonetheless corresponds with the dynamics of modernity's "coloniality of being" constituted by racialized dehumanization (Maldonado-Torres 2010) and the need to be recognized by the state in order to truly exist within civil society (Coulthard 2014; Dest 2020).

Assassinated Community leader Luis Eduardo Guerra implicitly signaled a racialized condition of constantly facing the possibility of death (Fanon 2008; Gilmore 2006; Maldonado-Torres 2010) when he infamously observed in the days before he was killed that "what we have lived during our entire history is that today we can be speaking, tomorrow we can be dead" (Red Italiana de Solidaridad 2005), as quoted in Chapter 2. Another member, Doña Fidelina Supúlveda, bluntly said that the war is a project to eliminate them and their way of life:

I asked, "And why is there this war?"
She responded, "In order to get rid of the campesino."
I followed up by asking, "They have not been able to take this land because of your resistance. Why do they want the territory?"
"To let it rot! Or bring in other people to work. Those people, I tell you, do not work or let you work." (personal interview 2013)

Considering the migratory experiences of both Luis Eduardo and Doña Fidelina, these narratives reflect a cumulation of knowledge as migrant settlers repeatedly facing armed and structural violence. These voices argue

3.1. CRIC booklet gifted to me by a member of ACIN: "Count on us for Peace . . . Never for War. End the war, defend autonomy, reconstruct civilian goods and build peace." Author photo.

that the violence is not only about resources and accumulation but is an anti-campesino war. While the term *mestizo campesino* as a means of anti-racialism serves to obscure ongoing racism, the war nonetheless remains an anti-indigenous process. Strikingly, whereas these antioqueños mestizos are supposed to have "moved up" in social status, what I heard over and over again were affirmations to similar conditions across indigenous, black, and campesino communities. Comparing their understandings of the war uncovers a shared racialized status.

TRANS-ETHNIC SOLIDARITY AGAINST MULTICULTURAL DIVISION

Declarations made in the Campesino University of Resistance enunciate perspectives about the war across ethnic and nonethnic groups. Participants come from an array of communities across Colombia, including campesino communities from Quindío, Antioquia, and Cauca departments as well as indigenous Wayúu, Wounaan, and Nasa communities from the departments of La Guajira, Chocó, and Cauca, respectively. Nasa communities in the Consejo Regional Indígena del Cauca (CRIC, Indigenous Regional Council of Cauca)[1] and the Asociación de Cabildos Indígenas del Norte del Cauca (ACIN, Association of Indigenous Councils in Northern Cauca)[2] are a particularly strong contingent in the Network of Communities in

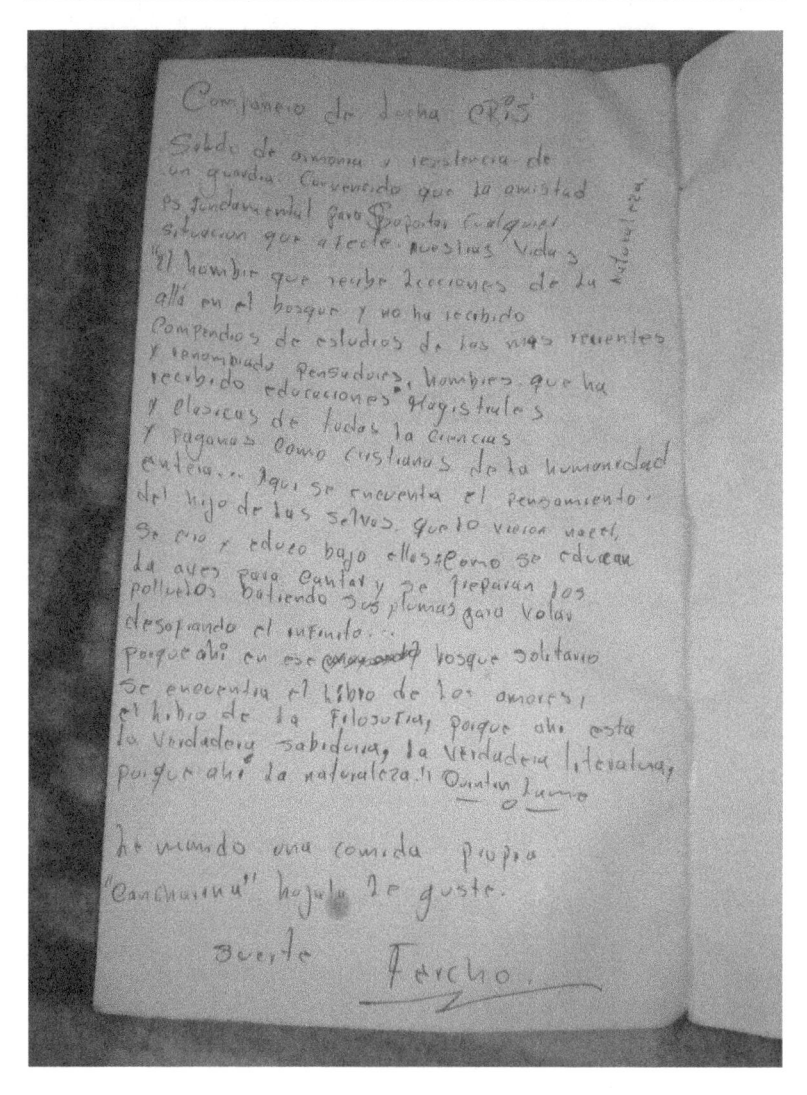

3.2. Lessons on ecological dignity: Quotation from Manuel Quintín Lame's book *The Thoughts of the Indian Educated in the Colombian Forests* included in a written letter inside the CRIC booklet. Author photo.

Rupture and Resistance (RECORRE). As we will see, while all communities affirmed the economic roots of war, Nasa and other indigenous representatives also identified the role of racism, which corresponds with racial analyses of Colombian violence that go back at least as far as the work of Manuel Quintín Lame and which inform their movements for life, land, culture, and autonomy (Lame 2004; Castillo 2004; Guzmán Campos, Fals Borda, and Umaña Luna 2008; Nene and Chocué 2004; Rappaport 1998,

2004). Comparing and contrasting narratives about the war across indigenous and campesino communities allows for an analysis of the ways that racism might affect even nonethnic groups.

During a gathering of the Campesino University in 2013, one participant reaffirmed the political economy of the war, where even legal recognition of indigenous space means little when it conflicts with the interest of the nation-state: "There is recognition of territories, of indigenous reserves. But for the state this has no value, only the riches that there are in the territory" (field notes 2013). A representative from an ACIN community in Cauca directly identified racism at the root of the war: "'Defending the civilian population,' say both the army and the guerrilla. From both of them: stigmatizations, assassinations, and threats. The war is not in order to protect, but a plan of territorial consolidation, as they call it. They have pit us against one another, our Afro, indigenous, and campesino comrades. The need that we all feel, the inhabitants of the national territory, is the same. There is racial persecution. This is not about a couple policies but a system" (field notes 2013). To affirm that the violence is systemic racial persecution, rather than an issue of individual policies or actions, is to confront the armed groups' dominant narrative of a "few bad apples" (Tate 2007) that erases the role of systematic and racial violence in Colombia's war. Moreover, she insisted upon the shared conditions faced by indigenous, black, and campesino communities, while also noting that racial or ethnic distinctions can allow the state to divide and rule.

While campesinos generally do not name racism in their explanations of the war, many Peace Community statements nonetheless affirm a shared condition with racialized ethnic groups. Recalling the words of a Peace Community leader related earlier that traced the war to neoliberal free trade agreements, notice the expression of a collective "we" to situate campesinos like himself alongside Afro-Colombian and indigenous peoples: "This whole war has an objective: free trade. To kill the people in the social organizations, to annihilate the indigenous communities and unions because *we* demand rights. . . . [A]s campesinos, we do not want to leave the land. . . . The government [therefore has] to kill us. . . . As campesinos, Afro-Colombians, and indigenous peoples, *we* do not need petroleum to live, according to *our ancestral practices*, but we are now obliged to because the United States and Europe need it. . . . But the communities are going to resist, although the others [have] the guns" (field notes 2012, emphasis mine). He therefore alluded to a shared subject position not merely due to indigenous or African ancestry, but to a shared project of political resistance through anti-extractivist territorial practices.

Also affirming this shared experience, a Campesino University participant from an indigenous community in Cauca said, "In my territory, we

3.3. Trans-ethnic solidarity: Painting by Doña Brígida González depicting the first gathering of the Campesino University in 2004. Author photo, with artist's permission.

live the same violence that all of us live" (field notes 2013). Another, from an indigenous community in Chocó, affirmed, "They are the same problems in each region, call them indigenous, campesinos, Afros. You want to see a place that is different, but you only see the same everywhere: the homes, the violence" (field notes 2013). These statements attest to the fact that regardless of whether a particular community mobilizes an ethnic identity, the conditions of violence they face are quite similar, taking place despite different local contexts and thus coinciding with theories of race as a global structure. As indigenous descendants in Colombia, whether or not you speak Spanish, practice Christianity, or identify with the Colombian nationality, it seems that if you do not cede to the needs of capitalism and the nation-state, you are nonetheless targeted as the "internal enemy."

Another member of an ACIN community shared with me in a personal conversation how "the guerrillas and the military soldiers come to an agreement. Each one positions themselves on a different side above the community [so that they can both attack us]" (field notes 2013). While some have theorized Colombia's violence as a "war against the society" (Pécaut 2001), these indigenous-campesino voices call for us to question the extent to which it is a war *of* modern society (by state-paramilitary *and* guerrilla forces) *against* racialized people. Another campesino delegate from Quindío argued, "The guerrilla does not want us to get organized either. We have to organize ourselves more strategically. To continue forward. We would like to accompany the Peace Community here with more people from my region. I will not leave you alone as long as I am alive" (field notes 2013). Amid war, communities face diverse options, which include co-optation, displacement, competition between ethnic and nonethnic groups for land, or resistance. Epitomizing the latter, the Campesino University network response is intercommunity solidarity. One of the aspects of dehumanization within the coloniality of being is to dismiss the possibility of racialized peoples' contributions to society by sharing knowledge and gifts (Maldonado-Torres 2010). In the sharing of seeds as well as knowledge about medicinal plants, agroecology, and human rights law, the Campesino University's mutual offerings refuse this dehumanizing racial regime and contribute to anticolonial rupture by supporting each community's respective autonomy. Trans-ethnic networks like RECORRE are also beyond solidarities based on shared ethnic identifications. They are rooted in political solidarities among ethnic and nonethnic communities which share a commitment to resist war and support one another in the process.

Unlike many communities amid the multicultural turn in Latin America, the Peace Community's reaction to violent attempts to displace them from their land is not to "legalize" a distinct identity (French 2009). They could have strategically sought rights to territory by demanding recognition from the state as "indigenous" descendants. Or they could join particular campesino movements who feel left out of the multicultural regime and are demanding recognition as a collective campesino subject with rights akin to ethnic black and indigenous communities (Dest 2019). Other Colombian communities often claim national citizenship by asserting racial and regional identities, such as antioqueño or caucano (Applebaum 2003). The Peace Community has opted for none of these. I recall in one meeting with San José's Internal Council when they mentioned a proposal made to them by a national human rights organization, which recommended that the Peace Community solicit state recognition as a collective territory along the lines of ethnic communities. Community leaders explained their decision to reject this option by arguing that to do so would pull them further into the state realms of politics, thus undermining their autonomy and dignity. The Peace Community's failure to identify along such ethnic lines implicitly eschews participation in the pluri-ethnic nation of Colombia, which is centered around political movements which seek inclusion through ethnic or regional identities. It is not that San José de Apartadó's campesinos reject their national identity as Colombians, but their politics is not ultimately concerned with inclusion within or recognition by the nation-state.

Instead it seeks to build a broader political movement of intercommunity self-determination that *transcends* the lines drawn by ethnic classifications. Nor do they fall into an anti-racism stance that negates the anti-racist claims by indigenous and black peoples. By working with indigenous and black communities without being part of them, the Peace Community undermines the racial hierarchy they "should" submit to, hence remaining the "enemy within." The Campesino University's work to unite those who are racialized, regardless of identity, is indeed an antiracist practice, which implicitly transgresses liberal identity politics' tendency to harden ethnic divisions without undoing racism (Moreno Figueroa 2011; Silva 2007). Seemingly foreseeing the dead ends of the "colonial politics of recognition" that so often institutionalizes, co-opts, disarms, and divides communities in resistance (Coulthard 2014; Dest 2020; Reyes and Kaufman 2011), the Peace Community exhibits a decolonial dismissal of the multicultural rights regime. If race serves to divide and rule (Zinn 1999), then these trans-ethnic solidarities between indigenous and campesino groups in the Campesino University that go beyond ethnic lines are implicitly an active rejection of the function of multiculturalism and racism that fetishize difference and impede collaborations among the subaltern.

To complement established scholarship on Colombia's war linked to political violence and land struggles, this chapter has offered a racial analysis to consider the extent to which violence against those who do not profess an ethnic identity can nonetheless be due to racism. Within the racial hierarchy of mestizaje, San José de Apartadó would be classified as a mestizo or "mixed-race" community. Yet theories of racialization as subject position rather than identity, the history of internal colonialism through state-Catholic missions and education in Antioquia, and Peace Community leaders' acknowledgment that they are of indigenous blood lead me to argue that the identifier *campesino mestizo* hides the process through which San José's farmers were historically "de-indigenized." Racially coded insults and the mass violence levied against them by the paramilitarized Colombian state both prior to and in the wake of asserting their self-determination from both state and non-state armed groups suggest that they remain racialized as the less-than-human "indigenous savage," to be exterminated as an impediment to state development (Rojas 2002; Wilderson 2010). While the rural organizations that comprise the Campesino University have different cultural practices and identities, the similar violence they face suggests an analogous racial subject position.

This demonstrates how categories such as mestizo and campesino, which in some nation-building views are seen as racially neutral or as transcending racial difference, can actually remain highly racialized and be the site of racial difference making. Diverse communities in the Campesino University, which ought to occupy distinct locations in Colombia's multicultural political landscape, perceive a common experience of racialized oppression and resist the divisive tactics of top-down multicultural governance. Repression visited upon mestizos or campesinos can in some cases be as racialized as that suffered by clearly identified indigenous and black people. Class-based oppression, displacement, and violence have an important racialized dimension, which legitimizes and justifies extreme violence.

Attention to race thus allows for a more complex analysis of the intersectional systems of oppression facing communities in resistance, while also revealing racial heterogeneities among those identifying as campesinos or mestizos (Moreno Figueroa 2008; Roitman and Oviedo 2017). The slipperiness of anti-indigenous and antiblack mestizaje versus multiculturalism's alignment with non-radical blackness and indigeneity is precisely what facilitates dominant actors' ongoing violence against "indigenous mestizos," whether it be the denial of indigenous rights for re-indigenized communities (Chaves and Zambrano 2006; Poole 2016) or the camouflaged racism against de-indigenized campesinos, as in San José de Apartadó.

When Apartadó mayor Gloria Cuartas sent buses to San José in the late 1990s to bring the displaced farmers to "safer areas," the campesinos refused. Their choice to remain was widely criticized at the time by national and international NGOs and governments. As explained by Juan Ricardo Aparicio (2012), "Some comments made about this decision made reference to its 'stupidity,' the possibility of 'a massacre foretold,' or the 'absolute irresponsibility of the Community regarding what could happen'" (239). Such views assume that there are "safe spaces" elsewhere, rather than recognizing the perpetuation of the colonialities of power and being against racialized campesinos. The displacements in San José de Apartadó during 1996 and 1997 were merely one chapter in a history of attacks against these indigenous-descendant migrants that can be traced at least as far back as the La Violencia period.

Yet if race is a question of who is threatened *by* but also threatening *to* the dominant society because of their intersecting phenotype, ancestry, and politics (Goldberg 2009), the Campesino University challenges racial divisions and violence. Mining and territorial titling have created land control conflicts elsewhere in Colombia among indigenous, Afro-Colombian, and campesino groups; meanwhile re-indigenization processes have induced conflicts with "traditionally-recognized" groups. Conversely, the RECORRE network unites groups divided by the dominant race lexicon. If racialization works to dominate but also divide the subaltern, then Campesino University participants' intercommunity network against what is a shared experience of racist violence both unveils and counters the racism of extractivism (Courtheyn 2019). To reword Silvia Rivera Cusicanqui's (1987) quote "Oppressed but Not Defeated," the Peace Community has been *de-indigenized, but not defeated*.

PART II

WHAT IS PEACE?

I'm just a wrinkly old woman. What would I have to say? *It's true.* I don't know what to say. Let's say I say something or another, but that's not how it is. So, I feel embarrassed.

                                      Nah. For example, I have a question . . .
Go ahead and ask.

                  This is called the *Peace* Community, so for you, someone who has participated in this process, what does "peace" mean?
Peace for me is to have, to have, how do I say it . . .
everyone being together with the same idea.

                                              Interesting . . .

Yeah? [Laughter!]
Yes . . . neither someone being upset, nor where one person is *here,* another *over there*, and another there. . . . That you are able *to do* what you need to do. . . . [If] one person comes *here,* but another moves *over there* . . . things *do not come together*. Instead everything *comes apart*. Right?
. . .

                                          So, peace is community?
Peace is *community*.
. . .

                     And how is it to *go* toward that peace? What is the *path*?
                          (Doña Fidelina Sepúlveda, personal interview 2013)

This was the first time I directly asked someone in San José de Apartadó about the meaning of peace. This interview deeply moved me, leaving a profound impression and spurring pages and pages of reflective field notes. I was immediately surprised and amazed by Doña Fidelina's framing of peace as "everyone being together with the same idea" in order to be "able to do what you need to do," which I subsequently interpreted as everyone working together toward the same goal.

    Her conception for me was a break from the common ways I had heard others theorize peace. She did not reduce peace to a material or societal condition and did not mention war at all. Instead she inferred unity and collective work among themselves. I began to see how peace could be defined independent from violence. It was only after she said that "peace is community" that I realized, unconsciously, that I was expecting her to define peace as living without war, harmony, or when people have their basic material needs met. Those visions corresponded with what I heard and read elsewhere until then, both in Colombia and in the peace literature: "negative peace" as the absence of physical violence and "positive peace" as the absence of structural and cultural violences as well as the integration of human society. These terms, coined by Johan Galtung (1964), have dominated peace theory for decades. Nor did her conception of peace as community directly map onto scholar Wolfgang Dietrich's (2012) categories of "modern" peace as security enforced by the state; normative "moral" peaces of justice, hospitality, or salvation in the afterlife; "energetic" peaces of fertility and cosmo-ecological harmony; or "postmodern" peace through the truth and imperfection of the many forms and definitions of peace.[1]

Interestingly, Nicole Laliberté (2014) cautions against asking people to define peace at all, arguing that they typically fall into simplistic claims or dominant clichés about tranquility or the absence of war. But as I proceeded to ask more and more people about their understanding of peace, both Colombians and international accompaniers responded with a wide array of diverse—and sometimes incredibly specific—understandings, proposals, and practices. I began the interview vignette above with Doña Fidelina's initial reluctance, as an elderly woman, to share her ideas in order to show how the "dialogic performance" (Conquergood 1985) of the personal interview (Pollock 2005) can break through such hierarchies of knowledge. "Experts" do not own a monopoly on thought, and communication itself is a means of knowledge production. In subsequent conversations I would remind her how her ideas were a breakthrough for my understanding of peace. The focus of Part II will be to render and analyze the significance of diverse expressions amid Colombia's peace process conjuncture to enrich peace theory.

Doña Fidelina's answer was also the first of what became a pattern among other Peace Community members. In subsequent interviews in San José de Apartadó, I continued to preface my question with "you call yourselves a Peace Community, so . . ." before asking what peace meant. I noticed that people would often answer by naming the Community's commitments, such as communal work and not collaborating with any armed group. I began to suspect that naming the Community in my formulation of the question, rather than asking about peace on its own, affected their engagement with the question. I felt that their statements could just as well have been answering "What is community?" or "What constitutes the Peace Community?" Yet, as the interviewee asserted above, the two are integral, which made me reflect on the significance of their naming themselves a "peace community" in the first place, and how that has affected their understanding and enactment of both concepts. Rather than a safe zone or "humanitarian space," for which there might be a temporal or spatial "peace" of refuge, the act of constituting an organization as a peace community demands a higher degree of unity, solidarity, and collective work within the group. It raises the stakes from physical survival alone and makes explicit the goal of constructing a particular sociocultural territory. Such a commitment and vision of peace comes through in members' definitions. For most of them, peace required *not* participating in the war and also *actively* participating in the construction of a community. In conversation, Community members frequently raised the question of what distinguished members who are committed to building community from other campesinos merely interested in surviving in the middle of war and have thus never joined, left, or been kicked out of the Peace Community. This alludes to the inherently territorial and political dynamic of peace and whether exclusions are also a part of living peace. How do such distinctions among campesinos in San José reproduce or subvert the exclusions and divisions of modern-colonial society?

In Doña Fidelina's statement about "everyone being together with the same idea," there is a sense of utopian conviviality and the need for a certain uniformity among the group. In practice, however, difference and conflict are central to the Peace Community process. In their founding document they name as core principles both the "respect of plurality" and the "freedom" of the Community and individual members to make their own decisions (Comunidad de Paz de San José de Apartadó 2005b). Such principles are epitomized by not automatically branding those who leave the Community as "guerrillas" or "paramilitaries" and by marching in solidarity with the rights and well-being of nonmember campesinos. In practice, to be "together with the same idea" has not been the result of a predetermined directive but rather of communal dialogue and decision. As Peace Community leader Berta Tuberquia Quintero described: "We always think and act in common. Even if we have different thoughts, and maybe even argue or disagree, in the end we end up uniting because it is a strength. What we have always said: strength is collective" (group interview 2014). As we will see in a multitude of members' reflections, peace, resistance, and creating an alternative to war requires unified organization, commitment, and work.

I ended the transcription that opened this part with the question I posed about the "path" *toward* peace. Doña Fidelina proceeded to narrate her personal journey migrating to San José from the Dabeiba region to the south, and how the Peace Community was founded. I included the question above because it reflects where my own conceptualization of peace was at the time. For me peace was still something "out there," to be achieved, for which there was a path or paths. When I began to write this part and returned to this interview, I noticed something else. She initially began her definition by saying that peace is "having . . ." without completing the sentence. When she finally articulated her vision, she switched to "being": "everyone being together." The former suggests peace as a condition, the point at which you have something; the latter speaks to peace as a process, as who and where we are is always becoming. This tension between condition versus process has been the focus of the recent geographies of peace literature (Williams and McConnell 2011; Loyd 2012), and the contrast of having versus being parallels what are characterized as normative "moral" peaces versus open-ended "energetic" cultures of peace within the "Many Peaces" framework pioneered by Dietrich (2012). Even at the time of the interview, I was struck by her sense that peace is not something that we can wait for from others. Instead we have to create and "be" it now.

Contemporary peace geographies scholarship has generated numerous critiques of the often undefined or vaguely used concept of peace. Yet most of this work has stopped short of proposing new definitions, as called for by Nick Megoran (2011). If we relegate ourselves to critically deconstructing dominant notions without proposing new framings, we are thus left with those limited mainstream concepts. New working definitions, which invite critique as well as imagine and articulate what peace "otherwise" can be, are necessary for further enriching peace scholarship.

My conceptualization of peace builds from critical theory on violence and politics, peace geographies, the transrational school of peace studies, and the praxis of the Peace Community and other Colombian social movements. I pose my own definition: Peace is a spatial process of creating self-determination and living with dignity that does not compromise the dignity of other people, places, and beings. I call this *trans-relational peace*, a term for which I am indebted to international accompanier Michaela Soellinger, from whom I first derived it.

Michaela's personal reflection on peace can be read in Chapter 4. When defining the concept, she used the word *transrational*, citing Dietrich's school where she studied. I was not yet familiar with the term and heard and transcribed it as *trans-relational*. It was only after I read Dietrich (2012) later and had a follow-up conversation with Michaela in which she clarified *transrational*—peacebuilding work that includes rational analysis but also goes beyond it to include emotional interconnections (Dietrich 2014)— that I returned to the interview audio and heard it correctly. Nevertheless, what I heard as trans-*relational* peace led me to conceptualize the latter term and in fact prefer it, given its inference of relational ontologies (Blaser

2010; de la Cadena 2015; Escobar 2018). Similar to the conversation with the Peace Community member that began this part, this was another example of "dialogic performance" (Conquergood 1985), where through the back-and-forth of inspirational conversations and clarifications, even misunderstandings are generative for producing new knowledge.

I propose this spatially practiced relational peace as a referential qualifier and normative framing for other theories and projects of peace. The concept of *trans-relational peace* is meant to invoke dignity rooted in relationality, but through particular forms of emancipatory solidarity that exceed mere interconnection. This perspective allows us to evaluate different forms of peace by always examining the relations at their heart, without idealizing every type of relationship to analyze the dynamics of power and politics regarding the experiences of and effects for those internal and external to them. Is such "peace" constituted by dignity? What are its spatial practices and politics? If a peace discourse is rooted in talk of freedom and self-determination, do these come at the expense of others? Or do they cultivate multiple praxes of ecological dignity that are networked together? One might argue, as some Colombian activists indeed do, that such a peace of dignity is impossible within the modern-colonial world permeated by intersectional violence. Therefore trans-relational peace must be constituted through a radical politics, in which there is a rupture with the violent divisions and demarcations of modern warfare and society (Fanon 2004; Reyes 2012a) by cultivating alternative "worlds" (Escobar 2018) and relations of radical solidarity.

Part II analyzes the implications of peace interpretations and practices. My concern here is the extent to which particular articulations of peace reproduce modernity-coloniality or foster ecological dignity. In Chapter 4 I present diverse understandings and practices of peace in Colombia during the "peace process" context, ranging from government officials to an array of people active in social movements. I argue that the struggle for peace in Colombia today is fundamentally an antagonism between divergent territorialities regarding state-driven peace, extractivism, and community autonomy. Chapter 5 analyzes peace according to the Peace Community of San José de Apartadó, explaining how its praxis inspired my conceptual articulation of radical trans-relational peace.

CHAPTER 4

"PEACE DOES NOT COME FROM THEM"

Antagonisms in Colombia's Peace Conjuncture

> Peace is having the consciousness amid the universe to know how small we are before the incommensurability of the universe.
>
> **JUAN MARTÍNEZ RESTREPO (*EL HERADO DE URABÁ* 2013)**

These are the words of the recognized poet and writer from the city of Apartadó in Urabá known as Juan Mares. The line above comes from a poem included in the book *Poesía por la paz* (Poetry for Peace) delivered to the Colombian government and FARC negotiating table in Havana. It was then published in the Apartadó-based newspaper *El Heraldo de Urabá*.

On the one hand, this statement speaks to thinking about peace beyond a specific individual experience and instead in relation to the larger universe encompassed by a multitude of beings. By stressing interconnectivity, it reflects Wolfgang Dietrich's (2012) notion of "energetic" peace. This might lead toward deconstructing the supposed individual liberal subject. On the other hand, this framing of peace lacks the vision of a politics of peace concretely created through commitment and organization. Such notions of passive peace seem counterproductive and even dangerous in a moment when actors across Colombia insist that peace is something that communities have to actively participate in and create. If the situation or "contradiction" (Mao 1937) in Colombia is fundamentally one of racist and patriarchal war, then the "politics" of rupture must be a peace that creates an alternative to that war. It is for this reason that the notion of *radical trans-relational peace* emphasizes an understanding of all beings' interdependence but combines it with a fundamental insistence on the radical political praxis necessary to break with modern state "peace" as war. Indeed, the current Colombian conjuncture reflects a scenario in which passive visions of peace are being challenged and alternative notions are being enunciated and practiced.

Given that peace is a strategic discourse used by a variety of actors (McConnell 2014), in this chapter I analyze an array of perspectives on peace in Colombia and whether or not they suggest alternatives to the war. I thus conceptualize peace in conversation with the thought and action of people who actually use and were asked about the term. Useful theories on peace have emerged from scholarship in contexts in which the term is not explicitly used by the actors involved (Dietrich 2012; McConnell, Megoran, and Williams 2014), but the Colombian case is especially fruitful for theorizing the concept because people are explicitly debating what peace means. This is due to the rich terrain of critique induced by the "peace process" between the FARC and Juan Manuel Santos administration.

Both state and non-state actors wield peace discursively, while also framing it at different geographical scales, including the interpersonal, communal, and national. Some assert that peace is assured when the state achieves a monopoly on the use of legitimate force, thus necessitating an end to what is often called Colombia's "internal armed conflict" between the guerrillas and the state. Others argue that consolidating peace requires reconciliation among the armed groups but also—and more importantly—among former combatants, communities, and civil society. Many affirm that peace requires the fulfillment of state-guaranteed rights to political participation, land, education, health, housing, and justice. Various actors conceptualize peace in relation to the country's dominant economic development model spearheaded by large-scale mining and agribusiness, with some affirming and others rejecting it. In addition, indigenous- and African-descendant communities consistently argue that peace requires autonomy for such groups. Finally, many people affirm that peace is constituted by conflict resolution through nonviolent interpersonal communication.

As we will see, most of the visions I encountered reflected "modern-liberal" or "moral" approaches to peace, through security as well as normative conditions of state order and rights. However, certain reflections also explained peace as an "energetic" or "imperfect-postmodern" process and experience, thus inspiring and guiding my notion of radical trans-relational peace. Attending to the too-often-ignored praxis of black, indigenous, and campesino social movements illustrates decolonial political understandings of peace that exceed a desire to "finally" achieve the supposed "order" and "security" of liberal democracy. While public attention to the conflicts surrounding Colombia's "peace process" tends to focus on the struggle between the "pro-peace" movement and the "No" movement's opposition to the Havana Accord led by the Democratic Center Party, this chapter illuminates less-discussed differences among sectors generally favorable to a cease-fire between the state and guerrillas. I argue that the struggle for peace in Colombia amid the "peace process" conjuncture is fundamentally a contestation between antagonistic territorializations regarding extractivism in which racialized communities' resistance to forced displacement confronts the state's extractivist development model. Indeed, the peace visions emanating from communities in resistance allow for a reconceptualization of peace beyond vague notions of "no war" or "tranquility," toward situated relational praxes of ecological dignity.

MILITARY AND NATIONAL GOVERNMENT PERSPECTIVES

I begin with the perspectives of state officials, including military officers and high-ranking officials in the Santos administration, whose perspectives were particularly influential in shaping the state's approach to peace. It was common to hear public security officers—along with many in the general public—define peace in parallel to its traditional, modern concept as the lack of direct violence and theft. A Colombian National Police officer expressed such a view in an interview: "Peace is living together peacefully. When people feel tranquility, safe, and that they aren't going to be robbed" (personal interview 2014). Members of the Colombian armed forces also described peace in terms of security and emphasized the role of the military. For instance, in a public interview then–minister of defense Juan Carlos Pinzón argued that "peace requires armed forces that are strong, equipped, and present in the entire national territory . . . with the capacity to face delinquency and the criminal organizations that might arise in the future. . . . Colombia is going to have peace either through reason or through force. . . . Today Colombia begins to have a hopeful future [because of] the presence of the armed forces. . . . With security, real peace will come to every Colombian" (*El Tiempo* 2014a). In this interview Pinzón asserted that, in fact, post-conflict had already arrived for the majority of Colombia's people and national territory due to the work of the armed forces. In so doing, the minister implicitly minimized the value of negotiations since state forces had supposedly already closed in on victory and would continue to assure peace militarily.

Yet all of the army officials I personally interviewed explicitly affirmed their support—and that of the National Army as a whole—for the "peace process" with the FARC. One pair of officers asserted, "The army is who wants peace the most. We are the ones who every day worry about our fellow soldiers and loved ones returning from the battlefield" (group interview 2014). This inferred a "negative peace" without open warfare and a "modern peace" of militarily enforced security.

Others were more explicit regarding their conception of peace and its political and economic implications. Note the following interaction I had with a colonel:

I asked, "What does peace mean to you?"

He responded, "Peace is comprehensive security. The soldier who provides security, [arm in arm] with the teacher, the businessman who provides work, and with the person who farms the land. But the land belongs to the state. *It decides what to do with it! And the land is to be exploited!*"

"What you do mean, 'exploited'?" I inquired.

"You know, exploited, where the people benefit!" (personal interview 2014)

These statements were accompanied by two notable gestures. First, as the officer spoke about the different actors, he raised his arms to simulate their standing together with their arms embracing one another, shoulder to shoulder. Second, when he repeated "exploited" in response to my request for him to qualify what he meant by "the land is to be exploited," he made a digging motion with his hands.

Both this army colonel and then–minister of defense Pinzón therefore framed peace as security enforced by the military. Pinzón expressed a top-down vision across the bounded nation-state, while the colonel affirmed the importance of integrated relationships between military officers and civil society groups. It should be noted that such a view inherently rejects proposals by certain indigenous groups and peace communities to not live alongside any armed group, including state forces. In addition, the colonel implicitly endorsed the state-driven political economy of extractivism, in which land is something to "to be exploited." Such views reflect a particular relationship with space and politics: a territoriality of domination over nature and population in which the state has ultimate authority. Despite the rhetoric of horizontal relations, this reflects the hierarchical political relations that constitute modernity-coloniality.

These positions spoke of and sought peace as the lack of open warfare, where the state achieved a monopoly on the use of armed force. Commonly held by members of the Colombian armed forces and also by sectors of society at large, especially the business community, this view of peace through force paralleled a more extreme view, the position of ex-president and current senator Álvaro Uribe, who opposed negotiations with guerrilla groups—and led the plebiscite "No" campaign to reject the Havana Accord—in favor of continued armed confrontation until the guerrillas' surrender or elimination. Even the very naming of the government–FARC negotiations as a "peace process" assumed that the demobilization of this non-state armed actor through negotiation constituted a form of peace. This follows the logic of Galtung's (1964) "negative peace"—the absence of open hostilities, in contrast to "positive peace" as the integration of human society through economic and social justice—but a supposed form of peace nonetheless. This is not to deny that the state–FARC accord included agreements on agrarian policy, victims, and oppositional parties' participation in electoral politics. But governments routinely legislate on land and justice policy without it being framed as "peace." What discursively constituted this negotiation as a "peace process" was not discussions on land or congressional representation but the goal of the guerrillas' demobilization. In fact, early indications showed that the government successfully implemented the disarmament process but has thus far failed to make substantial progress on its other commitments (Kroc Institute 2017). Future implementation became even less probable following the 2018 presidential election of the Democratic Center party's Iván Duque, a known critic of the negotiations and accord. It is for this reason that I prefer to refer to this process as the government–FARC *negotiations* or *accord*, and frequently write "peace process" in quotes. This "peace" of the state's monopoly on legitimate force is the modern-colonial liberal view of peace critiqued by a multitude of scholars (Daley 2014; Dietrich 2012; Foucault 2003; Gelderloos 2007; Loyd 2012; Ross 2011; Williams, Megoran, and McConnell 2014). It is state-centric, top-down, militaristic, and patriarchal (Daley 2014). It is often not even an effective strategy for obtaining so-called negative peace. Lotta Harbom, Stina Högbladh, and Peter Wallenstein (2006) point out that most liberal peace accords fail within five years, leading some scholars to assert that "peace" or "post-conflict" is merely the time between the last and the next war (Dalby 2014; Kirsch and Flint 2011). Nevertheless, or precisely *because of* the power relations enacted through it, the conception of peace as state forces achieving a monopoly on the "legitimate" use of force remains a ubiquitous concept and project.

Civilian state officials tended to speak about peace in a broader sense, beyond achieving the government's monopoly on the use of armed force. Voices from the administration of President Juan Manuel Santos were indicative here. Despite Santos's affirmation upon the FARC laying down their arms in June 2017 that "our peace is real and irreversible" (*El Tiempo* 2017), civilian government officials—including Santos himself—tended to claim that peace required more than the FARC's conversion from a guerrilla insurgency into a political party. For example, the Santos government's high commissioner for peace Sergio Jaramillo argued, "The base for constructing peace is citizen participation, of the communities in their territories" (*Semana* 2014). "It is increasing the reach and strengthening the effectiveness of institutions in the territories" (Vargas Velásquez 2015). Santos spoke further, "[Peace] is not limited to signing an agreement with the guerrillas. . . . Absolute peace is eradicating misery and Colombians having dignified shelter and employment. [We will progress when we are] together, united, in order to overcome resentments" (*El País* 2014).

Santos's and Jaramillo's proclamations thus appealed to national unity, local communities' increased participation within state realms of politics, and increased access to basic services. The message was strongly nationalistic, inferring that the country's lack of "progress" and peace is due to "resentments"—rather than structural violence—that can be solved through unification. These positions also spoke to citizens' rights and well-being, arguing that peace was constituted by meeting people's basic necessities, including their rights to life, food, housing, health care, education, and employment, which are either provided or guaranteed by the state. Meanwhile they accepted the role of the armed forces as security enforcers within the nation-state. This reflects what Dietrich (2012) categorizes as a moral peace of "everyone having enough" and a modern peace of "security." Marc Chernick (2009) reiterated this vision: "In Colombia, peace basically means the construction of a more participatory and inclusive regime and of a legitimate state presence throughout the national territory" (93–94).

It is important to gauge the extent to which popular demands for territorial autonomy from the state, such as by rural communities in resistance, are permitted within the Colombian state's vision of peace. I inquired into a Colombian policeman's interpretation of such proposals:

> I asked, "How do you understand those communities who demand 'territory'?"
>
> He responded, "The issue of community territories, here in Urabá, is a problem about the dispute over land. Here there has been follow-up on land restitution. This refers to those who had possession of their territories and have been displaced. Restitution is a mechanism to obtain that possession. Some landowners—people between a rock and a hard place—had to flee due to threats. We are all affected, because we are all one family. Land restitution is a process to resolve that problem. People present their titles and receive legal possession of the land." (personal interview 2014)

Referencing the Victims and Land Restitution Law of 2011, he thus agreed that displaced campesinos should be able to return to where they previously lived. But notice that he failed to mention anything about community autonomy. And his concept of territory equated this concept with a piece of land that is controlled à la "modern" rather than "energetic" peace.

Such views remain focused on the national polity and a liberal notion where the state guarantees that citizens' rights and basic needs are met. They are consistent with the theory that what plagues Colombia is a weak or absent state. They do not question the presence of state institutions—including but not limited to the military—as a force of violence (Ballvé 2020; Escobar 2008; Gómez Correal 2016; Hylton 2006). Rather, they insist that these institutions expand their reach and achieve legitimacy. This reflects the persistence of Thomas Hobbes's (1991) prescription that peace requires people's submission to the sovereign. However, the social contract in a rights-based state, à la Jean Jacques Rousseau (1968), in theory presumes a democratic and *legitimate* governmental system as well. Indeed, this legitimization of the state is what the Santos administration sought through the "peace process."

Yet the top-down and capitalist nature of the governing party's approach to peace is evident. Congruent with military officials, Santos affirmed, "We will achieve peace with the stick or the carrot" (*La Nación* 2014). In a presidential address after reaching agreements with the FARC on the four most disputed agenda items—making an eventual accord seem inevitable—Santos (2015) celebrated: "A Colombia in peace will shine like a fulgurous star in the international arena. . . . Make us safer. . . . Attract more investment and create more and better jobs. . . . Convert us into a tourist power. . . . Better protect the environment and that marvelous biodiversity we should preserve." Santos thus appealed to patriotism in relation to other nation-states, in which peace is achievable by disarming the guerrillas and advancing his "economic locomotives" development model, driven by agribusiness and mining (*El País* 2015). This was consistent with the export-oriented development model ubiquitous across Latin America, where extractive economies are the prime source of public income (Dávalos 2011; Gudynas 2015). The Colombian state's militarist and neoliberal form of "peace" is consistent with its standing as one the staunchest allies of the United States in Latin America (Tate 2015; Lindsay Poland 2018). As Diana Gómez Correal (2016) observes, for Santos, the "peace process" would inaugurate Colombia's arrival as a modern country, ignoring that Colombia's violence is already indicative of its peripheral situation within the capitalist world-system.

It seems contradictory to assert that post-accord Colombia will "better protect the environment" and "make us safer" when a prime sector for international investment that Santos sought was open-pit mining (Santos 2017; Ioris and Ioris 2018; Chagas-Bastos 2018). Large-scale mining correlates with high rates of ecological degradation, human rights violations, and forced displacement (Ramírez Cuéllar 2011; Torres et al. 2015). Municipal referendums across Colombia, such as the emblematic case in Piedras, Tolima, are increasingly defying state mining concessions by rejecting extractive projects (Hernandez 2017). And members of the political opposition within the Colombian government challenged the ruling party's militaristic peace by signaling the state's role as the root actor in the war. For instance, Iván Cepeda and Alirio Uribe of the Polo Democrático Alternativo (Alternative Democratic Pole) party spoke to an international delegation visiting Bogotá about how the "peace process" would be fruitless without a comprehensive "social transformation" and "justice against impunity" (field notes 2014).

Despite the FARC laying down arms, the military planned to *increase* its numbers and operations, which included "Security Cooperation agreements" where the military battalions' objective was to protect mining corporations from protests in order to ensure resource exploitation (Tierra Digna 2015). While international institutions such as the United Nations were expected to provide funding for "post-conflict" reintegration programs for ex-combatants, transitional justice tribunals, and victim reparations, government officials and journalists admitted that such programs would still depend on income generated by mining (*El Espectador* 2014b; Bermúdez Liévano 2015). In other words, the "peace process"—as envisioned and driven by the Santos administration—was designed to further entrench extractivism as the country's development model. This reflected a continuation of modernity-coloniality's exploitative environmental logics and hierarchical political structures.

INTRODUCING SOCIAL MOVEMENT PERSPECTIVES

Some social movement perspectives overlapped with state officials' framings, such as Juan Manuel Santos's recognition that peace would not be constituted by an accord alone. But, for the most part Colombian social movements presented a sharp contrast to state visions grounded in an ideology of state benevolence. In particular, almost all of those in Colombian social movements with whom I interacted challenged the position that the state's armed forces played a positive role in the production of "peace," however they defined the latter.

The primary exception among my interlocutors was one activist's assertion that "those who don't want peace are the illegal armed groups. We Colombians are those who want peace" (field notes 2014). Similar to state discourse, this problematic framing left out the state as a central actor of violence, while concurrently inferring that the members of the paramilitaries and guerrillas were not also Colombians. While an outlier among those whom I interviewed and worked with, I came across this sentiment frequently in the mainstream media and everyday conversations with taxi drivers, service providers, street vendors, and family members or friends of my interlocutors. It expressed a sentiment of "Can't we just have peace?!," which is in fact a reluctance and refusal to critically engage with the historical, cultural, and political conditions of the war. Lacking a politics of anticolonial rupture thus perpetuates the capitalist, patriarchal, and racist modern "peace" of state and military authority.

It struck me that no non-state actor whom I consulted argued that a government–FARC accord would constitute "real" peace. The quotations below demonstrate the extent to which debates about peace turned around the negotiations. They also exhibited Colombian human rights defenders and communities in resistance's strong critique of the framing of the accord itself as peace. However, from that common sentiment there was a variety of differing qualifications about what peace should mean.

Almost all of these social movement actors demanded more profound transformations, with respect to unequal distributions of land, wealth, and basic services; interpersonal conflict resolution; reconciliation with ex-combatants; re-subjectifications as individuals and communities; the demilitarization of institutions and minds; and finally, to the most radical view, of communities' autonomy and work toward an alternative world. These visions were reflective of popular social movements across the country who for decades or more had taken peace into their own hands as they resisted direct, structural, and cultural violences.

Of course some of these actors welcomed the negotiations to deescalate the armed conflict and as a political opening to write a new social agenda. Others asserted that the talks were merely an attempt by the two armed groups to divvy up the spoils of war. For some organizations and individuals, post-conflict was on its way as the government–guerrilla talks progressed, while others rejected such a framing. The latter position insisted that any "post-conflict" period that failed to face the social and economic contradictions at the root of the war would simply continue the war in a new way. According to this view, if politics is war by other means (Foucault 2003), this context looked like "peace as war by other means" (Escobar 2017). Let us proceed to explore these ideas in turn.

REJECTING PEACE DISCOURSE

Consistent with scholarly critiques of peace, one activist questioned the framing of peace altogether. Part of the Red Juvenil de Medellín (Youth Network of Medellín) comprised of conscientious objectors, urban community organizers, and feminists, he rooted his position in their philosophical position of nonviolence. For them this was not a pacifism that "turns the other cheek" but direct action to confront capitalism and sexism. In a rejection of the logics of armed struggle, he referenced one of the organization's slogans: "No army defends peace," adding that "you aren't going to solve anything by killing men and women" (group interview 2011). This corresponds with the concept of "principled" nonviolence that rejects all killing (Teixeira 1999), in contrast to a pragmatic "strategic" nonviolence that utilizes nonviolent direct action but does not necessarily repudiate armed resistance depending on the situation (Burrowes 1996; Schock 2005). Specifically arguing against "peace," this member of the Red Juvenil said, "The concept of peace is very relative. The United States lives peace internally. . . . Peace is something very romantic, uncritical. Because you speak about peace when the guns are silenced. But there are other issues, like a dignified life, that people in the [poor] urban neighborhoods have the minimum, basic services, human rights. I have problems with that concept" (group interview 2011). While ignoring racial and other forms of social violence within the United States, this is a useful critique of the way peace is used discursively as the opposite of direct violence without attending to structural violence. The statement reflects many social movement actors' disenchantment with the term in relation to the country's mainstream "peace movement" that arose in the 1990s to insist on a negotiated solution to the armed conflict between the guerrillas and government. Precisely due to the fact that this peace movement had generally focused on the guerrillas' demobilization without necessarily pushing for more structural changes (Isacson and Rojas Rodríguez 2009), many Colombians on the political Left commonly resisted framing their struggles through the terminology of peace. Instead, the latter distinguished themselves as a "human rights" or "justice" movement to challenge structural impunity and inequalities regarding land, income, and political participation (Koopman 2014). This reflects a rejection of "modern peace" as "security" provided by the military and also rebuffs the "negative" and "positive" peace duality: there is no reason to call *anything* peace—even a cessation of armed combat—unless it is constituted by dignity for the excluded and oppressed.

GUARANTEED RIGHTS AND SERVICES

Partially due to the "peace process" conjuncture, the majority of my interlocutors, rather than rejecting the concept of peace, looked to not only interrogate the dominant modern-moral "peace" but also to reframe and reinvent the concept by proposing alternative notions, arrangements, and practices.

For many, peace would be constituted through the fulfillment of socioeconomic and political rights. Historian Julián Londoño, from the political movement Congreso de los Pueblos (Congress of the Peoples), argued, "Nonviolence and peace [are] the guarantee that all civil rights will be fulfilled for everyone in a city, department, or country" (personal interview 2011). Edward Vergara of the Tejido Awasqa Conciente (Conscious Cultural Weave, commonly known as Awasqa) youth collective in Medellín expressed a congruent sentiment. He asserted that you could not talk about peace until people have their basic needs met—electricity and health care, for instance—and an appropriate education rooted in the will, skills, and knowledge of the local and national population (personal interview 2013). Speaking of Colombia's pervasive inequalities of land and wealth, Carmen Palencia (2012), then–legal representative of the land restitution organization Tierra y Vida (Land and Life), asserted, "Peace will not be constructed with the laying down of arms. It must be constructed by making life more equal in this country. . . . I speak about the construction of a social fabric with schools, highways, health centers, all those things that would make life easy for the campesinos." In other words, peace is a process of increasing equality, enacted through the delivery of basic rights and services, especially to campesinos. These views speak to a peace through the fulfillment of the promise of a Colombian civil society.

A congruent sentiment common in Colombia argued that unless there were economic opportunities for ex-combatants, especially rural and urban youth, they would merely form new or join existing armed groups (Chernick 2009). Indeed, many EPL guerrillas and AUC paramilitaries who demobilized in the 1990s and 2000s, respectively, followed this pattern. For instance, another member of the organization Tierra y Vida argued, "The government claims that peace is achieved through demobilizations. But that is not the case. Because you demobilize one group and from them arise five new [competing] groups. That is to increase rather than diminish [war]" (group interview 2011). A black community leader in Chocó from the Consejo Comunitario Mayor de la Organización Popular Campesina del Alto Atrato (COCOMOPOCA, Community Council of Campesino Popular Organization in the Upper Atrato River) concurred with that assertion. He also included reparations on the list of what would be required for peace in a legitimate state: "The topic of peace is extensive. For there to be peace in Colombia, the state has to recompense all the inhabitants of Colombia. It will be difficult for the conflict to end despite all of us saying that we want a peace agreement. There are some [preliminary agreements] but lots of nonconformity [or failure to follow through on them]. Peace is simple: education, housing, and health services. They will arrive at an accord, but it will only be peace for the armed actors. They will benefit and other [armed] groups who do not will emerge" (field notes 2014). It is notable how he affirmed that peace is both an extensive topic but also simple: state reforms and services that would ensure peace are substantial undertakings, but they are also quite obvious conditions for peace.

Defining peace in terms of a rights-based state conforms to a modern-moral vision, even as it attempts to break through the Hobbesian "security" state model. Of course the promise of liberal democracy is an alluring project. Yet trying to "fulfill" the promise of justice and equality from within a system that is structurally opposed or unable to guarantee and reach this promise has proved to be a limited strategy. For example, Wendy Brown (1995) warns how looking to the state for "justice" actually re-entrenches the very institution that is responsible for the injury. Modern "civil society" has never been a harmonious or equal structure. It has been structured by a racial hierarchy in which the well-being of the upper and middle classes as well as the white population was dependent on the subjugation of and gratuitous violence against black and indigenous peoples (Fanon 2008; Goldberg 2009; Wilderson 2010). Finally, finance capitalism, neoliberal structural adjustment, and the free trade agreements of past decades, attempting to make such reforms irreversible, have transformed many modern states (especially in the Global South) into "mafia" security states, in which the ability for redistribution or guaranteeing services within the state has increasingly been made a near impossibility; this racialized political economy blocks a potential return to the welfare state, even if desired (Estrada Álvarez 2006; Reyes 2015). That being said, demands for reforms remain crucial as part of a broader struggle for a different world, but this necessitates remaining cognizant of and pushing beyond the co-optation of struggle within those channels (Wolf 2009). The current conjuncture of the crisis of capitalist reproduction suggests that an alternative to "modern peace" requires decolonial imaginaries that go beyond state reforms. To this end the subsequent section turns to visions insisting on transformations of interpersonal relations.

INTERPERSONAL TRANSFORMATIONS

For many social movement actors, rather than a question of state building, peace was an issue of interpersonal communication and reconciliation. Take for instance Ricardo Esquivia, executive director of Sembrandopaz (Planting Peace) in Sincelejo, Sucre. A large part of this NGO's work is organizing campesino communities in the areas around Sincelejo, including the Montes de María region. This area's population lived through an intense period of mass forced displacement because of guerrilla, paramilitary, and army combat in recent decades. At the time of the signing of the peace accord in 2016, large-scale attacks had largely subsided, and the government named the area one of the country's exemplary laboratories for "post-conflict" in rural Colombia. This was despite the tenuousness of such a proposal, given that campesino livelihoods as subsistence farmers were still being undermined by the agrarian transformation to agribusiness through oil palm plantations (Berman Arévalo 2015). Sembrandopaz's work included small-scale agricultural projects and conflict mediation and reconciliation programs among campesino leaders from villages stigmatized as guerrilla or paramilitary hamlets. Speaking to an international delegation, Esquivia emphasized the need for agrarian reform and state reparations to the war's victims. However, he placed his emphasis on post-disarmament reconciliation *within* communities: "It is good for the guns to stop for our work to continue, that the armed groups find reconciliation. But *peace does not come from them*. For there to be peace, communities need to be prepared to receive the guerrillas who will demobilize in order to make the peace agreements a reality" (field notes 2014, emphasis mine). Without directly saying so, he alluded to the fact that many Colombian families include people who have fought on different sides of the war, some as guerrillas and others as paramilitaries, army soldiers, or police officers. Esquivia's was among the voices who supported the peace talks and an eventual accord. However, his assertion that "peace does not come from them" was a strong rebuttal of the dominant modern-colonial peaces that position state policy and action at the vanguard of peace making. His idea of reconciliation insisted on transformations that take place on individual and collective levels. Such a perspective speaks to the need to actually build a civil society at the grass roots, without which any peace accords will remain only on paper.

Also focusing on the scale of the local, a community leader from the campesino community of Macayepo in Montes de María located peace at the scale of the home. He affirmed that peace was a reconciliation process that must take place among family members: "Peace is harmony within the family, when you are able to talk through disagreements. Peace is not constructed in Havana; there they only leave behind the guns. Peace has to take place in families [through] reconciliation between parents and children" (field notes 2014). Of course such a comment implicitly implied that the accord *would* bring about a demobilization. He was obviously referring only to the guerrillas, rather than the neo-paramilitaries and public armed forces who remain active. As is clear from the quotes throughout this chapter, many other people and organizations strongly questioned that such an outcome was a given.

Another leader, also from Macayepo, agreed that the home must be considered when thinking about peace. He argued that poverty does not preclude peace, even if that is not to dismiss education and state rights: "Peace is when I can be in my home in tranquility, even if I'm poor. But education and granting rights [are] necessary. For there to be peace, we have to be prepared to forgive. And forgiveness comes from God" (field notes 2014). By inferring that peace requires not total equality but rather access to opportunities, this stance diverges from what we might call the Marxist peace where everyone is equal. Moreover, for him forgiveness and the divine were foundational to peace, reflecting what Dietrich (2012) deems a form of moral peace, which in this case comes through God.

The idea of peace through reconciliation and its mantra of "forgiving and forgetting" is a widespread vision in Colombia, largely traceable to the influence of the Catholic and growing evangelical churches. Such a perspective has been harshly critiqued by scholars and victims movements for perpetuating the judicial impunity at the root of the country's ongoing violence (Gómez Correal 2012, 2016; Gómez Muller 2008). I would argue that the "reconciliation" Esquivia spoke of was not the hegemonic form of reconciliation proposed by the Colombian elite, where guerrillas and other dissidents "reconcile" by simply joining mainstream society and renouncing their demands for justice and social transformation (Gómez Correal

2016). Esquivia's reconciliation with armed combatants must take place between and within communities.

The idea of peace constituted through interpersonal dynamics was also emphasized by historian Julián Londoño. Building from his comment about peace through civil rights cited earlier, he argued that peace was conditioned on nonviolent forms of communication to face and resolve differences and conflicts. On peace, he said, "It is having the ability to tell someone, calmly and not aggressively, that they made a mistake or that I don't agree with them. . . . It is to not aggravate anyone physically, economically, politically, or psychologically. . . . The state uses bullets to intimidate and disappear [people]" (personal interview 2011). Such a perspective mirrors "positive peace" or a civil society in which there is no direct, structural, or cultural violence. Additionally, he contrasted what is a dominant means of resolving conflict in modern-colonial societies—through force and guns, including the horrendous state practice of forcibly disappearing political opponents referenced by Londoño—with an alternative mode of interpersonal conflict resolution, where differences in opinion are respected and debated without killing the person with whom you disagree. Considering what Gómez Correal (forthcoming) signals as Colombia's and modernity-coloniality's "emotional habitus of hate" against the subordinated other, to insist that everyday disagreements are resolved through dialogue is in fact a radical proposal in the modern-colonial world. Of course such resolution is predicated on a situation of "conflict," in which mutual agreement is possible; the necropolitics at the root of modern-colonial "antagonism" (Mao 1937; Mbembé 2003) makes interpersonal communication insufficient for breaking with the contradiction of racist and classist dispossession. Yet the insistence on nonviolent communication is something that organizations can implement as part of their radical political praxis immediately without waiting for broader structural transformations (Gelderloos 2007).

Two of the international accompaniers I interviewed also affirmed the importance of interpersonal communication. FOR accompanier Gale Stafford argued that peace was constituted by eliminating automatic weapons and by resolving conflicts through dialogue. This included tempering impulsive reactions to things in order to respond to others thoughtfully (personal interview 2014). Such a view was another manifestation of "principled nonviolence," in which all physical harm with weapons is considered violence. Gale expanded on her concept at the end of her time in Colombia:

> I will no longer define peace as a lack of violence. Just on principle it's unfair to call peace just when people aren't killing each other. . . . I see peace as about building things, and creativity, and making communities that people have a space in and feel welcome to be a part of and can contribute to. Peace is about

choice and about play and enjoyment and about listening for the good, or helpful, or positive, or constructive in what people do. It is about belief in the value of forming things to be beautiful and taking the time to do so, and expressing what's important. And peace is about sharing. (Stafford 2015)

Another accompanier spoke to the importance of communication and building dignified societies: "Peace is where people are able to live where they are not harmed and not harming others, but that is still so complicated! [Peace is] the possibility and opportunity to have what we need: access to food, healthy and good food, water, and education. Peace can be conceived within a utopic vision that seems possible, but humans do thrive on conflict. Peace is having empathy and understanding for one another and communicating with one another in a way that doesn't harm others. And opening channels of understanding given our different upbringings and ideas" (personal interview 2014). Such views integrate both Dietrich's (2012) Marxist moral peace of "everyone having enough" and Francisco Muñoz's (2001) notion of an "imperfect peace," in which cooperation *and* conflict are constitutive to human interaction. Conflict can be a source of possibility, difference, and new ideas and ways of doing, albeit in situations in which such diversity is embraced and cultivated. The accompanier's reflection that this "is still so complicated!" was made in reference to how capitalism has made some people's social and material reproduction come at the expense of others' (Federici 2010), and gets to the heart of the impediments of dignified peace within the modern-colonial world-system, which is structured by oppression and exploitation.

Similarly FOR accompanier Luke Finn began from the theoretical position of "positive" peace and reflected on what he perceived as peace for the Peace Community and for himself. He argued that peace is the smooth working of human interaction without resorting to physical or group brute force; it is an egalitarian social and political structure, where people are able to achieve the livelihood they want, or that which makes them who they are as a person or as a community (personal interview 2013). Consistent with Julián Londoño's view, these accompaniers call for a balance between people being able to live and be who they are, but not at the expense of others. It requires intentional strategies of communication and conflict resolution.

To continue with the theme of balancing people's needs, a neighborhood community organizer in Medellín pointed to peace through "equilibrium." He questioned the utility of peace as a frame for organizational projects, preferring "life." He did not go so far as to deem peace a useless concept, but favored life as an open-ended, never-ending process of construction and reinvention:

> Peace is achieved through a cultural transformation, where we convince each other that neither they nor I have the only truth, but rather that we construct the truth together. Peace is not even a condition. It is something within each person. . . . Many say that peace isn't the absence of war, and they are correct. Peace is an equilibrium between all of the conditions of being a human being. Peace is achieved when I'm not hungry, or lack health care or education, but also an equilibrium among those things, on an equal plane. It doesn't only have to do with me but with the community. I can have money and all my basic needs met, but if I see my neighbor hungry, for me there isn't peace. Peace is achieved through everyone having their needs met in equilibrium. (personal interview 2011)

Therefore peace is only possible through material well-being, but there must be an equilibrium among the needs of everyone. Peace is also much more than everyone "having enough" with regard to material needs. There is a communal, subjective, and cultural aspect as well. His perspective reflected a "postmodern" and "transpersonal" peace (Dietrich 2012) constructed through relations within and among people. The way his community center emphasized "life" rather than "peace" correlated with Muñoz's (2001) project of a processual "imperfect peace." Dietrich's (2012) postmodern, transrational, and moral peaces are thus not necessarily mutually exclusive, and this community organizer's vision reflects what I might describe as a relational or transpersonal moral peace. Embedded within it is a postmodern critique of any one person owning "the Truth," yet there is the simultaneous insistence that there is "a Truth" to be constructed communally through the production of collective subjects.

Another international accompanier, Michaela Soellinger of FOR—and a former student of Wolfgang Dietrich—offered the following reflection. She began by referencing a definition of peace that she had heard during her studies: "'The breath of each individual in harmony with the holy one's breath.' I think that's something that sounds pretty cool. And peace, for me, is being centered, internally. . . . Peace is relational. . . . Transrational peace: I'm from that school. . . . So, peace is always between. It's never mine or yours. . . . And yet . . . an ability or an environment . . . not conflicting but creating a whole. . . . In every instance you are in relation with something, somebody. You are creating something. Because it's transforming" (personal interview 2013). What I find most significant from this imaginary of peace is how brilliantly it describes a "transpersonal" peace, in which peace is internal to each person, yet always interdependent with all others; there is no romanticization of the individual subject. This notion intimates that peace must always be thought of and practiced from a relationality between all human beings in which there is constant transformation of all.

Also speaking in terms of transformation like Michaela, Colombian nonviolence trainer Blas García from SERPAJ Colombia (the Colombian branch of Servicio Paz y Justicia or Service of Peace and Justice, which is the Latin American expression of the International Fellowship of Reconciliation, IFOR) framed peace from the perspective of nonviolence. He argued that we must transform both ourselves—à la a "transpersonal" peace—but also sociocultural institutions:

> Peace is derived from active nonviolence and demilitarization; it is integral. Peace is not only the absence of war. We must demobilize our consciousness and institutions—schools, churches, families—and the society in general. Within the concept of peace is the empowerment of communities to be able to demand their rights to health, education, housing, dignified employment. [It is] social, cultural, [and] environmental. What will be signed in Havana is not peace but a cessation of hostilities. We believe in an alternative power of the poor, the victimized, and the excluded. Nonviolence is a lifestyle. Those who look to make denunciations in this country are eliminated. (field notes 2014)

Similar to Londoño, who in his narrative about interpersonal communication included that "the state uses bullets to intimidate and disappear," García integrated the same critique. He inferred how the state apparatus—despite the Santos administration's leadership in the "peace process"—continues to react with repression against those who promote alternative social orders. Interestingly, he argued that the task is *demilitarization* rather than mere *demobilization*. Beyond the demobilization of the armed groups, the widespread demilitarization of minds, bodies, institutions, and places is the central task at hand, which is unlikely to be achieved by disarmaments alone. Here political and territorial subjectivity was again central to peace; this peace is not an abstract concept but is constituted by a concrete set of practices carried out by SERPAJ Colombia, including demands of the state, community organizing, and nonviolent communication.

I will conclude this section with a statement from Edward Vergara of Awasqa which synthesizes much of the sentiments that speak about peace as and through interpersonal transformation: "Peace is changes. Peace is transformation. For what? For satisfaction, love, well-being, life. For our maturation and fulfillment as individuals, as subjects, and as communities" (personal interview 2013). When we speak about peace as dignity, this is what is at stake: collective and personal transformation and love.

AUTONOMY AND RESISTANCE NETWORKS

Among the most comprehensive reflections on peace I encountered was composed in a workshop by the Movimiento de Víctimas de Crímenes de

Estado (MOVICE, Movements of Victims of State Crimes) in Bogotá. This workshop was organized and facilitated by anthropologist Diana Gómez Correal, who invited me to participate.[1]

The workshop began with participants seated together as a group offering ideas about what peace meant to them. Embedded within a critique of modern peace as security and of the discourse of Colombia's "post-conflict" present, one person opined, "They say that we live in peace. But if there's hunger, I can't live in peace." To the contrary, peace requires (to list a variety of people's responses): "Tranquility and the ability to work. The means to subsist. . . . An egalitarian government, where everyone shares the same fundamental rights and equality. . . . Territory. Without impunity or persecution. . . . We should live as if we are family, in community. . . . But the paramilitary groups are not welcome for me" (field notes 2013). Then Diana invited the participants to form small groups and create an artistic representation of their vision of peace. One of the groups drafted a statement that listed a multitude of conditions necessary for peace: "A country without hunger, with free education, dignified housing, social justice . . . [and] without discrimination. We contribute to peace in Colombia by working together in a united way, sharing ideas, in order to arrive at mutual agreements. We are in solidarity with all those who suffer attacks from the armed groups. We must participate in all the protest marches to demand what belongs to us." This statement accompanied their artistic piece, which depicted a circle of people comprised of campesinos, indigenous people, and Afro-Colombians. Imprinted on the work of art was the phrase "With Unity: Peace," in addition to "Pueblo [the People], Afros, Indigenous, Campesinos. With solidarity, with participation. With our human rights guaranteed. With equality of rights. With social justice" (field notes 2013).

In one sense these demands parallel common discourses about the importance of basic rights and services. However, in addition to the typical conditions mentioned by government officials—education, shelter, and employment—MOVICE's members also affirmed the importance of equality among Colombians, where equal rights "do not remain in theory," to use Peace Community leader Jesús Emilio Tuberquia's phrase (Moncada Hurtado, Ossa, and Caro Morales 2011a). They must be guaranteed and fulfilled. MOVICE's workshop participants also affirmed territory for campesinos to be able to provide for their own subsistence. By mentioning "impunity" and "persecution," they signaled the state's direct and institutional role in preventing what would be peace for them. Their art piece challenged the country's racist emotional habitus of hate by illustrating solidarity among racialized and subaltern groups. However, it was not a naive view of the national community, insisting that such a peace did not welcome the paramilitary groups who continued to operate across the country and assassinate social leaders (Programa Somos Defensores 2014). This parallels Ricardo Esquivia's idea of "reconciliation," which requires not only a guerrilla demobilization but also the dismantling of paramilitarism.

These are concrete ideas, proposals, and actions that combine demands on the state with a program of struggle by popular organizations. MOVICE's statement also went beyond Tierra y Vida's concept: peace is not achieved by "making life *more* equal" (Palencia 2012, emphasis mine), but where everyone *is* equal in fact. Rather than a vague appeal to national unity commonly found in state officials' pronouncements, this perspective affirms peace through unity and solidarity among social movements.

Edward Vergara of Awasqa also expressed this sense of a shared vision and project among popular movements: "Peace is used as a pretext by the state to advance its political and economic agenda. Peace for the rich is war for the poor. Peace for Santos means no protest against the government, and the continuation of the development model spearheaded by multinational corporations. But what the people want is sovereignty" (field notes 2013). This analysis refocuses attention on the elephant in the room: the link between the state-driven peace process and the extractivist political economy. President Santos himself was open about this connection. In his attempts to gain international and national support for the peace talks, he insisted that the development model was not under negotiation during the peace process, while also arguing that an accord with the FARC would allow for more multinational investment in agribusiness and mining (*El Espectador* 2014a; *El Tiempo* 2014b; *El País* 2015; Ortiz Gómez 2015).

Edward Vergara argued that the guerrillas laying down arms would not mean peace for most of the population unless social inequalities and the economic model of extractivism were rejected in favor of communities' and the Colombian people's self-determination. This declaration potentially overstated the shared demands of "the people," which in fact reflected different priorities, given the varied nature of people's definitions of peace. Nevertheless, this analysis importantly reiterated how "peace" is used as a discourse to advance particular goals (McConnell 2014). It signals the ways that actors define concepts according to their perspectives and interests (Fernandes 2009) and how the struggle for peace reflects conflicts over space, territory, and state–social movement relationships.

Indeed, some of my interlocutors were fiercely critical of the formal peace process. The following quote from a San José de Apartadó Peace Community member expressed a widely held sentiment within the Community: "The peace that the government talks about is the guerrillas not attacking the public armed forces. . . . However, the public forces can still attack the guerrillas if they see them. . . . But surely . . . there will be deaths. In the civilian population. . . . The peace that [Santos] speaks about is just that: where nobody denounces anything . . . where there aren't attacks against the public forces, but the state forces can still attack civilians. In reality, that is just trickery" (personal interview 2014). This individual thus affirmed that even if the guerrillas fully disarmed and the state lost its justification of "counterinsurgency" to attack supposed "guerrilla sympathizers," the project of the state is not limited to an antiguerrilla offensive. It is a project ultimately against civilian protest—and racialized peoples—whether dissidents organize into armed insurgencies or whether they struggle through nonviolent methods. Returning to a quote cited in the Introduction, a Peace Community leader stated during a Campesino University workshop on the state–FARC peace process that "people believe that in Colombia we are moving toward peace. But it is really to a peace of cemeteries" (field notes 2013). From the Peace Community's perspective, the Colombian government's peace is equivalent to a modern-colonial peace constituted by the victory of one armed group over another (Dalby 2014; Foucault 2003) and the violent repression of dissent against injustice (Ross 2011).

Many other rural Colombian communities resisting extractivist violence and forced displacement concurred. For example, a member of the Consejo Comunitario Mayor de la Asociación Campesina Integral del Atrato (COCOMACIA, Community Council of the Integral Campesino Association of the Atrato River), an Afro-Colombian community in Chocó, inferred that peace for her had to do with living according to their traditions: "We want . . . in Colombia and the department of Chocó that [all the violence] is ended. That the armed actors disappear. There was peace and tranquility before. We lived without electricity, in peace, without violence. We want to live like we did before. If God helps us, we will be able to return to that peace" (field notes 2014). Here peace is imagined as a harmonious "negative peace" condition that existed in the past and hopefully can be experienced again in the future. This peace does not require acquiring modern services like electricity but is instead about a return to past conditions and practices.

Peace for such communities was integrally connected to questions of territory. Correlating with an "energetic" peace, Father Albeiro Parra from the Catholic Pastoral Social (Pastoral Care Ministry) in Quibdó explained this eloquently to an international delegation visiting Chocó:

> For both indigenous and black communities, "There is no life without territory." For the indigenous, territory is *everything*. It is not a piece of land but rather a concept including everything: water, air, fauna, flora, themselves. They don't divide. Mother Earth, Pacha Mama, from which everything comes. Their uses and customs include rituals, spirits, and sacred land. When armed groups operate or there is mining, that is a violation. For Afro-Colombians, there is also

no life without territory. But due to the history of slavery and interactions with slave masters and the outside world, they don't have the same rituals, beliefs in spirits, or sacred places. Yes, it is true that many leaders of these groups have been co-opted or bought off. But the majority of the communities maintain that another world is possible and are building other networks, such as the Chocó Interethnic Solidarity Forum. (field notes 2014)

I will return to the divergent territorialities expressed here in Chapter 6. Suffice to say for now, there is a stark territorial contrast between such notions of ecological peace and the "modern peace" expressed by state officials.

Francia Márquez Mina of Proceso de Comunidades Negras (PCN, Black Communities Process) in Cauca placed this debate at the center of her definition of peace (Dest 2020). PCN is a network of Afro-Colombian organizations that emerged in the 1990s to defend black communities' rights to territory and culture. In a presentation at an international conference, Márquez Mina (2015) insisted that it was impossible to talk about peace when indigenous and black Colombians' livelihoods were threatened by large-scale mining projects as well as state, paramilitary, and guerrilla violence. She also reaffirmed indigenous and Afro-Colombian associations with collective land titles' constitutional right to prior consultation regarding any matter affecting an ethnic group's heritage and culture, such as mining or hydroelectric development projects. She defined peace in terms of autonomy: "That indigenous and Afro communities can live according to their traditional practices in their territories," immediately adding, "The question is if the development model is capable of [allowing] this. I do *not* believe so. We have seen in many press releases, by even the president himself saying that the prior consultation process is an obstacle to development. When prior consultation for us is what permits us to guarantee that we as people can continue to *be*, that we can continue to be here."

Proclaiming that the struggle over peace was a struggle over being and life itself—the existence of black communities—is to enunciate an ontological struggle (Escobar 2008; Gómez Correal, forthcoming). Rather than speaking from a perspective of civil society and how to strengthen or "rebuild" Colombian society, this comes from an excluded and racialized position of "non-being" (Fanon 2008), in which life itself is anything but guaranteed. Such denouncements call into question the "peacefulness" of an extractivist economy, even if used to fund social programs and the implementation of the Havana Accord. Such divergent peace imaginaries thus reflect not merely a conflict to be resolved within civil society or between the government and the guerrillas, but a modern-colonial antagonism among divergent territorialities related to state-driven disarmament, an extractivist political economy, and racialized communities' autonomy.

Most Colombians recognized the distinction between their ideas of peace and the negotiated "peace" of the government and the FARC. The latter signified the disarmament of one armed group, which would not end the fire of war unless the air and heat that fueled it were extinguished: inequality, unemployment, food insecurity, the dehumanization of black and indigenous peoples, and forced displacement. Peace is a strategic discourse precisely because of its universal appeal. Few are "against peace," with even the most brutal warlords often justifying their actions as pursuing "peace." We have to deconstruct peace discourses and practices, because behind even undefined or vague notions of peace are concrete political projects, as in the Santos administration's extractivist development model. Utopic rhetoric is easily manipulated to serve and maintain particular interests and power relations, which ultimately reproduces peace's conventional significance as simply the demobilization of one group and the victory of another.

Relative to peace discourses focused on ending the armed conflict or ensuring the fulfillment of state-guaranteed rights, the peace imaginary of autonomy receives scant attention in Colombia's mainstream media analysis. Disregarding rural resistance communities' alternative notions reflects and reinforces the racialized dehumanization of these groups since the colonization and modernization of Latin America. It appears that their proposals and knowledges remain ignored precisely because of the legacies of their constitution as "nonsubjects" within the modern-colonial world (Fanon 2004; Quijano 2000; Wilderson 2010). State and corporate mining and agribusiness projects are mutually exclusive with rural resistance communities' survival and subsistence (Dávalos 2011; Torres et al. 2015). Today's extractivism poses not merely a *conflict* resolvable through dialogue; it is an *antagonistic* contradiction if civil society's peace through basic rights and services is funded by extractivism, which comes at the expense of indigenous and African-descendant campesinos' lives and ways of life. While communities in resistance surely insist on representation within state institutions and utilize the international framework of human rights as strategies of survival (such as the Inter-American Human Rights system), to argue that peace is the *self-determination* to be able to live according to your traditions challenges the idea that *inclusion* or *assimilation* into liberal civil society is the ultimate answer for these groups (Coulthard 2014; Dest 2020). The struggle for peace in Colombia is not merely a geographical conflict between subsistence and extractive economies, but over the relationships to space, politics, and life that those entail.

Many groups in Colombia today—including various leftist, victims, and human rights organizations—demand "peace with justice and dignity." Yet similar to the idea of "negative peace," the phrase "peace *with* dignity" implies that there is also a form of peace without dignity. Conversely, human rights defenders who insist on interpersonal *and* social transformations, which are rooted in community struggles for autonomy and against extractivism, lead me to argue that "peace" *is* ecological dignity rooted in collective work, self-determination, and relational territorialities of solidarity. Of course, as Edward Vergara of Awasqa put it, "It's one thing to talk about peace, another to think about it, and another very different thing to have the vocation of peace" (personal interview 2013). To articulate what constitutes radical trans-relational peace, I now turn to a comprehensive exploration of the ideas of San José de Apartadó's campesinos, who in fact *define* themselves in terms of peace.

CHAPTER 5

THE POWER OF NOT PARTICIPATING IN WAR

Radical Trans-relational Peace

Today [a Peace Community leader] asked accompaniers from Palomas de Paz and me to accompany him to a Community farm above San Josecito, where a military troop had been camped. We were joined by his work group partner and a donkey, on which they were planning to load bananas.

To walk to the farm, we entered a trail from the road toward Apartadó, where three soldiers were on watch. After climbing up the hillside, we came across an army troop of at least seven soldiers. When the commander approached us, the Peace Community leader began to speak [to the troop commander]:

> [Community leader:] I come to ask that you retreat from here, since this is private property of the Peace Community, in which no armed actor is permitted. We demand respect. . . .
>
> Commander: Well, we are here by an order. It would be better that you speak with them at the [17th] Brigade [headquarters]. I will pass on this information to my major. . . .
>
> Community leader: But you all know very well that if you do not enter with a judicial order, you cannot be here on private property. Maybe you will leave an explosive here, like years ago, when a youth picked up a grenade and was injured.

As the conversation progressed, the Community leader and army commander frequently interrupted each other and spoke at the same time.

> Commander: But we do not leave behind explosives. And look, we are here precisely to protect the life and security of the civilian population . . .
>
> Community leader: We do not need the protection of any armed actor. You are here and then the guerrilla attacks. Look, you are the ones who are fighting, so do it elsewhere, not in the spaces of the civilian population of the Peace Community. You, together with the paramilitaries and the guer-

rillas, are the ones who have killed us. We number more than two hundred dead since 1997.

Commander: But you can't say that it is the same now as it was before. We are here in this position [above San José and San Josecito] precisely to protect the Peace Community, where there has been much suffering. We are responding to so much violence here. We have not seen any paramilitaries. We don't work with any illegal armed actor. Look, you can walk for two hours and not see an armed actor . . .

Community leader: Of course, because you all have everything coordinated. There are paramilitaries all over. . . . We are going to return later to see if you have left. How quickly can you communicate this to your supervisors?

Commander: We do an organizational plan at certain times, every four hours. . . . I will communicate it. . . . Look, we would prefer to be in Apartadó, but it is an order for us to be here. We are not complicit with the paramilitaries . . .

Community leader: It seems clear that it is the campesino who has clarity, not the people with guns in their hands.

And we left. We saw another three soldiers about a minute away in another camp. We hiked up further, where the Community members gathered some green bananas, which would serve as food for pigs back in San Josecito. (field notes 2013)

During my time in San José de Apartadó since 2008, I have witnessed such interactions on many occasions. When the military enters Peace Community spaces, Community members confront them. The interaction typically proceeds as follows: Community members remind the soldiers of the Peace Community's principles and insist that the soldiers leave, since their presence puts the Community at risk from immediate attack or subsequent retaliation from rival groups. Community members and international accompaniers frequently refer to Inter-American Court of Human Rights and Colombian Constitutional Court rulings that legitimize the Peace Community's position. The soldiers frequently challenge these demands and resist moving elsewhere. They assert their right, duty, and order to be there for the protection of the civilian population and, specifically, the Peace Community. They frequently argue that those guilty of killings are merely "a few bad apples," or that the military of today is not the brutal force that it was in the past. Eventually, the soldiers usually leave, after rounds of Community members' insistence or after international accompaniers begin to call the soldiers' supervising officers at the brigade headquarters. Peace Commu-

5.1. Overlooking San Josecito and the Apartadó River. Author photo.

nity members repeatedly say that these encounters proceed very differently when no international accompaniers are present: rather than affirmations that the soldiers are there to protect the community, campesinos say that soldiers usually threaten and accuse community members of being guerrillas. Negotiation of armed groups' presence and encroachment in these everyday interactions is a constant Peace Community task. This exemplifies the insistence that "the assassins should be the ones to leave, not us," as a Peace Community leader articulated during a public workshop (field notes 2010).

In the dialogue above notice how the army commander used the term "armed actor," saying "You can walk for two hours and not see an armed actor." He did not qualify the army's presence as an armed actor, inferring that the army and police are legitimate defenders of law, security, and life. In Colombian public discourse armed groups are typically qualified as either illegal or legal, in which paramilitary and guerrilla forces are rendered "illegal," whereas the public forces are "legal" and therefore legitimized.

The Peace Community calls this framing into question. Its principles demand that *all* armed groups respect their lives and land by not entering. For these campesinos the question is not whether a group is "legal" or "illegal." And Peace Community members understand that their denunciations of state violations are one of the reasons why they have been so fiercely attacked. To repeat a quote from Chapter 3, the war against them occurs "because the Community denounces what they do" (personal interview

2013); they are a target precisely because they are seen as a "threat" but also "threatening to" (Goldberg 2009) the state for denouncing the latter's supposed authority to legitimately wage war against its subjects (Finn 2013). According to the leader cited in the vignette above, campesinos are the ones who have "clarity [rather than] the people with guns," which refers to an ability to both understand the war and to make conscious and ethical decisions.

Beyond being armed or unarmed, the interaction above signals a political distinction between the farmers and the soldiers. The soldiers' position is indicative of modern-liberal peace through militarized security. The Peace Community leader personifies one of the two main ways Community members define peace: refusing to participate in the war. The principle of non-collaboration is not a passive act but instead involves constant confrontations with the armed groups, which is indeed a radical act of rupture not only with the armed groups themselves, but of resistance to modern-colonial state authority. The same can be said for the second way Community members tend to understand peace: as building community through solidarity work, which involves forging relational ties both within the Community and with allies.

This chapter surveys how Peace Community members conceptualize peace. Their concepts inspire my notion of radical trans-relational peace. This concept refers to radical ruptures with the logics of modernity-coloniality through solidarities and dignified relations within and across communities. These verbal articulations are obviously mutually embedded within their quotidian practice, which will be described and analyzed in more detail in Part III. This chapter focuses on the various ways that members explain what peace means to them.

DENOUNCING WAR, AFFIRMING SURVIVAL

There is a contingent of members whose thoughts on peace reflect its modern or "negative" conception. Similar to the critique of the concept and discourse of peace we heard from the Red Juvenil activist in Chapter 4, one Peace Community member argued against peace: "Peace is that there aren't armed groups. For the Peace Community, peace would be . . . a respect of life and land. But *I don't believe in peace*. [Despite a peace accord] *the state* will remain, who *is also an armed actor*, with its business, narcotrafficking" (personal interview 2014, emphasis mine). In other words, peace requires not only the demobilization of the guerrillas and the paramilitaries, but also of the state itself. This parallels Blas García's of SERPAJ prescription in Chapter 4 that peace requires a mass process of demilitarization. Peace is conditioned on true respect for the land and campesinos' way of life. Yet for this member, if modern peace is constituted by a supposed lack of war that

5.2. Maize. Author photo.

is guaranteed by a state, then no peace is possible within that sociopolitical system, because the state is an armed force structured to violate campesino autonomy.

Surely "the state" is not a monolithic entity (Brown 1995), but the Peace Community's narrative is not limited to particular government officials but the system—of modernity-coloniality—that the Colombian state represents and reproduces. Accordingly, Community leader Jesús Emilio Tuberquia (2011) denounced transnational corporations along with today's commodity chains central to this structure: "The consumption of Chiquita bananas, Coca Cola, and oil leaves rivers of blood in Colombia and so many other areas around the world, all in the name of development. This is not a question of changing presidents. We can change President Barack Obama or change President Juan Manuel Santos, but the problem is that everyone has become implicated in this system." Following this logic, the problem is capitalism itself, whose production and consumption processes are inherently violent. This reflects a global geographical imaginary that situates local conditions of war and peace in relation to the neoliberal political economy across the globe. Within this structure, changes in elected state representatives are insufficient without transforming the system itself.

Another voice skeptical of the possibility of peace in this world came from a deeply religious Christian member: "The peace of humanity is different from the peace of God. . . . Peace is what Jesus Christ gives at the end [in the afterlife]. There is only a passing peace here [in this world]. The Peace Community is a peace, but it's not a true one. It's momentary. . . . We are here alive. We are not [participating] in the war. . . . We don't go with the state, with armed people. . . . Peace is that there is food" (personal interview 2014). This view overlaps with Wolfgang Dietrich's (2012) "moral peace" in the afterlife through suffering and salvation in this life. For this campesino the only possible peace is through the divine or through forms of resistance that assure food security. Another member's conception concurred that peace as tranquility or a lack of war is only a temporary condition for them, although resistance is what creates spaces for such a "negative peace": "Peace is tranquility, but [we only experience it in certain] moments. The Community constructs a peace. Thanks to the Community, we have a level of tranquility" (personal interview 2013).

Referencing their organization's work was a common theme among Community members. Many defined peace explicitly in relation to their life and work as campesinos, where peace is a lack of war in which they are able to be who they are. For instance, one said, "What the campesino wants is that they are allowed to work their land. That campesinos can move around without worry, go to market, and sell what they have . . . and return to their home. This is not peace here. Peace would be living without all of this, living in tranquility" (personal interview 2013). Community elder Don Libardo Guzmán explained: "Peace is not running across any armed group, neither the army nor guerrilla. . . . Peace is that no armed actor enters here. That there are only families. And that we work. Being healthy we go to work to sow food: corn, beans, yucca, everything" (personal interview 2013). In Community narratives, even peace defined through the lens of tranquility is almost always immediately joined with assertions that this serenity is constituted by the active agricultural work of the collective. International accompanier Luke Finn articulated this dynamic:

> I think peace for them—obviously I'm not speaking for them—is more than just not fighting. Because they could go to Bogotá, where there isn't a war going on at the moment. They could go to Medellín. But it's not about that. It's about how they live together and their relationship with the land. I mean, to define campesino, it's about a relationship with the land. It's more than just "engaged in agriculture." It's about how your life and work cycle are engaged with the natural elements. . . . They are campesinos. And the peace they produce, a campesino peace, is why they aren't in Medellín or Bogotá. Because the peace they want is specific to their lifestyle and their social construct. (personal interview 2013)

5.3. Cacao. Author photo.

The Community's peace is not to merely live anywhere. It is to re-create a dignified campesino way of life. It is important to remember that the war also permeates cities, even if the dynamics of Colombia's armed conflict differ between rural and urban contexts. In the urban peripheries police and army forces conduct *batidas* (street roundups of young men to force them to settle their military service status) (Gil 2013); meanwhile paramilitary, guerrilla, and police forces compete, often brutally so, for socioeconomic control and legitimacy (Riaño-Alcalá 2002). To insist on a campesino peace is therefore a recognition that there are not "safe zones" awaiting them in cities, while also reaffirming their identity and life world.

Another Peace Community member, the elder known as Doña Diosa, repeated the idea of peace as a lack of war to allow campesinos to maintain their way of life. Yet she proceeded to insist on the importance of *internal* dynamics within the Community as well. For her peace meant "that there isn't anything here," referring to combat and violence. Doña Diosa continued, "That we do not do any harm against others. . . . That there are no weapons. [The members of the Community] are working hard. Men and women resisting . . . so that there is peace. Without peace, we will not live. So, God proposes that we live joyfully and help one another" (personal interview 2014). Again a connection is made between peace and the divine. As for PCN's Francia Márquez, who was quoted in Chapter 4, there is a correlation here between peace and life, where peace is predicated on survival. Peace Community member Montoya made a similar assertion: Peace is "that there isn't violence. That the poor person can work with tranquility, and maybe even receives assistance. . . . [It is] a respect of life. That we can all live" (personal interview 2013).

To insist that peace is life reflects the racialized positionality from which the Peace Community acts and thinks. They speak from an oppressed position in which their lives are constantly threatened. This implicitly infers a case in which the "coloniality of being" dehumanizes them (Maldonado-Torres 2010), thus making them disposable when the needs of capitalism and state power dictate. Indeed, in the political economy of Colombia's "war system," peace is more risky than war for the capitalist classes because of war's profitability (Richani 2002). This exhibits the "coloniality of power" (Quijano 2010), in which life and dignity are disregarded in favor of accumulation and sovereign power. Referring to the Zapatista struggle, among other examples of resistance by ethnic communities across the Americas, Mariana Mora (2017) speaks about the radical nature of merely living amid such contexts: "For indigenous Zapatista community members, as for many Afrodescendent and indigenous organized peoples throughout the continent, the very act of living as part of a dignified commitment to the reproduction of social life directly confronts the dehumanizing conditions of racialized colonial states of being" (23). Similar to black and indigenous communities, Peace Community members' framing of peace as life thus defines the concept in opposition to the modern-colonial war against them. Since such peace would require ending what appears to be a systemic war by the state, the members quoted above discounted any utopian hope of ending that war.

To summarize the statements of this group of Community members, peace would be constituted by respect for campesino life. However, within the current conjuncture such peace is impossible beyond limited moments. This can be partially explained by the Christian perspective from which many of these members speak, where life on earth is associated with struggle and there is only peace through God in the next life, à la Dietrich's (2012) "great moral peaces." I argue that this is also an indictment of the modern-colonial world and its concepts of peace, which include a seemingly never-obtainable "negative peace" but also a hollow "positive peace" rooted in a liberal "civil society" that excludes racialized people, such as these indigenous-descendant campesinos. Unlike indigenous and black communities opposing modernity-coloniality across the Americas (Coulthard 2014; de la Cadena 2015; Escobar 2008, 2018; Lame 2004; Mora 2017; Walsh 2010), the fact that the Peace Community does not profess an ethnic identity or name colonialism in their critiques might make the colonial relation here more difficult to see. But these statements implicitly reflect an affirmation about the coloniality of being at play here. It is as if to say, "There is no peace in this system for us!"

CREATING COMMUNITY

Nevertheless, the Community is not limited to critiquing modern peace. For many members peace is a much more comprehensive and communal process. The framings in the previous section reflect the diversity of ideas of those within this collective who, despite their lack of hope for "peace," nonetheless commit to work together in a peace community. But most members' framings diverged from these dismissive perspectives. Rather than rejecting the concept of peace, the majority strategically reinvented it, expanding how they define and perform peace beyond dominant moral and modern interpretations.

Most commonly, when asked about peace, Community members would respond by listing or inferring their organization's principles and rules. For instance, one member insisted, "Peace is the power of not being an armed group in the war. Not collaborating with any of the armed groups. It is the power to decide to not participate" (personal interview 2013). Here peace is described through the lens of power. Peace is constituted by nonparticipation in the war, but this is a refusal through which there is an active power of self-determination, which is the only means to an alternative within the modern-colonial power relations of domination and dependency. It is a peace that is not constituted by dominating or having hegemonic control over others, but instead a power of emancipation (Gutiérrez 2012) that frees oneself and one's community from subjugation. This radical trans-relational peace, as I conceptualize it, is thus rooted in a critique of state violence, capitalism, and hegemonic peace. But it most importantly affirms social movement power to rupture with the coloniality of power and freedom from subordination.

Other members described how such a peace is constituted not merely by the lack of violence or *refusal* to participate in the war but rather through the *construction* of internal unity and solidarity. Doña Fidelina Sepúlveda immediately referenced both: "To neither be with one side [of the armed conflict] nor with the other. That is one part. Now, another thing is to work in a group" (personal interview 2013). This second component specifically references their rule to be in an agricultural work group and alludes to the weekly community workday. For example, one member defined peace as "working together with a tight unity. And mutual respect. It's respect, love!" (field notes 2014). Another asserted, "Peace is that we are united. Because we are all children of God. White or black, we are all God's children. Because united we can work" (personal interview 2014). The latter, while the only member to allude to race in my interviews, enunciated the Peace

Community's core principles of plurality and antiracism (Comunidad de Paz de San José de Apartadó 2005b: 13). This solidarity, respect, and unity are what make collective work—and an alternative political process of anticolonial rupture—possible. By emphasizing communal work rather than mere cohabitation, this exhibits political solidarity rooted in shared goals and labor (hooks 1984; Scholz 2008).

A member defined peace as collective work, as he described his subjective transformation since joining the Community: "Before entering the Peace Community, my life was different, a different *world*! It was following that capitalist ideology. In the time I have been here, I have learned . . . to value what we have, like our lands. The right to life. . . . [Peace is] everyone together! When there is work to do, everyone goes! And always! Peace is not something you talk about. Rather, you *live it*" (personal interview 2014). In other words, San Jose's peace praxis overcomes individualism through collectivity.

For a sense of this community work, I will quote FORPP international accompanier Luke Finn at length. He described the first time he accompanied the comunitario, or weekly workday:

> My first accompaniment was for a comunitario two days after I arrived. They were working on improving the path from San José to La Unión. And, it was about forty people, kids, women, a comunitario where everyone was on the same team. And I went down there super early. I was there around 7 a.m., and already, [four men] were there. On what was just a patch of mud. And by the end of the day, they had built . . . the actual work involved first moving all the big rocks out of the way of the path where it was going to be, [toward] the river . . . [then] going to the river collecting small rocks, laying the big rocks down, laying the small rocks down, going to the river, collecting silt, like alluvial sand, and then covering the small rocks, and then lining the camino [path] with larger rocks. And I think most of this was done for the benefit of horses! That is a public good: the community came together, and there were children, old people, and there was one kid whose specific job was to chase wasps away! He had a palo [stick], and [one man] poured gasoline on top and the kid was chasing wasps away. . . . And that was his specific job. That was right after I first got here. It made an impression. It was really cool. Not only the Community uses that road, frickin' guerrillas use that road, the military uses that road. But it was a public good, and it benefited everyone. And it took a lot of work, from everyone in the community. If you added up all the work hours, there were like forty people, about twelve hours' worth of work. And that was just that day. The next week they did it for other parts. (personal interview 2013)

Peace is thus defined here not as some sort of tranquility or rest from work but *as* the work in community. The comunitario built from prior

5.4. Antagonistic peaces: The comunitario versus enforced "security." Doña Brígida González's painting depicts a Community workday of wood harvesting as well as army and police forces throughout the town despite signs reading "Unauthorized Entry Prohibited." Author photo, with artist's permission.

forms of collective work, such as the convite, in which groups of campesino families would join together to clear land or harvest crops. However, Peace Community members repeatedly affirmed to me that the comunitario was not simply a new form of the convite, because the former was predicated upon community-wide solidarity rather than simply collaboration between families. Catherine LeGrand (1986) describes the individualist and competitive nature of many convite-like systems: "They were . . . indicative of a strongly individualistic, competitive streak within colono [settler] society. To an undeterminable degree, such endemic frictions probably reduced the settlers' capacity to organize in their own defense when their claims to the land were challenged by outsiders in later years" (28). Epitomized by its collective workday, the Peace Community is an explicit attempt to resist and rupture with such capitalistic competition and individualism in order to nurture alternative logics.

One Community member, when asked what peace meant to him, immediately shifted to the terminology of resistance: "Resistance is good, because the Peace Community defends . . . and makes a very different world, without hunger, without deaths. Not like those [armed] people, a capitalist power" (personal interview 2013). Peace for the Peace Community is therefore explicitly about creating an *alternative world* different from capitalism. This is not to say that San José de Apartadó has severed its ties to the modern-colonial system altogether, as their international sale of organic cacao attests. However, Community leaders explain that their participation in fair trade markets is primarily for political reasons rather than economic ones tied to accumulating capital. For instance, San José sells cacao to the multinational corporation Lush for use in its cosmetic products, whose labels provide information about the Peace Community. In its stores Lush encourages customers to sign petitions to the Colombian government in favor of upholding human rights (Burnyeat 2018; Lush n.d.). Rather than an isolationist movement away from markets and a global system altogether, the Peace Community nonetheless seeks a decolonial peace that subverts capitalist logics. Such a power to resist displacement as well as refusing to participate in and escalate the war is dependent on and constructed through radical peace practices driven by unified organization and strategic alliances, which break with reactionary violence and oppressions in the modern-colonial world tied to individualism and state hegemony.

It is clear that peace for the Peace Community is not constituted by accords between armed actors. Peace is an everyday practice of collective work, driven by anticapitalist values. It requires creating a political and economic campesino alternative of autonomy to overcome dependency on the armed groups, the state, and capitalist enterprise for well-being. In the Peace Community's official declaration, core principles include justice (sanctions against victimizers), resistance (the right to work against hunger, death, and injustice), solidarity (collective work for the good of all), and liberty (communities' right to autonomy and for individuals to participate voluntarily—and not by obligation, as in the armed groups—in a given organization) (Comunidad de Paz de San José de Apartadó 2005b: 13–14). Such values are reiterated in the Peace Community's hymn, which they sing during gatherings. Written by leader Aníbal Jiménez, who was later assassinated, its lyrics speak of moving forward as campesinos; helping one another with care and love; honoring the dead; and following God's teachings to achieve civility, reconciliation, freedom, and peace.[1]

To refer back to Doña Fidelina's quote that opened Part II, it is not only about "acting" but also about "being." Note how in the following definition Community member and Doña Fidelina's son Bernardo inferred two community pillars—nonparticipation in the war and communal work—but also strived for a continual process of being a person of peace: "Peace for me means . . . not living in the war, not being part of the war, not supporting the state, but rather living in community. Peace comes from . . . dialogue. . . . Truly, I want to be a man of peace. . . . I do not like weapons. [All I want is] the tools in order to work" (personal interview 2013). While some Community members reflect a "strategic nonviolence" that deems nonviolent resistance prudent for them without necessarily condemning armed struggle everywhere, Bernardo's vision is another example of the Community's strong contingent of people who reject the use of weapons in one's life and organization on principle. His statement also reflects the creation and cultivation of a particular political process through everyday practice.

Deceased leader Eduar Lanchero was famous for articulating this idea. Father Javier Giraldo (personal interview 2013) recalled Eduar's 2010 speech during an intercommunity gathering in Sumapaz, where Lanchero argued, "Peace is not something of tomorrow but of today. There is peace because there is community." As another leader put it, "Peace is being in solidarity with one another.... It is making community.... What Eduar would say, we can make peace ourselves. We don't have to wait for the armed groups or a peace that comes from Havana" (field notes 2014).

This idea, that community itself can constitute peace amid overt warfare, is a contested one. I return to an exchange that I referenced to open the Introduction, which occurred during a Campesino University workshop on land defense strategies in 2013:

> A Peace Community leader stated that their strategy was "to keep working in our own community and with other communities. We are an example of peace, demonstrating that peace is possible."
>
> A former protective accompanier in attendance responded by saying, "But, forgive me. What peace can you really live in with all of these armed actors operating in the surrounding areas?"
>
> The leader responded, "We are not going to wait for the armed actors to come to an agreement. We are going to be an *example* of peace whether they continue to attack us or not. To show that, yes, *peace is possible*. You have a problem if you wait for it from them. Day-to-day, *we don't need the armed actors* to come to an agreement." (field notes 2013, emphasis mine)

The Peace Community frequently describes itself as an "example" or "experience" of peace, but not a "model" of peace to be followed like a formula. They commonly clarify that they do not call on others to replicate their neutral peace community strategy elsewhere in the same way. Rather, they hope that the Community serves as inspiration for others to work with them or create their own communities in resistance. The quote reiterates Ricardo Esquivia's assertion in Chapter 4 that "peace does not come from them" (field notes 2014). It calls into question forms of "peace" produced through post-conflict accords and for the needed imagination to *create* and *be* peace immediately in social movement.

Of course the international accompanier quoted above was correct: the war of the state and paramilitaries continues, despite the peace negotiations and the Havana Accord. One Community elder, Doña Jesusa Tuberquia, when talking about peace, recalled the early days of the Peace Community: "Eduar would say, 'You are going to return to La Unión, but it's not that

5.5. Radical trans-relational peace: Peace Community mural of collective work. Author photo.

there are not going to be blows. There will be blows in the surrounding area'" (personal interview 2013). This is thus not a utopian peace imaginary. It recognizes that peace requires struggle, likely provoking retaliatory attack, but that the violence itself does not diminish or eliminate the reality of "peace as community" being possible here and now. Building from the Peace Community's enunciation of its "rupture" with the state (Burnyeat 2018), such everyday actions that refuse to comply with racist and capitalist logics reflect ruptures with coloniality.

As a side note, comments by Community members referencing Eduar Lanchero's ideas exemplify the dialogical performance of knowledge production through the Community process between the farmers and this non-campesino leader, who came to San José in the Peace Community's early days. I would suggest that Eduar came to understand peace as "something of today [when] there is community" (Giraldo, personal interview 2013) through his experience struggling with the Peace Community. For instance, on Lanchero's (2000) learning from and with the Community, he wrote, "This historical process [of resistance] arises and develops in the communities who, from their reality of exclusion and minimal conditions of dignity, seize alternative positions where the present, past, and future of the achievable are conjugated. It does not mean futuristic or utopian positions" (75). "Achieving distinct alternatives is not an unreachable horizon; [the alternative is located] in the communitarian living of those peoples who resist" (74). There is congruency between what he wrote about the notion of dignity through community resistance—as an already-created and lived alternative to the modern-colonial world of exclusion and violence—and how he would conceptualize peace ten years later: as community itself. In Lanchero's writings and interviews, one can feel the process in which this "organic intellectual" (Gramsci 1971) came to theorize resistance, the state, and social transformation through his work in San José. Simultaneously Lanchero's interpretations of the Peace Community's experience rooted in critical theory resonated with and influenced the way its members understood their own struggle, which is illustrated by their frequent citations of his ideas.

I found another revealing example of this dialogical performance of knowledge production about peace in the narrative of a member who joined the Peace Community after Lanchero stopped visiting because of his struggle with cancer. This newer member had family in San José but had only recently come to live there at the time of our interview. I asked him what he had learned by participating in the Peace Community process. He responded, "The armed actors speak about a peace. But they do not live it. I learned how to search for peace and to live it" (personal interview 2014). A central transformation for him as a Peace Community member was his understanding of peace as something to be lived today, reflecting Eduar's contagious perspective of the quotidian life of communal work *as* the alternative and *as* peace.

Peace is therefore not a utopian condition, but a politically embodied and spatial process. In the words of Lanchero himself: "The logic of the system of death, of the paramilitaries, of the state, is to displace the people. They want to terrorize the people because it generates an individualism so strong that then you don't care about the life of the other anymore" (Buenaventura 2011). Therefore another world requires an alternative to the modern-colonial war advanced by the state and capitalist entities that individualizes subjects (Foucault 1982) and undermines resistance (Lanchero 2000, 2002). Eduar continued, "So, we had to create another way of living, where we were really against the war and against death. That's why the only way was to live in a community. If you live in a community you have different ways of relating to each other, of organizing, participation, of solidarity where everyone cares about the life of the other" (Buenaventura 2011).

Living in community does not mean the absence of conflicts. Rather, in the case of the Community, it encourages alternative forms of conflict resolution that take place autonomously from the armed groups. To that end the Peace Community has a conflict resolution committee to intervene when there are internal disputes between members or to address frictions related to a particular member's noncompliance with Community commitments, such as consuming alcohol or neglecting to participate in the weekly comunitario workday. In other words, peace is not constructed individually. Peace need not be limited to the afterlife or to peace within the self. Peace is relational (Michaela Soellinger, personal interview 2013), created through relationships of care (Gómez Correal, forthcoming). This radical transrelational peace of ecological dignity is built through collectivity, solidarity, and organization. What I find so significant is that, even for those members who do not believe in "peace"—the modern peace of state order—they in fact enact this other peace in their communal actions. They counter what for them is a false and violent "peace" with an embodied peace practice.

This articulation of peace with community is not a move toward isolationism. As Gwen Burnyeat (2018) elucidates, in the Colombian context this framing reflects an emancipatory politics intrinsically linked to fellow communities in resistance: "In Colombia the word 'community' is often associated with indigenous and afro-descendent ethnic communities which live together in geographically delimited areas and have collective identities which are connected to 'traditional' forms of living, especially regarding land use. . . . The word 'community,' therefore, is infused with connotations of emancipatory politics in Colombia. This doubtless influenced the Peace Community [in their decision to name themselves as such], especially considering the inspiration they took from indigenous communities' early declarations of neutrality" (234).

San José's community praxis extends to its solidarity alliances. These include the RECORRE network and protective accompaniment organizations such as FOR Peace Presence. Another example of collaboration is San José's partnership with a peace community located in Portugal, the Tamera Peace Research & Education Center. Tamera experiments with alternative energy technologies, agroecology, and interpersonal love.[2] The two organizations have conducted exchanges, where members of each community visit the other, to participate in and collectively design workshops about alternatives to militarism. A Peace Community leader explained how these were spaces of mutual learning with Tamera, but also served to meet other like-minded organizations and activists from Brazil, Mexico, India, and Palestine, among other countries. When I asked whether they would like to or have tried to visit those places, he responded:

> Yes, we have considered this. Going to Mexico, for instance, although we have not been able to do so just yet. We have had Skype conversations with people from Palestine, in which we have told them the history of the Peace Community. They have said that they wish to create a peace community there based on what they learn from us. And we learn from them, especially about other places that are much worse off economically than we are. The situation is very rough

there, worse than in Colombia. . . . Yes, [I would love to visit Palestine], but that is very complicated. [State officers there] would arrest us! (field notes 2018)

This sharing of ideas and experiences—whether in person or over the Internet—is key to the collective knowledge production of communities in resistance. It is a dialogical performance between social movements seeking to rupture with the logics and material conditions of war. Such solidarities inspire my emphasis on intercommunal relationality at the core of radical trans-relational peace.

A COMMUNITY OF PEACE AS RUPTURES

While the understanding of peace as community emphasizes collective work and collaboration in solidarity, it is important to recognize that this is not a purely "inclusive" or "harmonious" process. At odds with neoliberalism's ongoing "accumulation by dispossession" (Harvey 2005) through imposed dependency and extractivism (Bebbington 2009; Márquez Mina 2015; Laing 2012), I interpret it as a practice of rupture with Colombia's armed groups and the narcobourgeoisie, as well as the capitalist system more broadly. Various members' framings of peace included a rejection of extractivism and dependency, while also insisting on autonomy through food sovereignty. One member explained, "Peace for the campesino is that their life is respected. A respect for the land, which we should not exploit with mines. And a respect of freedom. We have sugarcane, so there is no need to buy it from outside. We can extract butter from the pigs and coconuts as well" (personal interview 2014). Another argued, "The state wants to be in control of everything, to maintain people in a relationship of dependency. What we want is to not depend on the state [because] you end up waiting. . . . We are autonomous. We want to have our own crops, food, and our own education. And we have them: alternatives of life. . . . We have a peace among ourselves. . . . If we unite, struggle, plant food, work, and have our daily bread, then there will be peace, even if we are attacked by the state" (personal interview 2014). In other words, peace as community is produced through political autonomy, food sovereignty, autonomous education, internal conviviality, and solidarity. By fusing internal practices with intercommunal networks, it is an attempted withdrawal from one particular "world"—that of modern-colonial-neoliberal war—but not a peace of resigned passivity or parochialism.

The conflicts related to this approach to peace are not limited to confrontations with armed groups and capitalist logics. The Peace Community process has also involved conflicts with some of their fellow campesinos in San José de Apartadó who are not Community members. There are a variety of reasons why some San José residents are not members. Some prefer to work individually, while others do not follow Peace Community commitments to abstain from consuming alcohol or receive assistance from the state, among others. Many nonmembers maintain friendly relations with the Peace Community, but tensions also ensue.

One emblematic example took place in La Unión in July 2008, when the Peace Community carried out what could be deemed a "sit-in" to prohibit nonmember campesinos from holding a meeting in a Community building. This standoff took place in the following context: The Peace Community had recently obtained organic certification of its cacao production, which was part of its strategy to sell to international buyers. This meant an increased price of 6,000 Colombian pesos per pound for organic cacao (approximately US$3 at the time) versus 4,000 pesos for conventional cacao, thus reflecting a dramatic 50 percent increase. The Peace Community continued to manage the Balsamar Cooperative, which they had legally administered since Apartadó mayor Gloria Cuartas had turned the cooperative over to the Community as the only remaining civilian authority in San José in 1997. In 2008 the Community began paying its members the higher price for organically produced cacao beans. They also bought as much organic cacao as they could from other, nonmember campesinos before shipping it to their buyer in Europe. But they did not have the funds to buy all the cacao available. Therefore those nonmembers unable to sell to the Peace Community were frustrated that they could not earn the higher rate. One group of nonmembers living on the outskirts of the Peace Community village in La Unión organized a meeting to discuss, among other topics, how to obtain a similarly high price for their cacao. This group was organized into a Junta de Acción Comunal (JAC, or Communal Action Board), which are organizations at the vereda or village level and are the smallest administrative unit in Colombia. After the extermination of the Patriotic Union party and the mass displacements of San José's farmers from 1996 to 1997, the JACs ceased to exist. After the installation of the police post in San José in April 2005 and increased social investment by the presidential agency Acción Social as of 2007, the state encouraged the reactivation of the JACs as a means through which non–Peace Community campesinos would be linked to the state's humanitarian and development assistance.

When the La Unión JAC organized its meeting in July 2008, they decided to meet in La Unión's school building within the Peace Community settlement. The JAC's coordinator did not ask the Peace Community for permission, however, merely receiving approval from the school's teachers, who were employed by the municipality of Apartadó. When the JAC members arrived and began their meeting in the school, La Unión's Peace Community members gathered together in the village's central gazebo.

One member came to the FOR house and asked us to accompany them, as they had decided to enter the school to block this unauthorized meeting. Once inside, we heard an Internal Council member explaining to the JAC coordinator, "You have not asked for permission to use this space within the Peace Community. The JACs are state-sponsored and the state is complicit with the paramilitaries. Therefore, given our principles, we do not approve of such a state-sponsored meeting to take place in our spaces. If you had asked for permission ahead of time, we could have vacated the village for you to hold the meeting. You are free to bring these requests to us, and we will deliberate in our general assembly. But you did not, so we cannot allow this meeting to continue." Outside the building other members of the JAC apologized to the Peace Community members, saying that they thought permission had been sought. Inside, however, after numerous heated exchanges, the JAC coordinator ultimately raised his voice and asked, "Well, what [good] has the Peace Community done over all these years, anyway?" The Internal Council member reacted: "We have paid with 140 deaths. But we have earned this space!" The other JAC members ultimately cajoled the coordinator to leave it be and exit. It is worth mentioning that many of the JAC and Peace Community members were members of the same families. In fact, the JAC coordinator and the member who petitioned FOR to accompany their sit-in were close relatives. This speaks to the ever-present tensions among families and communities in peace-building contexts. Such challenges are exacerbated by economic marginalization and the pressures of the armed groups who, as Peace Community members frequently assert, serve to divide and rule (field notes 2008).

To summarize, peace according to the Peace Community involves both resisting the modern-colonial war by refusing to participate as an armed actor in the war and creating dignity and a political alternative through communal work both within and beyond the Community. This radical trans-relational peace entails a variety of elements. First, it involves the consolidation of relations of solidarity internally. Second, it requires complex negotiations with neighboring people who do not join the struggle. Third, it is predicated on a rupture of relations with particular external actors, along with their corresponding practices and logics of modern-colonial domination.

This process of peace through autonomy, self-sufficiency, and creating dignified living conditions embodies an active and empowered perspective on peace. It focuses on what the Community can do immediately as an organized collective rather than being dependent on what state and armed groups should do. Rooted in a geographical political analysis that situates attacks against local communities amid global neoliberalism, it is an anticapitalist peace, which rejects being forced into an exploitative labor relation of wages and dependency. Here peace is the demand for and creation of self-determination and self-subsistence. Peace is about life but not "modern-liberal" peace's individualist approach that prioritizes the defense of one's mortality no matter the costs to the lives of others. The Peace Community defends a concept of life that emphasizes the dignity of all living beings, without which there is no peace.

Indeed, the Peace Community is less policy focused than the recent upsurge of Colombian organizations working for land restitution or the implementation of the 2016 peace accord. Rather, it focuses its energy on creating an autonomous alternative to war that integrates local place-based resistance within global solidarity networks. The Peace Community's legal representative, Germán Graciano, was among those who traveled to Havana as part of a victims delegation (*El Universal* 2014), but the organization has never been a leading actor in the national "pro-peace process" movement. Indeed, I have encountered certain Colombian and international scholars and activists who criticized this lack of engagement. While nowhere near as hostile, this is reminiscent of the Mexican Left's opposition to the Zapatistas and thus the latter's rupture with the Mexican political class, including its leftist party, the Partido Revolucionario Democrático (PRD, Democratic Revolutionary Party) (Mora 2017; Reyes 2015). Critiques of San José de Apartadó's supposed "naive parochialism" ignore that the Peace Community's task is not to reform or gain inclusion within liberal statism. Congruent with an alter-geopolitical imaginary from below, its objective is instead to contribute to the creation of an alternative system of collectivity and solidarity, where the social and ecological reproduction of some does not come at the expense of others (Federici 2010). They infer that real peace for all is impossible in the modern-colonial world-system, which is constituted by violent oppression and dehumanization. Resistance is dialectically produced against oppressive power (Foucault 1990), and this rupture is nonetheless predicated on the state itself, whose attacks induced the Peace Community's formation. Following the Community's logic, the first step is assuring a degree of autonomy from that state, which can be the beginning of an alternative peace, such as this case of communal solidarity.

We should not try to pin peace down to *either* an achieved (moral-modern) condition *or* a never-ending or never-to-be achieved "imperfect peace" (Muñoz 2001). It is short-sighted and politically dangerous to affirm either of these exclusively. On the one hand, to argue that peace is *only* constituted once we reach certain utopian conditions is a disempowering and futuristic perspective dependent on other groups; this approach leaves peace to be defined by dominant actors. On the other hand, claiming that peace is always an imperfect or never-achieved process forecloses a political imaginary that insists on building peace now, in which such peace should exceed one whose "imperfection" becomes an end in itself. There are certain ecological conditions more conducive to peace than others, while there *can be* peace through an immediate practice of "being" joined with a grander vision and guide toward a transformation of structural conditions. My ethnographic engagements reveal that for the Peace Community peace is both an immediate condition of self-determination, community, solidarity, and dignity, even as it is always a "processual peace," or an indefinitely renewed experience through social movement. Peace is perfectible, but you have to organize, struggle, and create solidarity.

My conception of a radical trans-relational peace across relations of solidarity and ecological dignity speaks to such a politics. *Being* that peace will not always mean or require the same action or strategy. It will always remain a contextual and political question. In the case of San José de Apartadó, this has meant an organization that, on the one hand, is voluntary. Only those campesinos committed to working communally are part of the Community, while those who prefer to work individually are not forced to join. Meanwhile, certain actors are strategically excluded, such as the state, armed actors, and people who break Community principles and undermine the praxis of peace. When faced with a so-called modern-colonial peace of genocidal order, security, and capitalism (Fanon 2004; Maldonado-Torres 2008), there are limits to what Dietrich (2002) deems "moral peace" as an all-inclusive hospitality and an "energetic" peace that welcomes all human and nonhuman elements. Strategic exclusions are also part of peace. That being said, while the Peace Community necessarily excludes particular actors and logics, its fundamental principles are not exclusion and division, as in the modern-colonial world. The Community's rupture with armed groups is not a dogmatic imposition on or violation of those actors; rather, it reflects a call for such actors to have their own transformations into subjects committed and contributing to dignity for all beings.

The Peace Community's peace is not rooted in a moral-modern Hobbesian fear of mortality, with its corollary violent defense of particular individual lives or "the nation" (Dietrich 2012). Surely, individual Community members fear being killed. Many international accompaniers like myself perceive a community-wide feeling where individuals constantly fear for their lives and for the lives of their fellow family and Community members. Yet this is why radical and reflexive political organization is crucial. As a collective they have committed to not letting fear be the ultimate determining element of their peace process by rejecting all forms of retaliatory violence, instead opting for an experience of unarmed solidarity, even if this costs certain individuals their lives.

From their principle of plurality, the Peace Community is thus not insisting on their practice as a "model" to be followed by others. Instead they frame their struggle as an inspirational experience to be in solidarity and collaboration with other groups. While recognizing the antagonism of resistance to the current world-system's war machine, San José's relational political imaginary and practices suggest hope for a planet in which multiple peaces can be possible. This struggle for communal autonomy and dignity is part of a broader movement for a "pluriverse," a world in which many worlds fit (Ceceña 2004; Escobar 2018; Subcomandante Insurgente Marcos 1997). To quote Ivan Illich (1981), "War tends to make cultures alike, whereas peace is that condition under which each culture flowers in its own incomparable way" (54). Peace Community conceptions reflect such an anticolonial peace. I offer the framework of thinking and enacting a radical and trans-relational politics of peace to enable us to evaluate different peace discourses and projects. The Peace Community demonstrates that peace "otherwise" is possible when people share a commitment to work together, resist war, and create community.

PART III

WHAT IS POLITICS?

April 16, 2014. It is afternoon in the village of La Unión. This is a common time for community members who have finished their work for the day to begin stopping by the FOR Peace Presence accompaniment house to say hello or chat. I am seated at a large table having an impromptu conversation with two men. I have known both of them since my first year living here in 2008. To my left is Community member Montoya, who is a resident of the village and one of my interviewees. Across the table is a man whose home and farm are an hour or so away on foot. I am excited to see him since we only get the chance to catch up every few weeks when he stops by the village. Like many of the campesinos living on the outskirts of the village center, he is no longer a Peace Community member. Sharing smiles and cups of *tinto* [sweet black coffee], we discuss updates about their crop harvests. Then, almost inevitably, the conversation turns to a prevalent theme in La Unión these days: who is a Peace Community member, who is not, and why.

The non-member explains: "I am no longer in the Peace Community. Because there are those people in the work group or in the Community who do their own thing. They fake being sick to get out of work or whatever, and *it's not equal like it should be*" [emphasis mine].

> Peace Community member Montoya [*smiling*]: *Yes*, what we have to do is *continue to motivate one another to work together*!
>
> Non-member: Surely! Without the Peace Community here, there wouldn't be any solution.

I ask what he means by "solution." He clarifies that he refers to the ability for campesinos to continue to live in the area without the armed groups exerting total control. Simultaneously, I remember another non-member, as he passed through the village the night before, saying something similar: "I don't want to work in the group when there is drama or a lack of full commitment. But without the Peace Community, none of us could be here in the surrounding areas. The army and paramilitaries would take over everything."

Montoya: Those who don't work (collectively), it's an issue of consciousness.

Me: But what distinguishes the two? What is the difference between those who stay committed despite the challenges and the others?

Montoya: It is about remembering what we've gone through, what we've suffered. You remember the past so as not to be fooled by what the state and the armed groups are up to. That memory keeps you working in community, as neutral, and autonomous. It's about *a love for the other and working together, a love to live with the other.* It's about remembering what you have lived, and that working alone is dangerous and not communal. It's not about re-creating the Community from scratch but *remembering* what it was like before. We are about to re-initiate our monthly training workshops, which are so useful for me because in them I have learned how to answer an armed actor when confronted by one: answering not being upset but rather explaining to them clearly what the Community is. (field notes 2014)

Building from its members' *definitions* of peace, this part turns to a more direct exploration of how the Peace Community *practices* peace. Imbued with power relations, peace is fundamentally a question of politics. Beyond the realm of state policies and representation, I understand politics as active self-transformation (Mahmood 2005) that challenges and reshapes the status quo, in which people exert their equality (Rancière 2010) to break relations of subjugation toward self-determination and dignified living conditions (Fanon 2004; Gutiérrez 2012; Ceceña 2012). This alter-politics depends on consciousness, commitment, organization, and solidarity.

The passage above exemplifies how constructing this politics of peace through collective work is an ongoing, daily struggle. Maintaining unity and a communal work ethic is a challenge every organization seems to face: people disagree on contextual analysis and what actions should be taken by the group; some individuals or subgroups dislike or mistrust others; and frustrations can abound regarding the extent to which certain people or the collective itself live up to identified goals. The Peace Community faces such conflicts on an ongoing basis.

It continues to strike me how its current members, exemplified by Montoya's statements, continue to affirm the need to maintain their organization by consistently motivating one another to build this communal alternative to the war. This is in sharp contrast to others who respond to internal difficulties by leaving the collective. Explaining what differentiates these two reactions, Montoya argued that it is a question of consciousness and memory. Many members say that "memory is the strength of the resistance" because it continually focuses one's commitment and analysis "not to be fooled by what the state and the armed groups are up to." Remembrance induces reflection about the necessity of "a love for one another and working together" because "working alone is dangerous and not communal," Montoya added. This memory and organization have to be continually produced through active remembrance as well as strategic workshops on how to act amid the war.

Montoya inferred that nonmembers lack "consciousness," which is a common assertion among members. However, I recall how in separate conversations with me, two leaders challenged this view. Berta Tuberquia Quintero and Jesús Emilio Tuberquia both argued that participating in the Community process is not a question of consciousness but of commitment itself. They said that all of San José's campesinos are conscious of their situation and the consequences of collectively organizing or not. As both members and nonmembers alike affirm, no campesinos could survive the narcobourgeoisie land grab in San José de Apartadó without an organization that defends their existence and way of life. Therefore it is less about an understanding of the situation and more about the decision and practice of commitment to building this organization, which is the basis for an always-ongoing peace of relational dignity and solidarity. Both surviving the war and creating an alternative to war require a strategic politics, rooted in the cultivation of collectivity and organization.

Another notable element of the conversation rendered above, although mostly lost in the transcription, was the complete lack of hostility or animosity between these two individuals. It was amazing the extent to which they explained their positions with smiles and acknowledgments of the other's ideas. This is not to deny that tensions exist among members as well as between the Community and some nonmember campesinos. But this conversation in particular exemplifies how the Peace Community is predicated on a respect for individuals' and families' decisions to voluntarily participate or not. Members, nonmembers, and the Community's official declaration of their organizational principles frequently proclaim that membership in the Peace Community is "*libre!*," a free decision (Comunidad de Paz de San José de Apartadó 2005b). The Peace Community's voluntary politics thus marks a key divergence from what is coerced participation in some guerrilla, state, and paramilitary units.

To paraphrase an international accompanier in San José de Apartadó, Gale Stafford, the Peace Community is more concerned with its members' active and conscious work and commitment than with how many members it has. They accept new members, but they do not organize missions to recruit additional people (personal interview 2014). On inclusions and exclusions: "There are more Community guidelines that tell you 'you *can't* be part of us' or cannot come back from. If someone breaks the rule about drinking, you can reassess, take a vow, and move forward. But [individual monetary] reparations [for victims from the government are a different story]: once you have accepted, you cannot undo accepting them. The movement gets smaller unless it actively gets bigger." She continued, saying that it is fundamentally about "consolidating who is actively making the choice to be here.... Being conscious about everything:... 'I'm making the decision to be here.' And then externally, so that anybody with arms... knows that there are still people there making this choice" (personal interview 2014). In other words, it is not that "members are conscious" and "nonmembers are not." Rather, the Peace Community's organizing and political work in response to forced displacement has continued decades of political education in San José by an array of actors, thus inducing a *concientização* or consciousness-raising process (Freire 1974) among the area's campesinos about the consequences of their decisions. I recall how jarred I was when I arrived for a fieldwork visit in September 2013 to find that a former Internal Council member and his family had left the Peace Community settlement of San Josecito for the police-occupied town of San José. They had decided to receive state reparation payments for the assassination of their son by the army, and thus left the Community.

While the Peace Community strives to build a strong and robust collectivity, it does not prioritize growing in numbers. As stated by deceased leader Eduar Lanchero, "It does not matter how many we are. What matters is that we really know and deeply live a different world" (Buenaventura 2011). But wouldn't more members increase the Community's ability to resist displacement and pressure the armed groups and Colombian state? Is the fact that they attempt to build a collective subject and yet lack a concern for increasing their membership contradictory? Doesn't the idea of a "collective subject" imply a multitude of people?

But the Peace Community embodies a collective subject not through quantity but quality: people who are committed to communal work. As such, this reflects a particular type of political movement. It diverges from a traditional leftist approach to political change focused on building a critical mass to counter-hegemonically occupy, reform, or potentially destroy dominant sites of power in order to build an alternative social order (Fals Borda 1968; Caycedo Turriago 2008; Ospina 1997). The Peace Community's goal is a collectivity not built on imposition and hegemony but instead is constructed through principled and committed solidarity. It is a political form of solidarity (hooks 1984; Scholz 2008) based on a shared commitment to peacebuilding and communal life. Such a praxis parallels other social movements across Latin America that are forging anticolonial ruptures through autonomous and emancipatory processes, which scholars have claimed embody an "other politics" (Grupo Acontecimiento 2012;

Denis 2012), "societies in movement" (Zibechi 2012), or "revolutions in the revolutions" (Reyes 2012b) amid the region's (post)neoliberal conjuncture.

When Peace Community members affirm that peace is refusing to participate in the war, along with dignity and solidarity through community organization, they inherently pose the question of power and politics, which refer to shaping and transforming reality. As the ethnographic vignette that opened this part illustrates, some campesinos respond to internal tensions by leaving the organization. Others face such challenges as opportunities to reenergize and motivate one another to nurture a collective process. I am unable to explain *why* certain individuals respond in these divergent ways, but it is clear that a key component of the Peace Community is precisely this commitment to building a campesino alternative by refusing to leave *where they are* and to do this *together*. This was so poetically rendered in Eduar Lanchero's (2000) narration of their 1998 resettlement of La Unión: "Terror was not superior to their desire to struggle for life, and the campesinos returned the same way they had left, that is to say, together; they knew that justice and the historical truth was with them" (69). Rather than an ethnic, religious, or national identity, the Peace Community's identity is explicitly political: those committed to and actively creating peace. Nevertheless, how do they nurture this togetherness in resistance? To what extent do particular Peace Community practices and places produce this "collective subject," "other politics," and a decolonial peace of radical relationality?

Part III analyzes the territoriality of the Peace Community through its experiments in food sovereignty and engagement in the trans-ethnic Campesino University of Resistance, before turning to the role of memorialization in the creation of peace. I argue that the Peace Community's set of spatial practices, places, and values through solidarity networks and food sovereignty projects illustrate a territory that produces a communal political subject who nurtures ecological dignity. Further, I examine the relationship between memory and peace in dialogue with the Community's affirmation that memory is the strength of their resistance. Indeed, their commemoration practices reinforce their commitment against retaliatory violence, reinvigorate communal cohesion, and consolidate their global solidarity network. Together these two chapters explore how the Peace Community practices its decolonial politics of peace through memory and solidarity networks.

CHAPTER 6

"LAND IS OUR MOTHER"

Alter-territorialities of Ecological Dignity

> Making our own *panela* [raw condensed sugar] gives me so much happiness. There have been many difficulties. People said that *"No, that is very difficult. You won't make* [sugarcane] honey or [condensed blocks of] panela."
>
> But some older men told me, *"Yes! It will work!* I worked with cane when I was a kid." And we began.
>
> Indigenous people came here to show us how to make panela.
>
> The first batch was a failure.
>
> Many people, you have to show them that, *yes*, things are possible. That they *see* because they don't believe: *"I* won't use that. No way." And the people are now happy, making their own panela; it has a *good flavor*.
>
> The Agricultural Center has enlivened many people. . . .
>
> It is important for communities to not depend on the outside world, to not depend on money. We are very far behind, but we have to *work really hard*! The first thing is being self-sufficient with our food.
>
> It makes me so happy when people [from other villages] tell me, "I have a fishpond and I learned how to make it in the *Agricultural Center*."
>
> That gives me a lot of strength to press on, looking for more alternatives.
>
> (Javier Sánchez, personal interview 2012)

I begin this chapter with the above passage because it speaks to self-sufficiency and solidarity, which are two core elements of the Peace Community and of the creation of an emancipatory politics more broadly. In 2009 in the Agricultural Center of La Unión village, they began preserving seeds, harvesting fish, and growing and processing sugarcane to produce their own panela, which spurred the creation of sugarcane-processing stations in other villages.

The Peace Community first began to pursue a project of food sovereignty following a series of paramilitary blockades of the Apartadó–San José road between 2002 and 2004 in which access to food and supplies from Apartadó was cut off. Many members refocused their attention on subsistence food crops and medicinal plants in the wake of two particular processes. The first was the Community's abandonment of a baby banana export project by 2012 following the failure to sustain the shipping and sales agreements with European buyers in addition to a paramilitary blockade of the port. The second was their participation in the Campesino University of Resistance, in which a collection of rural indigenous, black, and campesino groups have shared knowledge about agrarian, health, communication, and legal practices since 2004.

Self-sufficiency in a given community is produced through local practices but it is also the product of solidarity between different organizations. Javier Sánchez, the Community member quoted above, inferred the importance of mutual collaboration and training workshops in the Campesino University: "Indigenous people came here to show us how to make panela." Initiating and sustaining such programs is challenging, reflected by his allusion to contrasting subjectivities among community members. Some are skeptical about new ways and the possibilities for self-sufficiency: "'*No*, that is very difficult. You won't make honey or panela.... *I* won't use that.'" Others embody a "revolutionary enthusiasm" (Newton 2002) by harnessing their own knowledge and power: "'*Yes! It will work!* I worked with cane when I was a kid.' ... Many people, you have to show them that, *yes*, things are possible." The Peace Community's panela production reflects a trend among today's social movements to increasingly provide for their own subsistence (Federici 2010; Zibechi 2012). Breaking with material as well as subjective dependency on capitalist markets and state services is an immense task. Constructing such an emancipatory "other" politics of decolonial peace requires continual work and experimentation, not to mention passionate visionaries like Javier Sánchez to motivate new projects.

Such everyday political practices and spaces constitute a fundamental part of Colombian resistance communities' alter-territories, which counter the hegemonic territoriality of the modern state. "Territory" is typically understood as a bounded area controlled by a particular person or group, most often associated with the sovereign nation-state (Agnew 1994; Delaney 2005; Cowen and Gilbert 2008; Fernandes 2009; Elden 2013). All territories are tied to a particular "territoriality," the political relationship subjects have with space and exteriority (Raffestin 2012; Reyes 2015; Courtheyn 2018b), as in the modern state's territoriality of control over an area perceived as its "own" (Sack 1986). Yet recent scholarship argues that such notions are insufficient to capture what indigenous and black communities resisting land grabbing in Latin America mean with their increasing demands for "territory" rather than merely "land" (Gonçalves 2006; Reyes and Kaufman 2011; Haesbaert 2011; Liffman 2011; Clare, Habermehl, and Mason-Deese 2018). Rather than "bounded spaces of control," groups speak about territory as "life" (Ballvé 2013), "a living entity with memory"

(Ulloa 2012), or "biodiversity plus culture" (Escobar 2008). Building from this literature, if we reconceptualize territory broadly—as a moving set of practices, values, and places that cohere to produce a collective political subject—we are able to analyze the subjects who produce and are produced by a particular territorial formation (Courtheyn 2018b). Does a specific spatial and political arrangement produce individualistic or communal subjects? And what are the relationships among humans, nonhumans, and land/nature?

We are familiar with the collective subjects produced by the liberal-capitalist democratic nation-state's series of places, practices, and values: the promotion of a national history and patriotism; supposedly guaranteed education and employment; electoral party politics and representation; the values of competitiveness and wealth generation; top-down development projects, including mining and industrialized agriculture; and police and military forces which enforce those arrangements across a given area. Exhibiting a territoriality of control over nature and population, these cohere to produce nationalistic and capitalist subjects.

But not all territories are alike. This was made clear during a meeting of the Colectivo Agrario Abya Yala (Abya Yala Agrarian Collective), an interdisciplinary participatory action research collective which works in tandem with campesino, indigenous, and black groups by organizing seminars, conducting research, and publishing on land, territory, and social movements. In their 2013 seminar on territorial ordering,[1] a Nasa representative from Cauca challenged the state logic of territory as the demarcation of nature: "No había que ordenar el territorio sino el *pensamiento* [it is our *thinking*, and not territory, that should be (re)ordered] . . . to put ourselves in harmony with nature." Whereas state or liberal actors propose solutions to geographical conflict through land titling and demarcation, this perspective calls us to rethink modern-colonial territoriality. A congruent sentiment was expressed by the Colectivo de Sentipensamiento Afrodiaspórico (Afrodiasporic Feeling-Thinking Collective), which was founded in 2013 by various Afro-Colombian, *raizal* (inhabitant of the Colombian islands of San Andrés and Providencia), and *palenquero* (member of the Colombian maroon community San Basilio de Palenque) organizations to resist capitalism as well as the institutionalization and co-optation of the Afro-Colombian movement. They make a clear distinction between its concept of territory and the state's: "The notion of territory for the black population in rural areas who have been forcibly displaced to the large cities is distinct from the conceptualization that emanates from state institutions. Territory is conceived as an ancestral setting indispensable for the production and re-creation of life and culture. Land is not a resource for capital investment but instead *the space of relationality for collective being*"

(Colectivo de Sentipensamiento Afrodiaspórico 2015, emphasis mine). For these groups territory goes beyond a mere place but instead signifies a more complex spatial production of particular forms of life and collective subjects through corresponding places and values. Indeed, as Gilles Deleuze and Félix Guattari (1988) infer, "territorialization" is less about taking control of a place; it is a process of unifying bodies together into a "consistency" (145). Therefore, when Black Communities Process leader Francia Márquez Mina (2015) denounces military "helicopters bombing territories," this is much more significant than bombing a space or place. It is the bombing of the series of spatial practices, places, and values that constitute particular life worlds.

Attention to everyday political practices of peace allows us to see alternative territories even when people do not talk about it that way. Unlike many indigenous, black, and campesino communities demanding state-recognized "territories" (Fajardo Montaña 2002; Bocarejo 2012; Oslender 2016; Dest 2019), Peace Community leaders eschew such demands because they are skeptical of territory's loaded connotation as bounded spaces demarcated and enforced by violence. Opting against petitioning to create a zona de reserva campesina (campesino reserve zone) in Apartadó—which they have a right to demand—their divergence from the trend makes them a less obvious case of territorialization. But this community is clearly more than a mere set of places. It produces a complex geographical political structure and subjectivity. Other theorists are thus correct to consider territory beyond the "bounded and controlled area" of the nation-state, yet this scholarship has implications beyond the ethnic groups—indigenous and black communities—explored thus far.

This chapter illuminates the territoriality of the Peace Community's peace praxis by analyzing their understandings of land and territory as well as a number of Community spaces and practices: solidarity caravans with neighboring farmers threatened by armed groups, the Campesino University network, and food sovereignty initiatives in agricultural centers and self-sufficient farms. In contrast to state territoriality of control over land and population, San José's peace project produces a communal and solidarity subject who nurtures a relational territoriality between humans and nonhuman nature as well as across communities resisting the modern-colonial violence of state-corporate land grabbing. This alter-territoriality is foundational to its radical trans-relational peace of ecological dignity.

ON LAND AND TERRITORY

I begin exploring the Peace Community's territorial project by examining how they understand territory and land. While the Peace Community's zone of refuge for "non-combatant civilians" has been recognized as a new territoriality that challenges state sovereignty (Anrup and Español 2011), some interpret it as simply another form of creating a bounded space and sovereignty within the nation-state controlled by these farmers. This view is exhibited by fierce critiques by politician Álvaro Uribe (Asociación Campesina de Antioquia 2008) and Urabá media (*El Heraldo de Urabá* 2008) that denounced peace communities for supposedly striving to create "independent republics," which refer to communist enclaves in Colombian political discourse (Hylton 2006). Yet I argue that such an interpretation is incorrect. In fact, the Peace Community refuses the common practice of petitioning to become a state-registered collective territory, let alone demand a republic of their own. Instead they have *tierritas comunitarias* (little community lands under collective ownership) and individual members' plots, through which everyone has access to land. FOR accompanier Luke Finn observed, "There is land over there that technically someone owns. But in reality, no one owns it. It's just there and people can use it. I never really appreciated how important common land would be in another way of forming an economy, another society" (personal interview 2013). In other words, there are land titles and people know whose plots are where. Similar to indigenous and black communities' "overlapping territorialities" in Colombia's Pacific region (Agnew and Oslender 2013), San José's socio-territorial practice is one of shared access and use, which is an integral part of a collective Peace Community subject. The Community's divergence from the trend of marginalized groups demanding state-sanctioned "territory" allows us to analyze the potentials and limitations of territory and land as frames for resistance and autonomous politics, as well as the practices whereby land is materially and symbolically constructed as an alternative form of anti-state organization.

That is not to say that Community members never refer to territory. Some use *land* and *territory* interchangeably; Javier Sánchez explained, "When we and other communities talk about land and territory, we are talking about the same thing" (personal interview 2014). Similarly, leader Berta Tuberquia Quintero affirmed, "We struggle for the respect of life, for territory, that human rights are respected, for a number of things that all lead to the same point" (personal interview 2012). Berta also explained why they turned down proposals to declare themselves a collective territory, which is linked to a critique of the Colombian state's extractivist political economy:

> We don't believe that it's legal, the way the *territory* is administered. It has to do with the Colombian government's management of the subsoil. Because they go with their own interests. In contrast, we are not doing exploration or exploitation of mines.... The land, I compare it with the *body* of the human being.

> . . . If we strip it of minerals . . . we are stripping it of *life*. Like the indigenous peoples say, Mother Earth. . . . So, we have thought about having collective territories because it is a way of strengthening yourself to resist more. But governments are treacherous. They say, *"yes"* . . . and you get the collective land. But . . . they now have a window through which to enter. (group interview 2014)

Another leader expressed the same sentiment: "To get involved in [state-sanctioned] territory is dangerous, the law of extension and dominion. If we talk about territory, then the people are going to go work with the state. There are going to be those who grow coca. And the armed actors are always going to be in the zone. They need the territory and don't want us to prohibit them from passing through. We don't want coca, but since it will be a territory, the Peace Community will be responsible [for others growing it]" (field notes 2013).

A third leader reiterated the antagonism between the Community's understanding of land and state-corporate interests in San José de Apartadó, part of which was cited in Chapter 3: "Land is our mother. From her we were made. We were made from the dust of the land. And she gives us our food. . . . These lands are very rich. And for that reason, they are fighting over this land and want to kick us out, because of . . . pure air . . . water . . . coal, many minerals. Gold. . . . And they are already handed over to a multinational [corporation]" (Moncada Hurtado, Ossa, and Caro Morales 2011a). Member Doña Brígida González also affirmed that life comes from the land, of which people are merely a part. She insisted that we expand our analysis of the war in Colombia beyond its effects on humans: "We are at war in *every* sense. With nature. . . . People are killed as if they were any old animal. Animals *also* have a right to live. But as human beings, I believe that . . . the value of life has been lost, incredibly. . . . Without land we couldn't live. . . . From what air would we breathe? . . . Mother Earth gives us *everything*. She has water that is life. She has plants that are our daily food" (personal interview 2013). These quotes reveal how the Peace Community—seeing land as a living being—strives for a different relationship with the earth than the state has, manifested by their disagreement over extractivism. Without using the language of "earth-beings" (de la Cadena 2015) or practicing spiritual rituals to connect with Mother Earth (Vachon 2011), these campesinos' understanding of land is nonetheless similar to certain indigenous groups in the Americas. They infer a decolonial territoriality that is not about separating humans from space and land, but instead continually appreciating and reintegrating oneself with nature. This informs my notion of ecological dignity, building from what scholars have deemed "relational ontologies" (Blaser 2010; de la Cadena 2015; Escobar 2018; Oslender 2016) or "energetic peace," constituted by eternal experimentation toward harmony and equilibrium among all beings (Dietrich 2012).

While the Peace Community is skeptical of the dominant idea and practice of state territory, their insistence that armed groups keep out of their homes and farms should not be mistaken as a local-scale replica of state-like "sovereignty" over land and population. To the contrary, the Peace Community's rejection of extractivism and "more demarcation of land" by the state reflects a contrasting form of territory and territoriality. Given the Peace Community's decision to *not* pursue the creation of a state-registered campesino reserve zone in San José de Apartadó, their divergence from the trend toward demanding "territory" calls attention to the diverse understandings of land and territory *among* communities resisting land grabbing. The distinctions they describe are precisely why we need a broader conception of *territoriality,* as the political relationship between subjects and space, and *territory,* as an animated set of practices, values, and places that produce a collective political subject, in order to analyze diverse political arrangements of space. To illustrate the Peace Community's alter-territoriality through its places, practices, and values, I describe four elements of their Community process: solidarity caravans, campesino resistance networks, agricultural centers, and self-sufficient farms.

SOLIDARITY CARAVANS

The Community hosts various large gatherings annually in San José de Apartadó, such as their anniversary celebration each March 23 and the Mulatos–La Resbalosa massacre commemoration in February. Complementing those memorial encounters, the Peace Community also tends to organize an annual march in the latter half of each calendar year which is centered around a particular theme. For example, in October 2008 they hiked across five of their settlements within San José de Apartadó to accompany the recent returns of campesinos to La Esperanza, Mulatos, and La Resbalosa. The 2010 caravan began in Bogotá, where they carried out public demonstrations at government offices to denounce state violence and impunity, before proceeding to nearby Sumapaz, another place of armed conflict in recent decades, where an intercommunity conference was held. For clarity I use *pilgrimage* to refer to commemoration hikes to massacre sites and *caravan* to refer to solidarity marches farther afield. I use these terms to signal to the reader the motivating rationale for different types of marches, although Peace Community members tend to use both terms interchangeably, with the term pilgrimage being the most common.

The following is an ethnographic account of a caravan in which I participated in October 2013.[2] Due to paramilitary threats and kidnapping that displaced many families from neighboring Rodoxalí, the Community organized a caravan to confront the paramilitaries and state forces stationed there, even though it was not a Peace Community settlement. Communities in resistance utilized the presence of international accompaniers marching with them to increase their security and subsequently spread knowledge about the struggle to broader publics. My walking alongside them was an example of radical performance geography at work.

> "*Caminando la palabra*," or "walking the word," is how participants from indigenous communities in Cauca and Guajira departments described what we had done on our recently completed peace and solidarity caravan to the village of Rodoxalí, one of the thirty-two veredas in the rural district of San José de Apartadó.
>
> Organized by the Peace Community, it was named a "Pilgrimage for Life and against Displacement and Forced Disappearance." Rodoxalí's farmers are not part of the Peace Community. The pilgrimage was organized in response to reports that four people had been killed in the area and that paramilitaries had kidnapped a young man as well as demanded that the area's campesinos give them information and supplies. An estimated twenty-eight families subsequently fled their homes in fear. More than 150 people converged upon the village to confirm and confront the presence of a paramilitary death squad.
>
> The paramilitary group operating in the zone, who identify as the Autodefensas Gaitanistas de Colombia (AGC, Gaitanista Self-Defense Forces of Colombia), reacted with a press release dated September 28th, 2013, rejecting such accusations and affirming their commitment to land restitution and social justice for campesinos. The AGC is a neo-paramilitary group who announced its formation with a *paro armado* (armed shutdown) on October 15, 2008, in which all ground transport and commerce in Urabá came to a halt. In their first communiqué, they claimed to be victims of the state's failure to fulfill its promises made to the demobilized paramilitaries of the Autodefensas Unidas de Colombia (AUC, United Self-Defense Forces of Colombia). Their current name evokes the former Liberal and populist presidential candidate, Jorge Eliécer Gaitán, whose assassination in 1948 spurred the Bogotazo uprising and era of La Violencia. Local residents and analysts whom I spoke with while in the region during the AGC's armed shutdown of 2008 were surprised by the fact that this right-wing paramilitary group would name themselves after a leftist politician; it seemingly reflected a strategic effort to appeal to the popular classes (*El Espectador* 2008; Aparicio 2012).
>
> In response to the new wave of paramilitary attacks in 2013, the Peace Community invited journalists, members from its eleven villages, delegates from other Colombian campesino and indigenous communities, and international protective accompaniment organizations to join the caravan. I was the only academic.

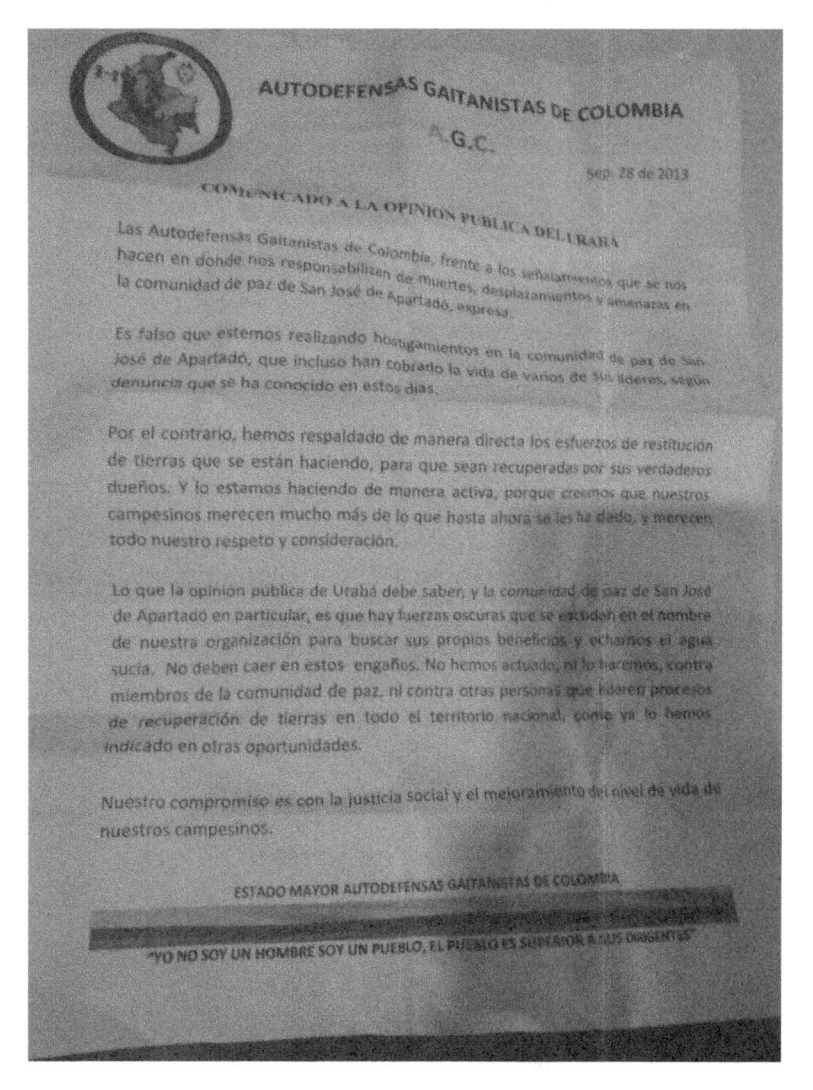

6.1. The narcobourgeoisie on the defensive: AGC press release. Photo by Luke Finn, with permission.

On October 7 three groups took different routes to reach Rodoxalí. Folks from La Unión left early in the morning and hiked four hours to the Peace Community farm in La Esperanza. They picked up additional caravanners and proceeded for another four hours to the small town of Nuevo Antioquia in the neighboring municipality of Turbo. There they waited for another contingent that had left San Josecito, took a public jeep to Apartadó, met up with visitors arriving from other parts of Colombia, and then took a bus to Nuevo Antioquia. This town is a notorious base for paramilitary fighters and operations, as

6.2. Mapping the caravan of October 2013: People converged in Rodoxalí from various directions. Map by author.

well as state police and army forces' collusion with them (Comunidad de Paz de San José de Apartadó 2014b). Those two caravan groups then marched together to Rodoxalí, another four to five hours.

I was part of the third group. The previous day, we made the five-hour walk from La Unión to the Mulatos Peace Village. After staying the night, we departed for Rodoxalí with residents of Mulatos and other campesinos who had arrived from neighboring La Resbalosa and villages in Córdoba. Soon after we set out a young woman whom I had known since she was a kid, asked me, "Why are we doing this?" referring to our caravanning through this rough and rocky river trail. I responded, "For dignity and to demand respect." "Yes," she replied, "solidarity. Resistance." I thought, "Consciousness among the youth about why we are doing this is impressive!" A bit later, when my boot became stuck in the mud and she lent a hand to pull me out, I said, "And this is solidarity also!"

Our group was the first to arrive to Rodoxalí. The place was largely abandoned. The FORPP accompaniers and I set out with a Peace Community Internal Council member to speak to the village's six remaining families. He proposed that we accompany them for a few days. They happily accepted, noting that such a large contingent of people had not been seen there for two decades. They revealed that, even before the most recent displacement of people, the village had been a skeleton of its previous self since the mid-1990s. It was once

6.3. Alter-territories in movement: FOR accompaniers walking alongside the Peace Community and its RECORRE network toward Rodoxalí. Author photo.

a thriving settlement that hosted local soccer tournaments before paramilitaries and the National Army displaced the local population, potentially linked with operations in preparation for the nearby Urrá hydroelectric dam project. In the process armed groups killed many residents and burned down most of the houses.

Rodoxalí's residents mentioned the heavy paramilitary presence currently in the region and the recently distributed AGC press release pamphlet claiming to support the campesinos, despite widespread beliefs in the region that paramilitaries were in fact carrying out a land grab. Our caravan would later encounter army soldiers comfortably camped between villages, as if they were on vacation. They said they had no specific knowledge of any paramilitary kidnapping or presence, suggesting at the very least a tacit collusion with the death squads.

Those of us who had arrived from Mulatos began to prepare the site for the others' arrival. As we fetched water from the riverbank, one of the members mentioned people who would arrive from an indigenous community in Cauca. "They are part of the Network," referring to the Network of Communities in Rupture and Resistance (RECORRE) which founded the Campesino University. "That network is very important because the problem in the country is not only in San José. We also do universities in their communities. This caravan shows the [armed] actors our strength and solidarity."

By late afternoon the other caravan groups began to arrive from Nuevo Antioquia. People converged to sit down on fallen trees placed for seating, and we would rest around a large pot of boiling water, covered with banana leaves. People shared stories of their respective walks. A group of young indigenous women from southern Colombia expressed their exhaustion: "We had no idea it would be so far! [*Laughter!*] We were told we needed hiking boots and we wondered, 'For what?' We live in a rural area but it's nothing like this!"

It was almost nightfall, and a lot of work was still to be done to accommodate everyone's sleeping arrangements. We accompanied an Internal Council member as he and a small team struggled to cut down large, dense bamboo trees at dusk. They then nailed them into a large, abandoned open-air building from which people would hang their hammocks. We were marching, back and forth, from one side of the settlement to the other, carrying bamboo trunks. People set up tents and hammocks in other vacant buildings. And a group cooked dinner, which featured rice and lentils brought on horses from Peace Community settlements, plus yucca, plantains, and pork purchased from local families. People gathered to eat and talk around the central water pot, illuminated by the burning coals underneath and people's flashlights. I wrote in my notebook: "Resistance is hard work. All the organization by the Community: invitations and coordinating everyone's arrivals, horses, food quantity, supplies, hammocks. Long walks. Taking care of everything, both people and the mules that can fall over on the trails. Then talking with the local residents, announcing our arrival, setting up accommodation in unoccupied homes, and hanging hammocks and mosquito nets. *And all this at night.*"

The FOR accompaniers and I were informed that we would stay with Father Javier Giraldo in the one house with a bedframe where he would sleep, albeit with no padding. This recently abandoned house was particularly chilling. In two rooms clothes that had been left behind were scattered and molding on the ground. In the kitchen there was a rotting box of spilled flour, and small ducks and chickens wandered outside under the lemon and cacao trees scavenging for food. One of the accompaniers became distressed, stalling to hang his hammock, and said, "You don't imagine that someone was tortured here, do you?"

When families are forcibly displaced, they take whatever they can carry on their backs and horses. This often means they bring only themselves and their children, plus any large animals, such as pigs, which serve as the primary savings for small-scale farmers. What is left behind is likely destroyed or lost forever. This unarmed pilgrimage of solidarity with these families was organized to confront the paramilitaries and complicit state forces and to assert the rights of the area's campesinos to work their farms without threats and killings by armed groups who compete to control the land.

However, the paramilitaries were nowhere to be seen. The following day, we walked to the adjacent settlement of Sabaleta where they were reportedly

6.4. Anticolonial peace: Marching to confront paramilitarism. Author photo.

camped. But they had retreated into the surrounding forest. Pilgrimage participants believed that this revealed the paramilitaries' own recognition that they lacked a valid verbal defense before such a civilian delegation. In the words of Father Giraldo, "They are unable to face their 'truth' with our truth." The Peace Community reflected on this in their subsequent communiqué: "We ask why they won't show their faces and the only answer that we can find is that they would never be able to justify their crimes" (Comunidad de Paz de San José de Apartadó 2013a). Participants also suspected that national police and army officials in nearby Nuevo Antioquia—through whose checkpoints the delegation had passed the day before—informed the paramilitary groups of the caravan so that they would hide their presence.

Since the supposed demobilization of the AUC in 2006, the Colombian government officially has claimed that "paramilitaries" who target political opponents do not exist. It asserts that, in addition to guerrillas, there are only drug trafficking *bandas criminales* (criminal bands), known as BACRIM, or *grupos organizados* (organized [armed] groups). Our large contingent of people from other regions and countries served to testify to our support networks in the diplomatic corps and human rights community about the reality of persistent paramilitarism. In the words of a Peace Community member, "The state officials probably told the paramilitaries, 'If they see you, we're screwed.'"

After returning to Rodoxalí by the afternoon, a heavy rainstorm hit. We huddled under roofs and some of us took a swim in the river. While swimming, campesinos from La Vega, Cauca, invited us to their upcoming November workshop meeting on water protection, given the threat of contamination from gold mining; each year they host an international gathering organized around the topics of water or seeds. It is through such encounters that solidarity networks are forged and enhanced.

During the early evening, a group of people convened for Father Giraldo's Catholic mass in Rodoxalí's decrepit but still standing chapel. He said mass in the dark, with only a flashlight to illuminate the Bible and a small altar. Rainfall continued to poor down outside. He opened by saying, "We are here in solidarity with those who were displaced and threatened by the presence of the paramilitaries. This violence has destroyed lives, and for that reason the Peace Community with its accompaniers within and outside the country have come here. Today we searched for the paramilitaries to confront their truth with our truth, to ask them why they are doing this. We could not find them because they hid, unable to face and reconcile their truth with ours."

He read from the Book of Isaiah and Gospel of Luke. In his homily he professed, "These are very symbolic texts, when Isaiah returns from exile and Jesus begins his mission in the synagogue. There is much work ahead: to come together to break chains, open paths, and that the ideas of humanity that we have elaborated will become reality one day."

To preface the mass's sign of peace ritual, he said, "Peace is a commitment of all Christians, that they be creators of peace. However, this is not a peace of resignation but a peace of justice. Let's share this peace." When mass had ended, people retreated under umbrellas and plastic sheets to their hammocks and tents.

On my walk back, I ran into a Peace Community leader making a phone call, since near the house I was staying in was the one place with cell phone signal, as weak as it was. He said, "I was just approached by an unknown man who asked me what I was doing, if this was a commission organized by the state. I told him, 'No, we are campesinos here accompanying these villages.' The man questioned, 'Walking through all these villages?' To which I replied, 'That's what we do. It's our work.' I suspect he was a paramilitary sent by their camp."

The next day, as we packed our backpacks and hammocks for departure, a Community member lamented the "poor little chicks and ducks" meandering around the grass adjacent to the house. She began to recount her own stories of forced displacement, with my corresponding field journal entry being titled "Being in those houses triggers one's own history." She described an occasion when her husband and daughters fled their home as paramilitaries approached, and in a frantic rush to leave, they actually left their baby daughter in a hammock, having to return to find her. Her elder daughter, who was also there with us, shared her version of those events a decade prior. The mother said, "Walking and visiting makes you remember what you lived through. You wonder, was it

6.5. "Walking the word": People helping one another cross a river on the trail from Rodoxalí to Mulatos. Photo by Luke Finn, with permission.

the same here as it was for us [during the mass displacement] in 1997? And if those times will return." Her daughter added, "Or be even worse." The mother continued, "In the past, when you would hear about a massacre, you would say 'That happened far away. It won't happen here.' But it does." I commented, "Everything is connected. Well-being and violence here affect everyone else." To which she concluded, "Yes, we must be in solidarity."

When we departed, Rodoxalí's residents said that they were energized by our visit, felt accompanied and not alone, and invited the Peace Community to return. A few hours after departure, we heard three gunshots back in the area toward Sabaleta and Rodoxalí. People in our caravan said, "It's as if the paramilitaries are saying, 'You did not see us, but we are here.'"

At the conclusion of the pilgrimage in the Community's Mulatos Peace Village, we reflected on what had occurred and what we had done. With local accounts, we had unfortunately confirmed the tragic forced displacements induced by the paramilitary presence with apparent government forces' backing. Additionally, the visit provided relief to those families who continued to resist fleeing their homes. This laid the groundwork for future visits. The hope was that paramilitaries and the army would respond to this act of civilian solidarity by abstaining from future killing and forced displacement, knowing that their actions would be reported to the outside world. Through greater visibility and a wider support network, including the Peace Community, journalists, and

"LAND IS OUR MOTHER" 173

6.6. This is peace: Community member guiding horses across a river. Photo by Luke Finn, with permission.

international human rights organizations, Rodoxalí's farmers could draw on a greater array of resources in their struggle.

To put it bluntly, our group of unarmed civilians caused an armed death squad to flee into the forest. People argued that without the accompaniment of organizations like FOR—which the Peace Community positioned at the front of the caravan to demonstrate international observation and lead the line in any encounter with an armed group—the paramilitaries probably would not have retreated. The pilgrimage demonstrated that the collective action of unarmed civilian campesinos and accompaniers walking together can open space for people to resist displacement and harvest the fruits of their agricultural labor with dignity. As stated in the Peace Community's subsequent press release: "Weapons will not intimidate us, and before the sowers of death, we will always choose life" (Comunidad de Paz de San José de Apartadó 2013a).

Just as significant was our walking itself. Parts of the path were brutal. There were long stretches of thigh-high mud, in which people's rubber boots got stuck. Others would move near to help pull them out of the ground. A horse carrying a Community member slipped as it climbed up rocks, resulting in a hard fall for both. Fellow caravanners carefully helped the woman and horse to their feet, both of whom luckily avoided serious injury. We also had to cross rivers multiple times, which became more challenging after an afternoon of thunderstorms and heavy rain raised the water level. People locked hands while leaping from rock to rock. At one deep crossing, a senior Community member immersed himself in the three-foot-deep water, literally pulling horses and people across to the other side. Prepared for the dangers presented by armed groups and the trails themselves, Peace Community leaders had made our commitment explicit at the outset: "We are in a war zone, but no one will be left behind."

This pilgrimage pointed to a more profound praxis of peace, signaled by some participants as Caminando la palabra. We walked the word. We did not merely profess to support some vague notion of peace, but actually generated relationships of care and love among ourselves as we marched in solidarity with the threatened families of Rodoxalí. A Colombian journalist in attendance said, "Many of the big-time university academics study violence and conflict. But they do so from books. They have never walked with the communities in a pilgrimage like this." As we walked together, we actually lived the peace we desire, rejecting the logic of modern-colonial competition and individualism while affirming that everyone's life must be defended by a collective political project. As a Community leader said during the closing reflection, "We are constructing the world that we want." We do it by walking and working together in solidarity, as campesinos, indigenous communities, academics, journalists, and international accompaniers. (edited from my field notes 2013)

Nine months later in a July 2014 meeting members of the Internal Council, international accompaniers, and I reflected on the situation in Rodoxalí. The Internal Council informed us that paramilitaries subsequently built a road and homes in the area, which pleased Rodoxalí's residents. My subsequent field note read:

Paramilitaries built a highway from Nuevo Antioquia, which passes through Sabaleta. I can barely believe it. Those villages are now reachable by *road*?! The paramilitaries then built many homes in Rodoxalí. A Council member reported, "The people are happy. They say that the paramilitaries are good now."

In our meeting, we reflected on the effects of the Peace Community caravan in October 2013. The march had pushed the paramilitaries to hide in the mountains. It then induced discussion with the Catholic Church to rebuild the chapel in Rodoxalí and create a neutral Humanitarian Zone, implying some type of relationship with the San José Peace Community. Subsequently, the paramilitaries began funding productive projects and house construction.

It is intriguing, because one theory is that the paramilitary development projects were a response to the caravan. Such direct cause and effect are difficult to ascertain. But it is logical to infer that the paramilitaries feared losing legitimacy and control given the possibility of a Humanitarian Zone linked to the Peace Community, thus provoking them to react with projects to legitimize their authority. This parallels the notion that large institutions only reform when presented with concrete, competing reforms, à la the United States government instituting the Head Start school breakfast program after the Black Panthers created their Breakfast for Children Program (Nelson 2011). While the Peace Community is obviously wary of such relations with the paramilitaries, Rodoxalí's residents received what they wanted: housing and funding for economic projects. We might say that the Peace Community caravan helped them earn those, even if that was not what the Peace Community wanted or intended to cause.

In my journalistic articles for *Upside Down World* and *Prensa Rural Periferia*, I wrote that the farmers of Rodoxalí could now draw on a wider network of organizations—human rights groups, the Catholic Church, and the Peace Community—in their struggle for survival. Indeed, they have a wider "support network," but with the paramilitaries! An Internal Council member said, "I don't think we can go back there for now, but we might organize another commission in the future." (field notes 2014)

On the one hand, this situation of campesino resistance to paramilitarism and subsequent re-entrenchment of paramilitary control is indicative of the period during and following the 2016 peace accord process, in which paramilitary groups such as the AGC have increasingly taken advantage of the FARC's decreasing presence in areas like San José de Apartadó to consolidate political control. On the other hand, these caravans exemplify the Peace Community's territoriality and practice of territory. This mobilization shows territory, rather than being limited to a marked place, to be a moving practice across space. Rather than a relationship with space rooted in control and domination, the Peace Community marched to express support for neighboring farmers and to open space for dialogue about future interactions, which initially included the possibility of forming a humanitarian zone. When Rodoxalí's residents ultimately favored roads and housing construction, the Peace Community respected their decision, even if it is wary of such projects linked to armed groups. This contrasts with the common treatment by Colombian state institutions. As Community members have frequently critiqued, agencies such as Bienestar Familiar (Family Well-being) often offer services to communities on the condition that they accept the presence of the state armed forces (field notes 2008, 2014). This again speaks to how the Peace Community's practice of territory and "community," to follow Silvia Federici (2010: 287–89), are "not intended as a gated reality" defined by ethnic or religious identities. Rather, they are concerned with building cross-community networks of solidarity in defense of commons and noncapitalist social relations. If the Peace Community was concerned with "controlling space and population," they would not walk in solidarity with nonmembers like those in Rodoxalí or would do so to impose their Community rules on these neighboring farmers. Instead these caravans are about nurturing particular values and creating political subjects committed to solidarity central to the alterterritory they produce.

CAMPESINO UNIVERSITY OF RESISTANCE

The day following the completion of the caravan to Rodoxalí, participants held a session of the Campesino University of Resistance, involving a day and a half of workshops. It began with a general conversation about the history of the University and individual communities' introductions. People then split up into three groups dedicated to land titling, communications, and health and medicine. The entire group then reconvened to share what each subgroup had done and conclude the session.

RECORRE, which was formed in 2003, inaugurated this University with a monthlong meeting in the Peace Community village of Arenas Altas in 2004. It has subsequently been held in other communities, such as San Vicente de Caguán in March 2005. Some of its planned meetings, such as one in the Sierra Nevada of Santa Marta, fell through because of lack of funds (Aparicio 2012), but various sessions have been held over the years, for example, in the Sierra Nevada in 2015. In the Peace Community alone gatherings have taken place in La Unión, San Josecito, and the Mulatos Peace Village, including the 2013 meeting following the Rodoxalí caravan.

In an interview one Peace Community member described the University using the metaphor of bees:

> Like honeybees . . . because . . . you always see a bee with flowers. Where it extracts its nectar. It then takes it to the hive. There they make honey. Honey is medicine, it's everything. It is healthy. I compare these people to honeybees. They bring new and good things so that we learn. And they also take from here to other places. People make creams for pain, powder for bad-smelling feet, and solar energy stations. Those knowledges that are so important. That way of behaving, that fellowship. It is sweet—I compare it with honey. This is different from flies . . . that all they bring and take is pure dirt, contaminating. The University serves as a journey of bees. Since it is *different* from other universities, we have made good use of it. (personal interview 2014)

Therefore this University is organized to share and produce tangible knowledge and products useful for people's health, energy needs, and general well-being. This implicitly rebuffs the "coloniality of being" that dehumanizes particular peoples to the point where they are branded as having nothing to offer other human beings (Maldonado-Torres 2010). Like the solidarity caravans, much of what constitutes the Campesino University is not only its explicit or practical objective. It is also about the form of fellowship nurtured in these spaces, which refer to the type of spatial practices and values that constitute such a territory.

What makes this University "different" from others? To open the 2013 session, Father Giraldo described its history and principles. He recounted how, after a series of discussions about forming a university among communities resisting forced displacement and political violence, they discerned:

> It is only worthwhile if it is completely different from the universities that we are familiar with. First, to not treat knowledge as merchandise, where one enters, registers, and pays for knowledge; afterward you graduate with a diploma, which you also sell as merchandise. That [this alter-university] refrains from being merchandise and becomes a sharing of knowledge. There is no payment or salaries but rather people who want to share. Second, no professors or students. To turn this scheme upside down, where everyone can contribute. Third, rather than a fixed site, to rotate it among different communities. And to be focused on the most affected and important sites: Afros, indigenous, and campesinos. (field notes 2013)

In other words, this University rejects the idea of education as a commodity. And it attempts to create horizontal social relationships: rather than teachers, there are "facilitators," and different organizations take the lead on facilitating each gathering. The University addresses a variety of themes central to campesino resistance: agriculture and food sovereignty, legal issues and human rights, health and medicinal plants, education, and media communications. Cartographic mapping and memory projects have also been proposed for future gatherings. Further, it is grounded in rotating community sites and experiences to address those groups' most pressing needs (Comunidad de Paz de San José de Apartadó 2004, 2006). Journalist Martha Ruiz (2005) remarked, "It is called a university (and not school or college) to recover the primary concept of the word. It is universal, humanist, and helps to transform reality." This speaks to the values of the Peace Community and this network's territory: collaboration, horizontality, dignity, and anticommercialism.

In the 2013 session's opening statements, representatives from different groups shared ideas. The following quotes provide a sense of common comments made in such sessions, which tend to express gratitude and solidarity for one another, as well as speak to each community's particular challenges and achievements. A representative of ACIN explained the relationship between autonomy and the University: "The Resistance University is to create another type of education that is more loyal to our needs as peoples. And change the system we are in. In our community, we have taken steps for autonomy in that we are now almost an [officially recognized indigenous] reserve. More practice, rather than theory. Sovereignty. Without food there

6.7. Dialogical performance for ecological dignity: Campesino University of Resistance workshop on medicinal plants. Author photo.

is no life. To have our own law and education" (field notes 2013). A member of the Guardia Indígena (Indigenous Guard) from ACIN opened with gratitude: "I give thanks to Mother Nature for allowing me to walk. And to our *compañeros campesinos*. . . . The *bastón* [baton] that I bring is to provide a message of the Nasa ethnic groups." Such batons are a symbol of protection used by the Indigenous Guard, which serves as a nonviolent defense force. Referencing the caravan we had just completed, another said, "The fear that we felt to come here because of the reports about the paramilitaries, we have converted into energy." Another man opened his statement in his indigenous language, Wayúu, before ultimately speaking in Spanish: "Spirituality is very important. Uniting ourselves to resist and listen to one another. This University of Resistance is to protect and respect our territories." A representative from a campesino community in Cauca emphasized a national struggle and the importance of water: "To traverse territories is an act of sovereignty and dignity. Thanks to these gatherings, the coming and going of leaders, we are constructing a space for a popular mandate of the people. In dialogue, we build friendship and the future of our nation that has been at war for so many years. This is a nation that deserves something different, with its tolerance, courage, and wisdom. . . . We must protect the water at whatever cost. Water is a right of all. It is not sold" (field notes 2013). While the lexicon of the representatives often differs—with indigenous communities talking about their "territories" and campesinos more often speaking of "the people" (*el pueblo*) and "the country/nation" (*el país, la nación*)—all express a sense of shared struggles, goals, and commitments to transforming the realities of their individual communities and of those in the network. Indeed, this reiterates my argument about these communities' shared racial condition.

The workshops are designed to cover specific themes. In the 2013 session participants split into three groups. Organizations with multiple representatives divided themselves among all three workshops. One group met to discuss the legal situation of each community's land titles (or lack thereof, in some cases) in preparation for a report on land challenges facing RECORRE's members amid the "peace process" conjuncture.

A second group, on the topic of health, took a walk outside the Mulatos Peace Village to collect medicinal plants. They then processed the plants into a variety of medicinal syrups, anti-inflammatory and pain creams, perfume, and antifungal powders. They put them in containers for delegates to take with them to their home communities. And they also put them to immediate use, treating one man who had cut his leg with a machete.

The third group did a workshop on community media. Led by the Bogotá-based Colectivo Sónica Sinfonía (Symphonic Sonic Collective), the group brainstormed goals, rationales, and strategies for community-generated communications. A Peace Community member argued that such media are needed to "manage our own image and show the work we are doing, since television sells an image of what we are not." Meanwhile a representative from an indigenous Chocó community alluded to the role of media in the struggle for existence, which infers resistance against capitalist logics and their erasure as racialized people: "To tell the government that, yes, we exist. That campesinos are the ones who provide everything to the cities. If we focus on bettering the economy, we will destroy the world. We should focus on culture, peoples' survival, and information about myths and legends: information that can change reality. Such as medicinal plants: to show that you can plant and harvest where you are, to not buy pharmaceutical drugs." The group then did interview and camera training. We learned practical skills, such as how to stand, look at the interviewee, ask questions, which buttons (written in English) to push on the camera, and how to position the camera stand. We had fun as we learned. And then people went to record interviews with folks from the other groups. I wrote in my notebook, "There is so much *life* here" (field notes 2013).

In the closing roundtable of the University, each workshop group shared with the others what they had done. Then there was a closing round of comments. It is striking how many opportunities these gatherings set aside to sit as a group and listen to any words or ideas anyone wishes to share, as an implicit alternative to the silencing of these racialized subjects by the dominant modern-colonial society. We heard "Thank you" over and over, as everyone expressed their gratitude for the invitation to participate in the caravan, with many acknowledging international accompaniment as well. Referring back to the caravan to Rodoxalí, one Peace Community member noted that we learned how "armed people are also capable of running from victims. Arms are very potent when we as people have stopped seeing one another as brothers [and sisters], when we lose our humanity." A representative from a Chocó community summed up the gathering's spirit and praxis: "We have to keep walking to continue struggling" (field notes 2013).

Asking participants what concrete things they have learned in the University, one man from Chocó told me, "That displacement is bad. We have never been displaced, but we can take precautions now to not be displaced in the future." I responded, "Such as not accepting offers to sell the land, for instance?" He replied, "Right. Someone comes to buy a plot with a wad of bills, but in our conversations with other communities, we learn that such bills are not actually much money. In the city, it runs out quickly" (field notes 2013). This alludes to San José residents' stories of displacement to nearby cities in 1996 and 1997 and their subsequent commitment to resettle their villages. Therefore these gatherings serve to generate collective analysis that helps to inform each community's strategy.

A Peace Community member explained things she learned from other communities in such encounters: "How to cure yourself with plants, to stop using pharmacy medicines. You use these remedies later. They are plants that we recognize [but did not necessarily know their properties or uses]. Others have learned how to use an electronic drying system for cacao. Solar energy also" (personal interview 2013). When I asked her what she thought others learn from the Peace Community, she said, "About resistance and living together. Collaboration. We have differences but learn to convivir [live together] with these differences. To be in solidarity: to take people down the hills [in hammocks when they are sick]. To cook for a large group of people, with everyone going to collect firewood together" (personal interview 2013). The Campesino University thus serves as a space of sharing practical knowledge. But these gatherings are not merely instrumental. They are just as much about enjoying life and spending time with and making new friends. "In the caravans, you have fun. You stay up late, meet new friends and go to new places. Indigenous people come and sometimes they teach you words in their language. That is learning as well" (personal interview 2013). Finally, the mobile nature of the Campesino University epitomizes how this territory is not a physical "area," even if the gatherings that rotate among different communities are one of this alter-territory's fundamental practices.

6.8. View from the highest gazebo in La Unión's Agricultural Center: Notice the sugarcane processing station (left), village cemetery in the background (middle), and thatch roof meeting-space gazebo (right). Author photo.

AGRICULTURAL CENTERS

One of the ways the Peace Community has replicated the Campesino University format within their own community and applied lessons learned from other communities is in agricultural centers, which were built in villages such as San Josecito and La Unión. Located next to the village's cemetery, the La Unión Agricultural Center stretched across various hillsides. It was inaugurated in 2009 with the construction of the library, named after Rigoberto Guzmán, the Internal Council member killed in the 2000 paramilitary massacre in La Unión. They also built fishponds and created an adjacent garden in which to store seeds, where a sign explicitly prohibited mineral exploitation. In 2010 they planted sugarcane within the Center and added the Peace Community's first sugarcane processing station, described in this chapter's introduction.

With architectural knowledge learned from indigenous communities, they constructed circular gazebos from local materials as meeting spaces. A shift away from square buildings made of concrete, these new constructions reflect the Peace Community's goals and principles: food sovereignty requires places for crop cultivation and spaces for collaborative discussion. And to create a communal subject, which is essential if peace is rooted in

6.9. Rejecting extractivism: "Agrarian Center Farm. Private Property. Free from Mineral Exploration and Megaprojects." Author photo.

community, you have to create places in that territory which nurture horizontality, in which people can sit in a circle and face one another.

The Peace Community frequently showcased La Unión's Agricultural Center to visiting delegations. During a 2012 visit by two members of the Catholic diocese in Apartadó, the bishop said mass in the Center's library. Afterward Community members took them on a tour. Beginning in the library, Community members highlighted its variety of books, including educational children's books as well as ones on agroecology. The Center's coordinator, Javier Sánchez, said, "This supports the Agricultural Center. People are now copying things from books and then implementing them" (field notes 2012). During our stop in the garden, Community members pointed out the different crops and seeds preserved there. Javier explained:

> Where the Agricultural Center is, the land was really depleted, just a grazing area. But now it is productive. It gives *lulo* fruit. Aloe. Amazonian wheat. It's beautiful! It grows more and more! The land liked it. Sorghum, as well. We have nineteen seeds of plantain and bananas, and different varieties of yucca. Cacao. Coffee. We plant seeds here to then transplant them, including medic-

6.10. Panela production: Community member tending to pots of boiling cane juice. Author photo.

inal plants. Many medicinal plants grow wild, but in the past, when a person was sick, someone would have to hike up the hills to find the appropriate plant. Now, they are all grown here for quick and easy access. . . . From a seed exchange in another region of the country, I brought squash seeds, huge squash! And people said, "Give me a seed, so I can plant one!" (field notes 2012)

We proceeded to pass by the fishponds, stop at the sugarcane-processing center for a taste of freshly made panela, and visit the different gazebos. Javier Sánchez described the philosophy of having an Agricultural Center:

> The fishponds are also an important food base for families. And we planted sugarcane, from which we have begun to make panela blocks and [sugarcane] honey. About 70% of the panela consumption in La Unión comes from here and not from outside. We have observed that birds have come to the Agricultural Center and stay. We also looked to having gazebos. In them, there are trainings. We choose a topic, say, coffee or panela, and among ourselves, we train ourselves. To learn from one another, where there aren't even teachers. The primary objective is that people can replicate what they learn in their own communities. Sometimes people say that they know how to plant, but we have seen failures. So, you have to not do like before, but adapt to the times. (field notes 2012)

6.11. Panela processing complete: Dried blocks ready for consumption. Author photo.

The agricultural centers thus serve as a more localized and communitarian version of the Campesino University.

These spaces of agricultural experimentation are part of the Community-wide project to nurture what they call *una agricultura profética* (a prophetic agriculture), in which the land becomes more fertile through cultivation (Brígida González, personal interview 2018). This relational practice of polyculture prioritizes planting diversified crops. Countering monocropping is rooted in an understanding of the earth as a living being, as one member explained: "The problem is that campesinos just want to cultivate one thing, and that's it. But I tell them, 'If a person only eats bananas, that is going to be bad for their health. Well, for the land it is the same. You have to plant many things, and in the same way, it feeds the land'" (field notes 2013). Like other Peace Community members and similar to certain indigenous and black communities, he expressed a communicative relationship with land. Land is not an inert object; it is a living being that requires nourishment and a "varied, healthy diet," just like humans. The quote signals how small-scale agriculture is not necessarily "sustainable": a relational territoriality is the product of political practice, not an "essence" of particular peoples. By focusing on embodied practices, we see how agricultural centers are places within the broader territory to nurture this anticolonial relationality and support their form of peace as self-determination.

6.12. Alter-territorialities: Harvesting squash in the Agricultural Center. Author photo.

SELF-SUFFICIENT FARMS

Applying lessons learned in the Campesino University and agricultural centers, as of 2014 there were at least two efforts within the Peace Community to create totally self-sufficient farms (*granjas autosuficientes*). The following narrative is composed from a series of conversations, interviews, and visits to a self-sufficient farm in 2013 and 2014 with food sovereignty pioneer Javier Sánchez (personal interview 2013; field notes 2013, 2014).

Javier began by situating the farm within the broader work and network

6.13. "Agricultura profética": Polyculture over monoculture. Author photo.

of the Community: "The idea behind this farm is very simple. This is a project that stems from the trajectory of the Peace Community over these sixteen years. I have had the ability to visit many other places in and outside Colombia. And the truth is that I have been able to look and learn. . . . Going to Cauca, indigenous communities, and Cali, for instance. I bring seeds and we exchange. I bring back other seeds. . . . This small farm that I am constructing with my family is the fruit of learning in other places." This speaks to the concrete effects of such solidarity networks: the sharing of seeds is a dialogical performance of knowledge production, in which campesinos learn from, with, and inspire each other.

He went on to emphasize the farm's goal—total self-sufficiency and food sovereignty—and why this was so important for campesinos in today's era of neoliberal free trade agreements (FTAs) and toxicity: "The fundamental idea is to make it self-sufficient as a family, which, in this region, I venture to say, does not yet exist. . . . That we have alternatives . . . to have our own food. To not depend on the outside world. This is a very complicated question today, now that there are the FTAs and the problem of genetically modified organisms. Because of the multinationals, our food is more and more poisoned." Despite these challenges, Javier also saw many opportunities for organic alternatives: "The idea is to cultivate without chemicals and genetically-modified seeds. Our advantage here is that we have so much land. And it is so fertile, producing without almost any fertilizer."

6.14. An alter-roof for an "other" politics of emancipation. Author photo.

We proceeded to a walking tour of the farm, including the thatched-roof house, water collection-storing site, fishpond, vegetable and fruit garden, and animal feeding stations. "Look here, the house's roof. The straw reeds are so simple. I have the tree that they come from planted right here. I will not have the problem of 'I have to go buy . . . ,' no. This is an alternative. It doesn't cost me anything. Besides, it is a tradition of our grandparents. It is an alternative, because this keeps the house cool and you can sleep, no matter how hot it is." I reacted by saying: "It is so interesting that your grandparents' technology is an 'alternative'! Modern technology has become so dominant, to where you need money to buy everything. A self-made and sustainable thatch roof then becomes an alternative, when it was a norm in the past." We continued as he responded:

> And I love it. Look here, these plants, including bamboo, which hold the hillside together and protect the water. We have about five hundred bamboos planted. It is also an alternative to build houses.
>
> What I need is a biogas system: you put animal excrement in a tube where it passes to a tank and ferments, and you have biogas. It is an alternative because you do not need to cut down wood to burn for cooking food. But to buy all the materials costs 2.5 million Colombian pesos [equivalent to approximately US$1,300 at the time], which I don't have. So, we are going to work with what we have.

6.15. Ecological dignity: Plant leaf boreh used as fish food after and before being fed to the fishes. Author photo.

>This is *boreh*. I feed it to the fish, and have it planted right here. The fish like to eat it. What I need is more fish, to have enough for our consumption.
>
>And this plant here, I brought it from an indigenous community in Cauca, to use as feed for chickens. It is a special food. And look at this portable pen for chickens to stay in. After a while, you move it and plant something there, since the chickens' manure fertilizes the land. So simple and useful!
>
>There are many fruit trees here: papayas, pineapple, tangerines, and oranges.... Look, a type of squash! Yucca. Beans. And up on that hillside I am going to plant food. I will rotate crops: yucca, rice, maize, and beans.... And this is the garden. Tomatoes, aloe, coffee, lulo, and medicinal plants: basil, ginger, lemongrass. See how wonderful coriander leaf smells!

Javier couldn't contain his enthusiasm, expressing that love of rural life that continues to drive the Peace Community's struggle. He also spoke to relationships with non–human beings: "I love the countryside. I love to plant. Look at all the wild animals around here. I take care of them, too, planting food for them—fruits—so that they enjoy themselves and come to sing in the surrounding area. I have fun along with them."

While it is an individual family farm, he envisioned the farm as a place of inspiration for other campesinos who need not become dependent on cash crops, markets, or external foundations. He lamented the fact that many farmers resigned themselves to mono-cropping, day labor, or the coca economy:

> I conceive of a project like this, which is also being carried out in other parts of the Peace Community, as a little school. Because various people come and learn, in order to then put in practice what they see here. It makes such a difference for people to see new alternatives. Even here, in this region, there are people and families who have fifty or even more than one hundred hectares of land. But often you see those youth merely work as day laborers on someone else's farm or even harvesting coca. Why don't they have enough food, despite so much land? It is a shame.

He continued, addressing the question of size and the need for strategic thinking: "This farm is four hectares. According to what I have seen and learned, you need only about two hectares to be able to be self-sufficient. Everything you see was constructed over the past two years. With this project people are going to realize that they do not need such large amounts of land to survive, even in the middle of a conflict like ours. We only need a small space. But we need to know how to work. And we have to know how to think." While some fellow campesinos similarly grow a variety of food crops, he turned to the fact that many community members continue to focus on harvesting cacao, the area's primary crop:

> Some think that it is all about going to the market. I have always said that communities need to think about food sovereignty. We have to change the mentality, the mentality of *everyone*, little by little, including community leaders. This is a cacao-growing area, and some people live off chocolate alone. They sell it and with those earnings buy everything else they need. Last year there was a good cacao harvest. But this year, it isn't producing. I spent three years in the baby banana project, which at the time sold for a good price. But that ultimately ended, and I returned to cacao. But we have to learn from those experiences and have another strategy.
>
> I love talking about a space that is small, but sustainable for a family. You notice that no one is investing money. This is to see what one family can do on their own. Without those moneys that finance projects, which sometimes do so much damage because there is money in the middle of everything.

His comments critiqued external financing that can incite internal divisions over money. If you are working for campesino dignity, autonomy, and community, then your political and financial strategies have to be consistent with those practices, subjectivities, and values. Ultimately they can cohere into a particular territorial process. By strengthening community autonomy, this farm facilitates the Peace Community's independence from—and refusal of—guerrilla, paramilitary, and army forces. Similar to how

San José de Apartadó has been inspirational for other peace movements in Colombia and beyond (García de la Torre et al. 2011; Nieri 2007), this self-sufficient farm is designed as a strategic place and practice to inspire other members *within* the community.

Javier explained the importance of food sovereignty in conversation with a critique of capitalism and the state:

> The idea is to think and act differently from a state. A state that all the time has trampled, killed, displaced us. It wants to exterminate us. I see that the grand capitalists, those who run this planet, want to make all of humanity submit to them. You are at their mercy if you have to, say, buy clothes or a car. In the city you have to buy everything. If I am able to stop going to the market, I would say that I am not supporting the state. Because everything that happens in cities is managed by the state. There you are always a slave to the state. I want to be independent and different from the state.

For him, as for so many Peace Community members, the state is understood as a capitalist institution that undermines self-reliance and autonomy, which correlates with the oppressive nature of modernity-coloniality. This is the system to which these farms are imagined as an alternative, in which there is a rethinking of money and what constitutes the "good life." As Javier asserted, "I think that with my thatched home and all the crops, it is a good life! A rich person that has lots of money and many things lives in fear that they will be kidnapped or that others will steal from them. That's not a good life. Because people are still interested in money." He continued, "The fact is, people live in that world," pointing over his shoulder toward San José town and Apartadó to symbolize urbanizing areas in accordance with the logics of capitalism and state power, as a contrast to where his farm was. "You work so much that you don't even have time to spend with your children. For me, that's not life! We have to live in another world, another way of living." Congruent with the World Social Forum's slogan of "Another World Is Possible," this vision infers that for campesinos to live dignified lives, there has to be a rupture with the state system, rather than mere reforms of the system. Dignity requires the creation of "another world" through an emancipatory "other" politics.

For Javier, key aspects of creating this other world include being open to new ideas, making mistakes, and learning within the family and the community. As another window into the Peace Community's embodied spatial practices, he described working with his preschool-age son: "Hopefully I will make mistakes so that I can learn. You have to make errors in order to learn. . . . You make your path by walking. . . . My son, he wants to do everything I do. . . . And he has an advantage: he asks questions. For instance, chopping down plants, he asks, 'And this one?' I say, 'Yes.' Then he says, 'And this?' I respond, 'No, that one is used for such-and-such.'" In other words, multigenerational and interfamily collective work and learning foment the innovation and sustainability crucial for a decolonial politics.

Surprisingly, these self-sufficient farms remain relatively invisible both in scholarship on the Peace Community and in the Community's own press releases. Appreciating the productive layers of this particular territory requires engagement with its "hidden transcript of resistance" (Scott 1990). As we overlooked the farm at the end of tour, Javier concluded, "This is a hidden place. It is like a secret place because you can't see it [from other farms or trails]. You only see it when you come here. And even if you just stumbled on this place, you wouldn't see all the things that are cultivated. But if they are shown to you, you begin to see. It's like entering into another world." I argue that the same kind of invisibility characterizes alter-peaces and alter-territorialities in communities like San José de Apartadó. A broader and more systematic approach to conceptualizing territory allows us to see the complexity of diverse productions of political space. If we reduce territory to a "place" or a bounded area controlled by a certain group, we can miss the social relations and political subjects produced by such a set of places and practices. If territory is reducible to "places occupied by violence to be fled from" (Connolly 1994)—like peace as repressive state "security"—then the term is obviously not one to guide an emancipatory politics. Yet through self-sufficient farms, campesino networks, and solidarity caravans, the Peace Community simultaneously creates an alter-peace and alter-territory.

If peace for the Peace Community means actively refusing to participate in the war and building community, then we see the politics of this peace through their territorial practices. The Peace Community's territorial formation is visible when we analyze the political subject who produces and is produced by its series of practices, places, and values. These include solidarity caravans, Campesino University gatherings, meeting places that are circular, and agricultural centers and self-sufficient farms. These manifest in concert with other aspects of their communal process, including their values of resistance, justice, and community; the weekly comunitario workday; autonomous education programs; and places of memory through stones and commemorations. Created through practice rather than being some kind of campesino or ethnic "essence," this territorial formation coheres to nurture a collective political subject. Rooted in valuing life over accumulation and collaboration over individualism, this is a relational subject, who seeks to not exploit human or nonhuman beings like objects. Rather, this subject seeks a reciprocal and embedded relationship with the land. San José's Peace Community thus exhibits a fluid and always shifting set of places and practices that forges a decolonial politics of ecological dignity in the process.

To social movements' insistence that peace depends on land, territory, and autonomy, the state has reacted with repression, given that the modern state interprets such movements "as a rival plan for division [rather] than to see division itself as the problem" (Elden 2013: 1). The Peace Community has a more fluid practice of both territory and peace, enacting both as an always-unfolding process, with no terminal point. This territoriality is not constituted by division and violence but by relationality with space, where community and space are integrated through common land, work groups, and human rights organization–campesino networks, which produce emancipatory and communal political subjects. Ultimately such relational territorialities nurture ecological dignity, where the lives of some are not reproduced at the expense of others. The Peace Community demonstrates how communities enact different geographies and territories without necessarily privileging the terminology of *territory*. Instead their territoriality emerges through practices of peace. By rejecting the dominant notion of territory as "demarcated and controlled space," the Peace Community allows for a broader conceptualization of territory. It allows us to attend to the territorial and political projects of an array of communities beyond those with an affirmative ethnic identity or demand for territory. Even where organizations such as the Peace Community eschew the language of territory, this concept remains useful precisely because it exceeds individual places or practices and thus speaks to a particular political design, which is not a design in the limited "modern" sense of a designer creating something outside of her/himself, but an "autonomous ontological design" (Escobar 2018) through practices, values, and places that cohere to produce an emancipatory collective political subject.

CHAPTER 7

"MEMORY IS THE STRENGTH OF OUR RESISTANCE"

An "Other Politics" through Commemoration

> What does memory mean,
> and why is it so important in Colombia,
> in the Peace Community,
> and for you?
>
> Memory, for me, is the strength of our resistance. *Why* is memory the strength of *resistance*?
>
> Because when you lose memory, you are condemned to repeat the same as before.
>
> We maintain memory and we always feel that someone who has passed away, all those very *important* people whom we have lost in the Community, continue to be with us.
>
> It's as if they didn't leave. They continue to be here.
>
> They continue to be here, from the *great beyond*. Their spirit is with us.
>
> And I believe that this has been what characterizes our Community, and that which gives us strength.
>
> (Brígida González, personal interview 2011)

Thus began my first official research interview in the Peace Community in August 2011. I conducted it with one of its most recognized members, Doña María Brígida González. Her immediate response about the meaning of memory immediately affirmed its importance as "the strength of resistance." She then asserted that the dead remain present. "Their spirit is with us," she said, stating not only once but twice that "they continue to be here." Doing so was seemingly an affirmation to this reality and to ensure that this truth would be heard. We proceeded to speak about the significance of memory for most of what became an eighty-five-minute interview.

Her opening statement immediately made clear that memory for the Peace Community is not something of the past or done simply to remember. It is about the present and completely integral to their political project.

In Doña Brígida's words, memory as an ongoing practice is essential in order to *not* "repeat the same as before," but instead create something new. Memory is a spatial and politicized performance in the present, rooted in place and landscape, that is related to the past and future (Bal 1999; Halbwachs 1992; Riaño-Alcalá 2002, 2015; Ricoeur 2004; Taylor 2003; Till 2005). Reading Diana Gómez Correal's (forthcoming) work on the "agency of the dead," I also began to engage with Peace Community members' comments on the active and present role of the dead, rather than simply people's remembrance of or "belief" in or about them.

This interview convinced me to make memory practices and objects a focus of this research project, and to continually question how memory is the strength of the Peace Community's resistance. Of the twenty Peace Community members with whom I addressed the topic of memory in interviews, only one person had no response when asked about it. The rest either brought up memory on their own, or immediately responded to my inquiry by affirming its importance and explaining how. This reflects the deep meaning that memory has for the Community, their internal work to create and maintain it, and how various members claim that memory is a fundamental part of what makes the Community what it is.

The Peace Community practices memory in a variety of ways. These include painting stones with victims' names, which are often placed together in monuments. They organize various commemoration gatherings each year, which include the anniversary of their founding on March 23; pilgrimages during *Semana Santa* (Holy Week), when they march to sites where they recount specific cases of assassination, nail crosses with names written on them onto trees, and speak about the significance of those people; the February pilgrimage to the sites of the 2005 massacre in Mulatos and La Resbalosa; and the June anniversary of leader Eduar Lanchero's death at his tomb in San Josecito. Another recurrent performance of memory is the frequent singing of the Community hymn during event gatherings. As part of their elementary education curriculum, Community children have a weekly class on memory in which they learn Community history. Meanwhile, Doña Brígida creates folk paintings of Community places and history, which are then gifted to people from all over the world to educate them about the Community's struggle. Finally, the Community periodically releases *comunicados*, or press release communiqués, through their website that document their history and armed groups' ongoing human rights violations.

To use Roger Simon, Sharon Rosenberg, and Claudia Eppert's (2000) terminology, memory can be a "difficult return" of bringing forth the presence of people and past events into the present through naming, images, sound, or symbols, as in Peace Community stones and massacre commemorations. Memory can also be a "strategic practice" in which a pedagogy or political deployment of traumatic history is deployed for sociopolitical goals. I posit that the notion of "difficult return" of living with loss subverts Sigmund Freud's (1917) false dichotomy of "melancholy" (never-ending attachment to what or whom is lost, prohibiting rehabilitation back into society) versus "mourning" (Freud's healthy response, ending in ultimate detachment). Memory as a "strategic practice"—which in the Peace Community's case includes demands of the state but also a nonviolent enacting of their own justice—provides an alternative to what Wendy Brown (1995) imagines as the insufficient yet only possible recourses for victims: forgetting (which is cruel and reinforces impunity), vindictive retaliation à la Friedrich Nietzsche's (2008) *ressentiment*'s moralizing revenge of the powerless (which fails to end violence), or capitulation to institutional state justice (that re-entrenches the very state responsible for harm).

Memory is best analyzed along with questions of peace and politics, because of the importance of memory work to speak to past and present realities of intersectional violences as well as its role as an integral action to create alternative forms of peace, justice, and social transformation (Courtheyn 2016). To separate peace, politics, and memory from each other unwittingly reinforces a discourse of post-conflict reconciliation state building where "justice" is often callously considered mutually exclusive with "peace" (Lederach 1997; Mertus and Helsing 2006). For instance, in her critique of peace discourse in Guatemala, Amy Ross (2012) argues, "The rich won the war, and the poor victims get to paint the memorials" in which "postwar peace" and memory work can serve as an obfuscation of persistent impunity and injustice. According to the dominant logic of transitional justice and post-conflict peacebuilding, you can have one or the other: either victims insist that war crimes be prosecuted, inducing armed actors to resist demobilization, or armed combatants agree to lay down arms to achieve "negative peace," but on the condition of amnesties and forgetting. According to the latter logic, the country in question must move *forward* toward reconciliation and not *backward* with vindictive and stagnant memory. These ideas problematically conform to the dominant, modern-colonial notions of peace as a lack of open warfare, justice as retributive punishment, memory as something of the past, and victims as stuck in the past (Gómez Correal 2016; Gómez Muller 2008).

I follow contemporary Colombian social movements' insistence on the importance of memory for peacebuilding (Argoty Pulido and Gómez Correal 2012; Díaz Montealegre, Pedraza, and de Pilar Suárez 2009; Riaño-Alcalá 2002, 2015). Karen Till (2012) argues that memory work as a "place-based ethics of care . . . might sustain more just possible futures" (5). Yet not all memory work is emancipatory. On the one hand, it can be mobilized for

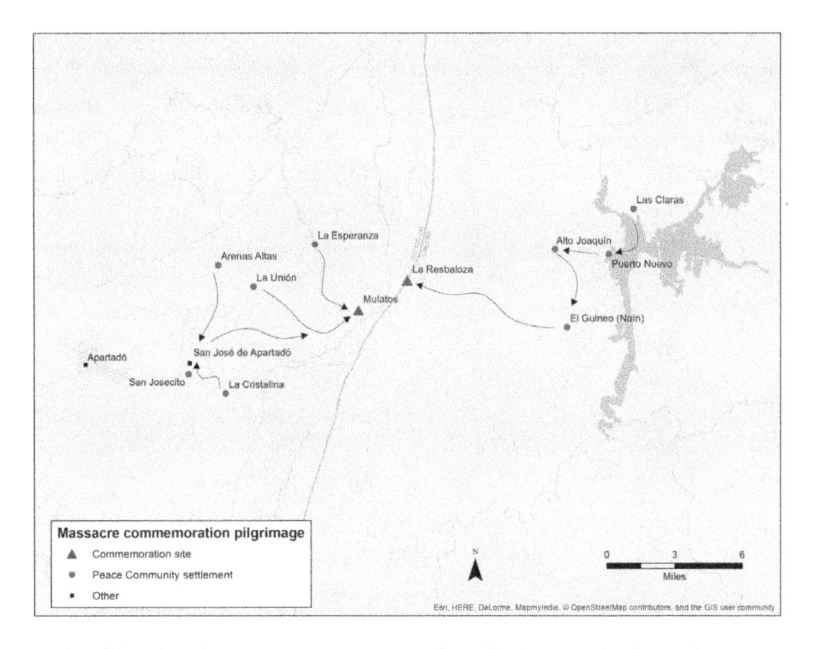

7.1. Mapping the massacre commemoration pilgrimage. Map by author.

xenophobic or other dangerous ends, resulting in reactionary violence and genocide (Bal 1999; Benjamin 2007a). On the other, it can serve to silence ongoing structural violence by presenting violent pasts as stark contrasts to a supposedly peaceful present (Tyner, Alvarez, and Colucci 2012). Moreover, disputes over memorialization can cause conflicts within social movements, as in the split within the Madres de la Plaza de Mayo movement in Argentina between Línea Fundadora's use of photos, assertion of their disappeared children's innocence, and support of state-sponsored monuments, and Asociación's insistence on a broader anticapitalist objective through educational and activist spaces in which the disappeared are recognized less as individual victims and instead as socialist revolutionaries (Bosco 2004, 2006). This begs the following questions: Which "just future" is imagined, by whom, and how might particular forms of memorialization contribute to such futures and to peace?

Building from my prior discussion of their alter-territoriality of ecological dignity, I trace in this chapter how the Peace Community produces radical trans-relational peace through their spatial, material, and embodied practices of memory. If Peace Community members define peace as both refusing to participate in the war and cultivating solidarity through community work, then what is the role of memory in the production of this peace? How do memory practices specifically contribute to this "other politics" of autonomy from state authority and capitalist dispossession at the

7.2. Memory materialized: Altar in the stone chapel in Mulatos, including pictures of Luis Eduardo Guerra and other victims. Author photo.

heart of modernity-coloniality? What is the role of memory practice in the production of a relational and collective Peace Community subject? Might their commemorations suggest forms of anti- or non-state justice?

I will proceed to explore different forms of San Jose's memory work and their significance for the Peace Community's political organization, defense of land, relationships with their solidarity network, and practices of justice. By exploring Community commemorations through pilgrimages, stones, and folk paintings, this chapter illuminates the ways they performatively embody and materialize an anticolonial emancipatory politics and geography of peace through memory.

EMBODIED AND PLACE-BASED MEMORY

This section offers an ethnographic account of what is often the Peace Community's largest annual gathering: the February pilgrimage to the sites of the 2005 massacre in Mulatos and La Resbalosa. A joint military and paramilitary operation killed eight campesinos. They included Peace Community founder and leader Luis Eduardo Guerra, Mulatos humanitarian zone coordinator Alfonso Bolívar Tuberquia, and three children. Every February 21, members converge from all of the Community's settlements at these sites. They are joined by representatives from other Colombian communities as well as accompaniers, lawyers, researchers, filmmakers, and journalists from Colombia and around the world.

While in Mulatos in 2013 Father Javier Giraldo (personal interview 2013) described how it became an annual event:

> Each February . . . on the 20th we hike up from San José, La Unión, et cetera. . . . The 21st, at the same hour when Luis Eduardo was assassinated—it was 7:30 or 8 a.m.—we say mass in the same site of the assassination. And after the mass, we go to La Resbalosa. We arrive at midday and we have a commemoration there where the other part of the massacre took place. . . . At that site there is another chapel, a site where [the army and paramilitaries] put the graves with the bodies. . . . And [ever since] we have never missed it. . . . Three months after [the massacre in 2005] . . . there was a pilgrimage . . . and the first chapel was inaugurated and, since then, the beginnings of recuperating this site.

I will proceed with a performative ethnographic account of the commemoration compiled from my audio recordings, field notes, and photographs from 2008, 2010, and 2014. To render the scene:

> The humid jungle air is filled with sounds of Spanish but also overlapping Italian, English, and German coming from the mix of brown, black, and white faces present. Do we number one, two, or three hundred who have walked hours through dirt, streams, mud, and rocky river paths? We are in La Resbalosa, named for the "slippery" and lush green hillsides we climbed to arrive here. The ground is covered with light green grass-like weeds, on which we stand or sit. Above a dark and dry brown dirt floor, the chapel around which we crowd stands with its gray tin roof and brown wooden walls and posts. A foot-long wooden cross and five half-foot crosses hang there. Below is a rainbow-colored flag ranging from purple to yellow to red; just above its white Italian letters spelling *PACE* is a picture collage of eight people. As Father Javier Giraldo solemnly takes the microphone, the sounds of dogs shuffling, and insects and birds chirping, fade away into the tropical forest. . . .

"MEMORY IS THE STRENGTH OF OUR RESISTANCE"

7.3. Decolonial peace: Enacting their own justice. Author photo.

"The workers cautioned him that if he returned, they would kill him, immediately.
Then, around two in the afternoon, they heard *how*
the arms became silent; you couldn't hear any more shots.
And Alfonso decided to return, to find out the fate of Sandra, and the *children*, and to face their same fate.
The workers waited, that night; he *didn't* come *back*.
The next day, through the entire morning, he *didn't* come *back*.
And so, they moved toward the house, slowly, with much caution.
They saw that there wasn't any movement in the house.
So, they began to enter.
In front of the house, they encountered a lot of blood.
. . .
And in this site
they found dried up cacao shells piled up
and they began to suspect that maybe the bodies had been buried.
. . .
And they sent a delegate to the Community to announce what had happened.
And the Community immediately began to organize a search commission.
More than one hundred people signed up to go the following day.
And they came first to this site, because they knew that *here*,
they were buried."

Father Giraldo proceeds to narrate their arrival to the sites. Military soldiers and lawyers from the Attorney General's office arrived simultaneously:

"Military soldiers began to call them *guerrillas*,
all the community members who were here,
and take their photographs, make jokes of them.
And the lawyers began the task of exhumation.
And one of the international accompaniers was able to *film*
some scenes of the exhumation, which are
horrifying
When they go pulling out the pieces of bodies.
And a lawyer
prohibited her, he told her that that was prohibited and that she could no longer continue filming.
And, she had to turn off her camera.
There remained here a *mystery*, about what happened
when Alfonso returned to his home,
his death, and the death of the children?
In the first two years afterward
the Attorney General's office's investigations
deviated toward a false account that attributed this crime to the *FARC*.
Two years later, the Attorney General's office,
due to *pressure* from a group of Congress members from the United States,
who had done their own investigation,
changed course and began to investigate the military soldiers
and the paramilitaries."

Citing declarations by demobilized paramilitaries, Father Giraldo then begins recounting details of the massacre.

"One of the paramilitaries, recounted that he *saw* the moment
when Alfonso returned, here to the house.
He came with the machete that all campesinos use.
At the moment when he returned, the soldiers hit him,
they made him kneel down on the floor
and insulted him.
But at the same time, the children, who were still alive
They moved toward him, to *hug* him.
Then, in that moment, the army soldiers and paramilitaries were discussing
if they would kill the children.
They were communicating by phone or radio with officers of the Brigade,
to consult about
what to do with the children?

The arguments that they put forth were that those children, when they grew up, could become guerrillas.
Others said that later,
the children would be able to *identify and recognize*
those who had committed the massacre.
And therefore it was better, to eliminate these possible witnesses."

My eyes water every time I hear, write about, or recount him talking about the killing of the children, a five-year-old girl and eighteen-month-old boy, and how they cut the bodies into pieces. Father Giraldo concluded:

"*This* was the terrible massacre that took place, at this site."
From portable speakers Father Giraldo plays a Catholic song whose lyrics sing: "When pain comes to your door, and sadness and oppression invade you, think about your pain, and that the Son of God also suffered."
He then asks me to read an excerpt from the Bible. References to the "struggle of good against evil" reverberate through my voice.
A Community leader had handed out postcards listing all 210 victims in San José de Apartadó to date, including photos of those killed in the 2005 massacre. After the mass one man from Córdoba who had recently joined the Peace Community remains there, holding his postcard. We speak as others drift away. His eyes water, holding and looking at the postcard. "The Colombian state has to be the most murderous of them all: it persecutes campesinos. But if we struggle in community, we can resist. . . . If I [had the opportunity], I would write in a book all of the atrocities, the things that have happened in this area. One day, I will have the opportunity to recount them."
We walk down the hillside from the massacre site. Community members take visitors to see their recently installed sugarcane-processing station. We smile as we look, and Community members tell us that the sugar we are consuming during the gathering was produced here. A Community leader asks Father Giraldo to bless the place, which he does with water and words: "From the beginning, the Peace Community has demanded and struggled for freedom, self-sufficiency, and solidarity." (field notes 2008, 2010, 2014)

A Community communiqué released in 2010, the day after the fifth annual commemoration of this massacre, ended with the following words: "In the midst of such sorrow, we are encouraged by the accompaniment of numerous groups from all the over the world, who share our unshakeable decision to not be crushed before death and shame, and share our love of life" (Comunidad de Paz de San José de Apartadó 2010).

This rendering is but a glimpse of what violence means and looks like to those resisting what Michael Taussig (1984) terms the "culture of terror" in zones of resource extraction and colonization. Through this performance

7.4. Co-performative witness. Photo by Gale Stafford, with permission.

of memory, the Peace Community levies its denunciation and at the same time enacts an autonomous form of justice through a "social sanction" (Javier Giraldo, personal interview 2013) of shaming the state's violence and impunity. A Community member stated that commemorations precisely "serve for other people to learn about what we have experienced and what war is like" (personal interview 2014).

Writing about Afro-Colombian communities in the Pacific region, Ulrich Oslender (2007) states that "narration itself, the message sent out into the world . . . is also resistance against the cultural elaboration of a generalized fear among local populations and breaks the silence that terror imposes as strategy of domination" (126). This is a deliberate process of memory making, which is not a "normal" reaction to violence, especially given the intense emotions and continued threats associated with retelling that can just as likely induce the person to want to "move away" from the harm, emotions, and violence rather than engage them (Ahmed 2004).

By voicing its recollections, the Peace Community harnesses the power of any production of history (Trouillot 1995) to reject the imposed state of modern-colonial dehumanization and "nonbeing" where racialized groups are deemed "other," subhuman, and expendable (Fanon 2008; Maldonado-Torres 2010). Like Línea Fundadora of the Argentinian Madres de la Plaza de Mayo, the Peace Community evokes the killings and the names of those killed. But they do not do so as a means to pressure state officials for offi-

7.5. Archived memories of the monument: FOR accompanier overlooks the central square of San José de Apartadó town in 2004, when the first victims monument (bottom left) still existed. Photo by Sarah Weintraub, with permission.

cial monuments. Rather, à la Madres' subgroup Asociación, this "difficult return" is part of an anti-state struggle.

In this difficult return of recounting the massacre details, the Peace Community reasserts the principles for which they have been attacked and continue struggling: freedom, self-sufficiency, and solidarity. In so doing they identify what members call their "project of life" in dialectical opposition to the state's "project of death," a reverse Manichaenism of defining what you are against as a necessary step toward building another world (Fanon 2004; Reyes 2012a). As Eduar Lanchero argued in his closing statement at the 2010 Peace Community caravan in Sumapaz, "Hope is when we no longer hate the murderer. Hope is when we build collectively. When we make life, from wherever we are" (Buenaventura 2011).

This autonomous politics is not isolationist; it brings people together to communicate across multiple organizations in a collective struggle. The commemorations are thus a dialogical performance among Community members and allies, in which Father Giraldo plays a central role and through which the Peace Community simultaneously writes and spreads their history. However, before expounding on these networks' significance in this memory project, I wish to turn to a second means through which the community performs its own history: painting stones.

ABSENCE AND PRESENCE THROUGH MATERIAL MEMORY

Another way Community members commemorate the dead is to take a rock from the river, color it with paint, and write the person's name on it. In the town center of San José, prior to the Peace Community's displacement from the town, they had constructed a monument of "stones arranged into three peaks to symbolize the Abibe mountain range. And with different colors, they had written the names of all of the victims, one on each stone" (Javier Giraldo, personal interview 2013). State forces destroyed this monument following the police's occupation of the town in 2005. But the Community continues to arrange stones in victims monuments in their new gateway village and at massacre sites. By continually remaking these monuments, they materially mark the landscape with their history, manifest their commitment to denounce injustice and impunity, and continually challenge the state's project to erase such traces of army-paramilitary violence.

Yet the stones, like recounting massacres, are not directed at the state alone. Father Giraldo discussed the role of stones in founding a new village: "When the displacement [from San José town] was immanent in Holy Week of 2005 . . . we picked up all the stones and marched toward San Josecito, which at that time was merely a field. We did this to bring the memory of the dead first. And we began to construct the village around the space where all the stones of the dead were. It was . . . the symbolic center of the Community's memory, you see? We build the life of the community around that center" (personal interview 2013). In other words, if peace for the Peace Community is not merely a question of non-collaboration with armed groups but also about creating community, then memory with stones is central to nurturing that solidarity and connection. I asked Doña Brígida:

> And the monuments of the victims.
> In San José you constructed *stone* upon stone.
> And here it is in a *circle*.
> And in the commemorations, you put down the stones.
> Why the stones and why the distinct ways
> of arranging and showing them?

Because . . . these stones have a deep meaning,
they, you can't destroy a stone.
A stone always remains intact.
You paint it and later it stays the same.
And in those stones *rests*
all the historical memory of compañeros y compañeras,
children, and adults who have fallen
for the construction of this world, alternative world.
. . .
We say that, even *by themselves*, the stones speak!
. . .
Therefore we believe that maintaining memory,
for example, the emblem of the Community. The memory museum.
The memory monument.
In them rests all of this remembrance,
of our compañeros.
Who . . . brought us together in meetings.
Who spoke to us about our construction, about our organization.
And how to obtain international support.
And I believe that, as for us,
this memory is as important for those who come from elsewhere.
Who look at how, we always maintain,
that memory is what strengthens us.

(González, personal interview 2011)

In what ways do "the stones speak?" I have held and painted such stones during commemorations in San José and in classroom and conference presentations about the Peace Community. After holding stones, fellow participants and I commonly express how we feel their weight. There is also a coldness and a silence to the stones. You see the name of the individual

7.6. "Even the stones speak." Photo by author, Julia Drude, and Moira Birss.

person written on it. This is a power of absence that can testify to particular realities—such as unrepresentable slavery, genocide, and massacres—with more meaning than a verbal articulation (Bernard-Donals and Glejzer 2001; Nyong'o 2009; Oliver 2001; Till 2005). Painted with the names of victims, these make memory into material matter (Saltzman 2006) in a way that makes an absence visible. Words definitely do something (Austin 2007), as in recounting the massacre, but objects and silences do things as well (Conquergood 2002).

The stones spatially imprint those people who have died upon the landscape, evoking their presence, wisdom, and contributions to the Community, which serve as the material, symbolic, and ethical base for communal life. They are material creations as a form of permanent remembrance against forgetting, yet reflect memory as always practiced in the present. I have noticed how painted stones, rather than staying the same, in fact change: the paint fades with time, weather, and humidity. This necessitates adults and children painting new stones. This speaks to how objects intended to be fixed or permanent are never fully so, but by fading can induce ongoing action and remembrance.

Another way the stones speak is by communicating history to others. A member stated, "Monuments testify to the fact that those people lived and struggled, for others to see and tell the truth about that reality. Those remains that are preserved there . . . are so that someone who comes from elsewhere looks and says, 'Oh, yes, they were massacred campesinos. They were people who struggled for peace, for life'" (personal interview 2014). Similar to the pilgrimages, the stones materially both denounce these assassinations and present their principles of life, peace, and small-scale farming

7.7. Embodied memory: Community member painting the names of the 2005 massacre victims onto stones during a commemoration at the site in Mulatos. Author photo.

that distinguish them from the armed groups. One man from Córdoba mentioned the stones when he described his first visit to San Josecito during the discernment process of deciding whether or not to join the Community: "In the meeting, I didn't understand the idea of being 'neutral.' And seeing the gringos [white foreigners], I thought, 'It must be that they bring in lots of money.' But I believed that this Community was good. They told me, 'The Community isn't about money. There have been many deaths.' And they showed me the stones. . . . [I said to myself] 'I'm in'" (personal interview 2014). He spoke both to the anticapitalist nature of the Peace Community process—focused on rupturing with modern-colonial subjectivities driven by accumulation and individualism—as well as the educative role of memory performance. In addition to honoring the victims, the stones and commemorations serve to educate children and new members about the history and ongoing stakes of the struggle, as well as to integrate them into the collective process. Another member from Córdoba who had recently joined spoke about the significance of attending his first commemoration: "I went to Mulatos, and wow, to see all of that about the massacre, the way that you don't forget, and how Luis Eduardo Guerra also died for me. It is similar to the death of Christ" (field notes 2010). This comment also signals the lens through which Father Giraldo and many Community members understand and frame their victimization as a corollary to the unjust yet necessary crucifixion of Jesus of Nazareth toward an alternative world. Another said, "Even though I didn't know him, I realized that Luis Eduardo died for me, too. I owe the benefits of being a Community member to him and other leaders" (personal interview 2014). Therefore the commemorations—in addition to their school curriculum on memory—serve to bridge new members with those who came before them.

If a liberatory decolonial politics requires the construction of collective rather than individualistic subjects, as necessary for sustained organization (Fanon 2004; Hallward 2011), then the material and embodied nature of the pilgrimages and painting of stones is a means through which a collective Peace Community subject is produced. This is true among older and newer members, children and adults, as well as between the living and the dead. It is to the production and reinforcement of this community's "collective consciousness" (Guha 1983), to which I now turn.

CONSCIOUSNESS AND COMMITMENT

Peace Community members tend to emphasize three themes when they talk about memory's significance: first, the duty of remembering and honoring the dead; second, its role in maintaining their commitment and strategy; and third, the importance of sharing this history with others. On commemoration as a duty, Doña Brígida stated, "To not commemorate means that the Peace Community is finished" (personal interview 2011). Another member said, "If we forget, we don't do anything. It is important that we have gone through difficult times. We cannot forget or go back to the same point" (field notes 2012). This is consistent with how "individuals and groups recall the past not for its own sake, but as a tool to bolster different aims and agendas" (Hoelscher and Alderman 200: 349). That being said, while commemorations occur in specific moments, they are not something "extra" added onto the Community's daily campesino life, as merely a "bolstering" or means toward a goal. Memory is a constitutive element of their consciousness: what defines their struggle and who they are.

At marked and unmarked sites throughout San José where people have been killed, it is common for community members to talk about those events. Being in those places evokes those people and stories about them (Riaño-Alcalá 2002; Till 2005). A member reflected, "On the commemoration pilgrimages, we are reminded of the paths that people walked by walking those same paths. You are reminded that you might face the same fate" (personal interview 2014). The act of walking in a pilgrimage reenacts the life path and struggle of those people, which induces reflection and can reinforce one's commitment to continue the struggle. Moreover, when former accompaniers return to visit San José, community members frequently say upon seeing us, "Ah, you remembered us!" As we often respond, "But I remember you every day, whether I am here or not!" What community members seemingly point to is how space, memory, and politics are mutually constituted. There is a something about memory—and solidarity—that requires being there, where returning evokes remembrance but memory also requires returning to particular places.

Members described their emotions associated with going to the massacre sites. Montoya shared, "We feel happy, because we are remembering that person who walked with us. . . . A joy. . . . It is a delight for us. Because we know that we went. We fulfilled that duty that we had. Because it is duty . . . to remember, in a walking caravan, go there with Father [Giraldo]. . . . I feel sadness, when we arrive there. Because . . . we go to see where they killed them, what they did, but later, we have that memory here" (personal interview 2012). Another member explained, "Personally, when I go on a commemoration, to where they have killed people, I feel bitterness, anger! I mean, how is it possible that we are living peace, struggling, and . . . [the government and guerrillas] who speak about peace [in the Havana negotiations] are killing us who are living it?" (personal interview 2014). Speaking to the intensity of the "difficult return," these emotions—notably sadness, anger, as well as joy and fulfillment—are harnessed toward reflection about those individuals' and the Community's history and ongoing work. At the 2014 gathering, a leader stressed the difference between commemoration and celebration: "February 21st is not a celebration. It is a *commemoration* to reflect on the work of the Peace Community. When you don't want to work collectively, in work groups . . . it is throwing away the sacrifice of these people. . . . Those who died did not do so in vain but because they believed in this. This is a time for reflection about the great difficulties and strength of this process. It is to feel the sorrow, those who have been tortured and assassinated, and to keep walking" (field notes 2014). Similarly, many organizations in Colombia and across Latin America talk about memory as connecting current movements to past resistance: its people, strategies, art, and culture (Gómez Correal 2012). Memory is not a limited "remembering" but rather an act of integrating struggles. By evoking fallen leaders' presence and principles into the present space as a continual guide, the Peace Community embraces the "agency of the dead" (Gómez Correal, forthcoming) and their speaking through the stones. This alter-territoriality of radical trans-relational peace is constituted through a relationality not only between humans and nature, but also between the living and the dead, in which there is dignity and solidarity not only among the living but with the dead. Here death is not an end point but a political beginning (Gómez

Correal, forthcoming) of an emancipatory decolonial politics of ecological dignity.

The commemorations result in regular gatherings throughout the year among Community members who live in dispersed settlements. For instance, relatives who live in different villages reunite, such as grandparents and grandchildren spending time together. Members and accompaniers also sing the Community hymn together and share communal meals. "The pilgrimages are good because you gather with many people and meet new folks, which is especially nice for those of us who live more far away and secluded from the rest" (personal interview 2014). Following the 2014 Holy Week pilgrimage, women played a soccer match, with music blasting in the background and the entire community cheering them on. While recounting the massacre details is very solemn, people tend to be happy during and after the gatherings, through which Community members, despite the ongoing war, nonetheless live "peace as community" in the present.

As a testament to the immense work involved with memory practice (Muzaini 2013), the pilgrimages require extensive planning and organization. In advance Community members build or renovate the chapels where the commemorations will take place as well as gazebos that serve as meeting places and where people can hang hammocks for sleeping. They organize visitors' arrivals and the transportation of food and supplies on people's backs and horses during and prior to the gatherings. The commemorations are thus manifestations of their commitment to "participate in community work."

Of course maintaining a collective work ethic over time is challenging. As illustrated in the opening vignette of Part III, a common response to internal disagreements and external threats is to leave the Peace Community. As described by deceased leader Eduar Lanchero: "It is very difficult to get up every morning and stay coherent in building a different world. There are so many things that attack us, so many ways of being discouraged. Even if the resistance is getting smaller, and many people get tired, it is up to all of us to help each other to carry on, to walk together through all difficulties" (Buenaventura 2011). This is a core constituent and challenge of a liberatory politics: maintaining collectivity and commitment amid challenging and seemingly insurmountable conditions. If the commitment to collective work makes an anticolonial politics of autonomy possible, then I argue that memory practice is precisely one way this cohesion is sustained. Community members frequently reference the strength they channel from the dead: "Memory is *important*. If you have a *fallen* leader or relative . . . it gives you strength to continue" (personal interview 2013).

It is worth repeating a quote from the introduction to this part. Alluding to people who have left the Peace Community to work independently or who have been excluded for breaking community rules, member Montoya affirmed that maintaining one's commitment "is about remembering what we've gone through, what we've suffered. You remember the past so as not to be fooled by what the state and the armed groups are up to. That memory keeps you working in community, as neutral, and autonomous. It's about *a love for the other and working together.* . . . remembering what you have lived, and that working alone is dangerous and not communal" (field notes 2014). This passage conveys two key elements: commemorations provide a space for historical and contextual analysis to guide the Community's work moving forward, and they inspire renewed motivation to work collectively. It speaks to how places of denunciation induce a space for new subjectivities to emerge (Ceceña 2012). In other words, "inhabiting the norm" (Mahmood 2005) of communal remembrance produces and nurtures this collective political subject. And as noted by Judith Butler (2004b), "Perhaps mourning has to do with agreeing to undergo a transformation (perhaps one should say submitting to a transformation)" (21). It is part of a subjective shift toward a "re-existence" as a community of peace (Gonçalves 2006; Hardt and Reyes 2012; Zibechi 2012).

These themes emerged when I asked Doña Brígida whether she perceived stronger commitment following the pilgrimages: "Yes, in the Community rules, for sure! You work with more zest, and with more strength, more definition. Because [during the gatherings] you can sketch many goals. That memory helps you awaken with more goals to continue building" (personal interview 2011). She also related outside witnesses' role in this co-performance of memory: "When you go to Mulatos you feel like, wow, there is so much life. There is so much life even in the midst of so many threats, so much adversity, but there is so much life. And even more so, when there are many people from around the world, you feel that joy. . . It gives you a lot of strength" (personal interview 2011). This renewed energy is something I have frequently witnessed over the years: more "revolutionary enthusiasm" (Newton 2002) in meetings and the weekly comunitario workdays in the wake of a pilgrimage. Again, memory here is not about recovering or going back to a nostalgic past, as is often the case in fascist or genocidal politics (Benjamin 2007b), but to simultaneously perform another history and produce another present and future.

The commemorations are frequently followed by general assemblies—in which the Community analyzes their context and makes collective decisions—as well as sessions of the Campesino University. In Montoya's words, commemorations are "so useful because there is a sharing with other communities who have close relationships with us" (personal interview 2012).

Hence the commemoration pilgrimages are spaces of cultivating collective cohesion but also contextual analysis and strategic direction. Such "reflexive dialogues within the movements that permanently look at and rethink their objectives, analyse reality and reinvent their action" (Holland and Gómez Correal 2013: 155) are indispensable for a liberatory politics' sustainability and effectiveness. The commemorations thus reflect and produce the collective consciousness (Guha 1983) and collective will (Hallward 2011) integral to members' ongoing politicization and emancipation.

DEFENDING LAND IN MOVEMENT NETWORKS

The commemorations are also an essential part of the construction of this alter-territory and "alter-geopolitics" (Koopman 2011) of transnational solidarity networks. They induce national and international witnesses to spread information about past violence, current threats, and the Peace Community alternative to war. They also increase security prior to, during, and potentially after the pilgrimage. Beforehand the Community and international accompaniers send letters to governmental authorities and human rights networks to raise the profile of the gathering. This focuses attention on San José de Apartadó, increasing the potential repercussions of armed groups' attacks committed in the presence of so many national and international witnesses. Members talk about how the armed actors tend to "retreat a bit" (Javier Sánchez, field notes 2013) during such gatherings: "Right now, it is so calm! Because of the pilgrimage. Maybe the paramilitaries will enter at a later date, but not for the time being" (personal interview 2013).

Therefore memory work is deeply embedded with their defense of land and life. Returning to the interview with Doña Brígida González, on the significance of the painted stones, I noted that:

> [A stone] is also something from the earth.
> For you, land is part of the resistance,
> and of the alternative.
> It's resisting being displaced again,
> and the alternative is working the land,
> and the stones come *from there*!

Of course!

> So, it's showing through things that you have here,
> and specifically, a stone,
> as you say, it lasts forever.

Well, the stones come from the land.
They are in the riverbanks, and they are in the soil.
But at the same time, we *struggle*
to take care of the land.
To *defend* the land.

7.8. Relational peace through pilgrimage: Walking between veredas in San José de Apartadó. Author photo.

Because of another intense war against the people. Why? Because in the land there are many mineral resources. There are so many national and international interests. In one form or another they want to take the land away from the people, and leave the people disadvantaged, without a place to work.

(personal interview 2011)

She veered away from my question about stones in the land to affirm their land struggle. And the pilgrimages, by mobilizing bodies across space, contribute to the defense of land in a particular way.

The following is an extended excerpt from a field note I wrote following the 2014 massacre commemoration:

Walking down from Mulatos, that military helicopter hovered in front of us. As we slid down the mountain and our boots got stuck in the wet mud, the helicopter lingered above, so close. Would they fire? Those who want this land (for oil palm or coca plantations, hydroelectric power, coal or gold mines) can *see* us, in different ways. The helicopter physically sees our bodies, but they also see us through the letters, embassy meetings, and accounts we spread before and after. This is radical performance geography.

It's less about the immediacy of the presence and dissuasion network, and more about constantly walking, continually having our bodies make the territory. People converged upon Mulatos from villages to the west, north, and east. In that movement, there is not only a different type of visibility that is created, but also transformations as people (Ceceña 2012; Fanon 1965; Mahmood 2005). When we work together in solidarity, care for one another, and reflect on the immensity of the struggle and our place in it, our bodies are pushed to certain limits. Our bodies are worn down, and made to ache and feel pain, but also strengthened. Like Father Javier said as we walked: "You can't explain what it's like to walk these trails. You have to experience it to know."

It's both, on the one hand, the internationals accompanying the Community in terms of providing encouragement, relegitimizing the struggle, sending letters to authorities, and being ready in case of confrontation with state armed forces on the trails, and also, on the other, the Community accompanying us, not letting anyone fall behind, getting horses for people who can't walk, and cooking the meals in Mulatos.

Again, of crucial importance to the pilgrimages: you walk to those sites. On the one hand, it is what happens there because of the "strategic practices" and "difficult return" (Simon, Rosenberg, and Eppert 2000) in those specific places, which include assemblies, Campesino University sessions, and people's conversations made possible by the memorial gathering. However, on the other hand, it's also about the *going there* itself, that transformational process of pilgrimage. Again, I'm convinced: "memory is the strength of the resistance."

[One international visitor] stated that she was not very impressed with or inspired by the commemoration pilgrimage: "Father Giraldo does almost all of the talking." Wow, that really jolted me. The Peace Community mobilized people from every one of its settlements and has refused to be silent for nine years about such a horrific massacre. Just the act itself of all these people moving in the land is amazing, as is building community across settlements during the assembly, not to mention the level of organization, commitment, and consciousness required for everything to take place.

To defend life and land, you have to walk and be the land, and live the transformation as our bodies, women, men, children, horses, and dogs move through it. This is a territorial practice: our bodies are in motion. (field notes 2014)

Through the commemorations and resettlements of these villages, they are converting spaces of death into spaces of life. This is epitomized by the inauguration of the Luis Eduardo Guerra Mulatos Peace Village in 2010, two years after they returned to re-create a Community settlement there. The families who have resettled the area grow corn, sugarcane, vegetables, and raise animals; they store their crops in a communal building—that was once a health center built by the Patriotic Union party—and there are a communal kitchen and library. This food sovereignty and commoning

7.9. From a space of death to a space of life: "Welcome to the Luis Eduardo Guerra Peace Village: Neutral zone." Author photo.

(Federici 2010) reflect and sustain their autonomous politics through an alternative economy. Many call the settlement the new "heart" of the Community, not only because it lies at a midpoint between dispersed settlements "where we have gatherings and community assemblies" (personal interview 2013) but also as a spiritual core. Doña Brígida commented, "In [Mulatos], there are so many people, invisible but they are there, because of a struggle. They are buried, where Luis Eduardo gave his life. . . . This land is so productive, and today Mulatos is the site of the Peace Village experiment" (personal interview 2011). During a public gathering at the site, Community leader Gildardo Tuberquia reflected: "Luis Eduardo himself said that we have to struggle for the land. When they killed him, I came here, and anyone could see the fertile, productive land. So, we had to return. . . . A site where there was death, [now] there is life" (field notes 2013). Many of those forcibly displaced from San José de Apartadó in the 1990s never returned to live there. Some have never even gone back to visit. One such relative of various Community members, now living in the city of Medellín, told me that he has terrible memories of the place and is too scared to ever return (field notes 2014). For him, as astutely noted by FOR international accompanier Gina Spigarelli (field notes 2013), the area remains a place of death, but the spatial practice of the Peace Community has created new memories and places. As one Community member argued, "Sharing those stories with other people—the massacres and also joys—is like reliving them, and to then continue forward" (personal interview 2014). The Mulatos Peace Village is a testament to the brutal violence they have suffered and continue to face, but also to their determination and alternative of communal work, food sovereignty, and remembrance.

Memory is thus part and parcel of the way this community recuperates and produces spaces. This occurs both through material objects, such as stones and chapels, as well as the embodied movement of the pilgrimages across villages. To use the terms of Gilles Deleuze and Félix Guattari (1988), there is a "reterritorialization" amid an ongoing "deterritorialization" by the war, in which the Peace Community reconstitutes itself as a collective. The Community thus insists that it is not through forgetting or repressing that modernity-coloniality's culture of terror and control is subverted or reversed. Conversely, the "difficult return" (Simon, Rosenberg, and Eppert 2000) of their dialogical memory performance signals how the "spectacle" of death through victims' and witnesses' bodies and consciousness (Taussig 1984) can in fact be re-performed in a way that counters that "space of death" with spaces of memory and life.

As Gómez Correal (2012) puts it, memory is a "political verb" (248). A Kankuamo elder in Colombia observed that memory "does not need to be reconstructed by you. You have to be reconstituted by it" (Maestre 2012: 111). Through stones and pilgrimages, the Peace Community creates memory narratives and objects to testify to their reality, but that memory practice also produces the Peace Community itself.

CREATING AND SPREADING HISTORY

Doña Brígida González's paintings of Peace Community places and events are another form of material memory that creates and spreads their history. Glued to a piece of wood and using a folk aesthetic, each painting depicts a particular scene, such as a massacre, displacement, Community village resettlement, or the area's geography. Doña Brígida has created hundreds of these paintings, gifting them to individuals and organizations in their solidarity network. For example, during a visit I made to her house in July 2014, Doña Brígida was sketching a painting featuring cacao trees, work groups, and the Community's chocolate processing machinery for international researcher Gwen Burnyeat, whose book explored the Peace Community's social, political, and economic project through the cacao production process (Burnyeat 2018).

This art is a means for Doña Brígida to contribute to the Community process through a creative activity that has particular meaning for her and for those who accompany the Community. Like the stones, the paintings materialize their memory and history. And like visitors' accounts and photographs of a commemoration, the paintings can be shared and gifted, and thus physically move beyond the Community.

So, the art projects
And all these *art* projects! [*smiling and laughing*]

Why are they important,
and how are they useful?
The drawings and handicrafts.

Because,
in the art,
although I don't write very well—I read well but I don't write well.
In the drawings I tell *everything*, all the work done in the Community.
And what I feel in my heart, I feel in order to make these drawings.
I make these drawings with deep love.
I put in all the dedication, love, and . . . service because I know that these drawings are going to go, to other places where people haven't been to the Community.
And where, through these drawings they are going to learn about the Community.
These paintings are all over, in Canada, Italy . . .
How? How do these drawings communicate *dignity*?
Because . . . many *people* have given their lives
in service, for this struggle, for this resistance.
But they remain with us, they continue giving us strength so that we continue moving forward, and that's what is told in these paintings.

[A MERENGUE SONG BLASTS IN THE BACKGROUND,
"¡¡POR UN MOMENTO, UN REMEDIO!!"]

To speak the truth, correct?
To speak the truth.
To speak the truth of what is going on, even though . . . the government goes to Europe or to the United States to say that in Colombia what exists is simply . . . *terrorism*, narcotrafficking.
We say,
something *else*.
Yes. Narcotrafficking, but because the state itself *is okay* with narcotrafficking.
Because if not, narcotrafficking wouldn't exist.

(personal interview 2011)

Along with their communiqués, painted stones, and commemoration pilgrimages, Doña Brígida's folk paintings are part of the Peace Community's struggle for truth. Enacting their commitment to "reject injustice and impunity," the paintings and the artist's corresponding interview narrative about them contest dominant discourses that Colombia's war is reducible

7.10. Memory and solidarity: Painting gifted to me by Doña Brígida González, whose caption reads: "San Josecito of dignity. Peace Community of San José de Apartadó invaded by the Public Forces causing the community's displacement to San Josecito." Author photo, with artist's permission.

to drug trafficking, "illegal" armed actors, or anti-state terrorism, while also implicitly denouncing alliances between state forces and narcotraffickers that comprise the narcobourgeoisie (Richani 2002).

These paintings are also representations of space that "say something else" in a particular and purposeful way. They are intentionally directed to the Community's solidarity network. They present allies with a material piece of artwork that serves to remind that person or organization of the Peace Community and their time in San José de Apartadó. To speak from my own experience, viewing such paintings hanging in my home or office often induces more frequent communication with Community members by phone, or serves as reminders of and motivation for political organizing. As Doña Brígida said, the paintings "go to other places where people haven't been to the Community. And where, through these drawings they are going to learn about the Community." Therefore they are a means for the person who received the painting to remember, and through which those allies can educate others about their experience and Peace Community history.

I have used the painting she gifted me in academic and activist spaces, and in informal conversations about San José and my research. In formal presentations I typically begin by asking participants to look at the painting and create a narrative about what they see. Common observations reference the rural people and landscape (rivers, trails, farms, and attires); the prevalent presence of what people identify as police officers or army soldiers, civilians moving away from the armed actor in different directions, and community members meeting in a gazebo. Participants often infer that it depicts a scene in Colombia or Guatemala. Starting from their interpretations of the painting, I then proceed to fill in details about Colombian politics, the Peace Community, and the specific details of the event depicted in the painting, which in this case, is the displacement from San José to San Josecito upon the installation of the police post in 2005.

The paintings are a way for this Peace Community artist to tell her stories even without being physically present. They also allow others to engage these stories through a performative medium that is an alternative to reading or listening. In this process of dialogical performance, viewers can construct their own narrative about what the painting reflects and its political importance. They are another means of materialized and embodied memory practice, through which Peace Community history is produced and moves through their alter-geopolitical solidarity network, which is fundamentally integral to its political strategy. In an impromptu interview that began one afternoon when I passed by her home and saw her weaving, Doña Brígida stated, "Here I am making this handbag because weaving is also resistance. I am also making bracelets. I am making paintings. Because all of this is resistance. And it is important, because one's creativity strengthens the Community" (personal interview 2014).

This chapter has investigated the role of memory in this "other politics" of emancipatory autonomy from state-paramilitary-guerrilla violence. I agree with Peace Community members that "memory is the strength" of this peace project, which is framed as both refusing collaboration with armed groups and constructing community. The commemoration pilgrimages, stones, and folk paintings are central to their decolonial politics because they assert the Peace Community's existence, write their own history, and enact their own justice in the face of state impunity and racialized dispossession; create material and symbolic traces in the landscape to honor and connect with the dead; bring the community together on a regular basis to contemplate and perform their history and present; cultivate internal cohesion and motivate continued work; serve to educate and integrate new members and children into the Community; create spaces of strategic planning and solidarity building with allies; mobilize those bodies across space to continually return to and defend their land; and facilitate the spreading of their history nationally and internationally through solidarity and media networks, which relegitimizes their struggle and increases their safety. Hence these memory practices and objects create this radical trans-relational peace of ecological dignity by integrating Community members internally—including across the living and the dead—as well as externally with its alliance network.

Memory and peace are dialectically relational. The Peace Community's approach to autonomy and peace also shapes the particular forms of memorialization they practice. Of course these or any other particular practices do not *inherently* or *inevitably* induce cohesion or anticolonial rupture, as evidenced by the disagreements, struggles, and organizational fissures over memorialization in Argentina (Bosco 2004). Yet in the Peace Community memorialization produces both analyses that reject reactionary and vindictive counterviolence and spaces in which they fully enact their principles of communal work, internal and external solidarity, nonparticipation in the war, and rejecting impunity.

In contrast to claims that ongoing remembrance and denunciation dangerously tend toward subjective stagnation (Freud 1917) or retaliatory vindictive violence (Brown 1995), Peace Community commemorations enact their own justice in a way that both denounces political violence and reasserts an alternative territorial politics through autonomy and collective work. They emphasize war's embodied reality and reinforce the Community's antiviolence ethic and practice, illuminating an alternative form of justice to state models of retributive and restorative justice. To summarize with the words of Doña Brígida González: "I believe that those who have fallen have given us that example, and they continue giving that example . . . constructing something different, a different world, a world without violence, a world without war, a world where we truly see each other as brothers and sisters, where we can work together, unified, and all share the fruits of our work" (personal interview 2011).

Memory is not a reactive political act anchored in the past; rather, it is a dynamic and forward-looking political discourse and practice. Memory is thus constitutive to the Peace Community's alter-territory and decolonial politics of peace: if peace for them is understood as building community and refusing to participate in the war, then the Peace Community creates this alter-peace and alter-territory of intercommunity self-determination, solidarity, and dignity through the spaces, practices, and values of commemoration. By thinking memory, peace, and politics together, we can understand the extent to which particular practices nurture solidarity, a refusal to enact retaliatory or offensive violence, and place-based ethics of care that are constitutive of a "more just possible future" (Alderman and Inwood 2013; Till 2012) or, I argue, this already-present emancipatory anticolonial politics.

EPILOGUE

This book has offered an ethnographic analysis of the Peace Community's radical vision and project of peace. My goal has been to illuminate the ways that the Community's understanding of peace and territorial practices—including massacre commemorations, food sovereignty projects, and solidarity networks—reflect an "other" politics of emancipation toward ecological dignity and thus anticolonial rupture. In this Epilogue I provide an update from San José de Apartadó since the peace accord was signed and when I completed my first draft of the manuscript in 2016. Drawing from media reports and yearly research visits from 2017 to 2020, I describe post–peace accord San José de Apartadó as a means to conclude with reflections on "post-conflict" Colombia and radical trans-relational peace.

San José de Apartadó, like the Urabá region as a whole, is not isolated from Colombia's national post-accord context. To date the most successfully implemented part of the peace accord has been the process of disarmament and political integration, in which the FARC-EP laid down their arms and converted into a political party named Fuerza Alternativa Revolucionaria del Común (Alternative Revolutionary Force of the Common), later renamed Comunes (Commons). Meanwhile the government has advanced some legal reforms at the national level to enable the execution of certain commitments, such as integral rural reform and political participation (Ioris and Ioris 2018). Regarding victims, the Truth Commission began conducting interviews in preparation for the writing and release of its final report in 2021. But implementation of most of the accord's stipulations—including illicit crop substitution, rural social development, transitional justice, and the creation of former conflict zone municipalities' special legislative seats—are either proceeding at a snail's pace or appear to have been discontinued altogether (Valencia Agudelo 2017; Kroc Institute 2019). Sustained reforms continue to be in doubt under the presidential administration of the Democratic Center party's Iván Duque, who has remained critical of the negotiations and accord. Unfortunately, the critique of the "peace process" as a government strategy to demobilize the guerrillas yet nonetheless inhibit the comprehensive sociopolitical transformations needed to undo the structural violences at the root of the war appears to be playing out as such (Chagas-Bastos 2018).

While overall levels of violence have fallen, human rights defenders and social leaders across the country were killed at an even higher rate in 2017 and 2018 than in the years during the peace negotiations (Programa Somos Defensores 2018, 2019). The army is implicated in some of these killings, and the rate of army assassinations of civilians could tragically rise even further, given a Colombian army chief ordering his units to boost their kill and combat numbers, even if they are still uncertain about whether or not their targets are indeed criminals. This is reminiscent of the doctrine that contributed to the illegal "false positive" killings in the 2000s, when thousands of civilians were assassinated and presented as guerrillas killed in combat to meet body count metrics (Casey 2019; Lindsay Poland 2018). Many assassinations of human rights defenders are attributed to neo-paramilitary forces, with the dominant group in Urabá since 2008 calling themselves the Gaitanista Self-Defense Forces (AGC, Autodefensas Gaitanistas de Colombia), otherwise known as the Gulf (of Urabá) Clan (Clan del Golfo). San José's post-accord reality is indicative of this dynamic, where threats against social movements persist as drug-trafficking paramilitary groups consolidate control after the FARC's disarmament. However, just as the Peace Community never waited for a government–guerrilla agreement to create peace in the first place, they continue to enact their own justice, irrespective of the (lack of) progress in accord implementation.

In April 2019 the Peace Community organized their annual commemoration pilgrimage during Holy Week. On Holy Thursday our group of Community members plus international accompaniers and researchers hiked six hours from the gateway village of San Josecito to Arenas Altas and then Arenas Bajas. The Community determined this route to demonstrate their persistent collective strength and international solidarity network following threats by the AGC paramilitary group against a family in Arenas Bajas who joined the Peace Community a couple years before, in whose homes we hung hammocks and stayed the night. On Holy Friday we made the return hike to San Josecito as a *Vía Crucis* (Way of the Cross) procession, following the Catholic tradition. Peace Community members and Father Javier Giraldo identified sites along the path where campesinos had been killed to commemorate the fourteen Stations of the Cross associated with Jesus Christ's path to crucifixion. At each stop a member of the group would read the biblical account of that station of the cross. Then another person would offer a reflection about the theme associated with it—such as torture, truth, or compassion—to speak to parallels between biblical and Peace Community histories. Finally, Father Giraldo and Com-

EPILOGUE

E.1. Radical peace: Stations of the Cross pilgrimage in Arenas Bajas, San José de Apartadó, April 2019. Author photo.

munity members would recount the killings of campesinos or events of the war that took place in that spot, while also nailing a cross onto a tree with the details.

For instance, at the fifth station about Pontius Pilate's judgment of Jesus, Father Giraldo invited FOR accompanier Tom Power and I to speak on the topic of justice. We reflected on how in commemorative pilgrimages such as these, despite the impunity of Colombia's judicial system, the Peace Community enacts its own justice through communal memory. This station took place at the site where in 2011 the Peace Community collected the bodies of AGC paramilitaries killed in combat and subsequently delivered them to their families. The Community has conducted such humanitarian missions on various occasions when state authorities fail to collect dead bodies, following the logic that a cadaver is no longer an armed actor and should be treated with dignity regardless of who that person was and what they did during their life.

A common thread in many other stations during the pilgrimage was the assassination of humanitarian zone coordinators. From 2005 to 2007 the military and paramilitary killed three such coordinators in Arenas Altas and Arenas Bajas alone. Often located in schools, these zones were envisioned as places where campesinos living outside Peace Community settlements could find refuge during army–guerrilla combat. However, the state officially refused to recognize them, arguing that such zones could be agreed on only between the government forces and the insurgency. Following the murder of the humanitarian zones' coordinators in villages across San José de Apartadó, they effectively ceased to exist. Yet the Peace Community continues to promote such spaces: for instance, as a participant in a victims' delegation to the peace negotiation table in Havana, Internal Council member Germán Graciano used the opportunity to insist that the government and guerrillas respect such civilian safe zones in accordance with international humanitarian law. These rights to humanitarian zones were reaffirmed during the 2019 Holy Week pilgrimage.

Ultimately the religious ritual of the Vía Crucis served the Community and its allies to memorialize its history as a means to a just present and future. Leader Gildardo Tuberquia reflected at one of the stations: "[Jesus Christ] died. But he returned and lives among us. I believe that we live the same in the Community. The victory of our compañeros who have fallen during this process, such as Luis Eduardo [Guerra], Ramiro [Correa], and all the other members, we believe that they have not died. They are still alive among us and continue to give us an example. They continue showing us the way of life and peace" (field notes 2019).

The Holy Week pilgrimage also provided a view of post-accord San José de Apartadó. After ceasing to be an armed actor in San José upon laying down arms in regional Transitory Normalization Zones (Zonas Veredales Transitorias de Normalización), such as in Dabeiba, some former FARC members subsequently returned to the area, settling in non–Peace Community villages. In the wake of the demobilization, the AGC paramilitary group consolidated their control by expanding into areas previously controlled by the FARC. According to local residents, some ex-FARC members are now on the payroll of the AGC, with reports of relatively high monthly salaries of approximately 2 million Colombian pesos (approximately US$700). This would not be the first case of ex-guerrillas in Urabá apparently switching their political allegiance and project from the left to the right; in the 1990s, facing attacks from the FARC, many demobilized members of the Popular Liberation Army (EPL, Ejército Popular de Liberación) joined the paramilitaries (Lindsay Poland 2018). Along with other AGC "employees," as of 2017 some of these FARC guerrillas–turned-paramilitaries operated checkpoints known as *puntos* along the trails between villages, many of which I passed through during my October 2018 visit. Yet by April 2019, on the pilgrimage to Arenas Bajas and my subsequent hikes to other villages in February 2020, there were no more checkpoints or visible AGC presence, apart from me coming across people in civilian clothing whom I recognized as paramilitaries. According to a Peace Community leader, this was an indication of consolidated control: "The paramilitaries no longer need as much armed presence or checkpoints, since [certain local leaders] are complying with their rule" (field notes 2019). AGC commanders recruit people to cultivate coca and work on the trails, levying fines for noncompliance. Consolidated control has not meant universal consent, however. Even some non–Peace Community households we visited during the pilgrimage expressed disapproval of the AGC and even went as far as to invite the Peace Community to return on a more consistent basis. Peace Community leaders subsequently reported that many people react with less direct but nonetheless subtle resistance to the paramilitaries by remaining quiet when questioned or evading payment when the AGC seeks to collect *vacunas* (tax-like payments to local armed groups).

With this paramilitary expansion threats and attacks against the Peace Community continue. In April 2016, as the government–FARC negotiations progressed into their final stage, the AGC made their territorial claim to San José clear by spraying graffiti of their acronym and writing "AGC is present and we came to stay" onto buildings inside the village of San Josecito (Comunidad de Paz de San José de Apartadó 2016b; *Noticias Uno Colombia* 2016a). Media interviews with AGC fighters confirmed the group's refusal of the Peace Community's demand that the paramilitaries evacuate the zone, with a commander admitting that they use the civilian population as a shield against attack (*Noticias Uno Colombia* 2016b). The AGC asserting a need for human shields was strange, however. Given tacit collusion with the local military and police forces, as well as the exit of the FARC, no armed opponents remained.

Before beginning the 2019 Vía Crucis on Holy Friday, the Peace Community family in Arenas Bajas took a group of Peace Community members and international witnesses to the cacao grove up the hill from the house where we had stayed the night. We found the sign there marking this as Peace Community land vandalized. "AGC" was written into the middle of the sign, while the "No's" to what Peace Community principles forbid were scratched out, so as to read: "The Peace Community freely: *does* not bear arms, *does* not consume liquor; *does* not plant illicit crops; *does* not give information to the [armed] parties; *does* not participate in the war," et cetera. The implicit message from the AGC was either to claim that the Peace

E.2. Vandalized neutrality: A Peace Community sign with the AGC paramilitary acronym etched onto it and with all of the Community's commitments to *not* participate in the war scratched out. Author photo.

Community's supposed neutrality is a farce or to assert that such nonparticipation is not allowed. This reiterated the message delivered by armed groups killing Peace Community members since its founding in 1997: neutrality is not permitted. Refusing to participate seemingly remains the most unforgivable crime. After laughing upon reading their "edited" principles, Peace Community members took the vandalized sign down, vowing to create and raise another. This almost nonchalant response, to simply replace the sign with a new one, is indicative of the Community's unrelenting reactions to attacks, such as responding to assassinations by commemorating the dead and to displacements by subsequently returning to their villages.

This resistance to aggressions was even more dramatically exhibited two years earlier. On December 29, 2017, two AGC paramilitaries armed with a gun, machete, and knife entered the storage center of the Peace Community's economic cooperative in San Josecito with the intent to assassinate their legal representative Germán Graciano and another member of the Community's Internal Council. Miraculously, Germán and additional Community members who converged on the scene were able to restrain the attackers and confiscate their weapons (Comunidad de Paz de San José de

Apartadó 2017a). During the struggle Germán was wounded by a machete cut to one thumb and barely evaded a gunshot, with the bullet hitting just a centimeter from his foot. Three other paramilitaries who had remained outside then fled to San José (field notes 2018).

The Peace Community informed the National Human Rights Ombudsman's office, while also spreading word to other people across the corregimiento. Upon hearing the news campesinos from various other settlements converged in San Josecito. There Community members held a vigil all night, during which they organized night watches to prevent another incursion into the village, attended to the detained paramilitaries, and conversed around large pots of brewing coffee. In their subsequent communiqué they expressed their gratitude for all those in solidarity with them:

> In the hours [after spreading news of the attack], innumerable messages of solidarity came from many corners of the world to the Community: parliamentarians, communities, councils, parishes, city councils, social movements. Everyone deplored and condemned the perversity of the victimizing facts; people rejoiced in the courage and values of the Community. . . . On this intense day again we highlight and thank the role played by our international accompaniers who extraordinarily showed the love with which they perform their work. We also appreciate the presence of the bishop of Apartadó, Monsignor Hugo Alberto Torres, as a qualified witness during the act of turning over the immobilized paramilitaries. To the immense network of our friends, our deep gratitude. (Comunidad de Paz de San José de Apartadó 2017b)

Nonetheless, many state authorities and public figures continued to remain hostile to the Peace Community and undermine justice. After the Community turned over the detained paramilitaries to the vice minister of the Interior Ministry and investigators of the Attorney General's office on December 30, residents of Apartadó reported that the attackers had been set free by local authorities. The three who had escaped from the scene in San Josecito subsequently held a meeting with fellow paramilitaries in the town of San José, without the police or army officers stationed there questioning or detaining any of them. Meanwhile local politician and cacao business group member César Jaramillo stated on the regional media station Teleantioquia that the attackers were not paramilitaries but merely cacao farmers whom he knew and who were innocent of any crime (Comunidad de Paz de San José de Apartadó 2017c). Finally, the governor of Antioquia, Luis Pérez Gutiérrez, responded by stating that the aggressors were not paramilitaries but instead Peace Community members carrying out an internal attack against the cooperative (Comunidad de Paz de San José de Apartadó 2018a).

In response to yet another case of the government denying the systematic nature of attacks against them, the Peace Community published the following denunciation:

> All these facts reflect the tragedy that Colombia lives: institutions that with silence, inaction, concealed complicity, and the systematic denial of reality cover up the most cruel sufferings of the social strata who do not participate in power; a corrupt justice system in all its instances; a law enforcement force in solidarity with the criminals and practically converted into their escorts; media that lies, deforms, distorts, silences, and conceals; a degenerated political class sunk in its own strong-man selfishness and eager for exclusive privileges. In the midst of this panorama, paramilitarism is the dominant force that relies on such complicity and the systematic denial of its actions by all of those in power. To uphold ethical principles in this context is to run the risk of extermination. (Comunidad de Paz de San José de Apartadó 2017c)

In spite of persistent state violence and impunity that replicate the coloniality of power, the Community responded by enacting their own justice once again through dialogical performance. In a public event recorded by news outlets such as *El Espectador* and *Noticias Uno*, the Peace Community destroyed the pistol, knife, two machetes, and two cell phones that they had confiscated from the paramilitaries. The remains of these items were then delivered to the National Human Rights Ombudsmen office (Comunidad de Paz de San José de Apartadó 2018b; *Noticias Uno Colombia* 2018).

The assassination attempt has become a rallying cry among the Peace Community. It became a key date in their history, memorialized with a wooden cross nailed next to the cooperative's entrance and subsequently referred to by members simply as "the 29th," similar to the way the 2005 massacre is commonly referenced as "the 21st of February." A communiqué expressed as much: "Since the massacre of Mulatos and La Resbalosa suffered on February 21, 2005, our Community had not collectively lived such a mysterious confluence of death and life that intertwined and defied each other in a moving way.... Without leaving puddles of blood, but safeguarding the integrity of all lives, we lived with the overwhelming emotion of those who open the way to life from corridors of death" (Comunidad de Paz de San José de Apartadó 2017b). The incident also made ripples beyond the Peace Community. One leader analyzed the reactions of nonmembers, including the attackers: "Our response to the attack has earned the respect of many people in the zone, even some of the paramilitaries themselves, who say, 'They/we went to kill them, and the Peace Community didn't do anything back to them/us. Wow.' The incident has made people rethink the meaning of the Community, to see it as an alternative" (field notes 2018). The Peace Community's response repeated their consistent reactions

E.3. Commemoration cross at the entrance to the Peace Community's economic cooperative, the site of the 2017 assassination attempt. Author photo.

E.4. Resurgent community: Communal garden in the Peace Community's newest settlement. Author photo.

to aggressions, which is to reaffirm both the systematic nature of violence against resistance movements as well as their peace politics through community and solidarity.

Indeed, the events of December 29, 2017, are indicative of the simultaneously persistent divisions and reconnections in the post-accord period. This so-called post-conflict era has definitively not eliminated the war dynamics of mistrust and fear. Rather, the AGC filling a vacuum left by the FARC may have intensified such phenomena, as the population adjusts to the consolidation of another armed group's territorialization. Some reaffirm their commitment to the Peace Community's project of autonomy. Others turn to new income opportunities offered by the AGC as coca growers or assassins. A third group tacitly and subtly resists while potentially reapproaching the Peace Community.

Spurred by divisions between members and nonmembers in the village of La Unión, over the course of 2016 and 2017 the Peace Community built an entirely new hamlet on a hilltop about fifteen minutes by foot up the mountain for members to all live together. They named it La Unioncita or "little La Unión." Although on a much smaller scale, this was similar to when the Community constructed San Josecito down the road from police-occupied San José in 2005. While certain amenities in this new settlement, such as concrete floors and individual bathrooms, were still in progress, a communal garden was already flourishing as of October 2018. In addition, Javier Sánchez's self-sufficient family farm was still thriving nearby.

Meanwhile the original village, despite some families still living there and various former FARC combatants having moved in, felt more like a ghost town as of 2018 than the thriving place it was when I first arrived in the region a decade earlier. In contrast to its time as a Peace Community village, various stores sold basic goods as well as beer and liquor. Families who moved out said that army soldiers frequently enter the village to buy snacks and supplies. And on each of my visits from 2018 to 2020, I encountered drunk men outside the stores. On one occasion, one of the men, someone I had known well, gestured to shake my hand and said he had something to tell me. As he pulled me in to listen, he struggled to speak and in fact said nothing. As I stared patiently into his bloodshot eyes, he eventually stammered through a slurred but revealing statement: "Silence says a lot . . ." Peace Community members living in the surrounding areas, when talking about the old village, commonly lamented those who "traded the Community for liquor" (field notes 2018, 2019).

The folks living in La Unioncita expressed pride and happiness to be living in a village where everyone was an active member, not to mention its stunning location with a view of the Gulf of Urabá. But certain Community members from La Unión conveyed deep levels of sorrow after having left the original village. It had also been FOR's home in the Community, so I felt this sadness myself and was brought to tears once when talking about it with a member. La Unión had been a heart of the Community's resistance, where they had withstood numerous attacks, including the paramilitary massacre of July 2000 when leader Rigoberto Guzmán and five others were assassinated. This massacre was commemorated periodically, such as during Holy Week pilgrimages or other gatherings in La Unión. However, an annual memorialization of the massacre at the site did not take place every July 8, like the Community does each February 21 for the 2005 massacre in Mulatos and La Resbalosa. Congruent with the Peace Community mantra about memory being the strength of resistance, Mulatos remained a Community stronghold as of 2020, despite persistent paramilitary aggression (Comunidad de Paz de San José de Apartadó 2019). Meanwhile they had retreated from La Unión not due to an armed incursion but because of inter-campesino divergences. I will always wonder whether a yearly commemoration of the 2000 massacre in La Unión each July 8 would have helped dissolve certain tensions and inspired reaffirmations of commitment by those drifting away from the Peace Community's principles. But the Community's politics is not rooted in a coercion that forces people to participate; an eviction campaign against what was a growing group of nonmembers in the village would have reproduced the logic of displacement. The construction of La Unioncita was a testament to the Peace Community's commitment to respect those who do not follow its principals, while assuring members' autonomous and communal living by creating new spaces when necessary.

Despite the lack of open warfare since the government–FARC "peace process," the situation was best described as a tense calm as of February 2020. People all over warned me to be careful when walking into and between villages, noting that not only some ex-guerrillas but also people whom I knew personally had switched sides to leave the Peace Community and work for the AGC. One person explained, "With the FARC's exit, the paramilitaries were finally able to enter the village. They were always around, but farther away. Now they are right here" (field notes 2018). Peace Community members also critiqued those nonmembers who interpreted the FARC's retreat as the end of the war and who are in favor of the development programs led by state and paramilitary forces, such as road construction expected to pave the way for mining projects (Comunidad de Paz de San José de Apartadó 2014c; Lindsay Poland 2018). Indeed, an increasing number of outsiders are purchasing land on the outskirts of Peace Community territory, including the area patrolled by the AGC in Arenas Bajas, where members expect multinational corporations to conduct extractivist projects (field notes 2019). Tensions over land ownership are also ensuing between Community and non-Community members, with some of the latter asserting their right to Peace Community–administered lands through the peace accord's rural land reform process (Aparicio 2020).

Given paramilitary control over much of the area, there is an even greater risk of violence if a rival group enters to dispute territory. As of 2018 people have relayed rumors of an oppositional armed group that is gathering its forces outside the limits of San José de Apartadó in order to challenge the AGC; reports call them "Los Caparros," short for "Caparrapos," meaning the men of alias "Víctor Caparrapo," formerly of the AUC, with the group comprised of paramilitary fighters who have forged alliances with some guerrilla factions (Carvajal Restrepo 2018; "Caparros" 2021). Others mentioned talk of the ELN guerrilla group potentially planning an organized entrance into San José. Community member Javier Sánchez said, "We are very familiar with all the problems that can arise when you hear of other armed groups planning to enter, who will deem this whole area and everyone in it to be 'paramilitary.' The same happened with the guerrilla [the FARC] beforehand. Now it flips to the other side" (field notes 2018). Whereas the Peace Community has been stigmatized for years by its critics—who notably include ex-president Álvaro Uribe—as merely an "auxiliary of the FARC," the post-accord paramilitary consolidation could have San José's residents now branded and targeted as "AGC sympathizers" by a rival group. For armed groups—including the state—there remains an inability to respect noncombatant civilians' insistence on nonparticipation and autonomy. It is quite possible that open combat will return to San José de Apartadó in the coming years, tragically confirming scholarly critiques that deem "peace" or "post-conflict" merely the time between the last and the next war (Kirsch and Flint 2011; Dalby 2014).

Over the course of the period during and following the Havana negotiations, in informal conversations with people working for or strongly supporting the government, I often encountered an assertion that "peace communities" were now obsolete, given the country's new "post-conflict" era. This discourse was commonly linked to an idea that there was no reason for communities to seek autonomy and resist state-driven "development." This follows the logic that the remaining threat is reduced to the still-active ELN insurgency as well as supposedly "apolitical" and "no-longer-paramilitarized" narcotraffickers or "criminal bands." The ongoing assaults against the Peace Community, including the vandalization of Community buildings and signs and the assassination attempt of its legal representative, are indicative of the unceasing attacks against social leaders across Colombia despite the peace accord. This situation is quite far from a "postwar" scenario, let alone "post-conflict."

In spite of—or precisely because of—the so-called end of the war, the Peace Community remains as relevant as ever. Its documentation and denunciation of ongoing human rights violations challenge the "post-conflict" discourse. San José de Apartadó shows how peace is a spatial process that can be produced by non-state actors through everyday ethical practices and places that cultivate dignified living conditions. How long the Peace Community will continue to survive is impossible to tell. Because of the Community's level of organization, courage, and commitment, until now they have been able to create peace without depending on armed groups' agreements or the implementation of their accords. They remind us that resisting war and forging alternatives amid the ongoing socioecological global crisis require not "post-conflict," but the conflict of radical politics itself, that which confronts injustice and oppression through anticolonial struggle. The Peace Community expressed this politics of peace in their communiqué prior to their anniversary gathering in 2019:

> Our Peace Community is close to commemorating 22 years of existence. On March 23, 1997, we made public our decision to not collaborate with any armed actor and to conjoin ourselves as a community of solidarity, by working and resisting together to safeguard our lives, our dignity and our territories. That same week (Week of the Passion of Christ in the Christian calendar), the Colombian State initiated a strategy of genocide to exterminate us. In these 22 years, it has murdered 307 comrades and friends, and has perpetrated 1,462 serious violations of human rights that are identified in international treaties as Crimes against Humanity for their systematicity. . . . At the same time it has developed 7 extermination strategies of the peace community, sustained

for many years: not only physical extermination (executions) but also media manipulation; ideological stigmatization; biological extirpation through rings of hunger and the violent elimination of food suppliers and transporters; legal criminalization based on false evidence and false witnesses; social exclusion and economic depredation that include the dispossession of territories. Faced with all these convergent and coordinated strategies to exterminate us, our decision has been to resist united, without backing down. We continue to build our life project facing all the storms. Facing perpetrators who invoke perverted powers to annihilate us, invaluable energy has been given to us by numerous solidarity communities in Colombia and in the world, which transmit permanent moral strength and political solidarity. (Comunidad de Paz de San José de Apartadó 2019)

Some studies of the Peace Community commonly interpret its significance as small-scale farmers "surviving" nonviolently amid civil war through momentary or localized ruptures (Anrup and Español 2011; Aparicio 2015; Masullo Jiménez 2015). Pushing further, this book traces how this community in fact enacts a coherent political structuring of space in its places, practices, and values to create an alter-territory. I relate how the Community's initial rationale of remaining alive and returning to their villages in the middle of warfare has transformed into a politics of decolonial rupture with modern-colonial logics of dehumanization and dispossession through autonomous commemorations of the dead, food sovereignty initiatives, and solidarity networks. Returning to the words of former Internal Council member Wilson David cited in Chapter 2, the Peace Community is not reducible to survival but is about creating another type of world: "We do not endure. We resist . . . because resistance means generating the possibility of another world different from the logic of death" (Comunidad de Paz de San José de Apartadó 2007: 80). Over the past decade, I have often heard critiques—even by scholars and activists sympathetic to their struggle—of the Peace Community's autonomist politics as "parochial" or "unrealistically utopian," especially with respect to their focus on grassroots peace instead of prioritizing leadership in the national-level "peace process" movement. It is true that the Peace Community has been unable to induce a structural shift in the policies and actions of global institutions and nation-states—as in the implementation of the 2016 peace accord—toward governance defined by social justice. However, I argue that this should not be interpreted as an indication of this community's ineffectiveness. Rather, it is an indictment of the modern world-system's incapacity to achieve its supposed guarantee of universal human rights, well-being, and freedom, despite the constant denunciations and demands by popular movements. The Peace Community has nevertheless demonstrated an adept ability to mobilize forces in the global system in support of its project, including international accompaniment and the Organization of American States' human rights system. However, along with other contemporary communities in resistance across Latin America and beyond, the Peace Community parallels critical feminist-indigenous-black scholars and social movements who ask us to think beyond the typical notion of politics as that which occurs only in the "halls of governance." We ought to look to and be inspired by such groups struggling to create new social relations, new political subjects, and, most importantly, alternative structures in the form of alter-territories.

The Peace Community's alter-territory of solidarity and community is not derived from any peasant "essence," but is produced through continual practice. Its identity is not nationalistically or ethnically defined but is an explicitly political one: those people actively committing to and working toward communal peace. This peace praxis inspired what I have called *radical trans-relational peace*: ecological dignity and solidarity through inter-community networks. According to members' definitions, peace for the Peace Community is not reducible to "security" or "tranquility." For them peace is a question of dignity, which member Brígida González explained in Part I as a question of conscience and truth, meeting basic material needs without compromising the dignity of others, and personal and collective transformation through resistance. This peace is trans-relational because it goes beyond mere relations to be constituted across and through solidarity both within the Community and with other organizations, especially across ethnic lines that can divide racialized groups, between the living and the dead, and through a noninstrumentalist relationality with land. It is radical by breaking dependency on the state and guerrillas for peace and by creating dignified living conditions as well as solidary—rather than competitive and capitalist—political subjects. In so doing, there is the production of a decolonial form of politics that transcends the dominant approaches to social change in the modern-colonial world, such as electoral party politics or armed struggle to reform or take over the state. I offer this ethnographic geography of peace as an invitation for further studies about the intersection of peace imaginaries, territorial practices, racial violence, memory performance, and radical political struggle, especially in post-accord contexts where this book signs off.

As final expressions of radical trans-relational peace, I will conclude with two quotes. First, the voice of Peace Community leader Germán Graciano (field notes 2018), who during a visit to Bogotá offered his reflection on the attack intended to take his life months before: "It was like a dream that nothing happened. They came to kill us. And we could have killed them. But no one died. Neither us nor them. We have to find other ways out of conflict if we want to end war. Without vengeance. And we are thankful to the many people who helped us arrive at this point, of creating community." And finally, consolidating and expanding on quotes of his throughout this book, the words of deceased leader Eduar Lanchero (Buenaventura 2011):

> The logic of the system of death, of the paramilitaries, of the state, is to displace the people. They want to terrorize the people because it generates an individualism so strong that then you don't care about the life of the other anymore, right? So, we had to create another way of living, where we were really against the war and against death. That's why the only way was to live in a community. If you live in a community, you have different ways of relating to each other, of organizing, participation, of solidarity where everyone cares about the life of the other. . . . It doesn't matter how many we are. What matters is that we really know and deeply live a different world. And we cannot build this different world tomorrow or in the past or something. We do it now.

APPENDIX

HISTORICAL TIMELINE

1960s Migrant campesinos from the Upper Sinú region of Córdoba and areas around the municipality of Dabeiba, Antioquia, to the north of Medellín, begin to settle in what would become the village of La Unión. Subsequently the town of San José was founded by Bartolomé Cataño and became a corregimiento (rural district) within the municipality of Apartadó, Antioquia.

July 19, 1977 The first documented massacre in San José de Apartadó takes place. Eleven campesinos are assassinated or forcibly disappeared by the National Army in La Resbalosa.

May 17, 1992 The first massacre in the village of La Unión occurs when army soldiers kill three campesinos.

1995 There are mass displacements of campesinos in the neighboring municipality of Tierralta, in the department of Córdoba to the east of Apartadó, thus clearing the area for the impending Urrá hydroelectric dam and reservoir.

1995–1996 Mayor of Apartadó Gloria Cuartas Montoya continues the Patriotic Union party's social investments in San José de Apartadó, including health centers, schools, and the first installations of running water and electricity.

June–September 1996 Due to paramilitary threats, campesinos from the majority of San José's villages are forcibly displaced from their lands.

June–July 1996 Over eight hundred campesinos march and occupy the stadium in Apartadó to denounce forced displacement and state crimes. A subsequent Verification Commission documents ninety-one crimes. All remain in impunity as of this book's publication.

August 16, 1996   Bartolomé Cataño—San José de Apartadó's founder, organizer of the June 1996 Apartadó march, and Patriotic Union councilor to the City Council of Apartadó—is assassinated.

September 7, 1996   Paramilitaries and army soldiers massacre four community leaders in San José town, including Balsamar Cooperative director Samuel Arias.

February 27, 1997   Paramilitaries massacre four more campesinos in San José town, including most of its remaining leaders, inducing most of the town's residents to flee.

March 23, 1997   The Peace Community is formally founded in the town of San José de Apartadó by 630 campesinos from over ten of the district's villages. Their declaration as "noncombatant campesinos" draws from support of the regional Catholic bishop, the Inter-ecclesiastical Justice and Peace Commission, and the Research and Popular Education Center (CINEP). In so doing San José de Apartadó rejects Antioquia governor Álvaro Uribe Vélez's proposal that San José become a Convivir, a so-called neutral zone (yet documented to be paramilitary controlled) that would inform state forces of guerrilla movements.

March–July 1997   Beginning the week after the Peace Community declaration, military and paramilitary operations forcibly displace the remaining campesinos from the villages of San José de Apartadó. Only five hundred remain, with all taking refuge in San José town. The International Red Cross provides humanitarian aid.

October 6, 1997   FARC guerrillas massacre three Community members during a community workday in La Linda, including Internal Council member Ramiro Correa.

December 1997   The Inter-American Commission on Human Rights adopts an interim protection injunction in favor of the Peace Community and recommends that the Inter-American Court of Human Rights open a case about San José de Apartadó.

1997   Paramilitaries carry out mass eviction campaigns across Urabá, notably of black communities in the neighboring Chocó department to the west. Many of those lands are subsequently transformed into mass oil palm plantations. Other peace communities are founded across Urabá, such as San Francisco de Asís.

1998   Nominated by the Colombia Support Network, the US branch of the Fellowship of Reconciliation (FOR) awards the Peace Community of San José de Apartadó its annual Pfeffer Peace Prize.

Peace Brigades International (PBI) begins to directly accompany the Peace Community in San José.

The Urrá dam is built in the neighboring municipality of Tierralta, Córdoba, following years of army and paramilitary evictions of that area's campesinos.

March 1998   On the Peace Community's one-year anniversary, a group returns to resettle the village of La Unión. Arenas Altas is resettled soon after.

June 1998   The Peace Community returns to La Esperanza village.

April 4, 1999   Aníbal Jiménez—Internal Council member, composer of the Community hymn, and training director—and two others are assassinated by paramilitaries in the town of San José.

February 19, 2000   Paramilitaries and military soldiers massacre five campesinos in the town of San José.

May 2000   Campesinos abandon La Esperanza due to fears of impending attack.

July 8, 2000   With an army helicopter hovering overhead, paramilitaries massacre six Community leaders in the village of La Unión, including Rigoberto Guzmán of the Internal Council. This causes another mass displacement from the village to San José town, before their return one and a half months later. After this massacre the Community stops meeting with military officials; a Special Investigation Commission is organized to document the systematic attacks against the Peace Community, although it never leads to any judicial sanctions or convictions; and the Peace Community begins a petition process with the Fellowship of Reconciliation to provide international protective accompaniment in La Unión.

November 2000   The Inter-American Court of Human Rights ratifies provisional measures of protection for San José and opens a case about violations against the Peace Community.

September 2001 Following the assassination of a Community youth by the military, the village of La Unión is displaced again.

January 2002 The Fellowship of Reconciliation's Colombia Peace Program (later renamed FOR Peace Presence) begins its protective accompaniment of the Peace Community with a team in La Unión.

March–June 2002 Paramilitaries blockade the Apartadó–San José road and assassinate three jeep drivers who worked the route. With the support of an archbishop of the Catholic Church and accompaniment by PBI, the Peace Community breaks the blockade with a caravan of motor vehicles and people marching up the road who bring supplies from Apartadó to San José.

October 2002 In a period without FOR accompaniment as the program transitioned between teams, paramilitaries enter La Unión and abduct a campesino. The entire village is displaced but returns when the next FOR team arrives two months later. As this book goes to press, La Unión has not been forcibly displaced since.

September 2003 The Network of Communities in Rupture and Resistance (RECORRE) is launched in a gathering in San José, comprised of campesino and indigenous communities in Colombia. They declare their refusal to participate in the Colombian judicial system until systemic impunity is addressed.

2003 Campesinos in neighboring Tierralta, Córdoba—who years later would join but at this point are not yet in contact with the Peace Community—begin to resettle lands not submerged by the reservoir from which they had been displaced in 1995.

August 2004 The first session of the Campesino University of Resistance, created by RECORRE, is held for one month in Arenas Altas.

September 2004 Paramilitaries erect another blockade of the Apartadó–San José road.

2005 The Peace Community announces the creation of humanitarian zones (mostly located in schools, where civilians can take refuge during combat) in different sites across the corregimiento. The Peace Community demands that the armed groups respect the humanitarian zones, even if residents are not active Peace Community members. The humanitarian zones eventually cease to function after many of their coordinators are assassinated in subsequent years.

February 21, 2005 During a paramilitary-military operation, eight campesinos are massacred in Mulatos and La Resbalosa, including three children and Internal Council member Luis Eduardo Guerra, who had only recently attempted to resettle the area. Families in surrounding villages flee.

March 20, 2005 President Álvaro Uribe, in a public address during a visit to Urabá, falsely claims that FARC guerrillas—rather than state forces—are responsible for the Mulatos–La Resbalosa massacre and claims that the San José Peace Community is an auxiliary to the FARC.

April 4, 2005 On orders from President Uribe, a police post is installed in the town of San José de Apartadó. Given Peace Community members' refusal to live alongside armed actors, they abandon San José and construct a new village fifteen minutes away by foot. Named San Josecito, its early years are plagued by malaria and dengue outbreaks before adequate sanitation infrastructure is built. Given the initial lack of health and school services, many leave San Josecito and the Peace Community in subsequent years to return to San José town, although the latter becomes plagued by frequent combat between the FARC and state forces stationed there.

In the wake of the February killing of Luis Eduardo Guerra (who was the Community's lead negotiator with the state), President Uribe's defamatory comments in March, the installation of the police post in San José in April, and no progress in any of the judicial investigations about human rights violations in San José de Apartadó, the Peace Community articulates four conditions for ending their ruptura (rupture) with the state. The first is a retraction by Colombia's president of stigmatizing comments against the Peace Community. The second is removal of the police post from San José town. The third is a Truth Commission comprised of national and international agencies to investigate why impunity persists for human rights violators in San José de Apartadó. The final stipulation is an end to military-paramilitary killings and harassment in Peace Community settlements and humanitarian zones. Subsequent rulings by the Inter-American Court of Human Rights and the Colombian Constitutional Court back the Peace Community's stance, calling on the state to make the first steps toward reestablishing dialogue. As of 2021, the state has yet to meet these conditions.

February 21, 2006 The Peace Community commemorates the one-year anniversary of the massacres in Mulatos and La Resbalosa with a pilgrimage to the sites, a tradition to be repeated every year since.

2006 An anticipated Peace Community return to La Esperanza is aborted due to FARC threats.

2007 A planned Peace Community return to Mulatos is aborted upon the insistence of the Colombian Armed Forces that they accompany a state-sponsored resettlement.

Peace Community members return to La Esperanza.

The San José de Apartadó Peace Community is nominated for the Nobel Peace Prize by the American Friends Service Committee.

January 2008 The Colombian Constitutional Court issues a ruling that upholds the Inter-American Court of Human Rights' provisional protection measures.

February 21, 2008 During its annual commemoration of the 2005 massacre, the Peace Community officially returns to Mulatos and La Resbalosa.

2009 The Peace Community expands beyond the corregimiento of San José de Apartadó. After a mutual discernment and initiation process, campesinos in the village of El Guineo (vereda of Naín) in neighboring Tierralta, Córdoba, join the Peace Community. Additional campesinos in Alto Joaquín, Las Claras, and Puerto Nuevo subsequently join.

The Italian-Catholic organization Operation Dove begins protective accompaniment in the Peace Community.

The Peace Community inaugurates the Agricultural Center in La Unión village.

February 2010 The Peace Community inaugurates the Luis Eduardo Guerra Peace Village in Mulatos during the fifth-year anniversary of the 2005 massacre.

2011 The Peace Community is comprised of 1,162 people across eleven villages, according to an internal census.

June 22, 2012   Peace Community leader Eduar Lanchero dies from cancer. A native of Bogotá, his family respects his wish to bury his remains in the Peace Community. A mass contingent of community members awaits the arrival of his casket and subsequently builds a tomb in the village of San Josecito.

December 2013   Colombian president Juan Manuel Santos offers an official apology for stigmatizing comments made by the previous president Álvaro Uribe against the Peace Community.

2017   In response to tensions with nonmember campesinos, the Peace Community leaves the village of La Unión and creates a new settlement farther into the hills, the Rigoberto Guzmán Peace Village, commonly known as La Unioncita.

December 29, 2017   Two AGC paramilitaries enter the Peace Community's economic cooperative in San Josecito and attempt to assassinate two members of the Community's Internal Council, including its legal representative, Germán Graciano. Community members restrain and disarm the paramilitaries. They subsequently release the attackers to the custody of the Attorney General's Office and Ministry of Interior before destroying the weapons they confiscated from the paramilitaries in a public demonstration accompanied by national institutions and media.

March 23, 2021   The Peace Community celebrates its twenty-four-year anniversary.

NOTES

INTRODUCTION

1. A literal English translation of the Spanish term *campesino* would be "person of the countryside" or "country-folk." It is usually translated as "peasant" to refer to rural farmers who cultivate food and/or cash crops on small plots of land that they either own or rent. However, I prefer to use the Spanish word *campesino* for a couple reasons. First, I am wary of the baggage associated with the term *peasant*, even as I disagree with this baggage. Peasants are often presented as nonsubjects, with pejorative connotations of ignorance, rudeness, and unsophistication *(New Oxford American Dictionary* 2012). Such belittling portrayals include the *Communist Manifesto* by Karl Marx and Friedrich Engels (1978), who infamously included peasants within those groups who they argued were "not revolutionary, but conservative. Nay more, they are reactionary, for they try to roll back the wheel of history" (482). This is not to deny that differing scholarly interpretations of Marx's view on peasants exist. For example, Michael Duggett (1975) is among those who argues that Marx's attitude was specific to the context in which he wrote and that he became more sympathetic to peasants in later writings. Second, as one alternative to *peasant*, I find the identifier *small-scale rural farmer* to be excessively general and verbose. I agree with Gwen Burnyeat (2013) who notes that "*campesino* is a whole cultural category in Colombia and other parts of Latin America that is not accurately conveyed by these translations" (437). Colombian campesinos are primarily descended from indigenous peoples and black slaves; when I specifically refer to "indigenous- and African-descendant campesinos," I am referring to all of those rural people whose ancestry can be traced to African or Amerindian peoples, whether they currently identify as black, indigenous, or campesino. In conversation with Frantz Fanon (2004), Ranajit Guha (1983), and León Zamosc (1986), I employ *campesino* in this book in order to analyze the racialized as well as political and social aspects of this subaltern subject position.

2. Of Colombia's guerrilla groups, the Fuerzas Armadas Revolucionarias de Colombia—Ejército del Pueblo (FARC-EP, Revolutionary Armed Forces of Colombia—People's Army) was Colombia's and Latin America's largest insurgency until they laid down their arms in 2017. It arose from rural farmers in the 1960s in the wake of the La Violencia era of civil war. This group, led by Manuel Maru-

landa, organized an armed struggle to defend themselves against military attacks and to advance left-wing goals of agrarian reform and political participation for campesinos and the poor (Ortíz 2006; Hylton 2006; Chernick 2009). The Ejército de Liberación Nacional (ELN, National Liberation Army) is Colombia's largest remaining guerrilla movement; a government–ELN "peace process" initiated on the heels of the peace accord with the FARC in 2017 had stalled by the time this manuscript went to press. Paramilitary groups refers to right-wing private armies which were created by the state, regional elites, drug traffickers, and large landowners to counter popular social movements struggling for land redistribution and sociopolitical reform, as well as the guerrillas' kidnappings, extortion, and attacks against corporate enterprises. While not called paramilitaries at the time, the contrachusma (against the uncivilized masses) and pájaros (birds) of the La Violencia era were manifestations of this phenomenon. Epitomized by the emergence in the 1980s of the group Muerte a Secuestradores (MAS, Death to Kidnappers), Colombia's current paramilitaries link drug traffickers and regional landed elites with a pro-state counterinsurgency ideology (Giraldo Moreno 1996; Taussig 2003; Romero 2006; Camacho Guizado 2006; Hylton 2006; Richani 2007; Hristov 2014). While the umbrella paramilitary organization known as the Autodefensas Unidas de Colombia (AUC, United Self-Defense Forces of Colombia) demobilized between 2003 and 2006, many of its members have rearmed or merely continued to operate as neo-paramilitary groups using a variety of names, such as Águilas Negras, Los Rastrojos, Los Urabeños, and Clan del Golfo (Human Rights Watch 2010). The two governmental forces of concern to this study are the National Police and National Army, which are closely allied with and receive aid from the US government in order to fight the "Drug War" and "War on Terror" (Murillo 2004; Tate 2015; Lindsay Poland 2018). The drug economy has been central to most of Colombia's contemporary armed groups since the late twentieth century, although paramilitaries are the most influential, having served as private armies for drug trafficking cartels and controlling most of the production and trafficking of cocaine. All of the armed groups have committed human rights violations, with the majority attributed to paramilitary groups (Grupo de Memoria Histórica 2013).

3. The Colombian public and many scholars tend to date the beginning of La Violencia to the Bogotazo of April 9, 1948. However, following particular studies (Hylton 2006; Roldán 2002), partisan violence began in 1946 that also contributed to trigger La Violencia.

4. I intentionally capitalize the word *Community* here. In Colombia, the term *comunidad* is a common way to designate a group of people living in the same place, such as a particular urban neighborhood or rural district. Rather than always using the full name—the Peace Community of San José de Apartadó—it is commonplace for Peace Community members, accompaniers, and others to refer to the organization as simply "la comunidad" without including "peace." However, this can cause confusion, since not all residents of the corregimiento of San José de

Apartadó are members of the organized collective known as the Peace Community. All of the district's residents can and are often referred to collectively as the "community of San José de Apartadó" since they live there. For clarity, I use the capitalized *Community* to refer to the Peace Community and lower-case *community* to refer to the term in its broader sense. A similar confusion is possible with regard to "peace communities." Following the same pattern of upper- and lower-case terms, my use of *Peace Community* refers to the organization in San José de Apartadó. When I write *peace community* or *peace communities*, I am referring to this *type* of organization abstractly (as civilian safe zones amid war) or to the historical social movement by various Colombian communities to brand themselves as such. Since San José de Apartadó is the only peace community I know of which still names itself as such, I deem the shorthand *Peace Community* appropriate when referring to the San José de Apartadó Peace Community. Additionally, paying attention to this word-use dynamic over the years, I have noticed that government officials and mainstream media tend to use "community of San José de Apartadó" rather than "the Peace Community" in their statements. For one of many examples, see Gómez Maseri (2013). While I cannot make a definitive claim regarding the deliberateness, intentionality, or consciousness associated with such framings, such language use can implicitly render the Peace Community invisible and nonexistent. For example, government officials—such as then–vice president Francisco Santos's statement during a visit to San José de Apartadó in 2008—frequently claim that "the Peace Community is only comprised of one settlement with barely twenty families" (field notes 2008). Therefore my capitalization of *Community* is my way of not falling into a similar conflation or erasure of the specific organization of interest here. For an assertion that explicitly denounces the Peace Community specifically, take the 2013 statement by ex-president Álvaro Uribe on San José de Apartadó: "I reaffirm that FARC and foreign terrorists have utilized certain people in the *peace* communities" (*El Tiempo* 2013, emphasis mine). Note how he did not vaguely refer to the "community" of San José de Apartadó but explicitly specified whom he was stigmatizing: the peace communities. I wonder about the extent to which actors who want to correlate the Peace Community with the guerrillas use the specific name, whereas if the speaker intends to obscure this organization's existence, they merely say "community." This topic warrants future analysis but is beyond the scope of this book.

5. Father Javier Giraldo has accompanied a multitude of other communities in Colombia as well. One notable example is his yearly accompaniment of the commemoration of the infamous 1990 massacre in the community of Trujillo, a site of recurrent killings in the department of Valle del Cauca (Giraldo Herrera 2012).

6. The Peace Community has had international protective accompaniment from three organizations: Peace Brigades International (PBI; see http://www.peacebrigades.org and http://pbicolombia.org); Fellowship of Reconciliation (FOR) / FOR Peace Presence (FORPP; see https://peacepresence.org); and Operation Dove (officially Operazione Colomba in Italian, but known in Colombia as Palomas,

the Spanish word for dove; see http://www.operazionecolomba.it and http://www.operazionecolomba.it/colombia.html).

7. The Partido Social de la Unidad Nacional, or Social Party of National Unity, is mostly referred to as the "U Party" or just "the U." The U Party was founded by ex-president Álvaro Uribe, who many Colombians believed to have named the U Party less after "unity" and more due to the politician's last name (field notes 2011). Due to Santos's dialogue with the FARC, Uribe broke with the U Party he had created, founding a new party under his leadership, the Centro Democrático (Democratic Center), whose principal slogan is "Mano firme, corazón grande" (Firm hand, huge heart) (Centro Democrático n.d.).

8. For scholarship on the negotiation process between the Colombian government and the FARC, the 2016 peace accord, and the post-accord context, see Rueda, Alvarado, and Gentili (2016), Valencia Agudelo (2017), Gómez Correal (2016), Gill (2017), Jimeno (2017), Tate (2017), Gruner (2017), Puerta Silva and Dover (2017), Dest (2019), and Morris (2019).

9. The colonial matrix of power also involves control over gender and sexuality (Quijano 2010; Lugones 2010; Maldonado-Torres 2010; Espinosa Miñoso, Gómez Correal, and Ochoa Muñoz 2014). As a feminist myself, I am attentive to the gendered dynamics of violence in Colombia because a gendered peace is central to creating ecological dignity. My intellectual project is rooted in feminist praxis in its attention to the power relations that shape and are shaped by embodied experiences in resistance, peace, and research. While gender and sexuality are not explicit analytical concepts in this book (due to my focus on other concepts such as race and territory), a feminist lens nonetheless operates implicitly in this critique of peace. I eschew patriarchal binary notions of peace where women are supposedly "peaceful" and "passive" and men are "aggressive fighters," while also subverting political and epistemological approaches that deem states to be the ultimate guarantors of peace rather than grassroots resistance communities. I hope to elaborate on such theoretical questions in relation to an explicit gendered analysis of the Peace Community in future scholarship. A different but related debate I had with myself in the writing of this manuscript was the question of using gender-neutral language for Spanish terms such as "campesinx" and "mestizx"—à la Latinx—to refrain from replicating the masculine-biased "campesino." I ultimately opted against this, because using the "x" for campesino and mestizo is not yet commonplace in Colombia, it is often distracting for readers in English, and this linguistic transgression would be most meaningful in a text in which gender is a central analytical category.

CHAPTER 1

1. All italicized words in my quotes indicate the stress of the speaker's voice, unless otherwise noted as my emphasis to highlight meaning.

2. For this framing, I am indebted to scholar and *camarada* Priscilla Ferreira. In a private conversation, she shared with me an interaction she had with a

group of colleagues. To her insistence on pursuing change beyond mere reforms and dominant institutional channels, they told her that she had to be "realistic" and "pragmatic." Inferring that small changes and thinking are not enough, she replied, "Then, I am *unrealistic*!" (personal communication 2010).

CHAPTER 2

1. For an analysis of the dynamics in which campesinos become guerrilla-supporting *milicianos* (armed militia members who provide provisions but are not full-time uniformed combatants), see "Apéndice: ¿Qué es un miliciano?" by Giraldo Moreno (2010: 413–29), who argues that becoming a miliciano is not ideologically motivated but is a strategy for victims' survival amid limited options in Colombia's rural war arena.

CHAPTER 3

1. See CRIC's website, http://www.cric-colombia.org/portal/.
2. See ACIN's website, http://nasaacin.org.

PART II

1. For examples of what fall under Dietrich's categories of "postmodern peace," see Muñoz (2001) and Koppensteiner (2011); for "moral peace," see Fasheh (2011) and Gebrewold (2011); and for "energetic peace," see Dietrich (2002), Esteva and Guerrero (2011), Jacobsen (2011), Rengifo Vásquez (2011), and Vachon (2011).

CHAPTER 4

1. For an extensive ethnographic rendering of this workshop and a rich analysis of this peace imaginary from the perspective of a decolonial anthropology of emotions, see Gómez Correal (forthcoming).

CHAPTER 5

1. The Peace Community hymn is available on YouTube—"Himno de la comunidad de paz," https://www.youtube.com/watch?v=KbtBWO5HlR0—while an interpretation of the hymn by the Orquesta Filarmónica de Bogotá can be viewed on the Peace Community's website, https://www.cdpsanjose.org/node/15.
2. See Tamera's website, https://www.tamera.org.

CHAPTER 6

1. For more information on this seminar, consisting of five sessions between April 11 and June 19, 2013, "Seminario Campesino Conflictos de Ordenamientos Territoriales en Colombia: Herramientas Para El Debate" (Campesino seminar on territorial ordering conflicts: Tools for debate), see http://colectivoagrarioabyayala.blogspot.com/2013/04/seminario-campesino-conflictos-de.html.
2. For a journalistic account, see Segura Álvarez (2013).

REFERENCES

Acevedo, Laura. 2009. "De la inmediatez de la opinión a la construcción de memorias como relatos del presente." In Díaz Montealegre, Pedraza, and de Pilar Suárez, *De nuestras voces*, 71–76.

Agnew, John. 1994. "The Territorial Trap: The Geographical Assumptions of International Relations Theory." *Review of International Political Economy* 1 (1): 53–80.

Agnew, John, and Ulrich Oslender. 2013. "Overlapping Territorialities, Sovereignty in Dispute: Empirical Lessons from Latin America." In *Spaces of Contention: Spatialities and Social Movements*, edited by Walter Nicholls, Byron Miller, and Justin Beaumont, 121–40. Aldershot, UK: Ashgate.

Ahmed, Sara. 2004. "Collective Feelings: Or, The Impressions Left by Others." *Theory, Culture & Society* 21 (2): 25–42.

Alberto, Paulina, and Eduardo Elena, eds. 2016. *Rethinking Race in Modern Argentina*. New York: Cambridge University Press.

Alderman, Derek H., and Joshua F. J. Inwood. 2013. "Landscapes of Memory and Socially Just Futures." In *The Wiley-Blackwell Companion to Cultural Geography*, edited by Nuala Johnson, Richard Schein, and Jamie Winders, 186–97. New York: Wiley-Blackwell.

Allen, Theodore W. 2012. *The Invention of the White Race*. Vol. 2, *The Origin of Racial Oppression in Anglo-America*. 2nd ed. New York: Verso.

Altieri, Rocco. 2007. "La fuerza de la solidaridad internacional." In Nieri, *Sembrando vida y dignidad*, 7–11.

Anrup, Roland, and Janneth Español. 2011. "Una Comunidad de Paz en conflicto con la soberanía y el aparato judicial del Estado." *Diálogos de Saberes* 35 (July–December): 153–69.

Aparicio, Juan Ricardo. 2012. *Rumores, residuos y Estado en "la mejor esquina de Sudamérica": Una cartografía de lo "humanitario" en Colombia*. Bogotá: Ediciones Uniandes.

Aparicio, Juan Ricardo. 2015. "El retorno a Mulatos y la Comunidad de Paz de San José de Apartadó: Contingencias y momentos de ruptura." *Antípoda* 21 (January–April): 73–95.

Aparicio, Juan Ricardo. 2020. "Cuando lo común no es común: Sobre leyes, territorios y lo campesino en la Colombia contemporánea." *Journal of Latin American and Caribbean Anthropology* 25 (3): 397–415.

Applebaum, Nancy P. 2003. *Muddied Waters: Race, Region, and Local History in Colombia, 1846–1948*. Durham, NC: Duke University Press.

Argoty Pulido, Victoria, and Diana Marcela Gómez Correal, eds. 2012. *Hescuela: Desaprendiendo para Liberar*. N.p.: Hijos e Hijas por la Memoria y Contra la Impunidad and United States Institute of Peace.

Asociación Campesina de Antioquia. 2008. *Detrás de Los Medios—San José de Apartadó—2de3*. Colombia: Producciones El Retorno. https://www.youtube.com/watch?v=AaPHM66cG94.

Austin, John L. 2007. "How to Do Things with Words." In *The Performance Studies Reader*, edited by Henry Bial, 147–53. New York: Routledge.

Bacchetta, Paola, Sunaina Maira, and Howard Winant, eds. 2019. *Global Raciality: Empire, Postcoloniality, Decoloniality*. New York: Routledge.

Bal, Mieke. 1999. "Introduction." In *Acts of Memory: Cultural Recall in the Present*, edited by Mieke Bal, Jonathan Crewe, and Leo Spitzer, vii–xvii. Hanover, NH: University Press of New England.

Ballvé, Teo. 2013. "Territories of Life and Death on a Colombian Frontier." *Antipode* 45 (1): 238–41.

Ballvé, Teo. 2020. *The Frontier Effect: State Formation and Violence in Colombia*. Ithaca, NY: Cornell University Press.

Bebbington, Anthony. 2009. "Latin America: Contesting Extraction, Producing Geographies." *Singapore Journal of Tropical Geography* 30 (1): 7–12.

Benjamin, Walter. 2007a. "Critique of Violence." In *On Violence: A Reader*, edited by Bruce B. Lawrence and Aisha Karim, 268–85. Durham, NC: Duke University Press.

Benjamin, Walter. 2007b. "Thesis on the Philosophy of History." In *Illuminations*, edited by Hannah Arendt, 253–64. New York: Schocken Books.

Berman Arévalo, Eloisa. 2015. "Intervention—'Land Occupations and Counter-Insurgency in the Colombian Caribbean: Will History Repeat Itself?'" Antipode Foundation, September 22. http://antipodefoundation.org/2015/09/22/land-occupations-and-counter-insurgency-in-the-colombian-caribbean/.

Bermúdez Liévano, Andrés. 2015. "¿Cuál debería ser el rol del sector minero en el proceso de paz?" *La Silla Vacía*, May 21. https://lasillallena.lasillavacia.com/la-silla-minera/cu-l-deber-ser-el-rol-del-sector-minero-en-el-proceso-de-paz.

Bernard-Donals, Michael, and Richard Glejzer. 2001. *Between Witness and Testimony: The Holocaust and the Limits of Representation*. New York: State University of New York Press.

Blaney, David L., and Arlene B. Tickner. 2017. "Worlding, Ontological Politics and the Possibility of a Decolonial IR." *Millennium: Journal of International Studies* 45 (3): 293–311.

Blaser, Mario. 2010. *Storytelling Globalization from the Chaco and Beyond*. Durham, NC: Duke University Press.

Bocarejo, Diana. 2012. "Emancipation or Enclosement? The Spatialization of Difference and Urban Ethnic Contestation in Colombia." *Antipode* 44 (3): 663–83.

Boothe, Ivan, and Lee A. Smithey. 2007. "Privilege, Empowerment, and Nonviolent Intervention." *Peace & Change* 32 (1): 39–61.

Bosco, Fernando J. 2004. "Human Rights Politics and Scaled Performances of Memory: Conflicts among the Madres de Plaza de Mayo in Argentina." *Social & Cultural Geography* 5 (3): 381–402.

Bosco, Fernando J. 2006. "The Madres de Plaza de Mayo and Three Decades of Human Rights' Activism: Embeddedness, Emotions, and Social Movements." *Annals of the Association of American Geographers* 96 (2): 342–65.

Brown, Wendy. 1995. *States of Injury: Power and Freedom in Late Modernity*. Princeton, NJ: Princeton University Press.

Bryan, Joe. 2009. "Where Would We Be without Them? Knowledge, Space and Power in Indigenous Politics." *Futures* 42: 24–32.

Buenaventura, Rafael. 2011. *Hope for Colombia: The Grace Pilgrimage 2010 Bogotá*. Video. N.p.: Grace Media Productions. http://www.youtube.com/watch?v=8vhh5KNnrxA&list=UUe8-23wgIRspP8paQif-6Vg&index=15.

Burnyeat, Gwen. 2013. "On a Peak in Darien: Community Peace Initiatives in Urabá, Colombia." *Journal of Human Rights Practice* 5 (3): 435–45.

Burnyeat, Gwen. 2018. *Chocolate, Politics and Peace-Building: An Ethnography of the Peace Community of San José de Apartadó, Colombia*. London: Palgrave Macmillan.

Burrowes, Robert J. 1996. *The Strategy of Nonviolent Defense: A Ghandian Approach*. Albany: State University of New York Press.

Butler, Anthea. 2015. "Shooters of Color Are Called 'Terrorists' and 'Thugs.' Why Are White Shooters Called 'Mentally Ill'?" *Washington Post*, June 18. http://www.washingtonpost.com/posteverything/wp/2015/06/18call-the-charleston-church-shooting-what-it-is-terrorism/.

Butler, Judith. 2004a. "Performative Acts and Gender Constitution: An Essay in Phenomenology and Feminist Theory." In *The Performance Studies Reader*, edited by Henry Bial, 154–66. New York: Routledge.

Butler, Judith. 2004b. *Precarious Life: The Powers of Mourning and Violence*. New York: Verso.

Camacho Guizado, Álvaro. 2006. "De narcos, paracracias y mafias." In *En la encrucijada: Colombia en el siglo XXI*, edited by Francisco Leal Buitrago, 387–419. Bogotá: Norma.

"Caparros." 2021. InSight Crime, June 2. https://insightcrime.org/colombia-organized-crime-news/los-caparrapos/.

Carvajal Restrepo, Estefanía. 2018. "Capturaron seis presuntos miembros del Clan del Golfo en Urabá y Bajo Cauca." *El Colombiano*, February 27. https://www.elcolombiano.com/antioquia/seguridad/capturas-del-del-clan-del-golfo-en-uraba-y-bajo-cauca-GY8265080.

Casey, Nicholas. 2019. "Colombia Army's New Kill Orders Send Chills Down Ranks." *New York Times*, May 18. https://www.nytimes.com/2019/05/18/world/americas/colombian-army-killings.html.

Castillo, Gonzalo. 2004. "Manuel Quintín Lame: Luchador e intelectual indígena del siglo XX." In Lame, *Los pensamientos del indio*, 13–49.

Caycedo Turriago, Jaime. 2008. "Procesos emancipatorios en condiciones complejas: La lucha por la unidad popular en Colombia." In *De los saberes de la emancipación y de la dominación*, edited by Ana Esther Ceceña, 217–38. Buenos Aires: CLACSO.

Ceceña, Ana Esther. 2004. "The Subversion of Historical Knowledge of the Struggle: Zapatistas in the 21st Century." *Antipode* 36 (3): 361–70.

Ceceña, Ana Esther. 2012. "On the Complex Relation between Knowledges and Emancipations." *South Atlantic Quarterly* 111 (1): 111–32.

Centro Democrático. n.d. "Centro Democrático: Mano firme, corazón grande." Accessed July 14, 2015. http://www.centrodemocratico.com.

Chagas-Bastos, Fabrício H. 2018. "Colombia's Peace in Tatters." *Journal of Peacebuilding & Development* 13 (2): 127–34.

Chaves, Margarita, and Marta Zambrano. 2006. "From Blanqueamiento to Reindigenización: Paradoxes of Mestizaje and Multiculturalism in Contemporary Colombia." *Revista Europea de Estudios Latinoamericanos y del Caribe* 80 (April): 5–23.

Chernick, Marc. 2009. "The FARC at the Negotiating Table." In *Colombia: Building Peace in a Time of War*, edited by Virginia M. Bouvier, 65–94. Washington, DC: United States Institute of Peace.

Churchill, Ward. 2007. *Pacifism as Pathology*. Oakland, CA: AK Press.

Clare, Nick, Victoria Habermehl, and Liz Mason-Deese. 2018. "Territories in Contestation: Relational Power in Latin America." *Territory, Politics, Governance* 6 (3): 302–21.

Clausewitz, Carl von. 1982. *On War*. Harmondsworth, UK: Penguin Books.

Colectivo de Sentipensamiento Afrodiaspórico. 2015. "Sentipensar la paz: Una paz pacífica es posible." Cali, Colombia. https://www.google.com/url?sa=t&rct=j&q=&esrc=s&source=web&cd=1&ved=0ahUKEwjZtJHf-s7QAhXG6iYKHRp0Cs0QFggcMAA&url=http://poderyunidadpopular.org/index.php/noti/item/download/6_998c3c5d3c2a45997994e8d9f772e891&usg=AFQjCNGef37EanvyUFUKOT-h3LcweUpQWw&sig2=7Dy.

El Colombiano. 2005. "La Comunidad de Paz debe replantear su proceso." March 23.

El Colombiano. 2015. "Polémica por propuesta de Paloma Valencia de dividir el Cauca." March 17. http://www.elcolombiano.com/colombia/polemica-porpropuesta-de-paloma-valencia-de-dividir-el-cauca-EL1519547.

Comisión Colombiana de Juristas. 2008. "Boletín No. 27: Serie sobre los derechos de las víctimas y la Aplicación de la ley 975." Bogotá. http://www.coljuristas.org/documentos/boletines/bol_n27_975.pdf.

Comunidad de Paz de San José de Apartadó. 2004. "La Universidad Campesina en San José de Apartadó se defiende del acoso de los medios." Agencia Prensa Rural, August. http://www.prensarural.org/apartado20040906.htm.

Comunidad de Paz de San José de Apartadó. 2005a. "La historia vivida." In *Noche y niebla: Caso tipo no. 6; Comunidad de Paz de San José de Apartadó*, 16–25. Bogotá: Centro de Investigación y Educación Popular. http://cdpsanjose.org/node/14.

Comunidad de Paz de San José de Apartadó. 2005b. "Nuestros principios en la Comunidad de Paz en San José de Apartadó." In *Noche y niebla*, 13–15. Bogotá: Centro de Investigación y Educación Popular.

REFERENCES

Comunidad de Paz de San José de Apartadó. 2006. "¿Qué es la Universidad Campesina de La Resistencia Civil?" Grupo Antimilitarista Tortuga, December 24. https://www.grupotortuga.com/Que-es-la-Universidad-Campesina-de.

Comunidad de Paz de San José de Apartadó. 2007. "Voces y reflexiones desde la Comunidad." In Nieri, *Sembrando vida y dignidad*, 76–82.

Comunidad de Paz de San José de Apartadó. 2008. "'La dignidad no se vende, crea vida.'" November 16. http://historico.cdpsanjose.org/?q=node/104.

Comunidad de Paz de San José de Apartadó. 2009. "Ignominia sin limites." January 28. http://historico.cdpsanjose.org/?q=node/106/.

Comunidad de Paz de San José de Apartadó. 2010. "Muertes anunciadas y responsabilidades del Gobierno y del Estado." February 21. http://historico.cdpsanjose.org/?q=node/158.

Comunidad de Paz de San José de Apartadó. 2011. "Fourteen Years of the Community with a New Murder." March 23. http://historico.cdpsanjose.org/?q=node/186.

Comunidad de Paz de San José de Apartadó. 2013a. "Sin armas en búsqueda de un ejército de asesinos armados." October 15. http://historico.cdpsanjose.org/?q=node/281/.

Comunidad de Paz de San José de Apartadó. 2013b. "El Presidente nos pidió perdón." December 16. http://historico.cdpsanjose.org/?q=node/290/print.

Comunidad de Paz de San José de Apartadó. 2014a. "Commander of the XVII Brigade Announces the Extermination of the Peace Community." Colombia Support Network, July 22. https://colombiasupport.net/2014/07/the-commander-of-the-17th-brigade-announces-the-extermination-of-the-peace-community/

Comunidad de Paz de San José de Apartadó. 2014b. "Bombardeos, espionajes, control y creciente poderío paramilitar: Así protege el Estado a sus ciudadanos." October 14. http://historico.cdpsanjose.org/?q=node/341.

Comunidad de Paz de San José de Apartadó. 2014c. "Paramilitares deciden plan de ordenamiento territorial de Apartadó y Turbo." December 11. http://www.cdpsanjose.org/node/4.

Comunidad de Paz de San José de Apartadó. 2016a. "Enfrentamiento armado coloca en riesgo a población civil." March 27. http://www.cdpsanjose.org/node/68.

Comunidad de Paz de San José de Apartadó. 2016b. "Se incrementa asedio paramilitar contra nuestra Comunidad de Paz." May 3. http://www.cdpsanjose.org/node/70.

Comunidad de Paz de San José de Apartadó. 2017a. "Announced and Tolerated Blow." December 29. http://www.cdpsanjose.org/node/121.

Comunidad de Paz de San José de Apartadó. 2017b. "Una noche de tensa vigilia solidaria." December 30. http://www.cdpsanjose.org/node/125.

Comunidad de Paz de San José de Apartadó. 2017c. "Paramilitarismo estructurado, protegido y en búsqueda de venganza." December 31. http://www.cdpsanjose.org/node/126.

Comunidad de Paz de San José de Apartadó. 2018a. "Caminos trillados de encubrimiento oficial." January 3. http://www.cdpsanjose.org/node/127.

Comunidad de Paz de San José de Apartadó. 2018b. "Destruimos pequeñas armas que de todos modos nos iban a masacrar, como signo de nuestro repudio a las cadenas de muerte." February 2. http://www.cdpsanjose.org/node/129.

Comunidad de Paz de San José de Apartadó. 2019. "Y ahora el silencio amordazante: Un sello en la boca." March 19. http://www.cdpsanjose.org/node/167.

Comunidad de Paz de San José de Apartadó, Consejo Comunitario de La Nupa, Asociación Campesina de Arauca, and Asociación Campesina del Valle del Río Cimitarra. 2003. "Comunidades campesinas declaran su ruptura con el sistema de justicia colombiana." Equipo Nizkor and Derechos Human Rights, December 9. http://derechos.org/nizkor/colombia/doc/apartado2.html.

Connolly, William E. 1994. "Tocqueville, Territory and Violence." *Theory, Culture & Society* 11 (1): 19–40.

Conquergood, Dwight. 1985. "Performing as a Moral Act: Ethical Dimensions of the Ethnography of Performance." *Literature in Performance* 5 (2): 1–13.

Conquergood, Dwight. 2002. "Performance Studies: Interventions and Radical Research." *Drama Review* 46 (2): 145–56.

Coulthard, Glen Sean. 2014. *Red Skin, White Masks: Rejecting the Colonial Politics of Recognition*. Minneapolis: University of Minnesota Press.

Courtheyn, Christopher. 2015. "Returning to Mulatos—A Reflection." FOR Peace Presence, February 19. https://peacepresence.org/2015/02/19/returning-to-mulatos-a-reflection/#more-3035.

Courtheyn, Christopher. 2016. "'Memory is the strength of our resistance': An 'Other Politics' through Embodied and Material Commemoration in the San José Peace Community, Colombia." *Social & Cultural Geography* 17 (7): 933–58.

Courtheyn, Christopher. 2018a. "Peace Geographies: Expanding from Modern-Liberal Peace to Radical Trans-relational Peace." *Progress in Human Geography* 42 (5): 741–58.

Courtheyn, Christopher. 2018b. "Territories of Peace: Alter-territorialities in Colombia's San José de Apartadó Peace Community." *Journal of Peasant Studies* 45 (7): 1432–59.

Courtheyn, Christopher. 2019. "De-indigenized but Not Defeated: Race and Resistance in Colombia's Peace Community and Campesino University." *Ethnic and Racial Studies* 42 (15): 2641–60.

Cousins, Peter. 2009. "Letter from the Field: The View from San José." Fellowship of Reconciliation Task Force on Latin America and the Caribbean Monthly Update, July.

Cowen, Deborah, and Emily Gilbert. 2008. "The Politics of War, Citizenship, Territory." In *War, Citizenship, Territory*, edited by Deborah Cowen and Emily Gilbert, 1–30. New York: Routledge.

Cuartas Montoya, Gloria. 2007. "¿Cuando hablamos de la Comunidad de Paz de San José, se habla de los vencidos?" In Nieri, *Sembrando vida y dignidad*, 68–70.

Cuartas Montoya, Gloria. 2014. "La guerra como práctica de adecuación de los lugares." *Criterio Jurídico Garantista* 6 (10): 12–33.

Dalby, Simon. 2014. "Peace and Critical Geopolitics." In McConnell, Megoran, and Williams, *Geographies of Peace*, 29–46.

REFERENCES

Daley, Patricia. 2014. "Unearthing the Local: Hegemony and Peace Discourses in Central Africa." In McConnell, Megoran, and Williams, *Geographies of Peace*, 66–86.

Darling, Jonathan. 2014. "Welcome to Sheffield: The Less-than-Violent Geographies of Urban Asylum." In McConnell, Megoran, and Williams, *Geographies of Peace*, 229–49.

Dávalos, Pablo. 2011. *La democracia disciplinaria: El proyecto posneoliberal para América Latina*. Bogotá: Desde Abajo.

de la Cadena, Marisol. 2000. *Indigenous Mestizos: The Politics of Race and Culture in Cuzco, Peru, 1919–1991*. Durham, NC: Duke University Press.

de la Cadena, Marisol. 2015. *Earth Beings: Ecologies of Practice across Andean Worlds*. Durham, NC: Duke University Press.

Delaney, David. 2005. *Territory: A Short Introduction*. Malden, MA: Blackwell.

Deleuze, Gilles, and Félix Guattari. 1988. *A Thousand Plateaus: Capitalism and Schizophrenia*. Minneapolis: University of Minnesota Press.

Denis, Roland. 2012. "The Birth of an 'Other Politics' in Venezuela." *South Atlantic Quarterly* 111 (1): 81–93.

Depelchin, Jacques. 2011. *Reclaiming African History*. Oxford: Pambazuka Press.

Dest, Anthony. 2019. "After the War: Violence and Resistance in Colombia." PhD diss., University of Texas at Austin.

Dest, Anthony. 2020. "'Disenchanted with the State': Confronting the Limits of Neoliberal Multiculturalism in Colombia." *Latin American and Caribbean Ethnic Studies* 15 (4): 368–90.

Dest, Anthony. 2021. "The Coca Enclosure: Autonomy against Accumulation in Colombia." *World Development* 137. https://doi.org/10.1016/j.worlddev.2020.105166.

Díaz Montealegre, Gabriela, Óscar Pedraza, and María de Pilar Suárez, eds. 2009. *De nuestras voces: Memorias para un nuevo caminar*. Bogotá: Hijos e Hijas por la Memoria y Contra la Impunidad.

Dietrich, Wolfgang. 2002. "Farewell to the One Peace." *Peace Review: A Journal of Social Justice* 14 (1): 49–55.

Dietrich, Wolfgang. 2012. *Interpretations of Peace in History and Culture*. New York: Palgrave Macmillan.

Dietrich, Wolfgang. 2014. "A Brief Introduction to Transrational Peace Research and Elicitive Conflict Transformation." *Journal of Conflictology* 5 (2): 48–57.

Dietrich, Wolfgang, Josefina Echavarría Alvarez, Gustavo Esteva, Daniela Ingruber, and Norbert Koppensteiner, eds. 2011. *The Palgrave International Handbook of Peace Studies: A Cultural Perspective*. New York: Palgrave Macmillan.

Dowler, Lorraine, and Joanne Sharp. 2001. "A Feminist Geopolitics?" *Space & Polity* 5 (3): 165–76.

Duggett, Michael. 1975. "Marx on Peasants." *Journal of Peasant Studies* 2 (2): 159–82.

Dussel, Enrique. 1985. *Philosophy of Liberation*. Eugene, OR: Wipf and Stock.

Dussel, Enrique. 2000. "Europe, Modernity, and Eurocentrism." *Neplanta: Views from South* 1 (3): 465–78.

Elden, Stuart. 2013. *The Birth of Territory*. Chicago: University of Chicago Press.

Escobar, Arturo. 1995. *Encountering Development: The Making and Unmaking of the Third World*. Princeton, NJ: Princeton University Press.

Escobar, Arturo. 2008. *Territories of Difference: Place, Movements, Life, Redes*. Durham, NC: Duke University Press.

Escobar, Arturo. 2017. "Habitalidad y diseño: Territorialidades y arquitecturas de la interdependencia y la complejidad." Presentation at the II Congreso Internacional de Educación para el Desarrollo en Perspectiva Latinoamericana: "Territorios y Éticas para la Vida," Corporación Universitaria Minuto de Dios, Bogotá, October.

Escobar, Arturo. 2018. *Designs for the Pluriverse: Radical Interdependence, Autonomy, and the Making of Worlds*. Durham, NC: Duke University Press.

El Espectador. 2008. "Alarma por rearme paramilitar en el país." October 24. http://www.elespectador.com/impreso/tema-del-dia/articuloimpreso85934-alarma-rearme-paramilitar-el-pais.

El Espectador. 2013. "Santos pide perdón a comunidad de San José de Apartadó." December 10. http://www.elespectador.com/noticias/paz/santos-pide-perdon-comunidad-de-san-jose-de-apartado-articulo-463333.

El Espectador. 2014a. "'Somos amigos de la inversión extranjera': Santos." August 26. http://www.elespectador.com/noticias/politica/somos-amigos-de-inversion-extranjera-santos-articulo-512951.

El Espectador. 2014b. "'El sector llamado a ser el gran jugador en el posconflicto es la minería.'" September 18. http://www.elespectador.com/noticias/economia/el-sector-llamado-ser-el-gran-jugador-el-posconflicto-m-articulo-517484.

Espinosa Miñoso, Yuderkys, Diana Gómez Correal, and Karina Ochoa Muñoz, eds. 2014. *Tejiendo de otro modo: Feminismo, epistemología y apuestas descoloniales en Abya Yala*. Popayán, Colombia: Editorial Universidad del Cauca.

Esteva, Gustavo, and Arturo Guerrero. 2011. "Guelaguetza and Tu Chha'ia: A Zapotec Perspective of What Others Call Friendship." In Dietrich et al., *Palgrave International Handbook of Peace Studies*, 352–72.

Estrada Álvarez, Jairo. 2006. "Las reformas estructurales y la construcción del orden neoliberal en Colombia." In *Los desafíos de las emancipaciones en un contexto militarizado*, edited by Ana Esther Ceceña, 247–84. Buenos Aires: CLACSO.

Fajardo Montaña, Darío. 2002. *Para sembrar la paz hay que aflojar la tierra: Comunidades, tierras y territorios en la construcción de un país*. Bogotá: Universidad Nacional de Colombia.

Fals Borda, Orlando. 1968. *Las revoluciones inconclusas en América Latina: 1809–1968*. México: Siglo XXI.

Fals Borda, Orlando. 1975. *Historia de la cuestión agraria en Colombia*. Bogotá: Punta de Lanza.

Fals Borda, Orlando. 2009. *Una sociología sentipensante para América Latina*. Edited by Víctor Manuel Moncayo. Bogotá: Siglo del Hombre; CLACSO.

Fals Borda, Orlando, and Muhammad Anisur Rahman, eds. 1991. *Action and Knowledge: Breaking the Monopoly with Participatory Action-Research*. New York: Apex Press.

Fanon, Frantz. 1965. *A Dying Colonialism*. New York: Grove Press.

Fanon, Frantz. 2004. *The Wretched of the Earth*. New York: Grove Press.
Fanon, Frantz. 2008. *Black Skin, White Masks*. New York: Grove Press.
Fasheh, Munir. 2011. "Shalom/Salaam: A Personal Palestinian Perspective." In Dietrich et al., *Palgrave International Handbook of Peace Studies*, 99–120.
Featherstone, David. 2012. *Solidarity: Hidden Histories and Geographies of Internationalism*. London: Zed Books.
Federici, Silvia. 2010. "Feminism and the Politics of the Commons in the Era of Primitive Accumulation." In *Uses of a Whirlwind: Movement, Movements, and Contemporary Radical Currents in the United States*, edited by Team Colors Collective, 283–93. Oakland, CA: AK Press.
Fellowship of Reconciliation. 2007. "Paramilitaries Kill Leader of San José de Apartadó Peace Community: TAKE ACTION." Task Force on Latin America and the Caribbean Monthly Update, July. http://forusa.org/paramilitaries-kill-leader-san-jose-de-apartado-peace-community-take-action.
Fellowship of Reconciliation. 2011. *Profits for Them, Destruction for Us*. Colombia. Video. https://vimeo.com/25264330.
Fellowship of Reconciliation and Colombia-Europe-U.S. Human Rights Observatory. 2014. *The Rise and Fall of "False Positive" Killings in Colombia: The Role of U.S. Military Assistance, 2000–2010*. Bogotá: Fellowship of Reconciliation.
Fernandes, Bernardo Mançano. 2009. "Territorio, teoría y política." In *Las configuraciones de los territorios rurales en el siglo XXI*, edited by Fabio Lozano Velásquez and Juan Guillermo Ferro Medina, 35–66. Bogotá: Editorial Pontificia Universidad Javeriana.
Finn, Luke. 2013. "The State and the Comunidad de Paz." *All Quiet on the Hillside*, blog, September 9. https://lukefinn.wordpress.com/2013/09/18/the-state-and-the-comunidad-de-paz/.
Fluri, Jennifer L. 2011. "Bodies, Bombs and Barricades: Geographies of Conflict and Civilian (in)Security." *Transactions of the Institute of British Geographers* 36 (2): 280–96.
Foucault, Michel. 1982. "The Subject and Power." *Critical Inquiry* 8 (4): 777–95.
Foucault, Michel. 1984. "What Is Enlightenment?" In *The Foucault Reader*, edited by Paul Rabinow, 32–50. New York: Pantheon Books.
Foucault, Michel. 1990. *The History of Sexuality*. Vol. 1, *An Introduction*. New York: Vintage Books.
Foucault, Michel. 2003. *"Society Must Be Defended": Lectures at the Collège de France 1975–76*. Edited by Mauro Bertani, Alessandro Fontana, and François Ewald. New York: Picador.
Foucault, Michel. 2007. "Questions on Geography." In *Space, Knowledge and Power: Foucault and Geography*, edited by Jeremy W. Crampston and Stuart Elden, 173–82. Burlington, VT: Ashgate.
Freire, Paulo. 1974. *Pedagogy of the Oppressed*. New York: Seabury Press.
French, Jan Hoffman. 2009. *Legalizing Identities: Becoming Black or Indian in Brazil's Northeast*. Chapel Hill: University of North Carolina Press.
Freud, Sigmund. 1917. "Mourning and Melancholia." In *The Standard Edition of the Complete Psychological Works of Sigmund Freud*. Vol. 14, *(1914–1916): On*

the History of the Psycho-Analytic Movement, Papers on Metapsychology and Other Works. Edited by James Strachey, Anna Freud, Alix Strachey, and Alan Tyson, 243–58. London: Hogarth Press.

Galtung, Johan. 1964. "What Is Peace Research?" *Journal of Peace Research* 1 (1): 1–4.

Galtung, Johan. 1996. *Peace by Peaceful Means: Peace and Conflict, Development and Civilization*. Oslo: International Peace Research Institute; Thousand Oaks, CA: Sage.

García, Clara Inés. 1996. *Urabá: Región, actores y conflicto, 1960–1990*. Medellín: Universidad de Antioquia.

García Agustín, Óscar, and Martin Bak Jørgensen, eds. 2016. *Solidarity without Borders: Gramscian Perspectives on Migration and Civil Society Alliances*. London: Pluto Press.

García de la Torre, Clara Inés, Clara Inés Aramburo Siegert, Diana Marcela Barajas, Daniel Valderrama, and Nicolás Espinosa. 2011. "El Urabá antioqueño." In *Geografías de la guerra, el poder y la resistencia: Oriente y Urabá antioqueños 1990–2008*, edited by Clara Inés García de la Torre and Clara Inés Aramburo Siegert, 263–487. Bogotá: Centro de Investigación y Educación Popular.

Gebrewold, Belachew. 2011. "T'ùmmu: An East African Perspective." In Dietrich et al., *Palgrave International Handbook of Peace Studies*, 428–41.

Gelderloos, Peter. 2007. *How Nonviolence Protects the State*. Cambridge: South End Press.

Gibson-Graham, J. K. 2006. *A Postcapitalist Politics*. Minneapolis: University of Minnesota Press.

Gil, Laura. 2013. "Batidas en Bogotá." *El Tiempo*, October 16. http://www.eltiempo.com/archivo/documento/CMS-13125593.

Gill, Lesley. 2004. *The School of the Americas: Military Training and Political Violence in the Americas*. Durham, NC: Duke University Press.

Gill, Lesley. 2017. "Another Chance for Peace in Colombia?" *Journal of Latin American and Caribbean Anthropology* 22 (1): 157–60.

Gilmore, Ruth Wilson. 2002. "Fatal Couplings of Power and Difference: Notes on Racism and Geography." *Professional Geographer* 54 (1): 15–24.

Gilmore, Ruth Wilson. 2006. *Golden Gulag*. Berkeley: University of California Press.

Giraldo Herrera, John Harold. 2012. "'Si esto sigue en el silencio, estamos sepultando la dignidad humana': Entrevista con el padre Javier Giraldo, asistente a la XI peregrinación en Trujillo, Valle, en homenaje a las víctimas de la masacre de 1990." *Semana*, August 28. http://www.semana.com/nacion/articulo/si-esto-sigue-en-el-silencio-estamos-sepultando-tambien-la-dignidad-humana-javier-giraldo/263718-3.

Giraldo Moreno, Javier. 1996. *Colombia: The Genocidal Democracy*. Monroe, ME: Common Courage Press.

Giraldo Moreno, Javier. 2007. "Imágenes interpelantes de un espejo retrovisor." In Nieri, *Sembrando vida y dignidad*, 52–59.

Giraldo Moreno, Javier. 2010. *Fusil o toga, toga y fusil: El Estado contra la Comunidad de Paz de San José de Apartadó*. Bogotá: Códice.

Giraldo Moreno, Javier. 2012. "Semblanza de Eduar Lancheros: Cuando un amigo se va." *Evangelizadoras de los apóstoles*, blog, July 5. http://evangeliza dorasdelosapostoles.wordpress.com/2012/07/05/semblanza-de-eduar-lacheros-p-javier-giraldo-s-j/.

Goldberg, David Theo. 2009. *The Threat of Race: Reflections on Racial Neoliberalism*. Malden, MA: Wiley-Blackwell.

Gómez, Jaime. 2007. *Tras la huella de la verdad: El caso Gloria Lara de Echeverri*. Bogotá: Fundación para la Investigación y la Cultura.

Gómez Correal, Diana Marcela. Forthcoming. *De amor, vientre y sangre: Politicización de lazos de parentesco en sujetos victimizados por la violencia estatal y paramilitar en Colombia en medio de la transición política y la construcción de paz*. Bogotá: Ediciones Uniandes.

Gómez Correal, Diana Marcela. 2012. "Enfrentando el pasado, pensando el presente e imaginando otros futuros." In Argoty Pulido and Gómez Correal, *Hescuela*, 239–61.

Gómez Correal, Diana Marcela. 2016. "El encantamiento de la justicia transicional en la actual coyuntura colombiana: Entre disputas ontológicas en curso." In *Victimas, memoria y justicia: Aproximaciones latinoamericanas al caso colombiano*, edited by Neyla Graciela Pardo Abril and Juan Ruiz Celis, 125–66. Bogotá: Universidad Nacional de Colombia.

Gómez Correal, Diana Marcela, and Óscar Pedraza. 2012. "Analizando para transformar." In Argoty Pulido and Gómez Correal, *Hescuela*, 63–85.

Gómez Maseri, Sergio. 2013. "Víctimas pedirán captura de dos generales (r.) por masacre de Apartadó." *El Tiempo*, May 14. http://www.eltiempo.com/archivo/documento/CMS-12799519.

Gómez Muller, Alfredo. 2008. *La reconstrucción de Colombia: Escritos políticos*. Medellín: La Carreta.

Gomez-Suarez, Andrei. 2017. *Genocide, Geopolitics and Transnational Networks: Con-Textualising the Destruction of the Unión Patriótica in Colombia*. New York: Routledge.

Gonçalves, Carlos Walter Porto. 2006. "A reinvenção dos territórios: A experiência latino-americana e caribenha." In *Los desafíos de las emancipaciones en un contexto militarizado*, edited by Ana Esther Ceceña, 151–97. Buenos Aires: CLACSO.

Grajales, Jacobo. 2011. "The Rifle and the Title: Paramilitary Violence, Land Grab and Land Control in Colombia." *Journal of Peasant Studies* 38 (4): 771–92.

Gramsci, Antonio. 1971. *Selections from the Prison Notebooks*. Edited by Quintin Hoare and Geoffrey Nowell Smith. New York: International Publishers.

Gregory, Derek. 2004. *The Colonial Present: Afghanistan, Palestine, Iraq*. Malden, MA: Blackwell.

Gruner, Sheila. 2017. "Territory, Autonomy, and the Good Life: Afro-Colombian and Indigenous Ethno-territorial Movements in Colombia's Peace Process." *Journal of Latin American and Caribbean Anthropology* 22 (1): 174–82.

Grupo Acontecimiento. 2012. "The Affirmation of an Other Politics of Emancipation." *South Atlantic Quarterly* 111 (1): 29–49.

Grupo de Memoria Histórica. 2013. ¡BASTA YA! *Colombia: Memorias de guerra y dignidad*. Bogotá: Imprenta Nacional.

Gudynas, Eduardo. 2015. *Extractivismos: Ecología, economía y política de un modo de entender el desarrollo y la Naturaleza*. Cochabamba: Centro de Documentación e Información Bolivia.

Guha, Ranajit. 1983. *Elementary Aspects of Peasant Insurgency in Colonial India*. Delhi: Oxford University Press.

Gutiérrez, Raquel. 2012. "The Rhythms of the Pachakuti: Brief Reflections Regarding How We Have Come to Know Emancipatory Struggles and the Significance of the Term Social Emancipation." *South Atlantic Quarterly* 111 (1): 51–64.

Guzmán Campos, Germán, Orlando Fals Borda, and Eduardo Umaña Luna. 1962. *La Violencia en Colombia: Estudio de un proceso social*. Vol. 1. Bogotá: Tercer Mundo.

Guzmán Campos, Germán, Orlando Fals Borda, and Eduardo Umaña Luna. 2008. *La Violencia en Colombia*. Vol. 2. Madrid: Taurus.

Haesbaert, Rogério. 2011. *El mito de la desterritorialización*. México: Siglo XXI.

Halbwachs, Maurice. 1992. *On Collective Memory*. Chicago: University of Chicago Press.

Hale, Charles R. 2006. *Más que un indio (More than an Indian): Racial Ambivalence and Neoliberal Multiculturalism in Guatemala*. Santa Fe: School of American Research Press.

Hallward, Peter. 2011. "Fanon and Political Will." *Cosmos and History* 7 (1): 104–27.

Harbom, Lotta, Stina Högbladh, and Peter Wallenstein. 2006. "Armed Conflict and Peace Agreements." *Journal of Peace Research* 43 (5): 617–31.

Hardt, Michael, and Álvaro Reyes. 2012. "'New Ways of Doing': The Construction of Another World in Latin America; An Interview with Raúl Zibechi." *South Atlantic Quarterly* 111 (1): 165–91.

Harney, Stefano, and Fred Moten. 2013. *The Undercommons: Fugitive Planning & Black Study*. Wivenhoe, UK: Minor Compositions.

Harvey, David. 2001. "The Marxian Theory of the State." In Harvey, *Spaces of Capital: Towards a Critical Geography*, 267–83. New York: Routledge.

Harvey, David. 2005. *The New Imperialism*. Oxford: Oxford University Press.

Harvey, David. 2012. *Rebel Cities: From the Right to the City to the Urban Revolution*. New York: Verso.

El Heraldo de Urabá. 2008. "ONG quieren formar república independiente." May.

El Heraldo de Urabá. 2013. "Poemas de Juan Mares irán a Mesa de Negociación en Cuba." September.

Hernandez, Camilo. 2017. "La minería va perdiendo 5 a 0 en las consultas populares." *El Tiempo*, July 10. http://www.eltiempo.com/colombia/otras-ciudades/rechazo-a-la-mineria-en-las-consultas-populares-107078.

Hernández Delgado, Esperanza. 2004. *Resistencia civil artesana de paz: Experiencias indígenas, afrodescendientes y campesinas*. Bogotá: Pontificia Universidad Javeriana.

Hernández Delgado, Esperanza. 2012. *Intervenir antes que anochezca: Mediaciones, intermediaciones y diplomacias noviolentas de base social en el conflic-*

REFERENCES 263

to armado colombiano. Bucaramanga, Colombia: Universidad Autónoma de Bucaramanga.

Hobbes, Thomas. 1991. *Leviathan*. Edited by Richard Tuck. Cambridge: Cambridge University Press.

Hoelscher, Steven, and Derek H. Alderman. 2004. "Memory and Place: Geographies of a Critical Relationship." *Social & Cultural Geography* 5 (3): 347–55.

Holland, Dorothy, and Diana Gómez Correal. 2013. "Assessing the Transformative Significance of Movements & Activism: Lessons from *A Postcapitalist Politics*." *Critical Practice Studies* 14 (2): 130–59.

hooks, bell. 1984. "Sisterhood: Political Solidarity between Women." In *Feminist Theory: From Margin to Center*, 43–65. Cambridge: South End Press.

Hristov, Jasmin. 2009. *Blood and Capital: The Paramilitarization of Colombia*. Athens: Ohio University Press; Between the Lines.

Hristov, Jasmin. 2014. *Paramilitarism and Neoliberalism: Violent Systems of Capital Accumulation in Colombia and Beyond*. London: Pluto Press.

Human Rights Watch. 2010. "Paramilitaries' Heirs: The New Face of Violence in Colombia." https://www.hrw.org/report/2010/02/03/paramilitaries-heirs/new-face-violence-colombia.

Hylton, Forrest. 2006. *Evil Hour in Colombia*. New York: Verso.

Illich, Ivan. 1981. "Peace vs. Development." *Democracy: A Journal of Political Review and Radical Change* 1 (1): 53–60.

International Displacement Monitoring Centre. 2020. "Global Report on Internal Displacement 2020." https://www.internal-displacement.org/global-report/grid2020/.

Ioris, Rafael R., and Antonio A. R. Ioris. 2018. "Colombia's Fractured History and Continued Challenges Following the Havana Accord." *Journal of Peacebuilding and Development* 13 (1): 79–83.

Isacson, Adam, and Jorge Rojas Rodríguez. 2009. "Origins, Evolution, and Lessons of the Colombian Peace Movement." In *Colombia: Building Peace in a Time of War*, edited by Virginia M. Bouvier, 19–37. Washington, DC: United States Institute of Peace.

Jacobsen, Elida K. Undrum. 2011. "Fridr: A Northern European Perspective." In Dietrich et al., *Palgrave International Handbook of Peace Studies*, 67–86.

Jimeno, Myriam. 2017. "Emotions and Politics: A Commentary on the Accord to End the Conflict in Colombia." *Journal of Latin American and Caribbean Anthropology* 22 (1): 161–63.

Junta de Acción Comunal—Corregimiento de San José, Municipio de Apartadó. 2009. "Carta a las Altas Cortes del Estado Colombiano." Comunidad de Paz de San José de Apartadó, November 27. http://historico.cdpsanjose.org/?q=node/143/.

Kalmanovitz, Salomón. 1995. "El desarrollo histórico del campo colombiano." In *Colombia hoy: Perspectivas hacia el siglo XXI*, edited by Jorge Orlando Melo, 257–307. 15th ed. Santafé de Bogotá: Tercer Mundo.

Kant, Immanuel. 2012. "Eternal Peace." In *Peace and Conflict Studies: A Reader*, edited by Charles P. Webel and Jørgen Johansen, 89–98. New York: Routledge.

Kirsch, Scott, and Colin Flint. 2011. "Introduction: Reconstruction and the Worlds That War Makes." In *Reconstructing Conflict: Integrating War and Post-War Geographies*, edited by Scott Kirsch and Colin Flint, 3–28. Burlington, UK: Ashgate.

Koopman, Sara. 2008. "Imperialism Within: Can the Master's Tools Bring Down Empire?" *ACME: An International E-Journal for Critical Geographies* 7 (2): 283–307.

Koopman, Sara. 2011. "Alter-geopolitics: Other Securities Are Happening." *Geoforum* 42 (3): 274–84.

Koopman, Sara. 2014. "Making Space for Peace: International Protective Accompaniment in Colombia." In McConnell, Megoran, and Williams, *Geographies of Peace*, 109–30.

Koppensteiner, Norbert. 2011. "Pagans and Nomads: The Postmodern Peaces of Jean-François Lyotard and Gilles Deleuze." In Dietrich et al., *Palgrave International Handbook of Peace Studies*, 525–47.

Kroc Institute. 2017. "Informe sobre el estado efectivo de implementación del Acuerdo de Paz en Colombia." Bogotá. https://kroc.nd.edu/assets/257593/informe_kroc.pdf.

Kroc Institute. 2019. "Estado efectivo de implementación del Acuerdo de Paz de Colombia 2 años de implementación: Informe 3 Diciembre 2016—Diciembre 2018." Bogotá. https://kroc.nd.edu/assets/316231/190410_informe_3.pdf.

Laing, Anna Frances. 2012. "Beyond the Zeitgeist of 'Post-neoliberal' Theory in Latin America: The Politics of Anti-colonial Struggles in Bolivia." *Antipode* 44 (4): 1051–54.

Laliberté, Nicole. 2014. "Building Peaceful Geographies in and through Systems of Violence." In McConnell, Megoran, and Williams, *Geographies of Peace*, 47–65.

Lame, Manuel Quintín. 2004. *Los pensamientos del indio que se educó dentro de las selvas colombianas*. Cali, Colombia: Biblioteca del Gran Cauca.

Lanchero, Eduar. 2000. *El caminar de la resistencia: Una búsqueda histórica*. Bogotá: Códice.

Lanchero, Eduar. 2002. *El amanecer de las resistencias*. Bogotá: Códice.

Lasso, Marixa. 2007. *Myths of Harmony: Race and Republicanism during the Age of Revolution, Colombia 1795–1831*. Pittsburgh: University of Pittsburgh Press.

Leal León, Claudia. 2010. "Usos del concepto 'raza' en Colombia." In Mosquera Rosero-Labbé, Laó-Montes, and Rodríguez Garavito, *Debates sobre ciudadanía y políticas raciales en las Américas Negras*, 389–438.

Lederach, John Paul. 1997. *Building Peace: Sustainable Reconciliation in Divided Societies*. Washington, DC: United States Institute of Peace Press.

LeGrand, Catherine. 1986. *Frontier Expansion and Peasant Protest in Colombia, 1850–1936*. Albuquerque: University of New Mexico Press.

Lewis, Laura A. 2016. "Indian Allies and White Antagonists: Toward an Alternative Mestizaje on Mexico's Costa Chica." *Latin American and Caribbean Ethnic Studies* 11 (3): 222–41.

Liffman, Paul M. 2011. *Huichol Territory and the Mexican Nation: Indigenous Ritual, Land Conflict, and Sovereignty Claims*. Tucson: University of Arizona Press.

REFERENCES

Lindsay Poland, John. 2018. *Plan Colombia: U.S. Ally Atrocities and Community Activism*. Durham, NC: Duke University Press.

Londoño, Ernesto. 2015. "Taking Stock of the $10 Billion Washington Spent on Colombia's War." *New York Times*, November 16. http://takingnote.blogs.nytimes.com/2015/11/16/taking-stock-of-the-10-billion-washington-spent-on-colombias-war/?_r=1.

Loyd, Jenna M. 2012. "Geographies of Peace and Antiviolence." *Geography Compass* 6 (8): 477–89.

Lozano, Juan José. 2006. *Hasta la última piedra*. Geneva: Earthling Productions.

Lugones, María. 2010. "The Coloniality of Gender." In *Globalization and the Decolonial Option*, edited by Walter Mignolo and Arturo Escobar, 369–90. New York: Routledge.

Lush. n.d. "Fair Trade Cocoa Butter from Colombia: In Spite of Political Turmoil, One Community Is Committed to Peace." Accessed December 21, 2020. https://www.lushusa.com/stories/article_peace-pioneers-community.html.

Madison, D. Soyini. 2010. *Acts of Activism: Human Rights as Radical Performance*. Cambridge: Cambridge University Press.

Madison, D. Soyini. 2012. *Critical Ethnography: Method, Ethics, and Performance*. 2nd ed. Los Angeles: Sage.

Maestre, Daniel. 2012. "Conversando sobre la memoria, o mejor, escuchando al viejo Lionso sobre qué es la memoria." In Argoty Pulido and Gómez Correal, *Hescuela*, 111–14.

Mahmood, Saba. 2005. *Politics of Piety: The Islamic Revival and the Feminist Subject*. Princeton, NJ: Princeton University Press.

Mahony, Liam, and Luis Enrique Eguren. 1997. *Unarmed Bodyguards: International Accompaniment for the Protection of Human Rights*. West Hartford, CT: Kumarian Press.

Maldonado-Torres, Nelson. 2008. *Against War: Views from the Underside of Modernity*. Durham, NC: Duke University Press.

Maldonado-Torres, Nelson. 2010. "On the Coloniality of Being: Contributions to the Development of a Concept." In *Globalization and the Decolonial Option*, edited by Walter Mignolo and Arturo Escobar, 94–124. New York: Routledge.

Mamdani, Mahmood. 2004. *Good Muslim, Bad Muslim: America, the Cold War, and the Roots of Terror*. New York: Pantheon Books.

Mao, Zedong. 1937. "On Contradiction." Marxist Philosophy. http://marxistphilosophy.org/oncontrad.pdf.

Márquez Mina, Francia. 2015. "Víctimas en el proceso de paz." Presentation at the Challenges of the Current Peace Negotiation Process in Colombia: Multiple Perspectives symposium, University of North Carolina, Chapel Hill, April 3. https://www.youtube.com/watch?v=MLqylICv8bA.

Martínez Hincapié, Carlos Eduardo. 2015. *De nuevo la vida: El poder de la Noviolencia y las transformaciones culturales*. 2nd ed. Bogotá: Trillas; Corporación Universitaria Minuto de Dios.

Marx, Karl. 1976. *Capital: A Critique of Political Economy*. Vol. 1. London: Penguin Books.

Marx, Karl, and Friedrich Engels. 1978. "Manifesto of the Communist Party." In *The Marx-Engels Reader*, edited by Robert C. Tucker, 469–500. 2nd ed. New York: W.W. Norton.

Masullo Jiménez, Juan. 2015. *The Power of Staying Put: Nonviolent Resistance against Armed Groups in Colombia*. Washington, DC: International Center on Nonviolent Conflict.

Mayer, Tamar. 2004. "Embodied Nationalism." In *Mapping Women, Making Politics: Feminist Perspectives on Political Geography*, edited by Lynn A. Staeheli, Eleonore Kofman, and Linda J. Peake, 153–67. New York: Routledge.

Mbembé, Achille. 2003. "Necropolitics." *Public Culture* 15 (1): 11–40.

McConnell, Fiona. 2014. "Contextualizing and Politicizing Peace: Geographies of Tibetan Satyagraha." In McConnell, Megoran, and Williams, *Geographies of Peace*, 131–50.

McConnell, Fiona, Nick Megoran, and Philippa Williams, eds. 2014. *Geographies of Peace*. New York: I.B. Tauris.

McKittrick, Katherine, and Clyde Woods, eds. 2007. *Black Geographies and the Politics of Place*. Cambridge: South End Press.

Megoran, Nick. 2011. "War and Peace? An Agenda for Peace Research and Practice in Geography." *Political Geography* 30 (4): 178–89.

Mertus, Julie A., and Jeffrey W. Helsing. 2006. "Introduction: Exploring the Intersection between Human Rights and Conflict." In *Human Rights and Conflict: Exploring the Links between Rights, Law, and Peacebuilding*, 3–20. Washington, DC: United States Institute of Peace.

Mignolo, Walter D. 2010. "Delinking: The Rhetoric of Modernity, the Logic of Coloniality and the Grammar of De-coloniality." In *Globalization and the Decolonial Option*, edited by Walter Mignolo and Arturo Escobar, 303–68. New York: Routledge.

Mills, Amy. 2010. *Streets of Memory: Landscape, Tolerance, and National Identity in Istanbul*. Athens: University of Georgia Press.

Mitchell, Christopher, and Sara Ramírez. 2009. "Local Peace Communities in Colombia: An Initial Comparison of Three Cases." In *Colombia: Building Peace in a Time of War*, edited by Virginia M. Bouvier, 245–70. Washington, DC: United States Institute of Peace.

Moncada Hurtado, Clarybell, Fabian Cristancho Ossa, and Agustín Mateo Caro Morales. 2011a. *Comunidad de Paz: Resiste (Parte 1)*. Universidad Católica de Pereira. https://www.youtube.com/watch?v=jkVDm4wsrb8&list=PL3cBDgCi9tR3D1zuCfZ3z2yG_fNQFNdfn&index=1.

Moncada Hurtado, Clarybell, Fabian Cristancho Ossa, and Agustín Mateo Caro Morales. 2011b. *Comunidad de Paz: Resiste (Parte 2)*. Universidad Católica de Pereira. https://www.youtube.com/watch?v=r-mhBRH9LRM&list=PL3cBDgCi9tR3D1zuCfZ3z2yG_fNQFNdfn&index=2.

Mora, Mariana. 2017. *Kuxlejal Politics: Indigenous Autonomy, Race, and Decolonizing Research in Zapatista Communities*. Austin: University of Texas Press.

Moreno Figueroa, Mónica G. 2008. "Historically Rooted Transnationalism: Slightedness and the Experience of Racism in Mexican Families." *Journal of Intercultural Studies* 29 (3): 283–97.

REFERENCES

Moreno Figueroa, Mónica G. 2011. "Naming Ourselves: Recognising Racism and Mestizaje in Mexico." In *Contesting Recognition: Culture, Identity and Citizenship*, edited by Janice McLaughlin, Peter Phillimore, and Diane Richardson, 122–43. Basingstoke, UK: Palgrave Macmillan.

Morris, Meghan. 2019. "Speculative Fields: Property in the Shadow of Post-Conflict Colombia." *Cultural Anthropology* 34 (4): 580–606.

Mosquera Rosero-Labbé, Claudia, Agustín Laó-Montes, and César Rodríguez Garavito, eds. 2010. *Debates sobre ciudadanía y políticas raciales en las Américas Negras*. Bogotá: Universidad Nacional de Colombia.

Moten, Fred, and Stefano Harney. 2011. "Politics Surrounded." *South Atlantic Quarterly* 110 (4): 985–88.

Muñoz, Francisco. 2001. "La paz imperfecta en un universo en conflicto." In *La paz imperfecta*, edited by Francisco Muñoz, 2–66. Granada: Universidad de Granada.

Murillo, Mario A. 2004. *Colombia and the United States: War, Unrest, and Destabilization*. New York: Seven Stories Press.

Muzaini, Hamzah. 2013. "Scale Politics, Vernacular Memory and the Preservation of the Green Ridge Battlefield in Kampar, Malaysia." *Social & Cultural Geography* 14 (4): 389–409.

La Nación. 2014. "Juan Manuel Santos: 'Colombia conseguirá la paz, con garrote o con zanahoria.'" February 7. http://www.lanacion.com.ar/1662215-juan-manuel-santos-colombia-conseguira-la-paz-con-garrote-o-con-zanahoria.

Nelson, Alondra. 2011. *Body and Soul: The Black Panther Party and the Fight against Medical Discrimination*. Minneapolis: University of Minnesota Press.

Nene, Yamilé, and Henry Chocué. 2004. "Las luchas de Quintín Lame." In Lame, *Los pensamientos del indio*, 103–10.

New Oxford American Dictionary. 2012. 3rd ed. Max OS X Version 10.9.5 Dictionary. s.v. "peasant."

Newton, Huey P. 2002. "Speech Delivered at Boston College: November 18, 1970." In *The Huey P. Newton Reader*. Edited by David Hilliard and Donald Wise, 160–75. New York: Seven Stories Press.

Ng'weno, Bettina. 2013. "¿Puede la etnicidad reemplazar lo racial? Afrocolombianos, indigenidad y el Estado multicultural en Colombia." *Revista Colombiana de Antropologia* 49 (1): 71–104.

Nieri, David, ed. 2007. *Seminando vida y dignidad: Comunidad de Paz de San José de Apartadó; 10 años de resistencia noviolenta a la guerra*. Pisa: Quadernia Satyagraha la forza della verità.

Nietzsche, Friedrich. 2008. *On the Genealogy of Morals*. Edited by Douglas Smith. Oxford: Oxford University Press.

Noticias Uno Colombia. 2016a. "Comunidad de paz de San José de Apartadó asaltada por presuntos paramilitares." April 17. https://www.youtube.com/watch?v=hB_fgLKNA9Q.

Noticias Uno Colombia. 2016b. "Neoparamilitares llegaron a comunidad de paz de San José de Apartadó." September 11. https://www.youtube.com/watch?v=ALtE7z8yt1s.

Noticias Uno Colombia. 2018. "Fueron destruidas las armas de supuestos paramilitares que entraron a Comunidad de Paz." February 17. https://www.youtube.com/watch?v=JcHXtyFjuAo.

Nyong'o, Tavia. 2009. *The Amalgamation Waltz: Race, Performance, and the Ruses of Memory*. Minneapolis: University of Minnesota Press.

Oliver, Kelly. 2001. *Witnessing: Beyond Recognition*. Minneapolis: University of Minnesota Press.

Ortíz, Román D. 2006. "La guerrilla mutante." In *En la encrucijada: Colombia en el siglo XXI*, edited by Francisco Leal Buitrago, 323–56. Bogotá: Norma.

Ortiz Gómez, Martha. 2015. "'El proceso de paz no resiste más tiempo': Santos." *El Colombiano*, July 12. http://www.elcolombiano.com/santos-en-entrevista-con-el-colombiano-hablo-sobre-proceso-de-paz-y-su-mandato-GB2289796.

Oslender, Ulrich. 2007. "Spaces of Terror and Fear on Colombia's Pacific Coast: The Armed Conflict and Forced Displacement among Black Communities." In *Violent Geographies: Fear, Terror, and Political Violence*, edited by Derek Gregory and Allan Pred, 111–32. New York: Routledge.

Oslender, Ulrich. 2016. *The Geographies of Social Movements: Afro-Colombian Mobilization and the Aquatic Space*. Durham, NC: Duke University Press.

Ospina, William. 1997. *¿Dónde está la franja amarilla?* Santa Fé de Bogotá: Norma.

O'Toole, Rachel Sarah. 2012. *Bound Lives: Africans, Indians, and the Making of Race in Colonial Peru*. Pittsburgh: University of Pittsburgh Press.

Pain, Rachel, and Peter Francis. 2003. "Reflections on Participatory Research." *Area* 35 (1): 46–54.

El País. 2014. "'Vamos por la paz total': Dijo Santos al inscribir su candidatura en la Registraduría." March 4. http://www.elpais.com.co/elpais/elecciones/noticias/juan-manuel-santos-y-vargas-lleras-inscriben-su-candidatura-presidencia.

El País. 2015. "Colombia ya vende la paz a los inversores extranjeros." May 15. http://www.elpais.com.co/elpais/colombia/noticias/colombia-plantea-avances-proceso-paz-para-lograr-inversiones-extranjeras.

Palencia, Carmen. 2012. "La voz de los ganadroes—PNP 2012." YouTube video. https://www.youtube.com/watch?v=SxNWwu26z84.

Pardo Santamaría, Rubén Darío. 2007. "Una lección de resistencia, dignidad y valentía." In Nieri, *Sembrando vida y dignidad*, 20–30.

Paschel, Tianna S. 2016. *Becoming Black Political Subjects: Movements and Ethno-Racial Rights in Colombia and Brazil*. Princeton, NJ: Princeton University Press.

Pécaut, Daniel. 2001. *Guerra contra la sociedad*. Bogotá: Espasa.

Pérez, Diego. 2007. "Geografía de la vida y la esperanza en Colombia." In Nieri, *Sembrando vida y dignidad*, 40–51.

Pollock, Della. 2005. "Introduction: Remembering." In *Remembering: Oral History Performance*, edited by Della Pollock, 1–17. New York: Palgrave Macmillan.

Poole, Deborah. 2016. "Mestizaje as Ethical Disposition: Indigenous Rights in the Neoliberal State." *Latin American and Caribbean Ethnic Studies* 11 (3): 287–304.

Povinelli, Elizabeth A. 2011. *Economies of Abandonment: Social Belonging and Endurance in Late Liberalism*. Durham, NC: Duke University Press.

Pratt, Geraldine. 2008. "International Accompaniment and Witnessing State Violence in the Philippines." *Antipode* 40 (5): 751–79.

Programa Somos Defensores. 2014. "D de defensa: Informe anual 2013 Sistema de Información sobre Agresiones contra Defensores y Defensoras de Derechos Humanos en Colombia." Bogotá. https://somosdefensores.org/wp-content/uploads/2018/08/Documentos/TODOS LOS INFORMES/informes en español/informes anuales/INFORME SOMOS DEFENSORES 2013 ANUAL_ESPAÑOL.pdf.

Programa Somos Defensores. 2018. "Piedra en el zapato: Informe anual 2017 Sistema de Información sobre Agresiones contra Defensores y Defensoras de DD.HH. en Colombia." Bogotá. https://choco.org/documentos/informe-anual-2017-piedra-en-el-zapato.pdf.

Programa Somos Defensores. 2019. "Clockwork Orange: Annual Report 2018 Information System on Attacks against Human Rights Defenders in Colombia." Bogotá. https://somosdefensores.org/wp-content/uploads/2019/04/informe-somos-defensores-2019-ingles_web.pdf.

Programa Somos Defensores. 2020. *Blindness: Annual Report 2019; Information System on Aggressions against Human Rights Defenders in Colombia*. Bogotá. https://drive.google.com/file/d/1vUnP57S1THj1wV7M0w_-2LMixvnP_FKD/view.

Proietti, Andrea. 2007. "Un extraordinario ejemplo de resistencia y esperanza: Presentación breve de la Comunidad de Paz de San José de Apartadó." In Nieri, *Sembrando vida y dignidad*, 12–17.

Puerta Silva, Claudia Patricia, and Robert V. H. Dover. 2017. "Salud, recursos naturales y el proceso de paz en Colombia." *Journal of Latin American and Caribbean Anthropology* 22 (1): 183–88.

Quijano, Aníbal. 2000. "Coloniality of Power and Eurocentrism in Latin America." *Neplanta: Views from South* 1 (3): 533–80.

Quijano, Aníbal. 2010. "Coloniality and Modernity/Rationality." In *Globalization and the Decolonial Option*, edited by Walter Mignolo and Arturo Escobar, 22–32. New York: Routledge.

Radcliffe, Sarah A. 2017. "Geography and Indigeneity I: Indigeneity, Coloniality and Knowledge." *Progress in Human Geography* 41 (2): 220–29.

Radio Macondo. 2015. "Continúa el desplazamiento forzado de los campesinos en San José de Apartadó." November 8. http://radiomacondo.fm/2015/11/08/continua-el-desplazamiento-forzado-de-los-campesinos-en-san-jose-de-apartado/.

Raffestin, Claude. 2012. "Space, Territory, and Territoriality." *Environment and Planning D: Society and Space* 30 (1): 121–41.

Rahier, Jean Muteba. 2014. *Blackness in the Andes: Ethnographic Vignettes of Cultural Politics in the Time of Multiculturalism*. New York: Palgrave Macmillan.

Ramírez Cuéllar, Francisco. 2011. *Gran minería y derechos humanos en Colombia*. Bogotá: Funtraenergética.

Rancière, Jacques. 2010. *Dissensus: On Politics and Aesthetics*. Edited by Steven Corcoran. New York: Continuum.

Rappaport, Joanne. 1998. *The Politics of Memory: Native Historical Interpretation in the Colombian Andes*. Durham, NC: Duke University Press.

Rappaport, Joanne. 2004. "Manuel Quintín Lame Hoy." In Lame, *Los pensamientos del indio*, 51–101.

Rappaport, Joanne. 2014. *The Disappearing Mestizo: Configuring Difference in the Colonial New Kingdom of Granada*. Durham, NC: Duke University Press.

Red Italiana de Solidaridad. 2005. "Ultima entrevista de Luis Eduardo Guerra." YouTube video. https://www.youtube.com/watch?v=xnCD3ksF0ZQ.

Rengifo Vásquez, Grimaldo. 2011. "Thaq: An Andean-Amazonian Perspective." In Dietrich et al., *Palgrave International Handbook of Peace Studies*, 373–86.

Restrepo, Eduardo. 2018. "Talks and Disputes of Racism in Colombia after Multiculturalism." *Cultural Studies* 32 (3): 460–76.

Reyes, Álvaro. 2012a. "On Fanon's Manichean Delirium." *Black Scholar* 42 (3–4): 13–20.

Reyes, Álvaro. 2012b. "Revolutions in the Revolutions: A Post-counterhegemonic Moment for Latin America?" *South Atlantic Quarterly* 111 (1): 1–27.

Reyes, Álvaro. 2015. "Zapatismo: Other Geographies circa 'the End of the World.'" *Environment and Planning D: Society and Space* 33 (3): 408–24.

Reyes, Álvaro, and Mara Kaufman. 2011. "Sovereignty, Indigeneity, Territory: Zapatista Autonomy and the New Practices of Decolonization." *South Atlantic Quarterly* 110 (2): 505–25.

Reyes Posada, Alejandro. 2009. *Guerreros y campesinos: El despojo de la tierra en Colombia*. Bogotá: Norma.

Riaño-Alcalá, Pilar. 2002. "Remembering Place: Memory and Violence in Medellín, Colombia." *Journal of Latin American Anthropology* 7 (1): 276–309.

Riaño-Alcalá, Pilar. 2015. "Emplaced Witnessing: Commemorative Practices among the Wayuu in the Upper Guajira." *Memory Studies* 8 (3): 282–97.

Richani, Nazih. 2002. *Systems of Violence: The Political Economy of War and Peace in Colombia*. Albany: State University of New York Press.

Richani, Nazih. 2005. "Multinational Corporations, Rentier Capitalism, and the War System in Colombia." *Latin American Politics and Society* 47 (3): 113–44.

Richani, Nazih. 2007. "Caudillos and the Crisis of the Colombian State: Fragmented Sovereignty, the War System and the Privatisation of Counterinsurgency in Colombia." *Third World Quarterly* 28 (2): 403–17.

Richani, Nazih. 2012. "The Agrarian Rentier Political Economy: Land Concentration and Food Insecurity in Colombia." *Latin American Research Review* 47 (2): 51–78.

Ricoeur, Paul. 2004. *Memory, History, Forgetting*. Chicago: University of Chicago Press.

Rivera Cusicanqui, Silvia. 1987. *Oppressed but Not Defeated: Peasant Struggles among the Aymara and Qhechwa in Bolivia, 1900–1980*. Geneva: United Nations Research Institute for Social Development.

Rivera Cusicanqui, Silvia. 2012. "Ch'ixinakax Utxiwa: A Reflection on the Practices and Discourses of Decolonization." *South Atlantic Quarterly* 111 (1): 95–109.

Robinson, Cedric J. 2000. *Black Marxism: The Making of the Black Radical Tradition*. Chapel Hill: University of North Carolina Press.

Roitman, Karem, and Alexis Oviedo. 2017. "Mestizo Racism in Ecuador." *Ethnic and Racial Studies* 40 (15): 2768–86.

Rojas, Catalina. 2007. "Islands in the Stream. A Compartive Analysis of Zones of Peace within Colombia's Civil War." In *Zones of Peace*, edited by Landon E. Hancock and Christopher Mitchell, 71–89. Bloomfield, CT: Kumarian Press.

Rojas, Cristina. 2002. *Civilization and Violence: Regimes of Representation in Nineteenth-Century Colombia*. Minneapolis: University of Minnesota Press.

Roldán, Mary. 2002. *Blood and Fire: La Violencia in Antioquia, Colombia, 1946–1953*. Durham, NC: Duke University Press.

Romero, Mauricio. 2006. "Paramilitares, narcotráfico y contrainsurgencia: Una experiencia para no repetir." In *En la encrucijada: Colombia en el siglo XXI*, edited by Francisco Leal Buitrago, 357–85. Bogotá: Norma.

Rosenthal, Caitlin. 2019. *Accounting for Slavery: Masters and Management*. Cambridge, MA: Harvard University Press.

Ross, Amy. 2011. "Geographies of War and the Putative Peace." *Political Geography* 30 (4): 197–99.

Ross, Amy. 2012. "(Putative) Peace and the Persistence of Conflict." Presentation at the American Association of Geographers conference, New York, February 26.

Rousseau, Jean Jacques. 1968. *The Social Contract*. New York: Penguin Books.

Routledge, Paul. 2008. "Anti-Geopolitics." In *A Companion to Political Geography*, edited by John Agnew, Katharyne Mitchell, and Gerard Toal, 236–48. Malden, MA: Blackwell.

Rueda, Eduardo A., Sara Victoria Alvarado, and Pablo Gentili, eds. 2016. *Paz en Colombia: Perspectivas, desafíos, opciones*. Ciudad Autónoma de Buenos Aires: CLACSO.

Ruiz, Martha. 2005. "La universidad de la resistencia." *Semana*, May 5. http://www.semana.com/on-line/articulo/la-universidad-resistencia/72716-3.

Russo, Chandra. 2019. "Solidarity Protests on US Security Policy: Interrupting Racial and Imperial Affects through Ritual Mourning." In Bacchetta, Maira, and Winant, *Global Raciality*, 195–212.

Sack, Robert David. 1986. *Human Territoriality: Its Theory and History*. Cambridge: Cambridge University Press.

Safford, Frank, and Marco Palacios. 2002. *Colombia: Fragmented Land, Divided Society*. New York: Oxford University Press.

Saltzman, Lisa. 2006. *Making Memory Matter: Strategies of Remembrance in Contemporary Art*. Chicago: University of Chicago Press.

Sánchez, Gonzalo. 2006. *Guerras, memoria, e historia*. Medellín: La Carreta Histórica.

Sánchez Ayala, Luis. 2015. "De territorios, límites, bordes y fronteras: Una conceptualización para abordar conflictos sociales." *Revista de Estudios Sociales* 53 (July–September): 175–79.

Santos, Boaventura de Sousa. 2006. *The Rise of the Global Left: The World Social Forum and Beyond*. New York: Zed Books.

Santos, Boaventura de Sousa. 2014. *Epistemologies of the South: Justice against Epistemicide*. Boulder, CO: Paradigm.

Santos, Juan Manuel. 2015. "Alocución del Presidente Juan Manuel Santos sobre el acuerdo en materia de justicia en el proceso de paz con las Farc." Presidencia de la República de Colombia, September 23. http://wp.presidencia.gov.co/

Noticias/2015/Septiembre/Paginas/20150923_07-Alocucion-del-Presidente-Juan-Manuel-Santos-sobre-el-acuerdo-en-materia-de-justicia-en-el-proceso-de-paz.aspx.
Santos, Juan Manuel. 2017. "Gobierno respalda consolidación del sector minero como impulsor de la economía." Presidencia de la República de Colombia, May 12. http://es.presidencia.gov.co/noticia/170512-Gobierno-respalda-consolidacion-del-sector-minero-como-impulsor-de-la-economia.
Schock, Kurt. 2005. *Unarmed Insurrections: People Power Movements in Nondemocracies*. Minneapolis: University of Minnesota Press.
Scholz, Sally J. 2008. *Political Solidarity*. University Park: Pennsylvania State University Press.
Scott, James. 1990. *Domination and the Arts of Resistance: Hidden Transcripts*. New Haven, CT: Yale University Press.
Segura Álvarez, Camilo. 2013. "Un río de vida buscando la muerte." *El Espectador*, October 12. http://www.elespectador.com/noticias/nacional/un-rio-de-vida-buscando-muerte-articulo-452056.
Semana. 2005. "Habla Vicente Castaño." June 5. http://www.semana.com/portada/articulo/habla-vicente-castano/72964-3.
Semana. 2009. "¿Por qué mataron a los niños?" April 11. http://www.semana.com/nacion/articulo/por-que-mataron-ninos/101939-3.
Semana. 2014. "'Tenemos que prepararnos para la paz': El alto comisionado para la paz, Sergio Jaramillo y el ministro del interior, Aurelio Iragorri, lanzaron la Red de Alcaldes y Gobernadores por la Paz." April 3. http://www.semana.com/nacion/articulo/tenemos-que-prepararnos-para-la-paz/382471-3.
Serje, Margarita. 2005. *El revés de la nación: Territorios salvajes, fronteras y tierras de nadie*. Bogotá: Ediciones Uniandes.
Sheriff, Robin E. 2001. *Dreaming Equality: Color, Race, and Racism in Urban Brazil*. New Brunswick, NJ: Rutgers University Press.
Silva, Denise Ferreira da. 2007. *Toward a Global Idea of Race*. Minneapolis: University of Minnesota Press.
Simon, Roger I., Sharon Rosenberg, and Claudia Eppert. 2000. "Between Hope and Despair: The Pedagogical Encounter of Historical Remembrance." In *Between Hope and Despair: Pedagogy and the Remembrance of Historical Trauma*, edited by Roger I. Simon, Sharon Rosenberg, and Claudia Eppert, 1–8. Lanham, MD: Rowman & Littlefield.
Smith, Christen A. 2016. *Afro-Paradise: Blackness, Violence, and Performance in Brazil*. Urbana: University of Illinois Press.
Springer, Simon. 2012. "Anarchism! What Geography Still Ought to Be." *Antipode* 44 (5): 1605–24.
Stafford, Gale. 2015. "4/5: A Peace of Happiness." *ReGale Me, Virginia*, blog, October 28. https://regalemevirginia.wordpress.com/2015/10/28/45-a-peace-of-happiness/.
Steiner, Claudia. 2000. *Imaginación y poder: El encuentro del interior con la costa en Urabá, 1900–1960*. Medellín: Editorial Universidad de Antioquia.
Subcomandante Insurgente Marcos. 1997. "Siete piezas sueltas del rompecabezas

REFERENCES

mundial (El neoliberalismo como rompecabezas: La inútil unidad mundial que fragmenta y destruye naciones)." *Chiapas* 5: 117–43.

Sullivan, Kevin, Mark Berman, and Sarah Kaplan. 2015. "Three Muslims Killed in Shooting near UNC; Police, Family Argue over Motive." *Washington Post*, February 11.

Tate, Winifred. 2007. *Counting the Dead: The Culture and Politics of Human Rights Activism in Colombia*. Berkeley: University of California Press.

Tate, Winifred. 2015. *Drugs, Thugs, and Diplomats: U.S. Policymaking in Colombia*. Stanford: Stanford University Press.

Tate, Winifred. 2017. "Post-accord Putumayo." *Journal of Latin American and Caribbean Anthropology* 22 (1): 164–73.

Taussig, Michael. 1984. "Culture of Terror—Space of Death: Roger Casement's Putumayo Report and the Explanation of Torture." *Comparative Studies in Society and History* 26 (3): 467–97.

Taussig, Michael. 1987. *Shamanism, Colonialism, and the Wild Man: A Study in Terror and Healing*. Chicago: University of Chicago Press.

Taussig, Michael. 2003. *Law in a Lawless Land: Diary of a "Limpieza" in Colombia*. New York: New Press.

Taylor, Diana. 2003. *The Archive and the Repertoire: Performing Cultural Memory in the Americas*. Durham, NC: Duke University Press.

Taylor, Diana. 2020. *¡Presente! The Politics of Presence*. Durham, NC: Duke University Press.

Teixeira, Bryan. 1999. "Nonviolence Theory and Practice." In *Encyclopedia of Violence, Peace, and Conflict*, vol. 2, edited by Lester R. Kurtz, 555–65. San Diego: Academic Press.

El Tiempo. 2013. "Estado rectifica acusaciones de Uribe contra San José de Apartado." May 29. http://www.eltiempo.com/politica/carrillo-dice-que-rectifica-acusaciones-de-uribe-por-san-jose-de-apartado_12832082-4.

El Tiempo. 2014a. "'El ciudadano necesita ver que se castiga a los que violan la ley': Pinzón asegura que si hay un escenario de paz es porque las Fuerzas Armadas lo hicieron posible." May 4. http://m.eltiempo.com/politica/justicia/el-ciudadano-necesita-ver-que-se-castiga-a-los-que-violan-la-ley/13928377.

El Tiempo. 2014b. "Acciones de la ONU en posconflicto se discutirán con las Farc: Santos." September 22. http://www.eltiempo.com/politica/proceso-de-paz/juan-manuel-santos-y-el-secretario-de-la-onu/14575935.

El Tiempo. 2015. "Cerca de 150 desplazados en San José de Apartadó por amenazas." November 5. http://www.eltiempo.com/colombia/medellin/cerca-de-150-desplazados-en-san-jose-de-apartado-por-amenazas/16422081#ancla_comentarios.

El Tiempo. 2017. "'La paz es real e irreversible': Juan Manuel Santos." June 27. http://www.eltiempo.com/politica/proceso-de-paz/discurso-de-santos-en-acto-final-de-la-dejacion-de-armas-de-las-farc-103190.

Tierra Digna. 2015. *Seguridad y Derechos Humanos ¿para quién? Voluntariedad y militarización, estrategias de las empresas extractivas en el control de territorios*. Bogotá: Centro de Estudios para la Justicia Social Tierra Digna.

Till, Karen E. 2005. *The New Berlin: Memory, Politics, Place.* Minneapolis: University of Minnesota Press.

Till, Karen E. 2012. "Wounded Cities: Memory-Work and a Place-Based Ethics of Care." *Political Geography* 31 (1): 3–14.

Tobón, William. 1997. "Urabá: Territorialidad privada y crisis regional." *Revista ANDI* 144 (January–February): 34–37.

Torres, Andrea, Johana Rocha, Diego Melo, and Rosa Peña. 2015. *El carbón de Colombia: ¿Quién gana? ¿Quién pierde? Minería, comercio global y cambio climático.* Bogotá: Centro de Estudios para la Justicia Social Tierra Digna.

Trouillot, Michel-Rolph. 1995. *Silencing the Past: Power and the Production of History.* Boston: Beacon Press.

Tsing, Anna Lowenhaupt. 2003. "Agrarian Allegory and Global Futures." In *Nature in the Global South: Environmental Projects in South and Southeast Asia*, edited by Paul Greenough and Anna Lowenhaupt Tsing, 124–69. Durham, NC: Duke University Press.

Tsing, Anna Lowenhaupt. 2005. *Friction: An Ethnography of Global Connection.* Princeton, NJ: Princeton University Press.

Tuberquia, Jesús Emilio. 2011. "Struggling for Peace amidst War: A Courageous Experiment in Nonviolent Resistance." Presentation at the Institute for the Study of the Americas, Chapel Hill, NC, April 4.

Tyner, James A., Gabriela Brindis Alvarez, and Alex R. Colucci. 2012. "Memory and the Everyday Landscape of Violence in Post-genocide Cambodia." *Social & Cultural Geography* 13 (8): 1–19.

Ulloa, Astrid. 2012. "Los territorios indígenas en Colombia: De escenarios de apropiación transnacional a territorialidades alternatives." *Scripta Nova: Revista electrónica de geografía y ciencias sociales* 16. http://www.ub.edu.libproxy.lib.unc.edu/geocrit/sn/sn-418/sn-418-65.htm.

El Universal. 2014. "Estas son las víctimas que viajaron a La Habana, Cuba." November 1. http://www.eluniversal.com.co/colombia/estas-son-las-victimas-que-viajaron-la-habana-cuba-175667.

Vachon, Robert. 2011. "Kayanerekowa: A Mohawk Perspective." In Dietrich et al., *Palgrave International Handbook of Peace Studies*, 330–51.

Valencia Agudelo, León, ed. 2017. *Terminó la guerra, el postconflicto está en riesgo: A un año del acuerdo de paz.* Buenos Aires: CLACSO.

Vargas, Joao H. Costa. 2004. "Hyperconsciousness of Race and Its Negation: The Dialectic of White Supremacy in Brazil." *Identities: Global Studies in Culture and Power* 11 (4): 443–70.

Vargas Quemba, Fernando. 2006. *Comunidades de Paz: Estrategia de guerra; Caso San José de Apartadó.* Bogotá: Litotécnica.

Vargas Velásquez, Alejo. 2015. "La paz territorial: ¿Eje fundamental para el pos-acuerdo?" Ola Política, February 2. http://www.olapolitica.com/content/la-paz-territorial-¿eje-fundamental-para-el-pos-acuerdo.

Vásquez, Teófilo. 2011. "Recursos, política, territorios y conflicto armado." In *Una vieja guerra en un nuevo contexto: Conflicto y territorio en el sur de Colombia*, edited by Teófilo Vásquez, Andrés R. Vargas, and Jorge A. Restrepo, 367–428. Bogotá: Centro de Investigación y Educación Popular.

Vásquez, Teófilo, and Andrés R. Vargas. 2011. "Territorialidades y conflicto: Hacia un marco interpretativo de las trayectorias subregionales." In *Una vieja guerra en un nuevo contexto: Conflicto y territorio en el sur de Colombia*, edited by Teófilo Vásquez, Andrés R. Vargas, and Jorge A. Restrepo, 343–65. Bogotá: Centro de Investigación y Educación Popular.

Vida, dignidad y territorio: Comunidades de paz y zonas humanitarias en el Urabá y Atrato; Memorias del seminario taller con comunidades en riesgo; Compilación de documentos. 2003. Bogotá: Fundación Cultura Democrática; Ministerio del Interior; Programa de las Naciones Unidas para el Desarrollo; Programa por la paz, Compañía de Jesús; Fondo de las Naciones Unidas para la Infancia; Instituto de Estudios para el Desarrollo.

Wade, Peter. 1993. *Blackness and Race Mixture: The Dynamics of Racial Identity in Colombia*. Baltimore: Johns Hopkins University Press.

Wade, Peter. 2016. "Mestizaje, Multiculturalism, Liberalism, and Violence." *Latin American and Caribbean Ethnic Studies* 11 (3): 323–43.

Wade, Peter. 2017. "Racism and Race Mixture in Latin America." *Latin American Research Review* 52 (3): 477–85.

Wallerstein, Immanuel. 2004. *World-Systems Analysis: An Introduction*. Durham, NC: Duke University Press.

Walsh, Catherine. 2010. "Shifting the Geopolitics of Critical Knowledge: Decolonial Thought and Cultural Studies 'Others' in the Andes." In *Globalization and the Decolonial Option*, edited by Walter Mignolo and Arturo Escobar, 78–93. New York: Routledge.

Warren, Jonathan. 2001. *Racial Revolutions: Antiracism and Indian Resurgence in Brazil*. Durham, NC: Duke University Press.

Washington Post. 2015. "Full Text: Obama's Remarks on Fatal Shooting in Charleston, S.C." June 18. http://www.washingtonpost.com/blogs/post-politics/wp/2015/06/18/full-text-obamas-remarks-on-fatal-shooting-in-charleston-s-c/.

Watanabe, John M. 2016. "Racing to the Top: Descent Ideologies and Why Ladinos Never Meant to Be Mestizos in Colonial Guatemala." *Latin American and Caribbean Ethnic Studies* 11 (3): 305–22.

Weber, Max. 1946. "Politics as Vocation." In *From Max Weber: Essays in Sociology*. Edited by H. H. Gerth and C. Wright Mills, 77–128. New York: Oxford University Press.

Welch, Sharon. 2007. "Dangerous Memory and Alternative Knowledges." In *On Violence: A Reader*, edited by Bruce B. Lawrence and Aisha Karim, 363–76. Durham, NC: Duke University Press.

Wilderson, Frank B. 2010. *Red, White & Black: Cinema and the Structure of U.S. Antagonisms*. Durham, NC: Duke University Press.

Williams, Philippa, and Fiona McConnell. 2011. "Critical Geographies of Peace." *Antipode* 43 (4): 927–31.

Williams, Philippa, Nick Megoran, and Fiona McConnell. 2014. "Introduction: Geographical Approaches to Peace." In McConnell, Megoran, and Williams, *Geographies of Peace*, 1–25.

Wolf, Sherry. 2009. *Sexuality and Socialism: History, Politics, and Theory of LGBT Liberation*. Chicago: Haymarket Books.

X, Malcolm. 2007. "The Ballot or the Bullet." In *On Violence: A Reader*, edited by Bruce B. Lawrence and Aisha Karim, 144–56. Durham, NC: Duke University Press.

Zamosc, León. 1986. *The Agrarian Question and the Peasant Movement in Colombia: Struggles of the National Peasant Association 1967–1981*. Cambridge: Cambridge University Press.

Zapata Olivella, Manuel. 1989. *Las clases mágicas de América*. Bogotá: Plaza y Janes.

Zibechi, Raúl. 2010. *Dispersing Power: Social Movements as Anti-state Forces*. Oakland, CA: AK Press.

Zibechi, Raúl. 2012. *Territories in Resistance: A Cartography of Latin American Social Movements*. Oakland, CA: AK Press.

Zinn, Howard. 1999. "Drawing the Color Line." In *A People's History of the United States*, 23–38. New York: HarperCollins.

INDEX

Acción Social. *See* Agencia Presidencial para la Acción Social y la Cooperación Internacional
accompaniers, 27, 34–38, 73, 198, 210; in action, 171, 173, 174, 212, 222; author, 23, 29, 34, 77; Community members and, 151, 227, 246n4; Peter Cousins, 75; FOR, 167–69, 203; former, 143, 209; international, 43, 48, 104, 131–33, 200, 212, 227; Mayra Sofía Moreno, 66; Tom Power, 223; protective, 15, 30; Gina Spigarelli, 215; Sarah Weintraub, 35. *See also* Burnyeat, Gwen; Fellowship of Reconciliation (FOR); Finn, Luke; FOR Peace Presence (FORPP); international accompaniment; Operation Dove; Peace Brigades International (PBI); Soellinger, Michaela; Stafford, Gale
ACIN. *See* Asociación de Cabildos Indígenas del Norte del Cauca (ACIN)
AGC. *See* Autodefensas Gaitanistas de Colombia (AGC)
Agencia Presidencial para la Acción Social y la Cooperación Internacional, 74, 75
"agency of the dead," 21, 49, 194, 209
agrarian reform, 51, 53, 58, 119, 246n2
agribusiness, 8, 17, 55, 56, 109, 119, 129; and extractivism, 11, 79, 114, 126; teak, 75. *See also* bananas; oil palm
agricultural centers, 14, 24, 77, 161, 164, 181–85, 191. *See also* La Unión Peace Village, Agricultural Center

agroecology, 3, 14, 99, 146, 182
alter-globalization, 6, 68
alter-territorialities, 21, 24, 158, 159, 161, 164, 185, 191, 196, 209
alter-territory, 168, 176, 180; in action, 168, 185; network of, 20, 212; of the Peace Community, 20, 24, 164, 191, 220, 234, 235; of radical trans-relational peace, 161, 209
Alto Joaquín Peace Village, 43, 46, 78, 79, 242
anticolonial politics, 22, 28, 50, 66, 79, 198, 210
anticolonial rupture, 6–7, 99, 115, 156, 220
antioqueño, 87, 89, 92, 95, 99
Aparicio, Juan Ricardo, 58, 65, 101
Areiza, Renato, 59, 62, 71
Arenas Altas Peace Village, 69, 76, 79, 176, 222, 224, 239, 240
Arenas Bajas Humanitarian Zone, 72, 222–26, 232
Asociación de Cabildos Indígenas del Norte del Cauca (ACIN), 32, 95, 97, 98, 177, 178, 249n2 (chap. 3)
assassinations, xv, xvi, 3, 7, 11–14, 35, 73, 77, 82, 97, 156, 237–41; attempted, 74, 226–29, 233, 243; commemorated, 194, 198, 206, 226; of a Community youth, 240; of humanitarian zone coordinators, 72, 224; of human rights defenders, 126, 222; of Bernardo Jaramillo, 66; in La Linda, 64; of Liberal guerrillas, 50; of Francisco Puertas, 72;

277

resistance against, 76, 80; of Bernardo Ríos, 74; of Arlén Salas, 72; selective, 65, 74; of Dairo Torres, 72; of UP party leaders, 52, 66; of Edilberto Vásquez, 72. *See also* Cataño, Bartolomé; Correa, Ramiro; Gaitán, Jorge Eliécer; Guerra, Luis Eduardo; Guzmán, Rigoberto; Jiménez, Aníbal

AUC. *See* Autodefensas Unidas de Colombia (AUC)

Autodefensas Gaitanistas de Colombia (AGC), 120, 246n2; and the FARC, 175, 224, 225, 230, 232; Peace Community and, 222, 223, 225–26, 243; press release pamphlet, 165, 166, 168

Autodefensas Unidas de Colombia (AUC), 10, 17, 56, 60, 70, 118, 165, 170, 232, 246n2

Awasqa. *See* Tejido Awasqa Conciente (Awasqa)

Balsamar Cooperative, 10, 58, 148, 238
bananas, 9, 54–56, 69, 90, 131, 132, 135, 159, 182, 184, 189
Brown, Wendy, 118, 195
Burnyeat, Gwen, 37, 66, 72, 146, 216, 245n1
Butler, Judith, 19, 211

cacao, 10, 14, 44, 69, 137, 142, 180, 182, 189, 199, 225; beans, 58, 148; farmers, 227; trees, 169, 216, 225
"Caminando la palabra," 165, 174. *See also* caravans; commemorations, and pilgrimages; Holy Week pilgrimages
Campesino University of Resistance, 3, 15, 76, 77, 95, 97–98, 100–102, 157, 176–80, 191; first sessions of 76, 240; network, 41, 99, 161, 168; sessions after commemorations, 211, 214; transethnic, 23, 28, 157; workshops, 4, 127, 143, 159
caravans, 3, 33, 204, 209, 240; solidarity, 24, 161, 164–76, 178, 180, 191
Cataño, Bartolomé (assassinated), 11, 55, 57, 91, 237, 238

Catholic Church, 11, 57, 58, 60, 62, 92, 100, 120, 174–75, 240; Bishop Isaías Duarte Cancino, 59; diocese in Apartadó, 182, 238; Father Albeiro Parra, 127; Monsignor Hugo Alberto Torres, 227; Sister Clara Lagos, 48. *See also* Giraldo Moreno, Father Javier
Center for Research and Popular Education (CINEP), 57, 63, 238
Chernick, Marc, 51, 113
Chiquita. *See* bananas
CINEP. *See* Center for Research and Popular Education (CINEP)
Clan del Golfo, 222, 246n2. *See also* Autodefensas Gaitanistas de Colombia (AGC)
coca, xix, 61, 78, 163, 225, 230; trade, 51–52, 189, 213, 246n2. *See also* crops, illicit; narcotrafficking
COCOMACIA. *See* Consejo Comunitario Mayor de la Asociación Campesina Integral del Atrato (COCOMACIA)
COCOMOPOCA. *See* Consejo Comunitario Mayor de la Organización Popular Campesina del Alto Atrato (COCOMOPOCA)
collectives: Colectivo Agrario Abya Yala, 160; Colectivo de Sentipensamiento Afrodiaspórico, 160; Colectivo Sónica Sinfonía, 179; Hurston Collective for Critical Performance Ethnography, 35; Peace Community, 136, 139, 151, 154, 162, 216, 247n4; urban Hip Hop youth, 31. *See also* Tejido Awasqa Conciente (Awasqa)
Colombian Congress, 17, 32
Colombian Constitutional Court, 72, 73, 132, 241, 242
commemorations, xviii, 37, 49, 53, 191, 197, 205–14, 229, 231, 233; of the dead, xvi, 20, 21, 226, 234; gatherings, 194, 198, 210; Giraldo and, 12, 247n5; and performance, 35, 204; and pilgrimages, 14, 24, 164, 196, 204, 207–14, 217, 219, 223; practices, 157; role of, 202, 211, 220, 221; of the 2005 massacre in

INDEX

Mulatos, 47, 164, 198–201, 242. *See also* Holy Week pilgrimages; painted stones

Community hymn, 142, 194, 210, 239, 249n1 (chap. 5)

comunitario. *See* workdays, comunitario

conflict resolution, 50, 109, 116, 121, 122, 145

conscientious objectors, 31–32, 116

Consejo Comunitario Mayor de la Asociación Campesina Integral del Atrato (COCOMACIA), 32, 127

Consejo Comunitario Mayor de la Organización Popular Campesina del Alto Atrato (COCOMOPOCA), 32, 118

Consejo Regional Indígena del Cauca (CRIC), 95, 96, 249n1 (chap. 3)

convite, 58–59, 141

*convivir*s, 60, 64, 238

Correa, Ramiro (assassinated), 64, 224, 238

CRIC. *See* Consejo Regional Indígena del Cauca (CRIC)

crops, 57, 68, 75, 77, 177, 147, 190, 214; avocado, 10; beans, 14, 75, 188; cash, 188, 245n1; coffee, 182; corn, 14, 214; diversified, 184; harvesting, xviii, 3, 69, 141, 153; illicit, 52, 61, 221, 225; maize, 10, 188; oranges, 188; papayas, 188; pineapple, 44, 188; plantains, 14, 182; rice, 44, 188; sorghum, 182; squash, 183, 188; subsistence, 158, 181; tangerines, 188; yucca, 182, 188. *See also* bananas; cacao; oil palm; seeds; sugarcane

Cuartas Montoya, Mayor Gloria, 55, 75, 101, 148, 237

Dabeiba, 9–10, 91–92, 105, 224, 237

David, Wilson, 68, 234

decolonial politics, 7, 41, 54, 220

decolonial rupture, 6, 15, 234

defamatory campaigns, 71, 73, 74, 77, 241

Deleuze, Gilles, and Félix Guattari, 161, 216

demilitarization, 116, 124, 134

Democratic Center Party, 16, 109, 112, 221, 248n7

Dest, Anthony, 51, 52

dialogical performance, 27, 29, 104, 107, 147, 178, 204, 219, 228; of knowledge production, 144, 145, 186; of peace, 22; of solidarity, 21, 28, 36

Dietrich, Wolfgang, 19, 104, 106, 108, 113, 123, 249n1 (part II); and "moral peace," 120, 122, 136, 138, 151

disappeared, the, 68, 196, 237

Doña Brígida. *See* González, Doña María Brígida (Doña Brígida)

ecological dignity, 6, 15, 23, 28, 40, 107, 163, 188, 209–10, 221, 248n9; and dialogical performance, 22, 178; examples of, 7, 96, 157; and memory, 220; and peace, 17, 18, 21, 110, 130, 146, 151, 161, 235; and relational territorialities, 192

Ejército de Liberación Nacional (ELN), 17, 51, 232, 233, 246n2

Ejército Popular de Liberación (EPL), 64, 118, 224

ELN. *See* Ejército de Liberación Nacional (ELN)

emancipatory politics, 21, 146, 158, 191, 198; as "other politics," 156, 159, 190, 219

"energetic peace," 19, 104, 108, 113, 151, 163, 249n1 (part II); correlation with, 127

EPL. *See* Ejército Popular de Liberación (EPL)

Esquivia, Ricardo, 119–21, 126, 143

extractivism, 83, 102, 107, 109–11, 115, 128–29, 147; rejection of, 21, 88, 126, 130, 163–64, 182

Fanon, Frantz, 54, 245n1

FARC-EP. *See* Fuerzas Armadas Revolucionarias de Colombia—Ejército del Pueblo (FARC-EP)

Father Javier. *See* Giraldo Moreno, Father Javier

Fellowship of Reconciliation (FOR), xviii, 32, 75, 124, 149, 173, 231, 239, 240,

247n6; accompaniers, 35, 38, 168, 169, 203
feminists, 25, 28, 116, 235, 248n9
Ferreira, Priscilla, 248–49n2
Finn, Luke, 63, 122, 136, 140, 162
fishponds, 158, 181, 183, 187
food sovereignty, 14, 20, 68, 177, 181, 189–90, 216; and autonomy, 147, 214; initiatives/projects, 22, 24, 28, 157–58, 161, 221, 234; pioneer Javier Sánchez, 183, 185–86, 230
FOR. *See* Fellowship of Reconciliation (FOR)
FOR Peace Presence (FORPP), 29, 34, 37, 44, 146, 153, 167, 240, 247n6
forced disappearance, 12, 82, 121, 124; pilgrimage against, 165
free trade agreements (FTAs), 83, 97, 118–19, 186
FTAs. *See* free trade agreements (FTAs)
Fuerzas Armadas Revolucionarias de Colombia—Ejército del Pueblo (FARC-EP), 10, 51–54, 70, 71, 75, 80, 200, 232, 241, 245n2; 5th Front, 56, 64, 77; former members of, 224–25, 230–31; founding of, 50, 64; killings/massacres/threats by, 12, 66, 82, 238, 242; laying down arms/disarmament, 112, 114–15, 221, 222; and "peace process," 4–5, 15–18, 24, 30, 32, 46, 108–11, 126, 127, 129, 175; political education from, 58

Gaitán, Jorge Eliécer, 53, 165
Galtung, Johan, 18–19, 104, 111
García, Blas, 124, 134
Giraldo Moreno, Father Javier, 177; and Lanchero, 67, 143, 144; and massacre commemorations, 12, 198–201, 204, 209, 214, 222–23, 247n5; and Peace Community, 48, 59–60, 61–63, 208; in Rodoxalí, 169, 170, 171
Gómez Correal, Diana, xviii, 84, 114, 121, 125, 194, 216, 249n1 (chap. 4)
González, Doña María Brígida (Doña Brígida), 29, 84, 93–94, 163, 208, 211–12; 215–20, 235; interviewed, xviii, 39–40, 193–94, 205; paintings by, xvi, 69, 98, 141, 216–18
Graciano, Germán, 150, 224, 226, 235–36, 243
Guerra, Luis Eduardo, 46–47, 59, 94, 207–8, 224; assassinated, xvi, 13, 70–71, 74, 78, 198, 241; commemorated in photos, 47, 197; interviewed, 54, 57, 60, 62, 65–66, 73, 76–77. *See also* Luis Eduardo Guerra Peace Village, Mulatos
guerrilla groups. *See* Fuerzas Armadas Revolucionarias de Colombia—Ejército del Pueblo (FARC-EP); Ejército de Liberación Nacional (ELN); Ejército Popular de Liberación (EPL)
Gulf of Urabá, 9, 10, 89, 91, 231
Guzmán, Rigoberto (assassinated), xv, 70, 181, 231, 239, 243. *See also* La Unioncita Peace Village

Havana Accord, 109, 111, 128, 143
Havana negotiations, 108, 120, 124, 143, 150, 209, 224, 233
Hobbes, Thomas, 90, 113, 118, 151
Holy Week pilgrimages, 33, 194, 210, 222–24, 231
humanitarian law, international, 57, 224
humanitarian space/territories, 57, 60, 105. *See also* humanitarian zones
humanitarian zones, 3, 13, 72, 174–75, 224, 240–41. *See also* humanitarian space/territories
human rights, xv, xviii, 3, 116–17, 125, 142, 162, 177, 234; community, 15, 170; defenders, xix, 4, 14, 16, 17, 32, 56, 115, 130, 222; Inter-American Human Rights system, 129; networks, 212; Organization of American States' human rights system, 235; organizations, 11, 16, 57, 99, 129, 173, 175, 192; United Nation's Universal Declaration of Human Rights, 57; violations, 7, 13, 32, 55, 70, 72–74, 114, 194, 233, 241, 246n2. *See also* Inter-American Court

of Human Rights; National Human Rights Ombudsman's office

"If We Remain on the Land" performance piece, 35–36
Inter-American Court of Human Rights, 72, 73, 132, 238, 239, 241, 242
international accompaniers. *See* accompaniers, international
international accompaniment, xix, 35, 46, 165, 180, 235, 239; protective, 146, 240. *See also* accompaniers

JAC. *See* Juntas de Acción Comunal (JAC)
Jiménez, Aníbal (assassinated), 142, 239
Juntas de Acción Comunal (JAC), 58, 75, 148–49

Koopman, Sara, 28, 37

La Cristalina Peace Village, 72, 79
La Esperanza Peace Village, 13, 44, 59, 69, 74, 79, 164, 166, 239, 242
La Linda, 64, 72, 238
Lanchero, Eduar, 46, 56, 62, 64, 66–67, 69, 77, 144–45, 156, 157, 204, 210, 236; buried in San Josecito, 48–49, 194, 243; Father Giraldo and, 67, 143
land restitution, 150, 165; activists, 31, 32, 117; and Victims and Land Restitution Law of 2011, 61, 113
La Resbalosa Peace Village, 43, 48, 78, 79, 164; commemorations in, 164, 167, 198–201, 242; massacres in, xvi, 13, 70, 74, 82, 194, 228, 231, 237, 241
Las Claras Peace Village, 44, 45–46, 51–52, 78, 79, 242
La Unioncita Peace Village, 230, 231, 243
La Unión Peace Village, 13, 56, 59, 79, 140, 148–49, 153, 176, 230–31, 237, 242; accompaniers in, xviii, 140; Agricultural Center, 158, 181–85, 242; and caravans/commemorations, 166–67, 198; killings in, xv–xvi, xvii, 69–70, 237, 239, 240; return to, 44, 67, 69, 143–44, 157, 239. *See also* La Unioncita Peace Village

La Violencia civil war/period, 9–10, 50, 58, 82, 91, 101, 165, 245n2, 246n3
Londoño, Julián, 117, 121, 122, 124
Luis Eduardo Guerra Peace Village. *See* Mulatos Peace Village

Madres de la Plaza de Mayo, 196, 202, 204
Márquez Mina, Francia, 128, 137, 161
Marx, Karl, 25, 120, 122, 245n1
massacres, xv, xx, 62, 65, 76, 101, 172, 206, 239, 241; and commemorations, 24, 33, 164, 194, 196, 204, 207, 209–10, 213–14, 216, 221, 242; first documented, 12, 82, 237; by FARC guerrillas, 66, 82, 238; in La Unión (2000) xv–xvii, 69–70, 181, 231, 239; in Mulatos and La Resbalosa (2005), xvi, 13, 46–47, 70–71, 72, 74, 78, 198–201, 228, 231, 241; in San José (2000), 70, 239; in Trujillo (1990), 247n5. *See also* commemorations; Holy Week pilgrimages; painted stones
medicinal plants, 77, 158, 177, 178, 179, 183, 188
memory work, 17, 21, 195–96, 197, 212; performance, 23, 194, 202, 207, 211, 216, 235; practices, 30, 194, 196–97, 210, 219, 220. *See also* commemorations; Holy Week pilgrimages; painted stones
mestizaje, 86–88, 91–92, 95, 100, 101
"modern peace," 109, 110, 113, 115, 117, 119, 125, 128, 134–35, 139, 146, 150
modern-colonial world, xix, 6, 20, 26, 129, 142, 145, 151, 235. *See also* modernity-coloniality
modernity-coloniality, 5, 7–9, 68, 107, 111, 135, 138; logic of, 15, 24, 115; oppressive nature of, 121, 190, 196–97, 216
Montes de María region, 119, 120
Montoya, Jesús Emilio, 58, 64–65, 83–84, 138, 153–55, 209, 211
Mora, Mariana, 6, 138
movements, various: Afro-Colombian, 160; agrarian reform, 58; anticolonial, 54; black liberation, xv; campesino,

79, 84, 99, 109; "communist," 51; Congreso de los Pueblos, 117; feminist, 28; guerrilla, 238, 246n2; Hijos e Hijas por la Memoria y Contra la Impunidad, 32; Landless Workers Movement, 15; networks of, 212–16; "No," 16–17, 109; Pastos of Putumayo and the Muiscas of Suba, Bogotá, 88; peace, 13, 53, 109, 117, 170, 190, 234, 247n4; political, 6, 22, 53, 99–100, 156; "re-indigenization," 88; repression of, 7; resistance, 28, 230; social, xix, xx, 6, 20–27, 30, 37, 38, 40–41, 106, 107, 115–16, 126, 139, 143, 147, 151, 159–60, 172, 192, 195, 222, 227, 235; solidarity, 28, 34; subaltern, 7; victims, 7, 32, 120. *See also* Madres de la Plaza de Mayo; Movimiento de Víctimas de Crímenes de Estado (MOVICE)

MOVICE. *See* Movimiento de Víctimas de Crímenes de Estado (MOVICE)

Movimiento de Víctimas de Crímenes de Estado (MOVICE), 32, 124–26

Mulatos Peace Village, 43, 55, 59, 79, 167–68, 172; Campesino University in, 176, 179; massacre commemoration in, 12, 47, 164, 194, 197, 198, 207, 211, 213–16, 242; massacre in (2005), xvi, 13, 46, 70, 72, 74, 228, 231, 241; return to, 44, 78, 242

Muñoz, Francisco, 122, 123

Naín Peace Village, 43, 46, 78, 79, 242

narcobourgeoisie, 7–12, 17, 46, 147, 218; consolidation of, 53, 56; land grab by, 15, 40, 79, 83–84, 155; press release, 165, 166

narcotrafficking, 7, 51–52, 90, 134, 170, 217, 218, 233, 246n2

Nasa, the, 69, 95, 96, 160, 178

National Army, 4, 7, 45, 50, 59–61, 66, 92, 97, 133, 136, 137, 141, 153, 167, 172, 189, 204, 224, 239, 242, 246n2; aggressions/harassment by, 54, 75; killings by 65, 82, 156, 222; massacres by, xv–xvi, 65, 198, 200, 237, 238;

officers/officials, 30–31, 52, 73–74, 110–11, 170, 227; 17th Brigade, 10, 56, 70, 74; soldiers, 3, 10–11, 12–13, 46, 62, 119–20, 131, 168, 219, 231

National Human Rights Ombudsman's office, 227, 228

"negative peace," 18, 104, 110–12, 117, 127, 129, 134, 136, 138, 195

neo-paramilitaries, 120, 165, 222, 246n2. *See also* Autodefensas Gaitanistas de Colombia (AGC); Clan del Golfo

Network of Communities in Rupture and Resistance (RECORRE), 13, 70, 76–77, 95–96, 99, 168, 176, 179, 240; unites groups, 101, 146. *See also* Campesino University of Resistance

neutrality, position of, 13, 59–60, 62, 72, 73, 75, 143, 146, 154, 174, 207, 211, 226

nongovernmental organizations (NGOs), 35, 57, 62, 101, 119; Paz Christi, 58

nonviolence, 32, 65, 116, 117, 121–22, 124, 142

nonviolent communication, 109, 121, 124

Paramillo, Natural Park, 45; Nudo de 91, 92

Nuevo Antioquia, 166–67, 169, 170, 174

oil palm, 8, 9, 11, 56, 119; plantations, 119, 213, 238

Operation Dove, 242, 247–48n6

painted stones, 14, 24, 204–8, 212, 217. *See also* memory work

Palestine, 146–147

panela, 158–59, 183–84

paramilitaries, 44, 46, 53, 54, 57, 59, 60, 61, 74, 79, 119–20, 131–32, 134, 143, 145, 149, 153, 168–75, 178, 212, 224, 227–28, 236, 246n2; and blockades, 67, 73, 158, 159, 240; death squads, 3, 4, 7, 10, 11, 165, 168; former guerrillas joining, 64, 224–25; hit lists, 34, 70; killing campaigns, 52, 56; killings by, 12, 72; massacres by, xv–xvi, 62, 70, 198–200, 231, 238, 239, 241. *See also* Autodefensas Gaitanistas de Colom-

INDEX

bia (AGC); Autodefensas Unidas de Colombia (AUC)
Partido Social de la Unidad Nacional (U Party), 16, 248n7
Pastrana, Andrés, administration, 15–16
Patriotic Union. *See* Unión Patriótica (UP)
PBI. *See* Peace Brigades International (PBI)
PCN. *See* Proceso de Comunidades Negras (PCN)
peace, politics of, 152, 154, 157, 220, 233. *See also* Dietrich, Wolfgang, and "moral peace"; "energetic peace"; "modern peace"; "negative peace"; "positive peace"
Peace Brigades International (PBI), 239, 240, 247n6
performance, 19–20; ethnography, 25, 35. *See also* dialogical performance
pilgrimages. *See* commemorations, and pilgrimages; Holy Week pilgrimages
Pinzón, Juan Carlos, 110, 111
police officers, 30, 52, 74, 110, 113, 119–20, 219
police post, San José de Apartadó, 71, 74, 75, 148, 241
"positive peace," 18, 104, 111, 117, 121, 122, 138
Proceso de Comunidades Negras (PCN), 28, 128, 137, 161
Puerto Nuevo Peace Village, 43, 45, 78, 79, 242

Quintín Lame, Manuel, 89, 96

racialization, xx, 85–86, 89–95, 100, 101–02
radical performance geography, 22, 25–27, 33–34, 38, 165, 213
radical trans-relational peace, 21, 24, 107, 108, 130, 139, 144, 146, 151, 209, 221; of ecological dignity, 161, 220; elements of, 149; inspiration, 109, 134, 147, 235; Peace Community produces, 196
RECORRE. *See* Network of Communities in Rupture and Resistance (RECORRE)

Red Juvenil de Medellín, 32, 116, 134
reparations to victims, 17, 61, 115, 118, 119, 156
resistance networks, 23, 24, 124–30, 164
Rigoberto Guzmán Peace Village. *See* La Unioncita Peace Village
Rivera Cusicanqui, Silvia, 25, 102
Rodoxalí, 164–76, 180
rupture, Peace Community's with the state, 41, 77, 78, 144, 190, 241; conditions for ending, 71–72, 241; and RECORRE, 13, 70, 240

Sabaleta, 169, 172, 174
Sánchez, Javier, 75, 158–59, 162, 182–91, 230, 232
San Francisco de Asís, peace community, 13, 238
San Josecito de la Dignidad Peace Village, 14, 75, 79, 131–33, 156, 176, 181, 207; attempted assassination in, 226–27, 243; and caravans, 166, 222; graffiti in, 225; Eduar Lanchero and, 48–49, 194, 243; and military camp, 131–32, 133; settlement of, 39–40, 71, 74, 204, 218–19, 230, 241
Santos, Juan Manuel, 15, 16, 72, 112–15, 126, 127, 135, 248n7; administration, 23, 61, 109, 110, 124, 129; apology, 72, 243
"savage territories," 8, 89–90
scholars: Nancy Applebaum, 90; Dwight Conquergood, 19; Glen Sean Coulthard, 72; Pablo Dávalos, 84; Arturo Escobar, 28; Orlando Fals Borda, 57; Silvia Federici, 175; Clara Inés García, 89; Lotta Harbom, 112; Stina Högbladh, 112; bell hooks, 28; Forrest Hylton, 50; Ivan Illich, 152; Nicole Laliberté, 104; Catherine LeGrand, 141; Soyini Madison, 26; Malcolm X, 79; Nick Megoran, 106; Kelly Oliver, 19; Ulrich Oslender, 202; Cristina Rojas, 89; Amy Ross, 195; Frank Safford and Marco Palacios, 62; Gonzalo Sánchez, 53; Sally Scholz, 28;

Margarita Serje, 90; Michael Taussig, 201; Karen Till, 195; Anna Tsing, 28; Teófilo Vásquez, 51; Peter Wade, 92; Peter Wallenstein, 112; Frank Wilderson, 85–86
seeds, 75, 78, 171, 181–82; sharing of, 15, 99, 158, 183, 186
self-sufficient farms, 14, 24, 77, 161, 164, 185–92, 230
Sembrandopaz, 32, 119
Sepúlveda, Bernardo, 142–43
Sepúlveda, Doña Fidelina, 94, 103–5, 139, 142
Servicio Paz y Justicia (SERPAJ), 32, 124, 134
Sinú River, 9; Project (Urrá II), 44–45; region, 70, 91, 92, 237
Soellinger, Michaela, 106, 123–24, 146
solidarity networks, 3–4, 20–23, 66, 175, 186, 197, 219–20, 221, 234; international, 14, 150, 157, 171, 212, 222; and paintings, 216–19; trans-ethnic, 28, 38, 80, 83, 95–100. *See also* caravans, solidarity
Stafford, Gale, 121–22, 155–56
Steiner, Claudia, 89, 90, 92
sugarcane, 6, 9, 44, 90, 147, 181, 201, 214. *See also* panela

Tejido Awasqa Conciente (Awasqa), 32, 117, 124, 126, 130
theories: critical, 25, 26, 27, 106, 145; of race and racialization, 98, 100; peace, 23, 103, 104, 107, 109; political, 38, 48
Tierralta, Córdoba, 79, 237, 239, 240, 242
Tierra y Vida, 32, 117, 118, 126
transnational corporations, 5, 84, 135
truth commissions, 71–72, 221, 241
Tuberquia, Gildardo, 215, 224
Tuberquia, Jesús Emilio, 27, 65, 76, 94, 125, 135, 155
Tuberquia Quintero, Berta, 75, 105, 155, 162–63

U party. *See* Partido Social de la Unidad Nacional (U Party)
Unión Patriótica (UP), 10, 11, 50, 52–56, 66, 214, 237, 238; exterminación of, 57, 66, 75, 148,
UP. *See* Unión Patriótica (UP)
Uribe Vélez, Álvaro, 10, 56, 60, 64, 71, 72, 111, 162, 238, 241; administration, 74; ex-president, 15–16, 232, 243, 247n4, 248n7
Urrá dam, 39, 44–45, 168, 237, 239; region, 46; reservoir, 42–43, 78–79

Valderrama, Diana, 67–68
Vergara, Edward, 117, 124, 126, 130

Wayúu, the, 95, 178
workdays, 14, 72, 139, 238; comunitario, 64, 68–69, 77, 140–41, 146, 191, 211

Zapatistas, 6, 15, 138, 150